THEORIES OF LOCAL ECONOMIC DEVELOPMENT

To my parents
Lester J. and Dorothy R. Rowe

Theories of Local Economic Development

Linking Theory to Practice

Edited by

JAMES E. ROWE

University of Auckland, New Zealand

Routledge

Taylor & Francis Group

LONDON AND NEW YORK

First published 2009 by Ashgate Publishing

Published 2016 by Routledge
2 Park Square, Milton Park, Abingdon, Oxfordshire OX14 4RN
711 Third Avenue, New York, NY 10017, USA

First issued in paperback 2016

Routledge is an imprint of the Taylor & Francis Group, an informa business

British Library Cataloguing in Publication Data
Theories of local economic development : linking theory to
practice
1. Economic development
I. Rowe, James E. (James Edward)
338.9

Library of Congress Cataloging-in-Publication Data
Theories of local economic development : linking theory to practice / [edited]
by James E. Rowe.
p. cm.
Includes index.
ISBN 978-0-7546-7305-7 (hardback) 1. Economic development. 2.
Community development. 3. Economic policy. I. Rowe, James E. (James
Edward)
HD75.T4773 2008
338.9009173'2--dc22

2008030030

ISBN 13: 978-1-138-27003-9 (pbk)
ISBN 13: 978-0-7546-7305-7 (hbk)

Contents

List of Figures

List of Tables

Notes on Contributors

Andrew Beer is a Professor in the School of Geography, Population and Environmental Management at Flinders University.

John P. Blair is a Professor of Economics at Wright State University.

Edward J. Blakely is a Professor and Chair of the Department of Urban and Regional Planning at the University of Sydney and is currently on leave from the University to serve as the Director of Recovery for the City of New Orleans as it recovers from Hurricanes Rita and Katrina.

Michael Carroll is an Assistant Professor of Economics and Director of the Centre for Regional Development at Bowling Green State University.

Paul Dalziel is Professor of Economics in the Commerce Division at Lincoln University.

Harvey A. Goldstein is a Professor and Dean of the Program in Public Governance and Management, MODUL University-Vienna, Vienna, Austria. He was formerly a Professor in the Department of City and Regional Planning at the University of North Carolina at Chapel Hill.

Michael Gunder is a Senior Lecturer in the School of Architecture and Planning and the National Institute of Creative Arts and Industries at the University of Auckland.

William Kaye-Blake is a Senior Research Officer in the Agriculture and Economic Research Unit at Lincoln University.

Richard Le Heron is a Professor in the School of Geography, Geology and Environmental Science at the University of Auckland.

Michael I. Luger is the Dean and Professor of Innovation, Management and Public Policy at the Manchester Business School at the University of Manchester and was formerly chairman of the Department of Public Policy and Professor of City and Regional Planning at the University of North Carolina at Chapel Hill.

Philip McCann is a Professor of Economics in the Waikato Management School at the University of Waikato.

Mark M. Miller is Professor in the Department of Economic and Workplace Development at the University of Southern Mississippi.

Martin Perry is a Senior Lecturer in the Department of Management and Enterprise Development at Massey University in Wellington.

Luke Pittaway is the William A. Freeman Distinguished Professor of Free Enterprise at Georgia Southern University and formerly a Senior Lecturer and Director of the Enterprise Education Centre for Regional Development at the University of Sheffield Management School.

James E. Rowe is a Senior Planner at the Manukau City Council and a PhD candidate at the University of Auckland. Mr. Rowe has submitted his thesis and is expected to graduate in May 2009. He is also the immediate past Vice President of the Australia and New Zealand Regional Science Association International and is currently the New Zealand Representative. He is an Accredited Economic Development Professional – AEcD (NZ), and a member of the International Economic Development Council.

Caroline Saunders is Professor of Economics and is the Director of the Agriculture and Economic Research Unit at Lincoln University.

Robert Stimson is a Professor in the School of Geography, Planning and Architecture at the University of Queensland and is the immediate past President of the Regional Science Association.

Roger R. Stough is a Professor of Public Policy and Associate Dean for Research, Development and External Relations at George Mason University and is the current President of the Regional Science Association.

Foreword

It's been 15 years since *Theories of Economic Development: Perspectives from Across the Disciplines* was published in 1993, and in that time span the world and the economic development profession have experienced tremendous change. Globalisation has presented a myriad of opportunities as well as obstacles to communities throughout the world, and as economic developers strive to improve the local and regional economies in which we operate, we are being forced to swiftly reinvent ourselves, keeping pace with the social, economic, and technological transformations that are altering our local business landscapes.

In the wake of globalisation and more than halfway through the first decade of the 21st century, the economic development profession has hit a critical juncture. With new rules and expectations, economic developers impulsively endeavour to become experts on issues of technology and entrepreneurship, developing local strategies to retain and expand business already in the region, rather than focusing on attracting new firms. All at once, our local businesses needed to become competitive in the global market, and we are courageously stepping ahead, dealing with the circumstances set before us, often without a clear route in place; however, in today's volatile economic environment, drawing from the old stockpiles of experience has not always fit.

The economic developer has been facing a quandary whereby the old methods may not be working, but new schemes have yet to be cohesively established. And while academics may eloquently explain how to achieve a certain result, the fact is that we are finding ourselves with a huge gap between economic development theory and practice, which is challenging our discipline as much as the market forces.

We have anxiously awaited the advent of a theoretic framework outlining the economic development practice and remedies on how to solve practical issues of this century, and now we have it. James Rowe's *Theories of Local Economic Development: Linking Theory to Practice* has filled the chasm. The book updates theories beyond concepts and defines the economic development profession, examining issues that economic development professionals around the world encounter day to day, proposing a link between theory and practice and ultimately offering a way forward.

With over 30 years in the economic development field, with experiences ranging from the US to Asia to New Zealand, James Rowe is in an exceptional position to edit this book, which includes insight from economic development icons such as Edward J. Blakely, Michael I. Luger and Roger Stough, to name a few. I applaud his efforts to bring this book to fruition at such a crucial time and consider it to be a valuable reference to economic developers worldwide. For all who struggle daily to make a positive impact on our localities and improve the wealth and quality of life in our communities, this is the book we have been waiting for. I wish all the best to James and thank him for this timely piece of work.

Jeffrey A. Finkle, President and CEO
International Economic Development Council

Preface

The need for this book became apparent during my research into alternative frameworks for understanding local economic development (Rowe, 2008). My research quickly led to Bingham and Mier's (1993) *Theories of Local Economic Development: Perspectives from Across the Disciplines*. This seminal publication was the first serious attempt to assemble a "practical framework for using theory in local economic development" (Bingham and Mier, 1993, p. xvi). This book is an update on their research and reflects my lifetime of working as an economic development practitioner.

I was first introduced to local and regional economic development when I accepted a position as an economic planner in Marion, Virginia, US in 1975. Despite being armed with a strong background in geography and a new master's degree in urban and regional planning from the University of Tennessee, I soon discovered that my knowledge and understanding of economic development was fundamentally lacking. In order to address my limited academic training in economic development, I joined and became an active member of the American Industrial Development Council. This body has since merged with the Council for Urban Economic Development to form the International Economic Development Council (IEDC).[1] I also completed the Basic Industrial Development Course (BIDC) at the University of North Carolina in 1976 and the Industrial Development Institute (IDI) at the University of Oklahoma in 1979. At the time, I thought that an understanding of basic economic geography and general planning principles were enough to conquer the discipline (and in that time period, it apparently was). From Virginia, I managed to gradually move up to management positions in various local government and regional economic development promotion organisations in five different countries.

During this odyssey of personal development I have become increasingly aware that I and other economic developer practitioners operate without a core theoretical frame of reference. On reflection, I was fortunate to be able to attend BIDC in Chapel Hill, North Carolina under the leadership of the late Barry Moriarty. Moriarty, being a good economic geographer, included several sessions on location theory in the programme. In contrast, the Oklahoma programme was a hands-on training course on how to be a practitioner. The key text for the course was Howard Bessire's (1970), *The Practice of Industrial Development*. Bessire's book and the

1 The Economic Development Association of New Zealand (EDANZ) has recently established a College of Practitioners and a professional certification programme that is recognised by the IEDC.

three-year programme were devoid of theory. Three decades later, when designing my research proposal for my thesis, I soon came to the conclusion that I have been operating for my entire career without a sound theoretical understanding of the discipline. This book is an attempt to fill the theoretical vacuum that constitutes the practice of local economic development.

Book Layout and Content

The book is divided into four parts. The first part introduces the book and the reasons why the discipline lacks a coherent theoretical framework for understanding the practice of local economic development. It continues by arguing for the necessity of linking theory to practice. It should be noted that the terms local and regional are often used interchangeably throughout the book.

Part 2 describes and defines the discipline through the eyes of Mark M. Miller, Ed Blakely and Andrew Beer from a regional and a local perspective. Most people would agree that the discipline is diverse, practitioners come from a variety of backgrounds and the field comprises many different activities. Miller's chapter provides a good introduction to the discipline by relating his experiences and views of the field as an academic and a practitioner. As his title suggests and this book will substantiate, despite 80 years of searching, no definitive all encompassing theory of local or regional economic development has emerged. Miller's reference to Ed Blakely's role as Director of Recovery for the City of New Orleans is especially pertinent because it illustrates where economic development theory is hitting the coalface of practice. In the Chapter 3, Blakely builds upon his interim role in New Orleans by defining the practice of local economic development from an historical perspective by focusing on the development of a strategic model for inner city economic development policy. In essence, Blakely argues for a locally based and controlled process that enables everyone to benefit from economic development. The final chapter in the section describes the theory and practice of developing locally. Andrew Beer's chapter is especially valuable because it examines the contributions of Michael Porter and Richard Florida and relates their theories to three case studies. Porter's and Florida's research on competitive advantage and creative cities have probably been the most significant new theoretical contribution to the discipline in the last 15 years. These three chapters together provide an excellent introduction to the discipline and sets the stage for an examination of the key theoretical concepts that underpins the practice of local economic development.

The numerous theories that are applicable to the profession are presented in Part 3. These nine chapters examine the traditional theories derived from across the complimentary disciplines of geography, economics, planning and regional science. The first five chapters can be classified as location and space theories. It is essential that every practitioner understands the forces of globalisation, the concepts of competitive advantage and the basics of location and cluster theories.

One also has to be able to apply research methodologies in order to assess their respective areas before drafting an economic development strategy. An understanding of globalisation and the fundamentals of competitive advantage are necessary for theorising local economic development because they directly influence corporate location decisions. A local economic development practitioner needs to grasp these essential concepts in order to influence, develop and adopt a strategy that is specifically designed for his or her local area. In Chapter 5, Richard Le Heron investigates the tensions between economic processes and institutional arrangements created by globalisation. He also traces the theory underpinning globalisation from Keynesian and the neoclassical political economic thought to Dicken's, Swyngedouw's and Amin's research on the capitalist crises and restructuring processes. Le Heron concludes by introducing the movement towards and the need for a poststructuralist interpretation of the globalisation process.

In my opinion; the most important task of an economic development practitioner is to enhance the competitive advantages of his or her area (Rowe, 2005, p. 1). In Chapter 6, Michael Luger introduces the fundamental concept of competitive advantage and explains why it is so important to the discipline. In a similar vein, since economic development is primarily concerned with the location of economic activity, an understanding of the fundamentals of location theory is as pertinent today as it was when I was entering the profession in the mid-1970s. In Chapter 7, Philip McCann presents a concise overview of the historical development of location theory by investigating the three major streams of research and how they interrelate. The first stream of location theory was developed out of the *regional science and urban economics* tradition, the second stream emerged out of a fusion of traditional *economic geography* and the *business and management* theory, and the third steam developed out of *trade theory*. This leads into the next chapter on the theory behind clusters. Perry expands McCann's introduction of agglomeration theories in order to explain the popularity of clusters and why they are not the panacea many commentators claim. In Chapter 9, Bob Stimson and Roger Stough investigate the theoretical shift from exogenous to endogenous factors. The two regional scientists go on to present a new model for conceptualising regional economic development and conclude by proposing a potential new paradigm for endogenous regional development planning.

The next four chapters include elements of labour, capital, political and social theories. In Chapter 10, Paul Dalziel and his colleagues investigate the importance of a research university to a community. It is generally agreed that creating a culture of entrepreneurship is a fundamental prerequisite for successful local economic development. Because it is such an important concept, I selected the most appropriate research on the topic and chose to include it as the only previously published research in this book. Luke Pittaway's chapter on the contending theories of entrepreneurship offers an excellent introduction to the numerous theories and philosophies of this growing subdiscipline. In Chapter 12, Harvey Goldstein discusses the interface between the theory of technology-based economic development and the practice. In Chapter 13, John Blair and Michael Carroll provide an overview of social capital and why it is important to local economic development. Their research supports Ed Blakely's earlier discussions in Chapter 3 of social capital and how to maximise its potential.

Part 4, the concluding section, will examine the importance of metaphors and introduce a poststructuralist alternative theoretical framework for understanding the practice of local economic development. Michael Gunder, one of the world's leading planning theorists, introduces poststructuralist theorising in Chapter 14 by examining the economic perspectives of a city or region created through globalisation. New insights can be garnered by comparing Gunder's discussion of Porter and Florida's theoretical contributions from a Lacanian perspective compared to Andrew Beer's in Chapter 4. In Chapter 15, I expand Bingham and Mier's commentary on metaphors and present the case for employing poststructural methodologies for developing new insights into the discipline.

In Chapter 16, I also introduce Deleuzian philosophy as an economic development concept. Gilles Deleuze (1925–1995) was one of the most influential philosophers of his time (Badiou, 2000, p. 97). Michel Foucault once remarked that the 21st century may become known as Deleuzian (Buchanan, 1999b, p. 1). Foucault was predicting that Deleuze's work would steadily grow in significance across a variety of fields and his work is especially noted in trans-or interdisciplinary work where theoretical innovation is often regarded as an end itself (Tormey, 2005, p. 415). Deleuze (with Guattari, 1994, p. 28), when discussing his place among the great philosophers, once stated that "is it to repeat what they said or to do what they did, that is, create concepts for problems that necessarily change?" and most commentators would agree that economic development is constantly changing. Since Deleuzian ideas, concepts and the terminologies are difficult to understand, I have also included an appendix of key terms. Finally in the concluding chapter, I offer a pathway towards developing an alternative theoretical framework for understanding the practice of local economic development.

This book has been written for the purpose of reviewing the changes that have occurred since Bingham and Mier's collaborative effort 15 years ago as it relates to a rapidly changing discipline. In the opening pages of the introduction, I assert that the discipline lacks theory. As can be seen by the table of contents, there are many theories that relate to and impacts on local economic development, but none that explicitly provides a framework for understanding the complex relationships that comprise this interdisciplinary field of endeavour. The purpose of this book is to fill that gap.

This book is designed for academics and practitioners seeking to understand the theory that informs the practice of local and regional economic development. It is intended for anyone involved in economic development and those seeking a realistic and understandable introduction to the theory that underpins the practice. The book is intended as the main text for a course in economic development theory and as a reader for courses in economic and community development, urban and regional planning, resource management or regional economics. It should be of interest to those concerned with the application of theory to practice and the development of alternative theoretical frameworks.

James E. Rowe
Manukau, New Zealand, 2008

References

Badiou, A. (2000), *Deleuze: The Clamor of Being* (L. Burchell, Trans.). Minneapolis: University of Minnesota Press.

Bingham, R.D. and Mier, R. (eds) (1993), *Theories of Local Economic Development: Perspectives from Across the Disciplines*. Newbury Park, CA: Sage Publications.

Bessire, H. (1970), *The Practice of Economic Development*. El Paso, TX: Hill Printing Company.

Buchanan, I. (1999b), "Introduction", in I. Buchanan (ed.), *A Deleuzian Century?* (pp. 1–11). Durham, NC: Duke University Press.

Deleuze, G. and Guattari, F. (1994), *What is Philosophy?* (H. Tomlinson and G. Burchell, Trans.). New York: Columbia University Press.

Rowe, J.E. (2005), "Economic development: From a New Zealand perspective". In J.E. Rowe (ed.), *Economic Development in New Zealand* (pp. 1–13). Aldershot, UK: Ashgate Publishing Limited.

Rowe, J.E. (2008), *Understanding the Practice of Local Economic Development: An Alternative Theoretical Framework*, Unpublished PhD Thesis at the University of Auckland, Auckland, New Zealand.

Tormey, S. (2005), "A 'critical power'?: The uses of Deleuze", A review essay, *Contemporary Political Theory* 4(4), 414–30.

Acknowledgements

This book would not be possible without the help of many different people. Firstly, I want to thank the contributors who wrote the various chapters. I am honoured that these leading international experts have participated in this project. I am fortunate to have been able to include three contributors who also wrote chapters for Bingham and Mier's iconic 1993 book. I especially want to thank and acknowledge Michael Gunder, my PhD supervisor, for introducing me to poststructuralism and the works of Gilles Deleuze. This book is designed to encourage innovative thinking and new ways of approaching the economic development. The book will be successful if traditional academics and scholars such as Ed Blakely, Bob Stimson, Andrew Beer and Lay Gibson consider the validity of and the possibilities offered by alternative philosophical approaches. I also appreciate and wish to thank Val Rose, Commissioning Editor for Ashgate, for her confidence in the merits of publishing this book. Finally, this labour of love would not be possible without the support of my wife, Tachaya.

PART 1
Introduction

Chapter 1
The Importance of Theory: Linking Theory to Practice

James E. Rowe

The discipline of local economic development[1] is a complex mix of concepts, practices and rhetoric. In this writer's opinion, the economic development discipline lacks a dedicated coherent body of theory. Some scholars, such as Bingham and Mier (1993, p. ix), disagree and maintain that the theoretical underpinnings of economic development are a compilation of numerous theories derived from a wide variety of disciplines[2]. Although academic disciplines[3] such as economics, geography, resource management, regional science and planning provide significant insights; understanding economic development requires a unique blending of all relevant disciplines (Shaffer et al., p. 72). As a result, Shaffer et al. argued that it is generally accepted, from a practitioner's perspective, that the concept of economic development as an interdisciplinary field of endeavour. In support, Koo (2005, p. 100) has noted that a "basic knowledge of economic and other related theories is a necessary condition for an in-depth understanding of the [economic] development process".

In economic development, as in many other areas of human activity, theory and practice exist as two seemingly separate realities. Academics strive to develop or refine theory and engage in the pursuit of disciplinary truths by drawing on abstract concepts about the way people behave and institutions work (Flyvbjerg, 2001, pp. 25–37; Moore, 1980, p. 19). Practitioners draw from a stock of experiences. The theorists often do not specify how theoretical frameworks relate to the real world and practitioners often do not understand or appreciate theory. The dilemma is accentuated because most theorists do not practice economic development and practitioners do not reflect on or consider the theoretical basis for their activities (Bourdieu, 1977, p. vii).

---

1 In this book, the term economic development refers to local economic development as practiced in most advanced western nations and does not relate to the literature on developing countries or to the theories of classic development economics (Perkins et al., 2001).

2 Some would argue that there are benefits from the creative tensions between the multiplicity of theories and from more than one theoretical framework (Austin, 2006).

3 An academic discipline is a field of endeavour that has specific degrees and qualifications conferred by universities plus recognised professional journals and associations devoted to its development.

The problem has been exacerbated by an absence of a general theory of local economic development (Reese and Fasenfest, 1997, p. 196). It is generally argued that developing economic development theory has not been a priority because economic development as a profession is a relatively young and constantly changing field of endeavour and is just emerging as an academic discipline. Mier and Fitzgerald (1991, pp. 268–9) have suggested that the borrowed theories from economics, planning, geography and resource management constitute flirtations with the establishment of a new academic discipline. Despite the lack of a specific general theory of economic development, this writer asserts that economic development is an emerging academic discipline and as such, would be further advanced by developing a theoretical base of its own. It appears that scholars have largely devoted themselves to developing the practical aspects of the profession while ignoring the theory. Knudsen (1997, p. 210) has argued that ignorance of theory by practitioners and of economic development practice by theorists have resulted in piecemeal practice and unrealistic theory. The reality of this is rarely acknowledged within the field because most practitioners have no appreciation of the need for a definitive theory of economic development. Yet this is not without cost.

Most early textbooks on economic development provided an excellent overview of practice with almost no original theory (Bessire, 1970; Fernstrom, 1976; Moriarty, 1980). Blakely and Bradshaw's (2002, pp. 53–74) iconic book *Planning Local Economic Development, Theory and Practice* devoted only 19 pages to theory in a book of almost 400 pages. The theoretical frameworks presented by Blakely and others are borrowed from regional science, regional economics or economic geography to explain location and business decisions (Bingham and Mier, 1993, 1997; Blair, 1995; Malizia and Feser, 1999; Stafford, 1979; Stimson, Stough, and Roberts, 2002). The framework for most of the theories is derived from the classic location studies of von Thunen and Christaller and the pioneering research of Isard and Hoover (Foust and deSouza, 1978; Hoover, 1975; Isard, 1960; McCann and Sheppard, 2003, Miller, 1977; Smith, 1971, von Thunen, 1966). In this author's opinion, the relevant literature neither develops nor presents a robust framework or theory to explain the process and practice of economic development.

This writer argues that traditional development theory has failed when it has been applied to local economic development because of its focus on abstract macro issues and not the specific. This is important because each city or region is unique and there are no clear blueprints (generic strategies or actions) that can be applied to an area that will guarantee success (Bellamy et al., 2003, p. 16; Bowles and Gintis, 2003, p. 429). Jun Koo (2005, p.100) further articulated the problem by stating that:

> Economic development professionals often lack a theoretical understanding of the regional development mechanism. As a result, many regions simply follow fashionable ideas or recent successes of other regions without paying a fair amount of attention to what role their strategies will play in the development process. Many previous failures of economic development strategies can be attributied to such ill-informed planning practices.

An example of a packaged solution would be Richard Florida's prescriptions of attracting talent by becoming more *Bohemian* and tolerant to in turn attract high-tech investment. Scott (2006) challenges this prescription by asserting that being Bohemian does not necessarily translate into new high-tech business locations in the communities that have adopted Florida's strategies.

This tendency to copy generic solutions has resulted in:

> cities adopt[ing] the same economic development tool-kit…at a time of theoretical emphasis on the role of innovation in [local] economic development; what actually emerges as local economic development policy lacks any real innovative, imaginative or original thinking because the policy priorities contained in the strategy documents are effectively identical (Boland, 2007, p. 1032).

Gunder (2008, see Chapter 14) builds upon this argument by stating that:

> compounding this lack of focus on site-specific uniqueness and creativity, local officials and politicians often do not actually understand the implications of their chosen policies, or the links of causality, or lack of them, underlying specific theories.

As Deleuze (1994, p. 23) cautioned, we learn nothing from those who say: "do as I do".

In my opinion, we need a theory for understanding the practice of local economic development because as an emerging discipline, practitioners and academics equally need a theory that underpins their activities, initiatives and strategies that will enable them to approach universal and particular problems with new and innovative solutions. In support of my position, Foucault (2005) stated that a discipline needs a theory that allows it to be codified so that it can be identified as a 'human science'. I believe that economic development does not have a general theory because traditional positivistic[4] approaches cannot adequately theorise the complexity of the chaos of markets, global forces and multiple actors. Foucault (2005, pp. 377) would have addressed this by focusing on the *differences**[5] instead of trying to classify diverse forces.

Taking Foucault's lead, this writer argues that a framework can be developed that is cognitive of practice by employing poststructuralist[6] methodologies as

4 'Positivist' is an epistemological assumption meaning that knowledge can be abstracted, measured and understood via mathematics (Pittaway, 2005, p. 218).

5 Key Deleuzian and other poststructural terms are defined in Appendix 1. The * indicates that the term is introduced for the first time and the reader should refer to the appendix for a definition.

6 Poststructuralism rests on an assumption that no-one can stand outside the traditions or discourses of their time. As Pratt (2000, p. 626) explains, "a poststructuralist conceptualisation both frames and regulates social reality, it literally brings reality into

espoused by Deleuze (who is often referred to as the Philosopher of Difference[7]). For Deleuze, "thinking differently, becoming different and the creation of difference" (Jeanes and De Cock, 2005, p. 3) are keys to understanding the philosophy of difference. This is important because with a Deleuzian poststructural methodology, the tools to address unsymbolic[8] differences will be identified and their usefulness as metaphorical analogies will be demonstrated in the last two chapters.

What is Economic Development?

The literature indicates that there is considerable disagreement as to what constitutes local economic development (Wolman and Spitzley, 1996). However, there is little doubt that economic productivity and productivity growth are fundamental drivers of prosperity and innovation in any capitalist society. Consequently, "the focus of economic development should be on supporting innovation and increasing prosperity" (Economic Development Administration, 2004). Most practitioners would now agree that the economic development process is an endogenous effort designed to enhance a local community's ability to create and retain employment. This observation is based on endogenous development strategies designed to encourage business start-ups, innovation, entrepreneurship and the growth of firms already existing within a region (Stough, 2003, p. 179).

Richard Florida's (2005, 2006) popular concept of knowledge workers moving between competitive cities in a globalised world is a good example of this emerging trend of thought. This thinking replaced the previous approach that attempted to attract firms into regions via cash incentives, tax breaks, the provision of land or buildings and other benefits (Tietz, 1994, pp. 101–106). All of which are embedded in unquestioned assumptions of the hegemony of the capitalist growth mode of infinite product substitution and consumption. However, it should be noted that many practitioners still believe that states should offer tax incentives to generate new jobs (Clower et al., 2004).

This writer believes that economic development can be explained as a complex process that is created from a successful fusion of entrepreneurship, education and skills of the community, driven largely by market forces. A favourable business environment and a supportive regulatory framework are important conditions of economic growth and development. It is generally accepted that the goal of economic development is to create new jobs, investment and improve the wealth of

---

being", and by doing so, "profoundly disrupts the distinction between representation and pre-discursive reality".

7 Deleuze, the author of *Difference and Repetition* (1994), was known as the 'Philosopher of Difference' because his writings produced a series of pairings and encounters of forces that resonated by aligning the reader with a new force and a new trajectory.

8 Unsymbolic means outside of language/words. For an explanation of unsymbolic differences see Alliez (2004, pp. 92–3).

individuals and the community, Others such as Ed Blakely (Blakely and Bradshaw, 2002, p. 375) described the practice of local economic development as being a "mixture of rational planning and salesmanship". As a further refinement, one learned colleague suggested that economic development is really about fostering 'entrepreneurial *immanence**'(Gunder, 2005).

What do Economic Developers Actually Do?

Deleuze once questioned what a philosopher actually does by asking "What is it I have been doing all my life?" (Deleuze and Guattari, 1994, p. 1). In a similar vein, Levy (1990) responded to the question in his article entitled, *What economic developers actually do: location quotients versus press releases*. Despite Levy's insightful analysis, most economic development practitioners would have a difficult time explaining what they do[9] (Friedmann, 1996, p. 94). This leads to the more complex questions of what should economic development practitioners be doing and why do they do what they do?

The literature indicates that the fundamental objective of an economic development organisation is to maintain and create jobs and regional production, to increase wealth (Stough, 2003, p. 179) and community well being. Therefore, the daily activities of a local economic development practitioner should be in doing tasks that lead to the creation of jobs[10] and wealth (or job retention). However, some cynics assert that generating job announcements is more important than creating jobs (Beer et al., 2003, p. 163). It has often become politically easier to garner support for a Foreign Direct Investment (FDI) marketing programme than to develop an entrepreneurial culture, despite the limited success of most industrial recruitment programmes (Loveridge, 1996, p. 155).

Many economic development programmes are under intense media scrutiny and as a result, many practitioners are under immense pressure to justify their positions[11]. When the economic development agency seeks renewed or additional funding they are often asked, 'What have you done for me lately?' As a result, many practitioners often "shoot anything that flies; claim anything that falls" (Rubin, 1988, p. 288). This often cited reference refers to the fact that many economic

9 For the purposes of this book economic development is defined as a subdiscipline within the greater body of planning. Relevant published statements by Friedmann and others originally describing wider planning and even pertinent geographical theory have been paraphrased and attributed to economic development.

10 The number of new jobs is a measurable outcome and is therefore often used as a benchmark for evaluating the effectiveness of economic development programmes. One of the key outcomes of this research is the development of an evaluation framework that enables one to assess the effectiveness of an economic development programme.

11 Economic development practitioners often have to seek funding approval every year from their main stakeholders.

development agencies claim credit for new businesses and facilities that locate in their area whether or not they actually had anything to do with the location decision making process. Rubin went on to say that, "I think a lot of people buy themselves with these retention surveys, whatever, and going to trade shows... [its] Good, [that at least they are]...out there marketing". As a result, Luke and his colleagues asserted that experience and working knowledge of the seasoned economic development professional are increasingly ineffective and, in many cases, even detrimental when applied to the new interconnected economic context. Competing with other cities for scarce industrial prospects creates adversarial, competitive relationships that can actually hinder future economic development (Luke et al., 1988, p. 227).

Many economic development initiatives, programmes and activities are designed to garner media coverage (such as FDI marketing trips and trade shows) to retain political support instead of enhancing the competitive advantage of the city or region. Many more activities are initiated in order *to be seen as doing something* (Isserman, 1994) and often economic development practitioners just *muddle through* (Fortun and Bernstein, 1998; Lindblom, 1959). Because economic development strategies and action plans are seemingly developed in a theoretical vacuum, Bartik (1991, p. 208) questioned if there is any reliable evidence that economic development programmes actually work. Consequently, some scholars have questioned the effectiveness of most economic development agencies and programmes (Blair and Kumar, 1997). In essence, Isserman (1994, p. 94) has concluded that for the most part economic development programmes have not had "any measurable economic effect and may merely constitute tinkering on the margins of massive market forces".

As a result, "it remains unclear whether policies and program[me]s attain even the basic local economic development goals such as job creation" (Felsenstein and Persky, 2007, p. 25) and thus, one must question if any of the programmes really make a difference[12] (Rowe, 2005, p. 230). Consequently, this writer argues that often economic development strategies have little effect on the occurrence of real world economic activities. This book (see Chapters 15 and 16) will endeavour to explain the apparent poor correlation by drawing on a poststructural theoretical framework based on Deleuzian philosophy. Yet, this position does not totally preclude a need for economic development programmes. This author argues that being seen to being doing something and being a point of contact, even if in a zero sum game, is still needed. This is because this author believes that an *effective* economic development practitioner can actually have a positive influence the location of economic activity and pragmatically, one has to be in the game in order to win.

12 The initiatives that practitioners believe are effective and which activities actually lead toward new job and wealth creation has been delineated by Beer et al., 2003.

What Constitutes Economic Development

This section will argue that the existing literature fails to develop a relevant theory for understanding the practice of local economic development. It will also introduce new key concepts in order to link the theory of economic development with practice as viewed through a Deleuzian lens. Significantly, it will explicitly tie Deleuzian concepts to the practice of economic development.

Because of its complexity, economic development practitioners enter the field from a variety of backgrounds. Most earn tertiary degrees in economics, geography, resource management or planning (Wilson, 2004). More recently, a limited number[13] of specialised programmes (and qualifications) have been developed to train economic development practitioners in New Zealand (Wilson, 2004, 2005). When preparing to become economic development practitioners, students must immerse themselves into the system of knowledge that constitutes the discipline (Gunder, 2004, p. 301). The process of transforming theoretical knowledge into practice is similar to when a person first enters the profession and undertakes an apprenticeship when learning to be a practitioner. The practitioner learns "by grasping [movements] in practice as signs" (Deleuze 1994, p. 23). A new person entering the field often does not have a firm foundation from which to proceed. Deleuze (1995) compared this learning experience to a novice learning to swim in the surf. In Deleuze's example, the swimmer has to experience the movement of the waves before he or she can learn to move with the waves instead of against them.

Lacanian social theory would suggest that most of this knowledge is derived from an unconscious interpolation of disciplinary knowledges, norms and values as to what constitutes *good* behaviour of a practitioner (Gunder, 2004, p. 304). Once employed, the new practitioners become responsible for reproducing, reinforcing and applying this knowledge. Economic development practitioners thus replicate the 'technical-rationality' of the knowledge based university discourse as the primary mode of the practice (Hillier and Gunder, 2005, p. 1057).

Schön and Rein, as discussed in Gunder (2003, p. 288), used the term *frame* to stand as a synonym for ideological perspectives or discourses attributable to a *master signifier**, that planners and policy analysts intrinsically identify with and which inherently shapes, or biases, their world view. Economic development also has master signifiers in the form of 'jobs', 'entrepreneurship', 'investment', 'economic prosperity', 'increased tax base', 'clusters' and 'globalisation'. These general and often fuzzy iconic terms refer to complex discourses that have become synonymous to 'successful economic development'. These terms, as *master signifiers*, are generally unquestionably accepted as valid and worthy of support

13 The only two US programmes that offer master degrees in economic development are the Universities of Arizona (Gibson, 2006) and Southern Mississippi, while other institutions such as the University of North Carolina offer master degrees in planning with an economic development focus. However, a number of continuing education programs are offered through the International Economic Development Council and the University of Oklahoma.

(Gunder, 2003, p. 282; Painter, 2005, p. 144). As a result, economic development policies and strategies always carry these coded *master signifiers*. However, most often these policies are not linked to or derived from theory. Thus, in this writer's opinion, there is a need to develop a theoretical framework that resonates with the practice and process of economic development. This is important because, as previously established; theorising is a blend of individualistic interpretation, paradigm and a practical context.

In my opinion, change does not occur in economic development practice because of shifts in the practitioners' conceptual equipment. Changes arise, rather, as adjustments to the unfolding realities within practice. According to Graham and Healey (1999, p. 27), "the realities of the open, dynamic, multi-layered and dialectically-constructed 'multiplex' circuitry of the contemporary world is reflected not in the practitioners' conceptions but in the evolutionary adjustments they have to make". The practice of economic development:

> vacillates between objectivitist and subjectivist epistemologies, with the contradictions often resolved in favour of privileged actors. The whole process, moreover, is greatly influenced by the need for action and a corresponding reliance on actors whose decisions are only partly motivated by analytical knowledge, resistant to government command, and tenuously linked to the spatial arenas in which policymakers operate. As a result, the path between knowledge and action is murky and discontinuous. The response is ideological formulations – the partitioning of economic development into routine activities and special projects, and a tolerance for epistemological conflict (Beauregard, 1993, p. 280).

Thus, "it is the practice, not theory, of the planning process that defines the roles and limits of the emerging professional economic developer", rather than any coherent body of theory (Blakely and Bradshaw, 2002, p. 376).

The question of whether theories can contribute to building a better understanding of the practice of economic development must be measured by their usefulness as tools of reading, seeing, inspiring and acting. Oettermann as quoted by Doel (2004, p. 452) stated that:

> theories never loom large and they are not of a piece: they are differentiated, mutable and dispersed. Nor do theories come as ready-mades: they are lent a certain situational consistency that works only insofar as it breaks down. Consequently, we should not be distracted by a mirage born of 'see-fever'.

In practical terms, this means that new insights are needed in order to understand the complexities of economic development because:

> New insights often arise as one reads a situation from 'new angles,' and that a wide and varied reading can create a wide and varied range of action possibilities…Our theories and explanations of organisational life are based on metaphors…that imply way(s) of seeing that pervade how we understand our world generally (Morgan, 1986, p. 12).

What constitutes economic development is constantly changing (Clower et al., 2004; Wolman and Spitzley, 1996). Therefore, from a Deleuzian viewpoint, the process and practice of economic development should be thought of as a philosophical problem that demands the creation of new concepts (Buchanan, 1999, p. 115). Every concept has components and is defined by them; consequently economic development is a combination or a *multiplicity** of concepts. Accordingly, a theory cannot dispense with concepts and for a theory of economic development, the central concept has to be economic development itself (Friedmann, 1987, p. 35). Deleuze argued that concepts are useful for creating "new connections for thinking" and opening up whole new *planes of thought* (Deleuze and Guattari, 1994). As a result, this book endeavours to develop an alternative theoretical framework utilising Deleuzian philosophy to gain new insights into, and a better understanding of, the practice of local economic development.

One has to understand the overarching desire and driving force behind such theories as they link and bind ideas together with minimum of constant rules of resemblance, contiguity, and causality in order to fight against chaotic reality, uncontrollability and unpredictability (Deleuze and Guattari, 1994, p. 201). Deleuze (1989, p. 280) stated that:

> For theory too is something which is made, no less than its object. For many people, philosophy is something which is not 'made', but is pre-existent, ready-made in a prefabricated sky. However, philosophical theory is itself a practice, just as much as its object. It is no more abstract than its object, it is a practice of concepts, and it must be judged in the light of the other practices with which it interferes…It is at the level of the interference of many practices that things happen, being, images, concepts, all the kinds of events.

From this perspective economic development theory can be developed that offers a new way of thinking about and seeing the everyday work of the practitioner. Such a theory should provide an explanatory framework to describe and interpret what economic developers actually do in practice and what economic development as a professional activity is. It should reinterpret the practice of economic development through a multifaceted prism of borrowed and appropriated concepts and reflect it back to the practitioners (Neuman, 2005, pp. 127–9).

Why is an Explanatory Understanding Important for Economic Development?

This section will suggest that theory is important for economic development. First it will explain the difference between the traditional or positivistic predictive and constructionist explanatory theories (the differences between traditional and constructionist theories are further elaborated in Chapter 15). This writer argues that it is impossible to develop an all encompassing predictive theory of local economic development. However, it is asserted that an explanatory theoretical framework can be designed by embracing Deleuzian poststructuralist methodology (see Chapter 16). Such a framework is useful in regards to the *real* reasons for economic development.

According to Flyvbjerg (2001, p. 167) the purpose of social science is not to develop predictive theory, but to contribute to society's practical rationality in elucidating where we are, where want to go, and what is desirable according to diverse sets of values and interests. Economic development, despite Flyvbjerg's rationale, may be argued by some to be a social science and as such requires a theoretical base, at least from a realist[14] or positivistic view. The positivistic (realist) traditional view of social science requires predictive theories or models, while constructionist theories are explanatory in nature. This book argues that an explanatory understanding would be more appropriate because of the complex transdisciplinary nature of the field. In this writer's opinion, a universal theory that covers all aspects of local economic development can never be achieved. Deleuze recognised the impossibility of developing such a universal theory and emphasised that it should not be considered a failure but a chance to experiment and to "grasp [the]...opportunity to accept the challenge to transform" (Colebrook, 2002a, p. 2) the discipline.

Friedmann (2003, p. 9) maintains that it is important to develop a theory of planning because it is essential to the vitality and continued relevance of planning as a profession. This writer suggests that Friedmann's assertion equally applies to local economic development. The development of discourse theories and analysis has been prompted by the failure of positivist and rationalist approaches to offer satisfactory explanations of social practices (Hillier and Gunder, 2005, p. 1062). Thus,

> A scientific theory does not necessarily assert that the world is so-and-so...rather, a theory is a recommendation that for some purposes it is convenient or useful to consider the world *as if* it were so-and-so...Or, to put the latter part of the sentence more precisely, the phenomena in the world are to be considered as they would be considered if the world were so-and-so even though, insofar as we can tell, it is not (Maki, 2004, p. 1724).

This turns a philosophical problem into a problem for theory and method. Social scientists develop ideas that can be represented and explained. However, representing and explaining a concept is only part of the equation. In making something 'make sense' one opens certain pathways and closes down others by defending our concepts because they extend our thinking beyond what is already known. Various epistemologies and methods point towards different kinds of explanation (Rose, 2004, p. 465). One has to develop a framework within the economic development discipline that allows for *thinking outside the square* by endeavouring to "change terrain in a discontinuous and irruptive fashion" (Derrida, 1982, p. 135).

---

14 'Realist' refers to the philosophical assumption that social 'reality' exists in a tangible way and that its underpinning rules can be identified.

In a globalised world what constitutes economic development has significantly changed in the last 20 years. The body of knowledge has expanded with numerous research articles in leading professional publications[15] and the development of new analytical tools and processes. However, as clearly indicated in the literature, no theoretical framework has emerged. Other planning fields, such as urban and regional planning, have evolved with the times and are constantly updating their often contradictory theoretical bases[16]. Local economic development, to the contrary, has lagged behind.

> Academic research has provided key ideas in several instances, but, on the whole, scholars have played a meager role in the design and evolution of economic development [theory]. Practitioners 'have had to learn by doing'[17] (Osbourne, 1988, p. 259).

This book argues that theory has to be developed for, and be applicable (relevant) to, it's professional field of practice.

Jacoby (1987) has asserted that planning theorists are not public intellectuals[18]. While many may disagree, he and others maintained that their work is written for and only read by other planning theorists (Yiftachel, 2006). Adding to the negativity, Beauregard (1991, p. 192) has published statements indicating that even planning practitioners avoid academic planning theory. Despite these comments, the planning profession has an active cadre of theorists that generates considerable debate and discussion. Planning theory is at least being read by a few, whilst economic development seems to be largely devoid of any theoretical debate. Hence, the *raison d'être* for this book is to stimulate more theoretical debate.

In conclusion, the field of local economic development is currently under-theorised. This writer maintains that a positivistic predictive theory may not be possible but a constructionist explanatory meta-theory of economic development can be developed by employing poststructuralist methodologies. After presenting the key concepts and the plethora of theories underpinning them, this book attempts to begin this constructionist process.

---

15 *Economic Development Quarterly, Local Economy, Applied Research in Economic Development, Economic Development America* and the *IEDC Journal of Economic Development* are the only journals exclusively devoted to the discipline while there are more than 20 planning journals with several dedicated to theory. However, numerous articles on economic development issues are published in planning, economic and geographic journals.

16 One could argue that planning still doesn't have a definitive base. There is always something lacking or incomplete in the theoretical base of any discipline.

17 This quotation, despite being published in 1988, is still relevant because scholars have not developed any applicable new theories.

18 A public intellectual was identified as an academic versed in social sciences who addressed issues of common interest or took a stance on an issue of the day and triggered public debates (Zizek, 2005, pp. 88–9).

Theory versus Practice

The accumulation of knowledge[19] consists of the process of gradual confirmation and/or modification of theories. Theory[20] and practice are related in a loose but important way. Theories suggest relationships that are consistent with their beliefs about the way the world works; and as the world changes, new theories are created and old ones are revised. The main purpose of developing theories is to explain complex issues; however such theories do not always reflect the real world (Shaffer et al., 2006, p. 71). Those writing theory have a "tendency to borrow, interpret, adapt, and occasionally misappropriate selective bits of theoretical concepts from others [as] standard practice in most intellectual endeavours" and, as a result, this method often advances knowledge (Neuman, 2005, p. 128).

Theory, under liberal modernity, is what you traditionally read and learn in university from studying scientific research[21] and then apply to the situations in your field of endeavour. The result is practice. People often talk about professional knowledge as if it were based on theory from which general principles (or rules) are derived. These in turn can be applied to the problems of practice. In this way, theory is *real* knowledge, while practice is the application of that knowledge to solve problems [hence the phrase 'applied social science'] (Smith, 1999). Richard Rorty has argued that "If we get rid of traditional notions of 'objectivity' and 'scientific method' we shall be able to see the social sciences as continuous with literature – as interpreting other people to us, and thus enlarging and deepening our sense of community" (Rorty, 1979, p. 203). This writer suggests that seeing the social sciences as 'continuous with literature' means, to paraphrase Rorty, seeing both science and literature as interpreting the earth to us and thus 'enlarging and deepening our sense of community' with the earth. This concept offers an opportunity to construct a framework that combines aspects of philosophy and science together into a coherent framework for understanding practice.

Historically, a contrast has often been made between theoretical and practical reason. Practical reason can therefore be defined as argument, intelligence or insight directed to a practical outcome. For Aristotle, praxis is guided by a moral disposition to act truly and rightly; a concern to further human well being and the good life. This is what the Greeks called *phronesis* (Flyvbjerg, 1992, 2001; Hillier,

19 There are five sources of knowledge: traditional, authority, trial and error, reasoning and the scientific method (Batavia, 2001, pp. 5–7).

20 Theory "is a set of related ideas that has the potential to explain or predict human experience in an orderly fashion" (DePoy and Gitlin, 2005, p. 56).

21 "The meaning of scientific research as a societal institution is to accumulate knowledge. The nature of knowledge to be accumulated varies, however, according to whether a theoretical or practical interest in that knowledge is to be applied. Plainly expressed, academic research strives for the accumulation of theoretical knowledge, i.e. the elaboration and refinement of scientific concepts, theories and models, tested by empirical research." (Bengs, 2002).

2005). The ingredients of *phronesis,* or practical wisdom, are complex. Practical rationality therefore, is best understood through cases, whether experienced or narrated, just as judgement is best cultivated and communicated via the exposition of cases (Flyvbjerg, 2004, pp. 297–8). This means that an explanatory framework should be developed through case studies with real world examples.

For this writer, theorising is an activity where truths are elusive phenomena, very much contextually and individually related. Accordingly, it makes sense to draw upon the concept of rhetoric (Throgmorton, 1996). With rhetoric, meaning is created through dialogue. One needs to communicate effectively in order to develop, together with others, meaningful solutions and answers to the many challenges facing the local economic development practitioner. Practical solutions can be derived as a result of traditional and poststructural research and from dialogues with other practitioners. Practical wisdom teaches us how to use experience and at the same time to evaluate a concrete situation on its own terms.

Aristotle, along with other classical Greek thinkers, believed that the appropriateness of any particular form of knowledge depends on the telos, or purpose, it serves. In brief:

> The purpose of a theoretical discipline is the pursuit of truth through contemplation; its telos is the attainment of knowledge for its own sake. The purpose of the productive sciences is to make something; their telos is the production of some artefact. The practical disciplines are those sciences which deal with ethical and political life; their telos is practical wisdom and knowledge (Carr and Kemmis, 1986, p. 32).

In praxis there can be no prior knowledge of the right means by which to achieve an objective in a particular situation (Flyvbjerg, 2001). As we think about what we want to achieve, we often alter our approach to the problem. As we think about the way we might go about something, our aim is often changed. There is a continual interplay between ends and means and a continual interplay between thought and action. The process involves interpretation, understanding and application. For Deleuze, philosophy and creative thinking involves the opposite thought process. According to Deleuze, one should not begin thinking from already defined terms. It is a mistake "to think of theories as commencing with the question of how minds or subjects can know the world; it is also a mistake to begin our thoughts from simple propositions or common sense" (Colebrook, 2002b, p. 66). As Pierre Bourdieu (1990) has argued, common sense[22] produces the strongest adherence of an established order. People act as they think they are supposed to; they do what they think is appropriate in places that are also appropriate.

---

22 "To have common sense is to recognize what is obvious" (May, 2005, p. 76). When applying common sense, one has already formed a general concept of what it means to think (Colebrook, 2002a, p. 14).

Underlying theories are paradigms[23] which are the fundamental models or frames of reference we use to organise our observations and reasoning. Paradigms are difficult to recognise as such because they are so implicit, assumed and taken for granted. They seem more like "the way things are than like one possible point of view among many" (Babbie, 2004, pp. 33–4). For Flyvbjerg, paradigms in social science that involve theory are derived from "practices in specific contexts while still working to achieve critical distance on [the] prevailing understandings" (Schram, 2006, p. 31). A paradigm is a model or an example, therefore *framing* offers an opportunity to conceptualise a discipline. Framing an action is defined as a set of tacit agreements without which action would not be possible. In economic theory framing is the study of relationships or externalities, the overflow is sometimes hard to identify because flows circulate, connect and link *actants** (Callon, 1997, p. 5). Analysis of this concept suggests that viewing the practice of economic development through a Deleuzian lens might contribute a different and unique (but very valid) theory for understanding the discipline.

For everyday use, a pragmatic definition of economic development is *what practitioners do* (Rowe, 2006). Consequently, practitioners can engage in the practice of economic development without having a clear definition of the term (Friedmann, 1996, p. 94). As a result, a theorist needs to delineate a general concept of a field before developing a theory. Zizek believes that when attempting to think the *new* when seeking creative transformation a shift in the coordinates of the prevailing frameworks of theory and practice occurs (Sinnerbrink, 2006, p. 85). With this in mind, a universal generic economic development theory is not and cannot be relevant, except for the particular forms of practice to which it happens to apply (Alexander, 2003, p. 180). Theorising, then, is a blend of individualistic interpretation, paradigm and a practical context (Hillier, 2002, p. 17).

In order to develop a relevant theoretical framework that practitioners can embrace, this writer examined the literature seeking the most appropriate way to bridge the gap between theory and practice. The literature led this writer to conclude that a poststructuralist methodological approach would yield the desired results. After a general survey of a number of poststructural writers, this author found that the Deleuzian concept of *geophilosophy** resonates with the practice of economic development. This concept will be further developed in the last chapter.

Deleuze's work is "truly inter-disciplinary and is not just a *theory* that can be applied to the arts and sciences. Each *event** in art and science is itself an opportunity to reinvent the whole process of thinking and living" (Colebrook, 2002b, p. 79). A theory of economic development requires *thinking out of the square* and *seeing the big picture*, therefore:

23 Paradigm is a model or framework for observations and understanding, which shapes both what we see and how we understand it. The term was first coined by Thomas Kuhn in *The Structure of Scientific Revolutions* published in 1962. Kuhn believed that in the natural sciences periodic conceptual transformations in the form of a paradigm shift occur that initiate new ways of understanding a discipline.

> Being inter-disciplinary does not just mean combining literary insights with philosophy, or using anthropology to enhance psychology; it means accounting for all the different ways in which thought produces order out of chaos. It requires thinking globally: not remaining within any one discipline, and not just combining disciplines, but crossing from discipline to discipline, to continually open and renew the very medium or 'milieu' with which we think (Colebrook, 2002b, p. 80).

Economic development is a synthesis of inter-disciplinary social sciences and it inherently conforms to Colebrook's injunction for inter-disciplinary thinking. In order to apply this synthesis of thinking, according to Deleuze and Guattari (1994), one has to create new concepts or modify old ones. Thus, concepts that give expression to the abstract machines, pure events and *becomings** on the plane of immanence are particularly important for establishing a new framework for understanding (Patton, 2005, p. 403) This equally applies to economic development because all these concepts resonate with the spatial aspects of the discipline.

Theory and practice are not opposites or separate entities. *Practice* cannot lack theory. To paraphrase Friedmann (2003, p. 8), there cannot be an economic development practice without a theory on how it ought to be practiced[24]. Deleuze echoed Friedmann with "theory does not express, translate, or serve to apply practice: it is practice" (Deleuze, 2006, p. 208). Similarly, it is difficult to conceive of 'theory' that is purely descriptive and devoid of reference to purposeful action. In other words, practice is underpinned by theory. There is a constant process of theory making and theory testing. Thus, it is in this sense that one can begin to talk about practice as praxis or informed action. As Freire (1972, p. 60) articulated "we find two dimensions, reflection and action, in such radical interaction that if one is sacrificed – even in part – the other immediately suffers". Deleuze further delineated the difference by stating that:

> Science or theory is an inquiry, which is to say, a practice: a practice of the seemingly fictive world that empiricism describes; a study of the conditions of legitimacy of practices in this empirical world that is in fact our own. The result is a great conversion of theory to practice (Deleuze, 2005b, p. 36).

As articulated by Murphy (1998, p. 214), Deleuze went on to insist that the relationship between theory and practice is a set of relays from one theoretical point to another as per the following quotation:

> far more partial and fragmentary. On one side, a theory is always local and related to a limited field, and it is applied in another sphere, more or less distant from it. The relationship which holds in the application of a theory is never one of resemblance…

24 This means that economic development practitioners have been practising with borrowed theories from other disciplines that often do not provide a clear theoretical framework for understanding the field or achieving their objectives.

> Practice is a set of relays from one theoretical point to another, and theory is a relay from one practice to another. No theory can develop without eventually encountering a wall, and practice is necessary for piercing this wall.

For example, Deleuze "takes solutions to particular problems he has encountered in the course of his own daily practice from other philosophers" (Buchanan, 2000, p. 12).

Some aspects of economic development can be considered one of the 'practical or applied sciences'. These were originally associated with ethical and political life. Their purpose was the cultivation of wisdom and knowledge. In the practical sciences, one has to consider the dichotomy between the particular and the universal. The particular can be equated to practice and the universal to theory (Butler, 2000, p. 33). The practice produces actions which need to be connected back to theory because the actions equate to values (Latour, 2005). The universal also has to be applied to a particular structure. They involve the making of judgments and human interaction. The form of reasoning associated with the practical sciences is praxis of informed and committed action. In order to understand, it is useful to reflect on what has already been said about the theoretical and the productive and to think about these in relation to what is meant by 'practice'.

> For theory too is something which is made, no less than its object. For many people, philosophy is something which is not 'made', but is pre-existent, ready-made in a prefabricated sky. However, philosophical theory is itself a practice, just as its object. It is no more abstract than its object. It is a practice of concepts, and it must be judged in the light of the other practices with which it interferes…It is at the level of the interference of many practices that things happen, beings, images, concepts, all the kinds of events (Deleuze, 1989, p. 280).

Practice is often portrayed at a very simple level as the act of doing something. It is frequently depicted in contrast to *theory* – abstract ideas about some particular thing or phenomenon. Or to phrase it differently,

> Practical activity, unlike *theoretical* activity, implies an engagement with a reality independent of ourselves and our thoughts…When we interact for practical purposes with the natural environment, which is profoundly independent of our thoughts, we do so collectively…That is to say: we know the world with our institutions, and by virtue of our institutions, not in spite of them (Bloor, 2001, p. 105 my emphasis).

Doing practice[25] for many practitioners "involves an appreciation of what matters and to whom" (Hillier, 1995, p. 292), however practice more often resembles the following:

---

25 Since economic development may be considered a subset of planning, an economic development practitioner and a planner have similar day to day activities.

> When we look at the day-to-day work of putting out brushfires, dealing with 'random' telephone calls, debating with other staff, juggling priorities, bargaining here and organizing there, trying to understand what in the world someone else (or some document) means, the first, means-ends, view quickly comes to be a tempting but inadequate reconstruction of what actually goes on. We might like to think that a straightforward rationale or goal justifies every action, but justifications are so diverse, so varying and wide-ranging, that no simple (and certainly no formal) coverall end helps us explain what [practitioners]...do (Forester, 1989, p. 15).

The practice of economic development is an "ensemble of social relations, networks and nodes of dynamic and often inventive social interaction, patterned by legal, governmental and professional systems, and by customs and habits build up over the years" (Healey, 1997, pp. 16–17). Economic development researchers have been "caught in the midst of accepting that the relation of theory to practice is one of either two approaches, namely: the priority of theory over practice, or vice versa" (Dewsbury, 2003, p. 1919). This relationship can be visualised as the "*fold** of theory and practice, of the conceptual and the empirical...[and] through this concept Deleuze argues that when we are at work in dealing with the world [as an economic development practitioner] we are working with 'concrete' *multiplicities**" (Dewsbury, 2003, p. 1918). The term 'concrete multiplicities' means that practitioners work in a complex world in which they have little control or influence. For example, a local firm may be forced to relocate to another city or nation where labour costs and tax liabilities are less because of corporate decisions made in oversea headquarters. This concrete real world example could adversely affect the performance rating of the local economic development practitioner if the local strategy's key goal was industry retention.

These 'concrete multiplicities' embody ways of thinking and ways of acting, which interact in complex and often ambiguous ways (Forester, 2001). The emergence of a new conception of the relationship between theory and practice can not be understood as an equally unified process of the application or implementation of theory, but as "a system of relays within...a *multiplicity* of parts that are both theoretical and practical" (Foucault, 1977, p. 206). Thus, as previously quoted, "it is the practice, not theory, of the [economic development] process that defines the roles and limits of the [practitioner] and the emerging economic development [discipline]" and not any body of theory (Blakely and Bradshaw, 2002, p. 376).

When discussing the link between theory and practice Butler has stated that theory should be applied to its examples and "is articulated on its self-sufficiency, and then shifts to register only for the pedagogical purpose of illustration an already accomplished truth" (Butler, 2000, p. 26). In this context, one must decide what truth is (Foucault, 1990). When describing truth, Foucault (1980, p. 132) once stated:

> by truth I do not mean the ensemble of truths which are to be discovered and accepted, but rather 'the ensemble of rules' according to which the true and false are separated and specific effects of power attached to the truth.

One should apply technical knowledge and skills according to a pragmatic instrumental rationality, what Foucault calls "a practical rationality governed by a conscious goal" (Foucault, 1984, p. 255). Practical rationality, therefore, is best understood through cases, whether experienced or narrated, just as judgement is best cultivated and communicated via the exposition of cases (Flyvbjerg, 2004, pp. 297–8). This means that an explanatory framework should be developed and tested through case studies with real world examples. Without such examples, the practitioner will not be able to connect the theory with practice.

When quoting Foucault, Deleuze once asked, "What is philosophy today…if it does not, rather than legitimising what one already knows, consist of an attempt to know how and to what extent it is possible to think differently?" (Macey, 1993, p. 471). Deleuze and Guattari saw their work as a breaking away from the traditional practices and structures of reading and writing.

> We're tired of trees. We should stop believing in trees, roots and radicals. They've made us suffer too much. All of *arborescent** culture is founded on them from biology to linguistics. Nothing is more beautiful or lovingly or political aside from underground stems and aerial *roots*, adventitious growths and *rhizomes** (Deleuze and Guattari, 1987, p. 15).

It is the rhizomatic structure of links, paths and lines of flight, which gives substance and meaning to the theory or framework of economic development. Deleuze once stated "…an AND, AND, AND which each time marks a new threshold, a new direction of the broken line, a new course for the border" (Deleuze, 1995, p. 5). The path could be disturbed, interrupted or lost, but there is always an alternative path to follow that continues the flow and connection of ideas and thoughts. Concepts, thus, are connective and not hierarchical but linking (Morss, 2000, p. 195).

Deleuze and Guattari offer a unique conception of the relations between theories and practice. This is a conception which understands such relationships:

> in a partial and fragmentary manner, not as determinate relationships between 'theory' understood as a totality and 'practice' understood as an equally unified process of the application or implementation of theory (Patton, 2000, p. 5),

but as a "system of relays within…a multiplicity of parts that are both theoretical and practical" (Foucault, 1977, p. 206). Adorno, as quoted in Buchanan (1999a, p. 103), stated that:

> The object of theory is not something immediate, of which theory might carry home a replica. Knowledge has not, like the state police, a rogue's gallery of its objects. Rather it conceives them as it conveys them; else it would be content to describe the façade.

What economic development practitioners actually do is more "fundamental than either discourse, text or theory because discourse is not life: regular, daily practice is" (Foucault, 1991, p. 72). Deleuze, in supporting Foucault, stated that "theory does not express, translate, or serve to apply practice: it is practice" (Deleuze, 2006, p. 208). Deleuze had earlier argued that "philosophy must constitute itself as the theory of what we are doing, not as a theory of what there is" (Deleuze, 1991, p. 133). Therefore, "theories can be thought of as tools which are grounded in everyday life and practice" (Hillier, 2002, p. 25). As a result, one can conclude "that theory and practice merge together in the application of knowledge…[and] that theory cannot be divorced from a practical grounding in the real world" (Gunder, 2006, p. 158) and thus, theory and practice must be linked.

References

Alexander, E.R. (2003), "Response to 'why do planning?'" *Planning Theory 2*(3), 179–82.

Alliez, E. (2004), *The Signature of the World, or, What is Deleuze and Guattari's Philosophy?* New York: Continuum.

Austin, P. (2006), *Personal Communication.* Auckland, New Zealand.

Babbie, E. (2004), *The Practice of Social Research* (10th edn). Belmont, CA: Thomson Wadsworth.

Bartik, T.J. (1991), *Who Benefits from State and Local Development Policies?* Kalamazoo, MI: Upjohn Institute.

Batavia, M. (2001), *Clinical Research for Health Professionals: A User Friendly Guide.* Boston: Butterworth-Heinemann.

Beauregard, R.A. (1991), "Without a net: Modernist planning and the postmodern abyss". *Journal of Planning Education and Research 10*(3), 189–94.

Beauregard, R.A. (1993), "Constituting economic development: A theoretical perspective". In R.D. Bingham and R. Mier (eds), *Theories of Local Economic Development* (pp. 267–83). Newbury Park, CA: Sage Publications.

Beer, A., Haughton, G. and Maude, A. (2003), *Developing Locally: An International Comparison of Local and Regional Economic Development.* Bristol: The Policy Press.

Beer, A., Maude, A. and Pritchard, B. (2003), *Developing Australia's Regions: Theory and Practice.* Sydney: UNSW Press Limited.

Bellamy, J., Meppem, T., Gorddard, R. and Dawson, S. (2003), "The changing face of regional governance for economic development: Implications for local government". *Sustaining Regions 2*(3), 7–17.

Bengs, C. (2002), *Let science have relevance!* Retrieved 21 January, 2006, from http://www.nordregio.se/EJSD/editorials.html.

Bessire, H. (1970), *The Practice of Economic Development.* El Paso, TX: Hill Printing Company.

Bingham, R.D. and Mier, R. (eds) (1993), *Theories of Local Economic Development: Perspectives from Across the Disciplines*. Newbury Park, CA: Sage Publications.

Bingham, R.D. and Mier, R. (eds) (1997), *Dilemmas of Urban Economic Development: Issues in Theory and Practice*. Thousand Oaks, CA: Sage.

Blair, J.P. (1995), *Local Economic Development: Analysis and Practice*. Thousand Oaks, CA: Sage.

Blair, J.P. and Kumar, R. (1997), "Is local economic development a zero-sum game?" In R.D. Bingham and R. Mier (eds), *Dilemmas of Urban Economic Development* (pp. 1–20). Thousand Oaks: CA: Sage Publications.

Blakely, E. and Bradshaw, T. (2002), *Planning Local Economic Development, Theory and Practice* (3rd edn). Thousand Oaks, CA: Sage.

Bloor, D. (2001), "Wittgenstein and the priority of practice". In T. Schatzki, K. Cetina and E. Savigny (eds), *The Practice Turn in Comtemporary Theory* (pp. 95–107). London: Routledge.

Boland, P. (2007), "Unpacking the theory-policy interface of local economic development: An analysis of Cardiff and Liverpool". *Urban Studies 44*(5), 1019–39.

Bourdieu, P. (1977), *Outline of a Theory of Practice*. Cambridge, UK: Cambridge University Press.

Bourdieu, P. (1990), *The Logic of Practice*. Stanford, CA: Stanford University Press.

Bowles, S. and Gintis, H. (2002), "Social capital and community governance". *The Economic Journal 112*, 419–36.

Buchanan, I. (1999), "Deleuze and cultural studies". In I. Buchanan (ed.), *A Deleuzian Century?* (pp. 103–117). Durham, NC: Duke University Press.

Buchanan, I. (2000), *Deleuzism: A Metacommentary*. Durham, NC: Duke University Press.

Butler, J. (2000), "Restaging the universal: Hegemony and the limits of formalism". In J. Bulter, E. Laclau and S. Zizak (eds), *Contingency, Hegemony, Universality: Contemporary Dialogues on the Left* (pp. 11–43). London: Verso.

Callon, M. (1997), *Actor-network theory – the market test*. Retrieved 31 March 2007, from http://www.lancs.ac.uk/fss/sociology/papers/callon-market-test.pdf.

Carr, W. and Kemmis, S. (1986), *Becoming Critical: Education, Knowledge and Action Research*. Lewes: Falmer Press.

Clower, T., Beer, A., Maude, A. and Haughton, G. (2004, August), *Multinational lessons from local and regional economic development agencies*. Paper presented at the European Regional Science Association, Porto, Portugal.

Colebrook, C. (2002a), *Gilles Deleuze*. London: Routledge.

Colebrook, C. (2002b), *Understanding Deleuze*. Crows Nest, NSW: Allen and Unwin.

Deleuze, G. (1989), *Cinema 2: the Time-image* (H. Tomlinson and R. Galeta, Trans.). Minneapolis: University of Minnesota Press.

Deleuze, G. (1991), *Empiricism and Subjectivity*. New York: Columbia University Press.

Deleuze, G. (1994), *Difference and Repetition* (P. Patton, Trans.). New York: Columbia University Press.

Deleuze, G. (1995), *Negotiations, 1972–1990* (M. Joughin, Trans.). New York: Columbia University Press.

Deleuze, G. (2005), *Pure Immanence* (A. Boyman, Trans.). New York: Zone Books.

Deleuze, G. (2006), *Foucault* (S. Hand, Trans. 7th edn). Minneapolis: University of Minnesota Press.

Deleuze, G. and Guattari, F. (1987), *Thousand Plateaus: Capitalism and Schizophrenia* (B. Massumi, Trans.). Minneapolis: University of Minnesota Press.

Deleuze, G. and Guattari, F. (1994), *What is Philosophy?* (H. Tomlinson and G. Burchell, Trans.). New York: Columbia University Press.

DePoy, E. and Gitlin, L.N. (2005), *Introduction to Research: Understanding multiple Strategies* (3rd edn). St. Louis: Mosby.

Derrida, J. (1982), *Margins of Philosophy*. Chicago: University of Chicago Press.

Dewsbury, J.-D. (2003), "Witnessing space: 'knowledge without contemplation.'" *Environment and Planning A 35*, 1907–32.

Doel, M.A. (2004), "Waiting for geography". *Environment and Planning A 36*, 451–60.

Economic Development Administration. (2004), *What is economic development?* Retrieved 21 December 2004, from http://www.eda.gov/AboutEDA/AbtEDA.xml.

Fernstrom, J.R. (1976), *Bringing in the Sheaves*. Corvallis, OR: Oregon State University Extension Service.

Florida, R. (2005), *Cities and the Creative Class*. New York: Routledge.

Florida, R. (2006), *What really drives economic development?* Retrieved 28 February 2007, from http://creativeclass.typepad.com/thecreativityexchange/2006/11/what_really_dri.html.

Flyvbjerg, B. (1992), "Aristotle, Foucault and progressive phronesis: Outline of an applied ethics for sustainable development". *Planning Theory 7–8*, 65–83.

Flyvbjerg, B. (2001), *Making Social Science Matter* (S. Sampson, Trans.). Cambridge, UK: Cambridge University Press.

Flyvbjerg, B. (2004), "Phronetic planning research: Theoretical and methodological reflections". *Planning Theory and Practice 5*(3), 283–306.

Forester, J. (1989), *Planning in the Face of Power*. Berkeley, CA: University of California Press.

Forester, J. (2001), "An instructive case-study hampered by theoretical puzzles: Critical comments on Flyvbjerg's *Rationality and Power*". *International Planning Studies 6*(3), 263–70.

Fortun, M. and Bernstein, H.J. (1998), *Muddling Through: Pursuing Science and Truths in the Twenty-First Century*. New York: Counterpoint Press.

Foucault, M. (1977), *Language, Counter-memory, Practice: Selected Essays and Interviews* (D. Bouchard and S. Simons, Trans.). Ithaca, NY: Cornell University Press.

Foucault, M. (1980), *Power/Knowledge: Selected Interviews and Other Writings 1972–1977*. Brighton: Harvester.

Foucault, M. (1984), "Space, knowledge, and power. Interview with Paul Rabinow". In P. Rabinow (ed.), *The Foucault Reader* (pp. 239–56). New York: Pantheon.

Foucault, M. (1990), *The History of Sexuality*. London: Penguin.

Foucault, M. (1991), "Politics and the study of discourse". In G. Burchell, C. Gordon and P. Miller (eds), *The Foucault Effect: Studies in Governmentality*. Chicago: University of Chicago Press.

Foucault, M. (2005), *The Order of Things: Archaelogy of the Human Sciences*. London: Routledge.

Foust, J.B. and deSouza, A.R. (1978), *The Economic Landscape: A Theoretical Introduction*. Columbus, OH: Charles E. Merrill Publishing Company.

Freire, P. (1972), *Pedagogy of the Oppressed*. Harmondsworth: Penguin.

Friedmann, J. (1987), *Planning in the Public Domain: From Knowledge to Action*. Princeton, NJ: Princeton University Press.

Friedmann, J. (1996), "The core curriculum in planning revisited". *European Planning Studies* 6(3), 245–53.

Friedmann, J. (2003), "Why do planning theory?" *Planning Theory 2*(1), 7–10.

Gibson, L.J. (2006, 3–7 July), *Geography learning: Building a research agenda for meeting societal needs*. Paper presented at the International Geographical Union, Brisbane.

Graham, S. and Healey, P. (1999), "Relational concepts of space and place: Issues for planning theory and practice". *European Planning Studies 7*(5), 623–46.

Gunder, M. (2003), "Planning policy formulation from a Lacanian perspective". *International Planning Studies 8*(4), 279–94.

Gunder, M. (2004), "Shaping the planner's ego-ideal: A Lacanian interpretation of planning education". *Journal of Planning Education and Research 23*(3), 299–311.

Gunder, M. (2005), Personal communication. Auckland.

Gunder, M. (2006), "Planning's perpetual twilight". *Urban Policy and Research 24*(1), 157–8.

Gunder, M. (2008), "Imperatives of enjoyment: Economic development under globalisation". In J.E. Rowe (ed.), *Theories of Local Economic Development: Linking Theory to Practice*. Aldershot, UK: Ashgate Publishing Limited.

Healey, P. (1997), *Collaborative Planning: Shaping Places in Fragmented Societies*. London: Macmillan Press Ltd.

Hillier, J. (1995), "The unwritten law of planning theory: Common sense". *Journal of Planning Education and Research 14*(4), 292–6.

Hillier, J. (2002), *Shadows of Power: An Allegory of Prudence in Land Use Planning*. London: Routledge.

Hillier, J. (2005), "Straddling the post-structuralist abyss: Between transcendence and immanence?" *Planning Theory 4*(3), 271–99.

Hillier, J. and Gunder, M. (2005), "Not over your dead bodies! A Lacanian interpretation of planning discourse and practice". *Environment and Planning A 37*(6), 1049–66.

Hoover, E. (1975), *An Introduction to Regional Economics* (2nd edn). New York: Alfred A. Knopf.

Isard, W. (1960), *Methods of Regional Analysis: An Introduction to Regional Science*. Cambridge, MA: MIT Press.

Isserman, A. (1994), "State economic development policy and practice in the United States: A survey article". *International Regional Science Review 16*(1 and 2), 49–100.

Jacoby, R. (1987), *The Last Intellectuals*. New York: Basic Books.

Jeanes, E.L. and De Cock, C. (2005, 23–24 March), *Making the familiar strange: A Deleuzian perspective on creativity.* Paper presented at the Creativity and Innovation Management Community Workshop, Oxford, UK.

Knudsen, D. (1997), "Response: What works best? Reflections on the role of theory in planning". *Economic Development Quarterly 11*(3), 208–211.

Koo, J. (2005), "Technology spillovers, agglomeration, and regional economic development". *Journal of Planning Literature 20*(2), 99–115.

Latour, B. (2005), *Reassembling the Social: an Introduction to Actor-Network-Theory*. Oxford, UK: Oxford University Press.

Levy, J.M. (1990), "What local economic developers actually do: Location quotients versus press releases". *Journal of the American Planning Association 56*(Spring), 153–60.

Lindblom, C.E. (1959), "The science of 'muddling through". *Public Administration Review 19*, 79–88.

Loveridge, S. (1996), "On the continuing popularity of industrial recruitment". *Economic Development Quarterly 10*(2), 151–8.

Luke, J.S., Ventriss, C., Reed, B.J. and Reed, C.M. (1988), *Managing Economic Development: a Guide to State and Local Leadership Strategies*. San Francisco: Jossey-Bass Publishers.

Macey, D. (1993), *The Lives of Michel Foucault*. London: Hutchinson.

Maki, U. (2004), "Realism and the nature of theory: A lesson from J.H. von Thunen for economists and geographers". *Environment and Planning A 36*, 1719–36.

Malizia, E. and Feser, E. (1999), *Understanding Local Economic Development*. New Brunswick, NJ: The State University of New Jersey Press.

May, T. (2005), *Gilles Deleuze: An Introduction*. New York: Cambridge University Press.

McCann, P. and Sheppard, S. (2003), "The rise, fall and rise again of industrial location theory". *Regional Studies 37*(6 and 7), 649–63.

Mier, R. and Fitzgerald, J. (1991), "Managing economic development". *Economic Development Quarterly 5*, 268–79.

Miller, E.W. (1977), *Manufacturing: A Study of Industrial Location*. University Park, PA: The Pennsylvania State University Press.

Moore, M. (1980), *Social Science and Policy Analysis, Some Fundamental Differences*. Cambridge, MA: John F. Kennedy School of Government.

Morgan, G. (1986), *Images of Organization*. Newbury Park, CA: Sage.

Moriarty, B.M. (1980), *Industrial Location and Community Development*. Chapel Hill, NC: University of North Carolina Press.

Morss, J.R. (2000), "The passional pedagogy of Gilles Deleuze". *Educational Philosophy and Theory 32*(2), 185–200.

Murphy, T. (1998), "Quantum ontology: A virtual mechanics of becoming". In E. Kaufman and K.J. Heller (eds), *Deleuze and Guattari: New Mappings in Politics, Philosophy, and Culture* (pp. 211–29). Minneapolis: University of Minnesota Press.

Neuman, M. (2005), "Notes on the uses and scope of city planning theory". *Planning Theory 4*(2), 123–45.

Osbourne, D. (1988), *Laboratories of Democracy*. Boston: Harvard Business School Press.

Painter, J. (2005), "Governmentality and regional economic strategies". In J. Hillier and E. Rooksby (eds), *Habitus: A Sense of Place* (pp. 131–57). Aldershot, UK: Ashgate Publishing Limited.

Patton, P. (2000), *Deleuze and the Political*. London: Routledge.

Patton, P. (2005), "Deleuze and democracy". *Contemporary Political Theory 4*(4), 400–413.

Perkins, D.H., Gillis, M., Snodgrass, D.R. and Roemer, M. (2001), *Economics of Development* (5th edn). New York: Norton.

Pittaway, L. (2005), "Philosophies in entrepreneurship: A focus on economic theories". *International Journal of Entrepreneurship and Small Business 11*(3), 201–221.

Pratt, G. (2000), "Post-structuralism". In R.J. Johnston, D. Gregory, G. Pratt, M. Watts and D.M. Smith (eds), *The Dictionary of Human Geography*. Malden, MA: Blackwell Publishers.

Reese, L.A. and Fasenfest, D. (1997), "What works best?: Values and the evaluation of local economic development". *Economic Development Quarterly 11*(3), 195–207.

Rorty, R. (1979), *Philosophy and the Mirror of Nature*. Princeton, NJ: Princeton University Press.

Rose, M. (2004), "Reembracing metaphysics". *Environment and Planning A 36*, 461–8.

Rowe, J.E. (2005), "Lessons learned and future directions". In J.E. Rowe (ed.), *Economic Development in New Zealand* (pp. 221–34). Aldershot, UK: Ashgate Publishing Limited.

Rowe, J.E. (2006, 4–7 July), *What economic development Practitioners actually do and why?* Paper presented at the International Geographical Union, Brisbane.

Rubin, H.J. (1988), "Shoot anything that flies, Claim anything that falls: Conversations with economic development practitioners". *Economic Development Quarterly 2*(3), 236–51.

Schram, S. (2006), "Return to politics: Perestroika, phronesis, and post-paradigmatic political science". In S. Schram and B. Caterino (eds), *Making Political Science Matter: Debating Knowledge, Research, and Method.* New York: New York University Press.

Shaffer, R., Deller, S. and Marcouiller, D. (2006), "Rethinking community economic development". *Economic Development Quarterly 20*(1), 59–74.

Scott, A.J. (2006), "Creative cities: Conceptual issues and policy questions". *Journal of Urban Affairs 28*(1), 1–17.

Sinnerbrink, R. (2006), "Nomadology or ideology? Zizek's critique of Deleuze". *Parrhesia 1*, 62–87.

Smith, D. (1971), *Industrial Location: an Economic Geographical Analysis*. New York: John Wiley and Sons.

Smith, M.K. (1999, 9 July), *Knowledge*. Retrieved 20 January, 2006, from http://www.infed.org/biblio/knowledge.htm.

Stafford, H.A. (1979), *Principles of Industrial Facility Location*. Atlanta: Conway Publications Inc.

Stimson, R., Stough, R. and Roberts, B. (2002), *Regional Economic Development*. Berlin: Springer-Verlag.

Stough, R. (2003), "Strategic management of places and policy". *The Annals of Regional Science 37*, 179–201.

Throgmorton, J. (1996), *Planning as Persuasive Storytelling*. Chicago: University of Chicago Press.

Tietz, M. (1994), "Changes in economic development theory and practice". *International Regional Science Review 16*(1), 101–106.

von Thunen, J.H. (1966), *Von Thunen's Isolated State* (C. M. Wartenberg, Trans.). Oxford, UK: Pergamon Press.

Wilson, D. (2004), "Professional education for economic development practitioners in New Zealand". *Sustaining Regions 4*(1), 41–9.

Wilson, D. (2005), "Economic development education for New Zealand". In J.E. Rowe (ed.), *Economic Development in New Zealand* (pp. 205–219). Aldershot, UK: Ashgate Publishing Limited.

Wolman, H. and Spitzley, D. (1996), "The politics of local economic development". *Economic Development Quarterly 10*(2), 115–50.

Yiftachel, O. (2006), "Re-engaging planning theory? Towards 'South Eastern' perspectives". *Planning Theory 5*(3), 211–22.

Zizek, S. (2005), *Interrogating the Real*. London: Continuum.

PART 2
Defining the Discipline

Chapter 2

Theory and Practice in Economic Development: Eighty Entangled Years in Search of Panacea

Mark M. Miller

Nothing is as practical as a good theory.

Kurt Lewin

In theory, there is no difference between theory and practice; in practice, there is.

Chuck Reid

Over more than two decades of higher and continuing education in regional economic development (ED), I have always found greater interest in theory among ED practitioners than my ED students. The students, of course, are more interested in the concrete tools that will lead them to their first job in the field: industrial recruitment, impact analysis, and the like. The practitioners, meanwhile, spend most of their professional careers reacting to immediate crises, opportunities, and political demands. For the typical practitioner, it is a luxury to sit back occasionally in a seminar room and reflect on what it all adds up to: how do we make sense of the ED forest amid all the trees? It is when I am discussing theory with a class of professional colleagues that I am most likely to find the "aha!" moment: when the light bulb comes on, and years of professional experience come together in a clearer, more coherent picture.

The ED profession is often derided for mere, opportunistic "smokestack chasing." In reality, our profession has a very long and distinguished (well, let us settle for "long," at least, at this point) tradition of theory – at least to the extent that theory can be loosely defined as organized and widely recognized models or patterns of practices. Over at least the past eighty years, these theories or models of ED have had tremendous influence in informing and shaping our professional practice.

On the other hand, is the reverse also true? To what extent has ED practice informed and shaped our bodies of ED theory? This, too, has been significant, I believe, though often through more informal channels of feedback. It is the practitioner, after all, along with his or her job, who is truly on the front lines of field evaluation of ED theories. Enthusiasm for enterprise zones, for example, seemed to fall in decline long before the results of more rigorous academic evaluation became available.

Often, too, the actual implementation of ED theories – e.g., industrial clustering – becomes a much different animal in the cold reality of practical application, due to the influences of political considerations, available financing, random effects of good and bad luck, et al. As such, the theories we end up evaluating are generally much different from those we originally dreamed up from atop the ivory tower. Further, most of our academic ED theories (enterprise zones, industrial clusters) derive from descriptive and explanatory studies of what seems to have worked well in particular locations largely without deliberate ED intervention: for instance, Hall's studies of Singapore and Hong Kong's entrepreneurial environments, or Porter's observations of shoe-manufacturing industrial regions of Italy. While interesting and valuable, such studies remain a long leap of faith from the more definitive tests of scientific theory: can these ideas be translated into policies and practices with similar – and, especially, predictable – results?

Of course, every new theory is going to be the solution to everything, from the perspective of the theorist as well as the practitioner. Recall, for example, that industrial clusters only recently contained the seeds of prosperity for everything from university research parks to inner cities (Porter, 1997). Some of this overbounded enthusiasm may result from the relatively small number of tools available to us to cover every community's every economic need. As they say, if all you have is a hammer, then everything looks a lot like a nail. Also, I am not convinced we are more given to this tendency than those in other fields of study. (Note to health sciences: weren't steroids going to solve all of our ailments not so very long ago?)

In our professional collective defense, I recall a long-ago discussion on National Public Radio concerning, essentially, stuff that is really hard. We commonly refer to readily doable tasks in terms of "it's not brain surgery." The NPR correspondent ran with this idea, interviewing brain surgeons on the expressions that they use. They tended to use the other common expression: "it's not rocket science." So, the intrepid reporter next interviewed scientists engaged in rocket-related technology, asking what they refer to as being especially difficult, in comparison with their work. One such interview subject responded by saying that he had always been daunted by the tasks confronting those who study economies. Trying to figure out an economy and help make it work better – I recall him saying – now that's a complicated and difficult task.

I agree. We plowing the ED field are not working in sterile operating theaters, nor laboratory conditions, nor within readily specifiable parameters of reality. We are trying to make this ED stuff work amid a thousand poorly-defined and constantly shifting variables; determined in large measure through human and social irrationalities; buffeted by continuous pressures of politics and public opinion; across thousands of community cases that vary wildly from one another in terms of size, demographics, cultures, and other geographic characteristics.

I cannot think of a better example of this grand challenge than the Hurricane Katrina-affected region from which I write this chapter. Our colleague Ed Blakely – widely respected in our science and profession for his academic and pedagogical writing – toils away in nearby New Orleans as I write this now, trying to implement our collective eighty-odd years of wisdom to the practical test of rebuilding a major city's shattered economy and community. We have been working at similar tasks over the past two years here in multiple southern Mississippi communities. I can't speak for Ed, but here in Mississippi it looks a lot different on the ground than the view from within the ivy-covered walls. On the other hand, through it all, theory (e.g., New Urbanism on the Mississippi Gulf Coast) has provided us with constant touchstones against the temptations of frantic, haphazard, and ultimately unproductive attempts at redevelopment. Other similarly besieged colleagues have also attempted to confront economic disaster recovery with the few tools of ED theory and analysis available to us (Henthorne, George, and Swamy, 2006; Clower, 2006; Webb, 2006).

Yes, ED is hard – and confusing and frustrating more often than not. On the other hand, though, ours will always be a fascinating and eternally challenging field of both academic study and professional development.

Drawing on work by Friedmann and Weaver (1979), Bradshaw and Blakely (1999), and many others, Figure 2.1 offers – at best – a straw man to encourage consideration of the long relationship between theory and practice in the field of ED.

To offer up further cowardly caveats, I should note that this chapter limits itself to the relationship between practice and theory in *regional* ED: the attempt to foster job creation, wealth accumulation, and occasionally even social equity within particular regions, states, districts, communities, or even individual neighborhoods. There does exist a significant relationship between the regional and national levels of ED in theory and practice, but the relationship can be tenuous and at times even hostile.

In particular, this chapter focuses on regional ED theories concerned primarily with *where* ED tends to occur naturally and where interventions can and should potentially be implemented to influence its geographic direction. One of the most age-old questions of our field is, for example, do we try to bring jobs to people who need them (such as inner-city and rural residents), or do we try to bring needy people to places more likely to provide them with jobs jobs (such as thriving urban industrial centers)?

Other vast bodies of ED-related theory are concerned with *why* we should intervene at all or *what* sorts of practices should be implemented in these places, but this particular geographer is content to leave those sorts of questions to other chapters or perhaps other texts. For example, market failure theory concerns, quite appropriately, the question of why we good capitalists should concern ourselves with economic interventions at all, instead of relying on the "invisible hand" or "miracle of the marketplace." Suffice it to say for now that none of us in ED, practitioners nor academics, would have jobs for long if we did not subscribe to the widespread need for market interventions.

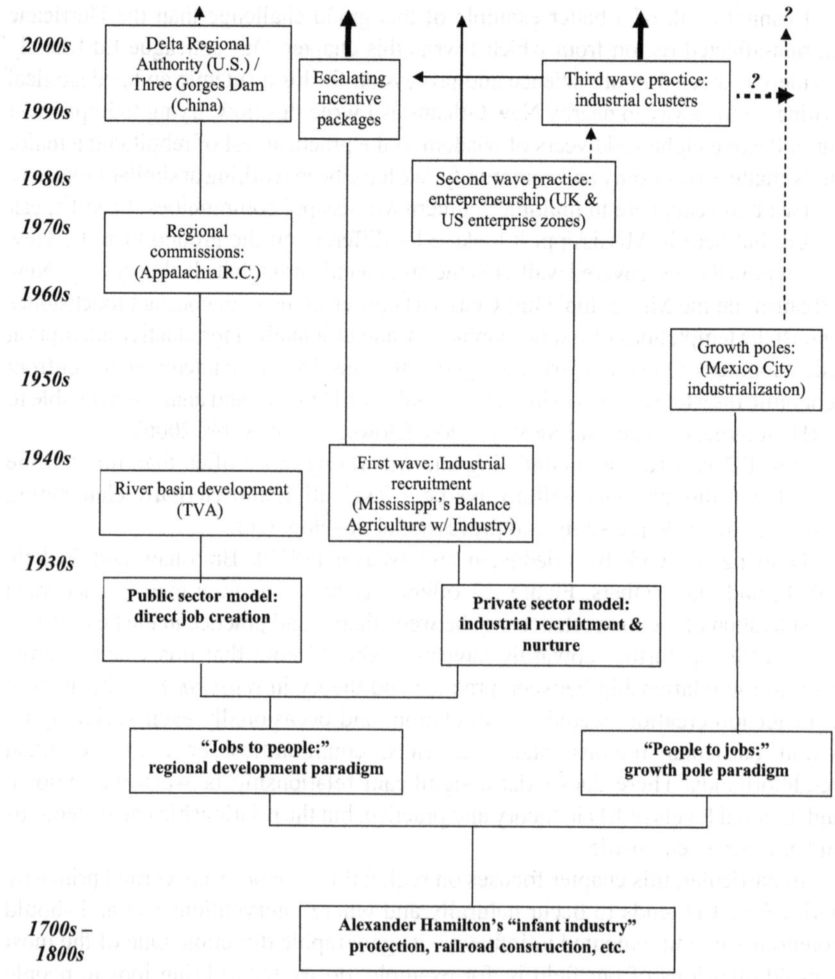

Figure 2.1 The relationship between theory and practice

I have also made life easier for myself by – arbitrarily, some of my colleagues would argue – devoting the lion's share of my timeline to the period from 1920s through the present day. Yes, I am willing to concede without a fight the title of "Father of ED" to Alexander Hamilton (Hamilton 2001, Chernow 2004), with the line of patrimony extending through canal builders, railroad developers, and assorted other robber-barons through the centuries. The period from the 1930s through the present day, however, I believe incorporates a reasonably coherent, well-documented, and evaluated body of work.

Furthermore, Figure 2.1 is United States-centric in the extreme. Despite our best efforts to assert our rightful position as the world's epicenter, though, the recent history of ED in the US has been strongly characterised by diffusion of our ideas throughout the world (e.g., the Tennessee Valley Authority), as well as our own appropriation of innovations gathered from around the globe (e.g., enterprise zones, industrial clusters).

All of that said, what remains in Figure 2.1 still covers a very broad and impressive progression of though and action within our field. Working up from the bottom of the figure, the first bifurcation is the grand jobs-to-people vs. people-to-jobs division mentioned above. The theoretical foundations for this debate were not really codified until the 1950s (Perroux, 1950; Friedmann and Weaver, 1979), however, the concept was made explicit throughout our policies and practices as early as the 1930s. The Tennessee Valley Authority and Mississippi's Balance Agriculture with Industry program both were entirely explicit efforts to influence ED toward targeted lagging regions.

True, the countervailing process of channeling mass numbers of needy people to jobs was beginning in roughly this same period – for example, the mass migration of rural African-Americans from the Mississippi Delta region to northern industrial cities. However, I am not aware of deliberate government policies or programs in the US that were designed to encourage this process. More explicit people-to-jobs programs emerged much later, and largely outside the US – especially beginning in the 1950s, directed toward regions such as the Mexico City metropolis.

Later in this chapter, I will argue that ED theories since the 1990s – such as industrial clusters and technology-based development – may be resulting in the effect of steering people to jobs. However, the overwhelming thrust of ED policies and practices in the US since the 1920s has been focused on steering jobs to people in particular regions. The result has been a true *paradigm*, in Kuhn's (1962) conceptualization: what has been almost universally accepted as "normal" science and practice in our field. Even in the darkest moments following Hurricane Katrina, for example, the overwhelming concern of the country was to reverse the "diaspora" of population from the Gulf Coast region and rebuild the economies of these severely damaged communities. Advocates of abandoning these regions, or generally uprooting people in poor regions and directing them to more prosperous communities, exist but tend to be dismissed or even ridiculed as extremists – even though their arguments might be more economically rational.

If the people-to-jobs branch of our heritage largely went the way of *Australopithecus* (or perhaps *Homo Growthpolecus*, in our case), the jobs-to-people side of our professional gene pool continued to thrive, evolve, and differentiate. The two major *genera* characterizing our profession today both emerged during the 1930s: the public sector model, embodied by the Tennessee Valley Authority (TVA, n.d.) – and the private sector model, the origins of which are generally credited to Mississippi's Balance Agriculture with Industry program (Mississippi Historical Society, n.d.).

The line of the TVA model continued on through the creation of other regional commissions in the US: most notably the Appalachian Regional Commission (ARC, n.d.), and perhaps most recently in the Delta Regional Authority (DRA, n.d.). The TVA model was clearly embraced outside the US in various Mexican development plans, Venezuela's Ciudad Guyana, and arguably – for better and for worse – China's monstrous Three Gorges Dam project. Interestingly, among the US's first impulses following Hurricane Katrina were Congressional calls for a federal regional commission for the Gulf Coast disaster zone. The genetic strands of this field of theory clearly still run deep in our collective professional body.

The dominant and most dynamic line of ED theory and practice, on the other hand, clearly runs from the private-sector model. Building on the work of Herbers (1990) and many others, Bradshaw and Blakely (1999) introduced the metaphor of ED "waves" into our professional and public lexicon. In Bradshaw and Blakely's conceptualization, the Mississippi's BAWI initiated the "first wave" of private sector ED practice, which emphasises the use of ever-expanding and ever-growing incentives to attract (typically) manufacturing development to particular regions, states, or communities.

The terminology of the "wave" is perhaps misleading to the extent that it implies a phenomenon that rises then falls back again under its own weight. This clearly has not been the case with industrial incentives, which continue to characterise and to some extent dominate our professional practice of ED to date – despite the best efforts of ED academics to discredit them.

The "second wave" of private-sector-based ED is characterised by Bradshaw and Blakely as emphasizing the retention and expansion of existing local firms. This may be the case "in theory," but in reality – in mine and perhaps most minds – the defining symbol of the 1980–1990s second wave was the enterprise zone. The reality of the enterprise zone tended much more toward – no surprise – industrial attraction: just toward poorer places, and on-the-cheap through such incentives as tax and regulatory relief. Enterprise zones live on today (USDA Rural Development, n.d.), throughout the US and beyond, but the concept no longer receives much attention within the larger profession.

In large part, the demise of enterprise zones was due to the emergence in the early 1990s of the much larger and much more expensive "third wave," symbolized by Porter's (1990) industrial cluster concept. After nearly two decades, the cluster concept remains our latest and biggest idea in the field of ED, with an extensive literature, but still has received surprisingly little evaluation. This may be because, as discussed earlier, the reality of a cluster as a result of professional ED policy and practice tends to be (a) exceedingly rare, and (b) very unlike Porter's nice, tight diamond diagram. Instead, in practice the cluster concept in many cases has provided little more than another justification for – yes, you guessed it – industrial attraction and incentive-giving on an even more massive scale than before.

The numbering of waves has naturally led to considerable anticipation – among academics, students, and practitioners of ED – of what we all hope will be a forthcoming fourth wave. So far, we're still on the shore waiting. There has been considerable discussion of "technology-" or "innovation-based" ED in recent years, but it's not at all clear in scholarly or professional circles that this has coalesced into what clearly is a new and coherent wave in the field. To my mind, at least, it is reminiscent of much that was promised of the second wave, which was distracted away by the enterprise zone furor. Further, within the third wave, Porter emphasized the element of technology with regard to virtually every region and every industry about which he wrote.

Regardless of which wave we're riding at the moment, nonetheless, technology is an important part of it, and of course the higher the technology the more excited we get about it. Furthermore, despite Porter's protestations to the contrary, any clusters that are appearing in reality are doing so in what are already fairly well developed regions. The South's persistent efforts to develop automotive manufacturing clusters, for example, have resulted in major automotive plants outside places like Nashville, Tuscaloosa, Jackson, and Tupelo. I am not expecting many major developments in places like the Mississippi Delta, on the other hand.

The result has been a pronounced tendency toward ED in urban areas, especially those with major research universities as well as relatively well-educated and technology-literate populations. Similar is the recent enthusiasm for Richard Florida's (2003) creative communities. What, then, of the poor people in poor places? Does all of this imply an implicit return to the people-to-jobs paradigm? Frankly, my best advice to a Delta resident for career enhancement would be to enroll in a good university and plan on moving elsewhere. I do not see any new or alternative theories contending these days for the advancement of lagging regions, although I would be delighted to be enlightened by my peers on this point.

Furthermore, what of the economic equity concerns in general that originally motivated and drove the theories of our field: from the TVA and ARC and BAWI on through the enterprise zones of the 1980s? Although both cluster and technology-based theories of ED are exciting and remain promising, what do they have to do with anything concerning regional or social equity considerations of ED? Not much, that I can find, other than creating greater needs somehow to address the woes of lagging regions and populations that increasingly find themselves on the wrong side of the "digital divide." I can only remain watchful and hopeful that our ED theorists will rise to the occasion, as they have throughout the decades.

References

Appalachian Regional Commission. About ARC: History. Retrieved 29 August 2007: http://www.arc.gov/index.do?nodeId=7.

Bradshaw, T.K. and Blakely, E.J. (1999), "What are 'Third-Wave' state economic development efforts? From incentives to industrial policy". *Economic Development Quarterly* 13(3): 229–44.

Chernow, R. (2004), *Alexander Hamilton.* Penguin.

Clower, T. (2006), "Economic Impact Analysis for Disaster Assessment and Planning: A Review of Tools and Techniques". *Applied Research in Economic Development* 3(1): 19–33.

Delta Regional Authority. "About DRA". Retrieved 29 September 2008: http://www.dra.gov/about/.

Florida, R. (2003), *The Rise of the Creative Class: And How It's Transforming Work, Leisure, Community and Everyday Life*. Basic Books.

Friedmann, J. and Weaver, C. (1979), *Territory and Function: The Evolution of Regional Planning*. University of California Press.

Hamilton, A. (2001), *Writings*. Library of America.

Hebers, J. (1990), "A third wave of economic development". *Governing* 3(9):43–50.

Henthorne, T., George, B. and Swamy, A. (2006), "Social capital and local community support for post-tsunami economic recovery in India". *Applied Research in Economic Development 3*(1): 34–47.

Kuhn, T. (1962), *The Structure of Scientific Revolutions*. University of Chicago Press.

Mississippi Historical Society. Mississippi History Now. Retrieved 29 August 2007: http://mshistory.k12.ms.us/features/feature52/economic.htm.

Perroux, F. (1950), "Economic space: Theory and applications". *Quarterly Journal of Economics* 64: 89–104.

Peters, A. and Fisher, P.S. (2002), "State Enterprise Zone Programs: Have They Worked?" W.E. Upjohn Institute.

Porter, M. (1990), *Competitive Advantage: Creating and Sustaining Superior Performance*. Free Press.

Porter, M. (1997), "New strategies for inner-city economic development". *Economic Development Quarterly* 11(1): 11–44.

Tennessee Valley Authority. "From the New Deal to a New Century: A short history of TVA". Retrieved 29 August 2007: http://www.tva.com/abouttva/history.htm.

US Department of Agriculture Rural Development. Home of the Rural Empowerment Zone and Enterprise Community Program. Retrieved 21 September 2007: http://www.rurdev.usda.gov/rbs/ezec/.

Webb, G. (2006), "Unraveling the Economic Consequences of Disasters: Sources of Resilience and Vulnerability". *Applied Research in Economic Development* 3(1): 3–18.

Chapter 3
The Evolution of American (Spatial) Local and Regional Economic Development Policy and Planning

Edward J. Blakely[1]

Spatial Economic Development as Public Policy

All spatially based economic development, whether it's local, urban or regional, is based on a long US set of public policies that started with the earliest Colonial experience when toll roads, canals, and bridges were built by locals in response to the need to move local goods to market. The fledgling Republic when it was only 13 colonies entered almost immediately on policies designed to develop each colony and each town maximizes its economic form. The early American Republic embarked on policies and programs to assist local areas shape markets. Local towns formed a variety of organizations from farmers unions to merchants clubs to promote their communities or crops. Finally, the Louisiana Purchase in 1803 and the building of the railroads in epitomize national policy promoting local economic development as the nation moved from Colony to nation. This same pattern was followed with national policy reinforcing local development with the formation of the Tennessee Valley Authority in 1933 as well as later projects through the Depression and post-World War II eras.

Our current notion of local economic development is based on more recent issues related to the transformation of the national economy from one based on industrial base to one that is based on the quality of the human social base in a locality as the basis for forming a competitive local economy.

As we enter a new century, the American economy has globalized, national demography transformed and spatial economy changed forever. Thus a new national economic form is leveraged by understanding the means to deal with and respond to the changes in inner city and poor communities. Terms like inner city and empowerment are useful ways to frame the socio-political actions of the past four decades; these old lexicons poor, disadvantaged, low-income, have been eclipsed by the current economy. Each of the former terms has deep and compelling meanings.

1 Professor Blakely in addition to being Professor of Urban Policy and Planning at the University of Sydney is currently on leave from the University to serve as the Director of Recovery for the City of New Orleans as it recovers from Hurricanes Rita and Katrina.

Each has generated specific politico-economic actions. Local communities including inner city disadvantaged neighborhoods have now to compete in a global economy so the old words are liabilities and no longer fit the current situation or the intended goals of local economic development. New terms have evolved with changed rhetoric to reflect a new paradigm or model for a social and not merely and industrial base to forge a socio-economic development paradigm.

An Evolving Pattern of Local Economic Development

Words are more than a means of communication. They are powerful even over powering means of conveying deep-seated notions of the nature and response to socio-political forces. Metaphor is a powerful tool for translating and transmitting difficult and complex issues of human relationships. No arena better exemplifies the lexicon power of the metaphors than the terms used to describe the conditions of the less privileged in 20th-century America. Both the conditions of people and places have been the subject and object of powerful language aimed at altering the national psyche and transforming national politics (see Chapter 15 for a detailed discussion on the importance of metaphors in understanding local economic development).

In the early part of the 20th century the nation was transfixed by the images of tenement houses and urban squalor of the *working classes* in cities. Epic work on these conditions by Upton Sinclair and Jane Addams (Christenson and Robinson, 1989) provided a new national image-able vocabulary for dealing with the issues of the poor in cities. This literature, buttressed by early social science research, created the social construct of noble poverty. Jane Addams nobilized the poor and poor places as needy of mere physicals and social rehabilitation. Settlement houses, Addams contribution to urban decay strategies, were to help restore communities by altering the emotionally crushing circumstance of poverty (Christenson and Robinson, 1989). While this portrayal, may be an over simplification of the Addams concept, it is a good representation of the underlying metaphor, "nurture and not nature" can transform both the poor person and poor communities. This was revolutionary thinking at the turn of the century since the operating prior concept was that poverty was a personal condition related to family breeding and intractable to any interventions. A host of government reforms were built on the Addams Settlement House formula and exist to this day in the form of a wide range of accepted poverty treatments ranging from inner city Y's to parole and rehabilitation for prisoners and government sponsored community centres.[2] The power of this concept of making better places as the means to alter social conditions

2 The first Settlement Houses started in London in 1884 based on the work of Arnold Toynbee. Jane Addams and Gates adapted this form of project in Chicago with founding of Hull House to Americanize immigrants by providing a combination of community organization and social work for newcomers to large cities.

remains deep in the national psyche. The Addams notions are responsible for such basic approaches to poverty such as public housing and aid-to-families with dependent children (AFDC – welfare). In New Orleans, Chicago, Seattle have with federal assistance through HOPE VI and other initiatives razed public housing and replaced it with mixed income communities in which the poor are not concentrated in the same physical space. The local inner city-based economic development theory here is based on the Jane Addams social reform model.

The Villains and Victims in Economic Development Evolution

Until the Great Depression of the 1920s and 1930s the notion that the poor were merely noble citizens trapped in poor circumstances was the operating conceptual framework. One must keep in mind this same concept was the springboard for important political changes including Prohibition, Women's voting rights and a myriad of programs to aid Negroes. In the Depression, this concept is too weak to deal with the changed circumstances. No longer could individual behavior or local conditions be seen as the sole rationale for poverty and economic distress. Indeed, Karl Marx pioneering work and that of the early socialist saw the economic system itself as creating "winners" and "losers" – villains and victims. Corporations and the very rich were depicted as creating the conditions of poverty for their own gain.[3] As a result, new operating for local economic development aims at reallocating both wealth and power. Franklin Roosevelt was able to invoke the "middle class" metaphor in his drive to redistribute assets via such devises as the income taxes, social security and the Workers Progress Administration (WPA), the Housing Act of 1937 as well as other schemes were designed to create middle class communities. As Alice O'Connor says, "The overarching goal of the (Roosevelt) New Deal... was to promote homeownership among working and middle class Americans..." (O'Connor in Ferguson, 1999, p.91). The class local development has served the nation well for most of the century. Crafting a notion of solidarity based on the movement to the "middle class" for all Americans is deeply ingrained in much post-World War II American legislation dealing with poverty. The middle-class local economic base embraced minorities as well. As a result, the NAACP aimed its considerable energies on creating opportunities for "Negroes" to enter white neighborhoods, white schools and white jobs. We will not recite here the depth and emotional energy devoted to advancing this "equality" for Black Americans. However, it is inconceivable that the Civil Rights movement could have been successful without the generally accepted middle-class local economic goals for all American accepted in the North and the South. Achieving middle class was a right of Black Americans, women and other minorities in any community – even if it is not in my neighborhood.

---

3 Karl Marx and Frederick Engels summarize this theory in the *Communist Manifesto* in 1848.

The villains and victims approach for local economic development is a particularly strong ingredient in the notion of ghetto and rural modernization that started with Lyndon Johnson and lasted until the Nixon Administration when finally *Negroes* were *Black* and needed wealth and not just opportunities to succeed. By the time Nixon left the Presidency Negroes became Black and later Afro-Americans an important change in nomenclature that underscored a dramatic alteration in expectations by African-Americans (O'Connor in Ferguson, 1999, p.109–112).

A War on Poor People, Poor Places or Poor Circumstances

Lyndon Johnson in 1963 announced a dramatic and some say catastrophic War on Poverty. Johnson aimed his War for the "people and places left behind" in the national march to the middle class, (President's National Advisory Commission on Rural Poverty, 1967). While the War targets were people its ground action was places. Over 500 rural counties and nearly every urban center in the nation were considered ground zero for this combat. The war metaphor lasted three decades. Nicholas Lemann in a scathing indictment of the thesis of the War on Poverty says,

> It took only a few months for the War on Poverty to started being perceived as a failure. In retrospect, the poverty warriors were always swimming upstream against public opinion and politics…So, to try to create a lot of new economic activity in poor neighborhoods is to swim against the great sweeping tide of urban life in America. Inside the ghetto, it usually does no harm – but it doesn't help much either. Outside the ghetto, though it does a great deal of harm…other efforts would do a great deal more good (especially improving schools, housing and police protection)… (Lemann, 1994, p. 28).

The Johnson War created elaborate machinery called community based development organizations. These organizations, as Avis Vidal (1995), a leading researcher on the topic says,

> CDCs show considerable promise as agents promoting effective targeting of public development dollars. Even though they are small, it is increasingly clear CDCs draw strength from their numbers and in doing become more effective representatives of the interests of their neighborhoods – precisely the sort of social and political capital these neighborhoods lack (Vidal, 1995, p. 217).

At the zenith of the War on Poverty hundreds of communities were provided multiple forms of social and economic aid to transform their own economic vitality. The war metaphor was based on a deficiency model. That is, if the correct social and economic organization could be put in place, then the residents of distressed communities could eradicate all local deficiencies, including gaining political control for themselves.

Community Development Corporation (CDCs) the main instruments of the War on Poverty provided, at their zenith, more than eighty percent of low income housing in the nation (Vidal, 1995). Moreover, some very large and prominent CDCs became major forces in the economic revitalization of portions of cities like Newark, New Jersey, Oakland, California and New York City in the Bronx, Brooklyn and Harlem.

Attendant to the War metaphor was the notion of "dis-investment". That is, poor communities are not poor by accident but by design. Building on and similar to the villains and victims was the notion that corporate America was re-allocating the assets of the poor communities to wealthy ones. Banks, in particular were deemed as taking money from low-income communities and using these funds to build suburban areas and businesses. Poor neighborhoods in central cities were dramatically affected by dis-investment strategies. After the Watts and subsequent urban riots in the late 1960s, inner city area supermarkets, banks, clothing stores and convenience stores disappeared. So did inner city jobs. William Julius Wilson (1989) provides a compelling analysis of how inner city areas were stripped of both their economic and social assets. He says,

> Social isolation deprives residents of certain inner city neighborhoods not only of the resources and conventional role models whose former presence buffered the effects of neighborhood joblessness, but also cultural learning from mainstream social networks that facilitate social and economic advancement in modern industrial society.
>
> I argue that the lack of neighborhood material resources, the relative absence of conventional role models, the circumstances cultural learning produce outcomes or concentrations of effects that restrict social mobility (Wilson, 1989, p. 11).

Dis-investment of human, economic and social assets made inner city areas breeders of poverty. The underclass approach became the unfortunate symbol of the conditions of much of inner city America. This was a crippling concept since it implied that the inner city areas were devoid of assets that the best approach to dealing with the situation was to move people out, break the communities up and end the support structures – namely welfare dependency that promoted these conditions. This was the formula that the Clinton Administration embarked on when it came into office in 1992. Chicago became the experimental center for many of these programs. The Gautreaux program moved low-income residents from inner city Chicago to surrounding suburbs. Chicago, Philadelphia, Detroit, Seattle and Milwaukee embarked on the largest destruction and renewal of public housing in the nation's history re-settling poor families into mixed income communities as part of a strategy to break up the ghettos (Wyly and Hammel, 1999).

A New Local Economic Development Structure for Old Places

The Clinton Administration combined several old notions of people and place deficiency to craft a national anti-poverty strategy. The Administration ended forty years of social welfare supports for needy families and concocted something called Empowerment Zones for poor places. Clinton Administration metaphor nomenclature "empowerment" tells the story. Empowerment Zones view poor places as structural. That is, poor communities have to be totally restored and redesigned to recreate the physical and social fabric so local poor people's institutions can deal effectively with deep-seated poverty and social disorganization that generate poverty (Lemann op.cit, 1994).

The operating concepts under girding structural strategies of the last decades are based on the notions disorganization, fragmentation and internal social malaise. From the vantage point of this notion is most of inner city America's underclass conditions are epidemic with local institutions as carriers of this socially debilitating disease through the schools, housing projects, gangs and welfare culture. As a result, existing local organizations, people and institutions are poor investments. Therefore the best economic and social development approach, according to Henry Cisneros, Clinton HUD Secretary, is to disperse the residents and break up these communities and then reconstitute them (Rosen and Dienstfrey in Ferguson, p. 441). It is against this background that inner city poor communities and institutions are viewed. The collective actions of the last forty years combined with large-scale immigration along with more than a decade of sustained economic growth lowering poverty rates and increasing incomes of all races and classes have changed template for the economic development of poor places and the opportunities structures for poor people. Only time will tell if these are permanent changes but no matter their longevity, the view of poor people and places has undergone a permanent conceptual transformation.

Building Models for Local Economic Development

Models that guide policy actions in the same way plans provide implementation guides for builders. In this case, we are describing a policy building process, "Being a Conscience and a Carpenter" as Herbert Rubin describes it (Rubin, 2000). Models, like metaphors, are translations of complex phenomena into more easily digestible depictions of the situation and sometimes provide the means to attack the underlying problem. Models are descriptive manifestations of the problems and provide the guides or plans for policy prescriptions. Several models provided the underpinnings for current anti-poverty/inner city revitalization policies. These models interrelate people and place characteristics.

Conceptually there are three basic models form the base of most urban poverty theory – Structural, Causal, and Pathological. I will not try to re-produce every known poverty or inner city model but use general systems descriptions as illustrative.

Urban Structure

The plight of urban and even the rural poor cannot be disassociated from the socio-economic changes in the conditions of the United States spatial economy in the middle of the 20th century. Suburbanization and industrial transformation have changed spatial economics for good and ill. Suburbs created the spatial base for urban economic modernization, globalization and middle class expansions. But many urban theorists have identified the systematic increase in metropolitan areas as undercutting the chances of urban communities. Myron Orfield (1997); Ewing (997), Rusk (1995) point out that metropolitan spatial relocations unleashed a set of un-intended consequences that have been destructive to cities, suburbs and rural areas.

In this model suburbs are no accident. Public and private investments in highways, home loans and other subsidies created an unprecedented transfer of wealth from city to suburbs. Not only were the cities left with a smaller population but they also were also left with a poorer one. As a result, of suburban processes the underlying conditions of central cities are structurally unsound. Cost of civic services rose in cities because needy populations increased while tax rolls plummeted. Moreover, the characteristics that made central cities unsound as shown below in Figure 3.1.

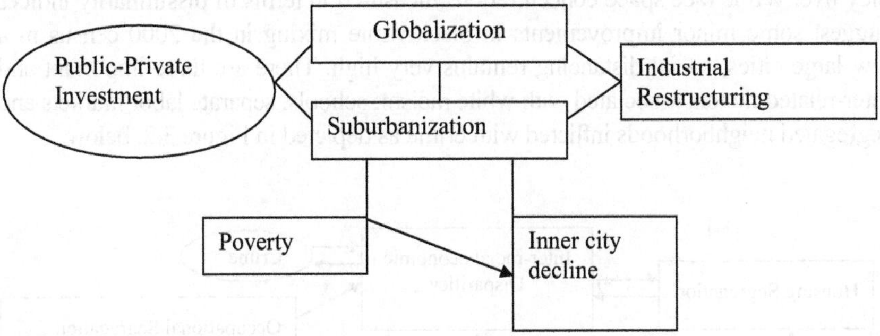

Figure 3.1 Urban restructive model

The forces of globalization, suburbanization and socio-economic polarization created separate spatial economies and societies (Goldsmith and Blakely,1992). In this model economic opportunity cannot be repaired until the system is balanced. This would require equalization of resources and investment between urban core and peripheries through tax structures and other forms of reallocation including limits on suburban development.

The latest waves of regional development labeled variously as “smart growth”, “regional management” and “regional governance” aim to restore the imbalances between central cities rural and peripheral suburban development. The mechanisms to promote this form of urban transformation aim at dealing with the underlying economic malady of urban decline versus attacking the manifestations like race and spatial inequality. One can consider this an indirect approach to the issue or the most direct means of arresting urban decline. Proponents of this approach suggest that both urban and rural poverty is more easily dealt with through a regional economic balance approach than by any attempts to invest in low-income communities or poor people. This is because unless the outward disinvesting forces of suburbanization are thwarted urban and rural poor people and poor places cannot compete or survive.

The Apartheid Race-Space Causal Model

Racism is various guises are considered the principle culprit in the disintegration of urban America. Numerous researchers have tracked race-space issues over more than five decades. Race and class dramatically segregate American cities. Racial isolation has economic consequences. Jobs, social networks and wider opportunities are directly related to the degree of separation or hypersegregation from the white population (Bullard, Grigsby and Lee, 1994).

Thus race space debates are not idle discussions of some ideal state but pre-requisites to dealing effectively with the problems of people of color no matter where they live. While race space concentrations measured in terms of dissimilarity indices suggest some minor improvements in black-white mixing in the 2000 census in a few large cities, social distancing remains very high. There are three important and inter-related factors associated with white racism; schools, separate labor markets and segregated neighborhoods inflicted with crime as depicted in Figure 3.2, below.

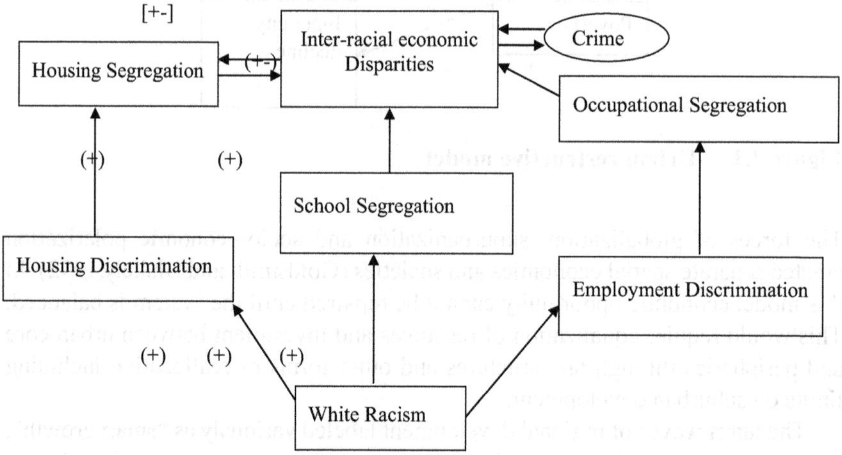

Figure 3.2 Apartheid race-space model

The Racism Model infers that the problems of cities cannot and will not be dealt with until racism is reduced or eliminated entirely. While few local economic development policies can correct attitudes and it is clear that public policy cannot effectively deal with the consequences of racial prejudice. Affirmative action in housing, employment and education has had some dramatic impacts on both attitudes and results of racism (Bluestone, 2000). Nonetheless, serious disparities continue between Blacks and whites. This model for local economic development requires more vigorous application of affirmative action and anti-discrimination laws with aggressive enforcement. This model is almost too dependent on a combination of good will and good government.

Urban Pathology Model

Urban inner city and rural distressed areas have a very clear culture. This culture is deep and not susceptible to simplistic inducements to change behavior. Dropping out of school, having a baby out of wedlock, taking drugs or not working appear to be self defeating behavior and irrational. But in impoverished communities these behaviors are rational and conforming. Breaking these cultural patterns is difficult because they have deep roots. The interaction among family, community and social structures prevent positive or greater cultural frameworks to become the norm. As Kenneth Clark pointed out in 1965,

> The culture of the ghetto must be reshaped so as to strike at the very roots of the ghetto's social malaise. Nothing short of a concerted massive attack on the social, economic and cultural roots of the pathology is required…in the development of remedial stratagems, even if the major concern is the 'elimination of juvenile delinquency' rather than the 'building of a better life' for the people of the ghetto, stress on the latter is more likely to accomplish desired ends than too narrow a concern with the problem, be it homicide, gang fighting, burglary, drug use or unwed motherhood…It is clear, moreover that the continued existence of social pathology…increases the proportion of human casualties (Clark, 1965, p. 109–110).

There is no easy way to change a culture. Current welfare to workfare policy embraces a cultural shift by changing the welfare supports structure. Under the new welfare (TANIF) rules work and school are the cornerstones to self-sufficiency. As President Clinton, said, "welfare has changed forever". The question is whether the cultural supports evident in the impoverished ghettos and rural areas have been erased or just temporarily covered up by a robust economy. No one argues against the basic notion of promoting personal responsibility and community self-sufficiency, the question is whether current policies deal with the symptoms or the cause. The policy goal is to build communities with increased social capital as the base ingredient in total community transformation. Local economic development emphasizes community social cohesion or social capital through micro-enterprise, community cooperative and enterprise models are central to this approach.

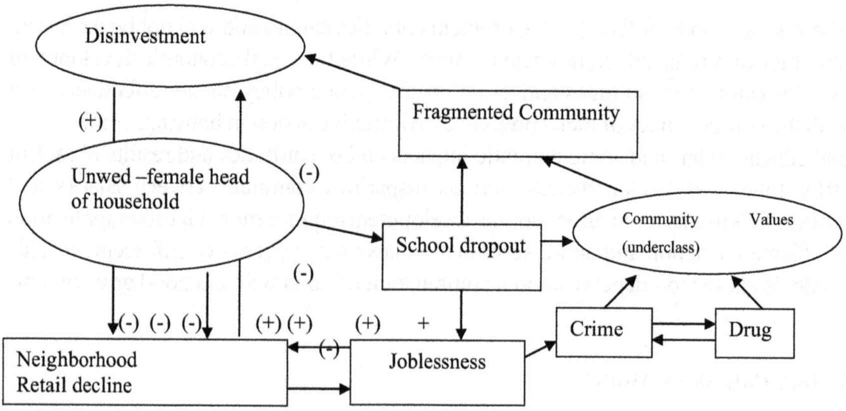

Figure 3.3 The underclass pathology model

Constructing the New Models for Urban Economic Development

Creating inner city policy is confounding and complex because the operational conditions that produced the ghettos and urban decline have changed. In a cyber-age, location does not mean nearly as much as it did in recent times (Blakely, 2001). Nearly a decade of economic expansion, full employment and rising incomes for all groups is an unusual period to construct policies for poor places and/or poor people. Can we assume these times will last forever? Economist and social policy advocates take both sides of this debate (*The Economist*, 27 May–2 June 2000, p. 82). However, it is clear in the waning years of the Bush Administration that the stresses of a prolonged War in the Middle East, rising oil prices and poor fiscal policy have placed new pressures on urban economies. Poor Blacks, the objects of most urban inner city policy are only a portion of a larger and more diverse tapestry of poverty and low-income communities. In fact, some policy analysts argue that Black gains into the middle class should be the focus of national policy. The conditions of female-headed households were central to Black poverty now cross all races with very similar outcomes (Jencks and Peterson,1991) This is not to say that racism is not of consequence in dealing effectively with urban poverty. It is merely an observation that policies aimed at only one group and not the larger conditions may well have perverse impacts on the rising Black middle class with few gains for urban neighborhoods.

As we enter a new century, the relationships between space and race are not firm. Urban space is the subject to new and intense competitive forces. Gentrification is a real or perceived threat in some inner city areas (Wyly and Hammel, 1999 op.cit). As a result, of these changes in objective reality what metaphor applies that stimulates positive formulas and plans/models for policy action.

The George W. Bush Market Approach for Urban Reform and Development

As we discussed earlier, inner city communities are no longer isolated or insulated from the larger forces of the global economy. Macro, not micro, economic activity is the most powerful force on urban space and people. Immigration is one of the best illustrations of these epiphenomena. Large-scale new immigration has regenerated the inner city housing market in most cities throughout the nation. Asian and Latin immigrants have moved into former space vacated by both Blacks and Whites creating a new market for urban real estate. More importantly, these new immigrants are not suburbanizing very rapidly for a host of reasons related to the formation of new linguistic and cultural enclaves as well as the creation of internal social support networks that would not be possible in the suburbs. As a result, there is a nascent revitalization of inner city areas by these newcomers. There is also a competition for cultural and physical space among groups as well. Gangs are one manifestation of this competition. The forces that made urban communities vital are beginning to re-manifest themselves with enclave commercial centers emerging that serve immigrant populations, capture local wealth and generate jobs. This is precisely what the old ethnically segregated neighborhoods did at the beginning of the 20th century. As these forces shifted and inner cities became more useful and useable space public policy has shifted away from enhancing fringe development for a host of environmental and economic reasons. Now in the beginning of the 21st century national public policy programs like HUD's Hope VI initiative, replaces public housing with new mixed income housing, aims at stimulating neighborhood gentrification processes rather than avoiding them as mentioned earlier is the primary tool of the George W. Bush Administration approach to urban ills (Wyly and Hammel, 1995, op. cit.). Thus, the Bush approach is to create or restore market forces in the inner city.

Five factors anchor the new markets approach to inner city development. Each of these has been commented on in the policy literature as single forces or in some combinations but seldom altogether.

1. Changing demography – The 2000 census reveals a much larger and more diverse population that forecasted. The nation has a new base population of 300 million significantly larger than the estimates. The composition and location of this population is the important factor. Increasing numbers of new immigrants from Asia, Russia and Latin America (over 1 in 10 American are now foreign born) are moving into cities. This fresh and young population is a market for housing, retail services and jobs. While incomes in this group are low, they are working. As a result, they create a new market potential. Food retailers were the first to take advantage of this opportunity.

Another force in city demographic resurgence is senior citizens preference for city living and services. As the children move to the "burbs", seniors are returning to the cities where they can reach stores and medical care. While the numbers are not large the trend is clear, larger numbers of seniors prefer the mobility options of the inner city to the immobility of senior suburbs.

2. The new economy is a new user of city space. Dot.coms and their off shoots are city located for a variety of reasons, not the least of which is the innovation worker preference for urban space and urban life styles.

City economies are also improving because of the resurgence of the old industrial base. Technological change has benefited many old industries like oil, agricultural processing, chemicals, furniture, and related firms that remained city based. In addition, finance and insurance along with health care industries have expanded in the cities absorbing city workers and recreating a city human capital economy.

Finally, cities are the beneficiaries of past investments in cultural, sports and entertainment facilities that have been revitalized and are attracting suburbanites and tourist to them.

3. The role of non-profits in inner city development. Non-profit organizations entered low-income areas as investors of first and last resort. Government and foundation funding underwrote much inner city commercial and housing development. These investments stabilized and in some cases revitalized inner city real estate as well as act as the base for commercial development.
4. Environmental attacks on suburban development are a new boon for inner cities. The dis-economies of suburbanization have been well documented. While there is considerable dispute over the links between suburbanization and inner city deteriorization,[4] the reaction of the real estate development community to increasing public acrimony over suburban building has been to shift focus to easier and frequently subsidized options in the cities.
5. Improved city government and regional planning are changing the opportunity landscape in core urban areas. Inner suburbs and inner cities share the same fates, so there is increasing collaboration and cooperation across jurisdictional lines to lower crime, consolidate transportation and other urban infrastructure.

Downtowns in many American cities are safer (both crimes to persons and property have dropped in the last decade[5]), and also aim are urged to provide robust city service improvements to rising city incomes and better city management at every level. In short, cities are back and the Bush Administration assumes this is enough. Young people increasingly prefer the city as the place to live, work and play.

All five of these factors are linked as shown in the diagram (Figure 3.4) below to form a new operational metaphor for the competitive city.

---

4 Anthony Downs provides an excellent assessment of the link between sprawl literature, policy and prescription in "Some Realities about Sprawl and Urban Decline" in *Housing Policy Debate* vol. 10 no. 4, 1999, pp.955–74.

5 US Crime Statistics, 1960–2006 US Crime Statistic Center, 2007.

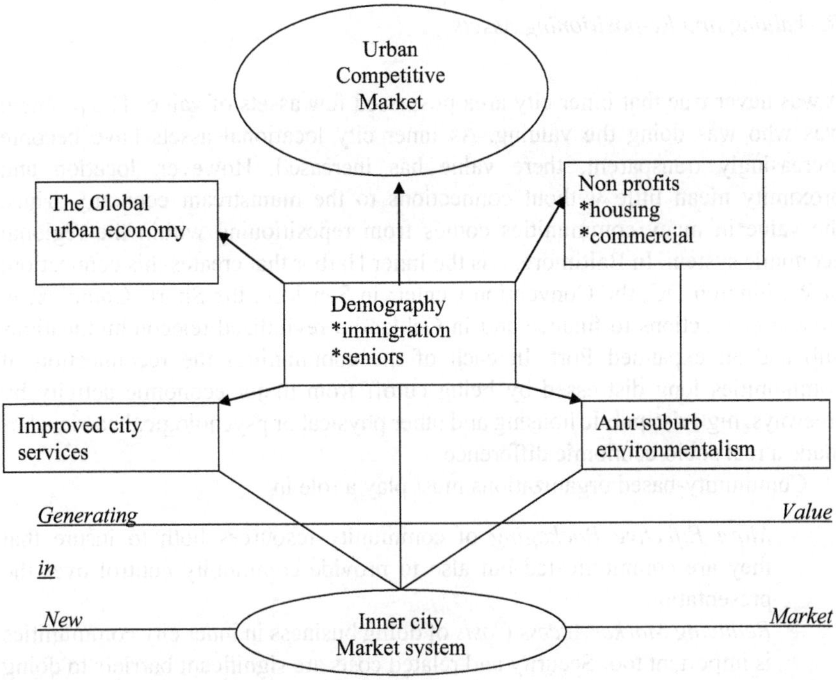

Figure 3.4 Urban competitive market

A Strategic Competitive Model for Inner City Economic Development Policy

Michael Porter was the first well-known scholar to observe that conceptualizing inner city areas through the deficiency lens limited their value and retarded development. In his now famous paper in the *Harvard Business Review* in 1995 he correctly observed, "the ability to access competitive clusters is a very different attribute-and one much more far reaching in economic implications-than more generic advantage of proximity to a large downtown with concentrated activity" (1995 p. 60).

Since Porter, the notion of recognizing and re-positioning inner city areas from a competitive framework builds wealth rather than strips or merely transfer funds within the government structures to external markets. Retaining value and building both jobs and wealth, Porter (1995, op. cit.) pointed out, has to be the fundamental tenant of any form of economic development. Thus, inner cities have to be more than competitive enclaves but they must be connected to and take advantage of the larger urban regional, national and international markets too. Subsequent work by James Carr (1999) and Franklin Raines (2000) as well as Andrew Cuomo (2000) have built on Porters work and reflect it in their models for inner city development. Here we attempt to design an implementation model based on this work and the market construct discussed previously.

Re-Valuing and Re-positioning Assets

It was never true that inner city area possessed few assets of value. The problem was who was doing the valuing. As inner city locational assets have become increasingly transparent, there value has increased. However, location and proximity mean little without connections to the mainstream economy. Thus, the value in many communities comes from repositioning within the regional economic system. In Baltimore, it is the Inner Harbor that creates this connection; in Washington DC, the Convention Center; in San Jose, the Sports Complex; in Boston connections to finance and in Oakland a revitalized telecommunications hub and an expanded Port. In each of the communities the reconnection of communities long distressed by being cutoff from major economic activity by freeways, high rise public housing and other physical or psychological barriers has made a real socio-economic difference.

Community-based organizations must play a role in:

- *More Effective Packaging* of community resources both to insure that they are communicated but also to provide community control over the presentation.
- *Reducing Market Access Costs* of doing business in inner city communities is important too. Security and related costs are significant barriers to doing business in inner city areas. These can be reduced through community sponsored business improvement districts (BIDS) and similar mechanism that provide both the appearance and fact of greater community territorial control.
- *Dynamic Value of Assets* is more important than having assets. A landmark building, theater or other important asset has to be made part of a wider economic system to have real value. Communities that have connected their landmarks to historic tours, use theatres for school and community events etc. create dynamic and not merely static values for these assets.
- *Expertise Assets* are very much under stated and scarcely valued in many inner city communities. Expertise can range from knowledge of local history or specific cultural information such as Asian medicines and healing arts or foods. This expertise, along with financial and management expertise has to be magnified in inner city areas for the community to develop a self sustaining future based on its values and not merely another location for national retail outlets.

Building New Market Combinations

While changing demography can create marketing opportunities this does create a self-sustaining market. Markets are interconnected economic activities that form nodes for goods and services. In the current global economic environment this means dynamic clusters of economic activities that form a rich mix of human and physical capital that has a role in the world or regional market place. Inner city areas, Porter, has suggested can and should be formed re-conceived as a network of enterprises that can act collectively through supply and information chains to compete.

To date, economic development energy as been directed at promoting small and minority businesses that can absorb local spending power. Too little emphasis has been placed on the need to generate a collective economic system with competitive capacity. Such as system would be composed of:

- *Organized industrial and commercial institutions* in the community that can act as voice for the economic community.
- *Capturing local cash flows in the community to build and retain local wealth.* This means inner city areas must have sophisticated financial institutions that can both act to finance local business but can equip these firms to move beyond local demand to compete in the larger economy. In far too many cases local community banks and credit unions are far too weak to handle the needs of new or expanding ventures.
- *Community Image management* is as important as any asset. Markets are images. In fragmented communities this can be a contentious issue but it is important because image is reality – Silicon Valley or Silicon Alley, Back Bay are important image assets that attract economic activity.

Re-creating the Development Base

Considerable emphasis has been placed on inner cities as housing and retail markets. Inner city areas have a larger set of development potentials than these. Inner city areas can and should become hosts to new technology and transformed industrial sectors as well. To be involved in the new enterprise development, inner city areas have to prepare human resources and re-configure existing physical assets. Clearly, it is important to prepare people for entry level trades at the bottom of the economic ladder but growing economies are based on advanced trained workforces. Human resources generate economic activity and not new businesses or plant re-locations. Inner city economic development needs to be re-thought to build human skills and provide quality living environment to retain such skilled persons and the firms they create. Inner cities are of course ripe for other development opportunities such as:

- High-density mixed-income development will become increasingly popular and profitable. Inner cities will be the objects of this development or the beneficiaries of it.
- Transfer of development rights within the city and across jurisdictional lines will create inner city development rights as well.
- Human resource development that creates specialty workforces can attract and grow new businesses.

From Funding to Financing

Funding need rather than justifying financing opportunity has been the mode of development for inner city areas. Non-profits took on this form of development because it was viewed as unprofitable. Since development was need driven assets were purposely down graded and deficiencies magnified. This method of obtaining resources has created a psychology of presenting problems rather than opportunities. A competitive marketplace operates on the opposite principles of government and foundation funding. Community assets need to meet market tests and the opportunity structure needs to show promise. Thus, finance has to create new value and build new assets that are capable of returning to investment to the lender of investor. This mode of operation and philosophy for inner city economic development will take totally new approach on the part of all parties involved in the inner city. Community-based development organizations will need to think of themselves as strategic intermediaries for financing difficult projects for which their expertise is critical. They will earn their return on the basis of their astute risk taking and not on the basis of how desperate the situation is both before and after their involvement. A financing approach will provide:

- Financial packaging and engineering plans need to be designed bundling of assets and cross collateralizing community assets.
- Creating arbitrage opportunities by holding under valued community assets in various forms including high risk loan portfolios for later re-sale.
- Creating instruments to hold community assets collectively to re-capture the value for future generations.
- Enhancing the financing climate in the community by acting as intermediary of conduit for various forms of government funds.
- Promoting micro-financing projects and programs to widen the opportunity structure for community group members to become entrepreneurs.
- Building a new generation of community finance expertise.

These are not the only financing opportunities that can be employed to alter the inner city economic development-financing paradigm. However, both government and foundations will have altered their current approaches to investing in low-income communities to make this possible. But lead institutions such as Fannie Mae can play and important role here as anchor investors in these catalytic institutions thus paving the way for others to follow.

Wealth Building

Economic recovery has been the operating approach for inner city areas. While government agencies like the Small Business Administration have preached minority wealth creation via small business, their practices have severely limit wealth generation opportunities. As he points out in a very direct attack on the SBA's minority lending programs, "...SBA has not been traditionally been interested in the viability of the MESBIC (Minority Enterprise Small Business Investment Company)..." (Bates, 2000, pp.239) In fact, such organizations with the goal to capitalize inner city businesses are under funded and too poorly operated to meet their intended objective of generating new wealth or new business opportunities in the inner city that might produce good jobs (Bates, 2000).

Moreover, there are few mechanism for the community to gain or retain the wealth generated with it own resources. Value recapture as, James Carr (op. cit.1999), labels it is aimed at retaining some of the wealth created by nee market activities in the community from which it originates. William Schweke of the Corporation for Enterprise Development (in Boston, 1997) and others and others have called for such strategies for many years. Clearly, individual risk needs to be rewarded. However, in low income communities' wealth stripping is far easier than re-investment. Much real income from inner city investments necessarily escapes to outside suppliers and investors. However, there are instruments to maintain some of this wealth in the community and to allow community members to retain some of it so that they can re-invest internally or externally. The instruments available for community wealth retention are imperfect at best. They include:

- Land trusts are one means of community wealth retention in the land value arena. Land trusts retain the underlying land asset in housing programs and recapture the value of the land as houses are resold in the community. Land trusts are more acceptable in some communities than others.
- Community trusts are similar to land trusts in that they hold assets collectively.
- A new generation of community-oriented but regional financial investment institutions need to be developed to allow residents opportunities to have ownership stakes in both local and national firms that do business in their neighborhoods.

Even if these and similar mechanisms are designed, the real need is to create wealthy people in wealthy communities. Wealth in this sense means owners of real transferable assets such as businesses, real estate, stocks and bonds etc. Real wealth is almost non-existent in historic minority communities except Asians (Bluestone and Stevenson, 2000). Therefore, active means to promote wealth building and transfer need to be undertaken so that Blacks and Hispanics can take their rightful place as generators of real wealth and economic opportunity. This will never be and can never be the role of government but it can and must be a role that the private financial markets taken on not as charity but as a reasonable means to diversify their own portfolios. The above factors create a simple but compelling model for inner city economic development shown above (Figure 3.5).

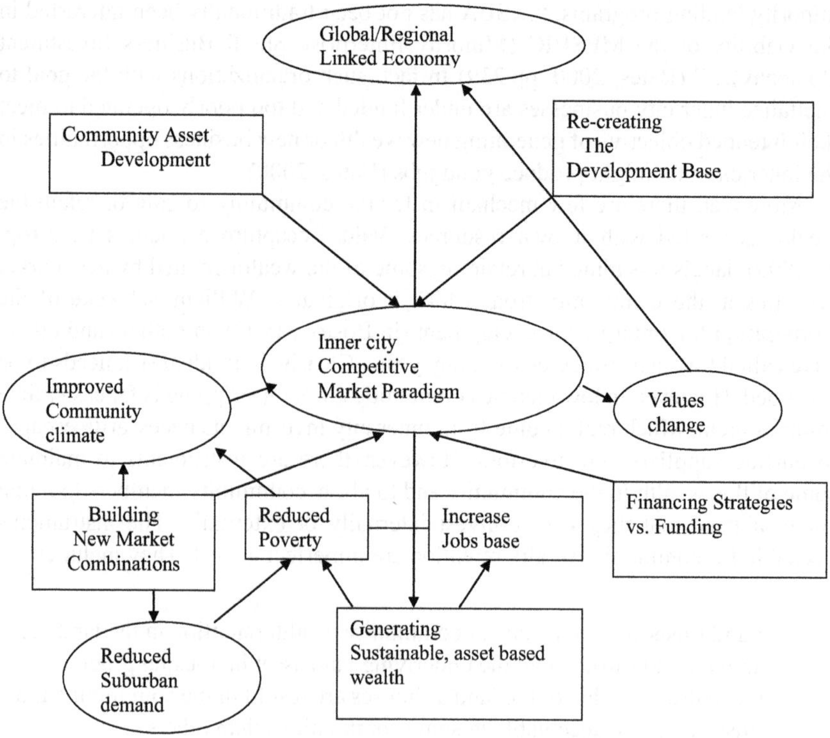

Figure 3.5 Global city competitive market model

Arguing for Locally-based and Controlled Economic Development

In our text Planning Local Economic Development (Blakely and Bradshaw, 2003) we argue that the evolution of urban and rural economic development requires a new conceptualization of the notion of local and the structure of economic development. We acknowledge the issues addressed above by suggesting that economic development must be based in merging local indigenous resources both human and material into what we call a "third wave" form that using new technologies both hard "telecommunications" and soft "human social and political capital" to form new links between communities both inner city urban and or rural in a definable region to forge a new economic engine that improves the opportunity structure for all. The form of this newly evolved model is articulated opposite in Table 3.1.

Table 3.1 An evolved model of urban economic development

Economic Development Component	Old Concept	New Concept
Geographic Base	City or town	Global regional network of collaborating communities
Industrial/Business Base	Recruiting firms	Building economic activity that has global reach from the community assets and regional network
Employment/Human Capital Goals	Fitting or training local people to imported or industrial activity	Generating jobs within communities that match or matches can be created for local population
Structures for Local Economic Development	Chambers of Commerce and Redevelopment agencies	Collaborative regional consortia aimed a socioeconomic renewal

Source: Adapted from Blakely and Bradshaw (2003) p.67.

Conclusions

As the 20th century began a theoretical framework was needed to both explain and ameliorate urban poverty as a component of an industrializing society. An original thesis with companion architecture was forged a movement to deal with it. By mid century the problems of inner cities had transmuted to the point that theorists opined that the residents themselves have more knowledge of the problems and could design their own blueprints to success. The new millennium brings a restructured socio-economy creating internal and external forces on cities in general and inner city disadvantaged communities in particular. This market-competitive situation requires a model like its predecessor with specially designed implementation vehicles. In the era of social welfare ala Jane Addams, the social acculturation institutions of the Settlement Houses and Y's were the vehicle for inner city renewal. These institutions still have their place in the arsenal of social pathology solutions to the problems of an underclass culture. Clearly, social services were weak instruments as the nation moved to urban renewal strategies. Community development corporations were the natural out growth of this new wave of "development" as opposed to service. Development has taken on many forms, not the least of which has been real estate and economic development. Now, social capital formation seems to be central to the notions of development but the exact institutional vehicles to carry this message are not clear other than the neighborhood church. There is some risk in a pluralist democracy of expecting faith-based organizations to meet total community needs both social and economic will be troubled.

At this juncture in the evolution of inner city development theory, social supports need to be combined with market economic positioning. Viewing communities as needy or deficient of social or economic assets will not draw capital to these communities. For the first time in over one hundred years, inner city communities are viewed as locals with possibilities. This potential springs in large measure because inner city, no longer means, Black or only Black. Inner cities now contain very viable populations and are potential strong economic and human resource markets. Thus, the paradigm shifts from "need" to opportunity and from moving away from and destroying to rebuilding and celebrating.

At the same time we have to examine the institutional means to carry this message. Community-based development organizations present one strand of a model. However, their early mission of social service and political action creates internal tensions and external credibility problems. As we examine a new model as a plan of policy action, we have to look for a new means of carrying out this architectural design. Some form of new hybrid public-private institutions will have to be created or evolve to meet these changed circumstances. It is by no means certain that such organizations need to be physically located in the communities they serve. Their mission is to capitalize, connect and build market structures and access for inner city communities. Already the signs of such institutions are on the horizon. BRIDGE Housing Corporation, headquartered in San Francisco but servicing low-income communities throughout California is one model. Other approaches are emerging in the form of new inner city capital organizations such as Michael Porter's own *ICI Capital Fund* and Henry Cisneros *New Vistas Corporation* and DC Agenda in Washington DC are a new breed of publicly supported venture companies that focus on inner city social and economic renewal. These are sign that a model is emerging that combines public goals with private capital and sees the restoration of people and places as the ultimate goal for development.

As CDCs became development institutions a new class of intermediary was formed to capitalize them such as LISC and Enterprise Corp. and the like. This next class of development institution requires a similar vehicle for government, foundations and private capital to use for economic and social investments in the inner city and disadvantaged rural areas. The Community Development Finance Institutions CDFIs may be the first wave of such institutions. At present, CDFIs are too varied and too weak to play any role with private capital. However, the CDFI may be the first of the next generation of institutions that will operationalize the competitive in changing communities. One very promising implementation model is "The Double Bottom Line: Investing in California's Emerging Markets" spearheaded by Philip Angelides, The California State Treasurer. This program steers state investment capital such as state pension funds and infrastructure financing to inner city areas with social and economic returns benchmarked to national levels.[6] No one has the ultimate answer or the key to all of the problems of poverty in any society. We have learned through all previous efforts that we have to give every place and every person the option and opportunity to succeed anywhere. As Alexis de Tocquville observed in 1831, "Nothing struck me more forcibly than the general equality of conditions." We start the 21st century placing resources in the community to gain equality of opportunity is part of a new asset based market approach. In this century we must build resources for the community; it now seems possible for both regional and local community to be allies in building a competitive future for the nation's communities no matter where they are. As Lester Thurow said of the current economy, "How does one preach political equality in an economy of ever growing inequality".[7] The role of the new model is to understand the market to design positive opportunities to achieve economic, social and political equality.

References

Bates, T. (2000), "Financing the Development of Urban Minority Communities: Lessons of History" *Economic Development Quarterly* vol.14 no. 3, pp. 227–43.

Beauregard, R. and Body-Gendrot, S. (1999), *The Urban Moment: Cosmopolitan Essays on the Late 20th Century City* (Thousand Oaks, Calif: Sage Publications).

Blakley, E.J. (2001), "Competitive Advantage for the 21st Century: Can a Place Based Approach to Economic Development Survive in a Cyberspace Age?" *Journal of the American Planning Association.* Spring.

Blakely, E.J. and Bradshaw, T.K. (2003), *Planning Local Economic Development* (Sage Publications).

Bluestone, B. and Huff Stevenson, M. (2000), *The Boston Renaissance: Race, Space, and Economic Change in an American Metropolis* (New York: Sage Foundation Press).

Bullard, R.J., Grigsby, E. and Lee, C. (1994), *Residential Apartheid: The American Legacy* (Los Angeles: UCLA, Center for Afro-American Studies).

Carr, J. (1999), "Community, Capital and Markets: A New Paradigm for Community Reinvestment" *The NeighborWorks* Summer.

Christenson, J. and Robinson Jr, J. (1989), *Community Development in Perspective* (Ames, Iowa: Iowa State University Press).

6 The State of California program directs more than $7 billion in state resources for "smart investments" that increase jobs in inner city areas, revitalize inner cities, improve schools and slow outward suburban development by financing new higher density mixed urban development.

7 Lester Thurow cited in Philip Angelides, *The Double Bottom Line: Investing in California's Emerging Markets* (Sacramento: Office of the State Treasurer), 2000.

Cuomo, A. (2000), *The State of the Cities 2000: Megaforces Shaping the Future of the Nation's Cities* (Washington DC: US Department of Urban Development).

Downs, A. (1999), "Some Realities about Sprawl and Urban Decline" in *Housing Policy Debate* vol. 10 no. 4, pp.955–74.

The Economist (2000), "Growth is Good" 27 May–2 June.

Ewing, R. (1997), "Is Los Angeles-Style Sprawl Desirable?" *Journal of the American Planning Association* vol. 63, no. 1, pp. 107–126.

Galster, G. (1998), "An Econometric Model of Urban Opportunity Structure: Cumulative Causation among City Markets, Social Problems, and Underserved Areas" *Urban and Metropolitan Issues* (Washington DC: Fannie Foundation Monograph).

Goldsmith, W. and Blakely, E.J. (1993), *Separate Societies: Poverty and Inequality in the US Cities* (Philadelphia: Temple University Press).

Jencks, C. and Peterson, P. (1991), *The Urban Underclass* (Washington DC: Brookings Institution Press).

Kasarda, J. and Kwok-fai-Ting (1996), "Joblessness and Poverty in America's Central Cities: Causes and Policy Prescriptions" *Housing Policy Debate* vol.7, no. 2.

Lemann, N. (1994), "The Myth of Community Development" *New York Times Magazine* 9 January.

O'Connor, A. (1999), "Swimming Against the Tide: A Brief History of Federal Policy in Poor Communities" in Ferguson, R.F. and Dickens, W.T. *Urban Problems and Community Development* (Washington, DC: Brookings Institution Press).

Orfield, M. (1997), *Metropolitics: A Regional Agenda for Community and Regional Stability* (Washington, DC: Brookings Institution Press).

President's National Advisory Commission on Rural Poverty (1967) (Washington DC: US Printing Office).

Raines, F. (2000), "Playing from Strength: The Market Power of Cities" *Brookings Review*, Summer pp. 16–19.

Rosen, K. and Dienstfrey, T. (1999), "The Economics of Housing Services in Low-Income Neighborhoods" in Ferguson and Dickey op.cit pp.437–72.

Rubin, H. (2000), *Renewing Hope Within Neighborhoods of Despair* (Albany: State University New York Press).

Rusk, D. (1993), *Cities Without Suburbs* (Baltimore, Md.: Johns Hopkins University Press).

Schweke, W. (1997), "Making Comparative Advantage Work for Economic Opportunity" in Thomas Boston and Catherine Ross *The Inner City: Urban Poverty and Economic Development in the Next Century* (New Brunswick: Transaction Publishers).

Vidal, A. (1995), "Reintegrating Disadvantaged Communities into the Fabric of urban Life: The Role of Community Development" *Housing Policy Debate* vol. 6, no. 1, pp.169–230.

Wilson, W.J. (1987), *The Truly Disadvantaged: The Inner City, the Underclass and Public Policy* (Chicago, Ill.: University of Chicago Press).

Wilson, W.J. (1996), *When Work Disappears: The World of the New Urban Poor.* New York, Vintage Books.

Wyly, E. and Hammel, D. (1999), "Islands of Decay in Seas of Renewal and Resurgence of Gentrification" *Housing Policy Debate* vol. 10, no. 4, pp.711–72.

Chapter 4
The Theory and Practice of Developing Locally

Andrew Beer

The Theory and Practice of Developing Locally

Policies and practices that seek to promote or sustain local or regional economic development are a feature of virtually all developed economies (OECD, 1997, 2001, 2005; Statskontoret, 2007; Halkier et al., 1998). Government agencies or community groups operating at the regional or local scale seek to foster growth through a mix of strategies including: encouraging inward investment in the region, fostering innovation, nurturing a 'creative city' environment, promoting new business start ups, engaging in regional economic planning, coordinating infrastructure investment, assisting small businesses gain access to capital and acting to facilitate development applications through the approval process (Beer et al., 2003a). In some nations, actions and strategies intended to encourage growth at the sub-national scale are considered regional policies (for example, Australia) but elsewhere (for example, the United States of America) comparable programs are referred to as local development initiatives. For this reason this chapter will refer to both local and regional economic development.

There is a substantial theoretical literature that addresses the growth of regions and local economies (see, for example, Haughton, 1999; Cooke and Morgan, 2000; MacLeod, 2001; Jacobs, 2007). A key marker of the strength of the theoretical debate on regional or local development has been reflected in the burgeoning number of new academic journals focussed on some aspect of this field of intellectual endeavour. This chapter argues that while there has been a highly visible programmatic effort in local or regional development, the links between the practice of regional development and theories of regional development are themselves under-developed. At a fundamental level, the evidence base on the practice of regional development – what 'works' and what doesn't – is absent. This gap reflects failings both in the way governments pursue economic development and in the constitution of academic interest in questions of local or regional development.

Many local economic development programs are based on one or more theories of economic development but the multiplicity of theoretical perspectives results in confusion amongst practitioners on the purpose and justification for their programs. These issues are examined in this chapter through the review of some of the key theoretical influences on the practice of local and regional economic development. The chapter also examines how both the practice of local economic development and academic writing on local or regional development are constructed socially. It argues that there are processes operating on both the development of theory and the practice of local development that serve to drive the two sets of interests in diverging directions. The chapter then goes on to consider the role of inward investment strategies with the suite of economic development programs deployed by three cities: Winnipeg, Canada; Sheffield, England, and San Diego, United States of America. The chapter uses the examination of these three case studies to demonstrate the diverse pathways to economic development and the degree to which a number of theoretical positions can be used to justify economic development practices. The chapter then concludes with a discussion of the need for a more rigorous evidence base on the practice of local or regional development.

Theoretical Perspectives on Local Development and Linkages with the Practice of Economic Development

A cursory examination of any text book (Armstrong and Taylor, 2000; Stimson et al., 2006, Beer et al., 2003b) on regional development will uncover a wealth of theory on the drivers of local or regional growth. From the perspective of economics, theoretical positions include neo classical models, endogenous growth models, demand led models, cumulative causation models and new institutional economics (North, 1990) to name but a sample of approaches. These constructs variously emphasise the role of capital, labour, productivity or productivity growth, technical knowledge and innovation. Export base theory, for example, suggests that regional specialisation will occur over time and that regions will specialise in products for which the factors of production are abundant. This theory proposes that demand for a region's product will be seen to drive the region's development while cumulative causation models (Kaldor, 1970; Dixon and Thirwell, 1975) highlight feedback loops in the development process and their contribution to both regional disparities and industry specialisation. Other disciplines have contributed to the development of theory around local development with various authors focussing on the role of the state (Jessop, 1990, 1997, 2002; Jones, 1997, 2001), regulation theory (Peck and Tickell, 1992, 1995, 2002; Goodwin and Painter, 1996), 'new regionalism' (McLeod, 2001; Rainnie and Grobellar, 2005), and more recently 'city regionalism' (Harrison, 2007) as well as perspectives based on the work of Deleuze (Jacobs, 2007).

All theoretical approaches have implications for local development practice: for example, regulation theory approaches emphasise the creation of appropriate institutions for regional or local development; neo classical models highlight the need to attract capital and/or labour to the region or locality; new regionalism perspectives emphasise encouraging growth locally; while new institutional economics draws the attention of the economic development practitioner to the need to encourage information and infrastructure provision in order to reduce transaction costs. Economic development practitioners can argue a theoretical basis for such wide-ranging actions as the provision of subsidies to incoming firms, regional planning, cluster formation, the establishment of business incubators and support for small business generally. In many cases, while the link between theory and practice can be argued, the evidence on the success of such programs is often missing or adverse (Isserman, 1994; Freebairn, 1998, 2003). Multiple theories on the drivers of local development represent a challenge for the practice of local economic development as practitioners may struggle to understand, or have difficulty in awarding priority to, one perspective over others. In short, the burgeoning of theories around developing locally has created a 'crowded' marketplace, where one set of ideas displaces or cramps the other and practitioners are inclined to ignore all perspectives because of the absence of a consensus.

The linkages between the theories of local or regional economic development and programs delivered 'on the ground' are weak because of a complex of factors. Importantly, both the 'supply' by researchers of ideas and information on local and regional development practices is tenuous, as is the demand from regional development practitioners and government sponsors.

On the supply side, the institutional environment in which academics undertake research has not encouraged them to directly address the practicalities of local development. Academics work within a setting which provides rewards commensurate with the quality and quantity of their outputs – essentially tangible research outcomes such as refereed articles, books and book chapters – as judged by their peers, who are other academics rather than economic development practitioners. This, inevitably, results in a focus on theory building and the writing of manuscripts that will be acceptable to the most prestigious journals or book publishers. Such outputs will have an academic rather than practical orientation and this is reinforced by the promotion practices of universities, as well as government quality assurance processes, such as the Research Assessment Exercise in the United Kingdom. It is important to acknowledge that some institutions – and some groups within universities – have an explicit mandate to engage with their community but such activities are often focussed on teaching and consulting activities that have limited capacity to be generalised to a wider stage. The land grant universities in the United States are often very active with their local communities, as are some institutions in other developed nations. There are, of course, notable exceptions of which Blakely's (1994) work and the journal *Economic Development Quarterly* are the most prominent. But work of this nature tends to be the exception, rather than the rule, and even then, publication in any form cannot be guaranteed a readership by economic development practitioners.

Local and regional development does not attract the substantial research funding found in health research where there is a very strong tradition of evidence based research. As O'Dwyer (2004 p. i) notes, evidence based policy is 'based on research that has undergone some form of quality assurance or scrutiny' and such evaluations usually follow a protocol such as those established by the Cochrane or Campbell collaborations. The Blair Labour Government in the United Kingdom expressed considerable concern for evidence based policy but its application to other jurisdictions has been episodic at best. Researchers interested in the practicalities of local and regional development practice have failed to develop an evidence base comparable to that found in health-related research because they have struggled to find programs and contexts which are comparable, as well as secure sufficient funding to allow either large scale research or a quality assurance process to take place. As Lovering (1999) noted, much regional development research and theory development is based on limited case studies rather than a systematic collection of data and the testing of theories. Indeed, Lovering (1999) commented that many of the propositions posited by 'new regionalists' are essentially untestable. In sum, the linkages between the theory and practice of local development are weak on the supply side because the majority of researchers working on regional issues are concerned with the development of theory rather than practical knowledge and because they lack the resources to undertake the large scale studies or program reviews needed to establish an objective and proven evidence base.

There are significant demand side impediments to the establishment of stronger linkages between the theory and practice of local or regional economic development. Governments at national, state/provincial, and local levels often make decisions on regional development issues on the basis of political expedience rather than a proven track record of success (Beer et al., 2003b, pp. 197–8; Australian National Audit Office, 2007) and the development of a more strongly grounded local development practice may call into question such actions. While governments have a vested interest in not encouraging scrutiny of their actions, they are also reluctant to shed too harsh a light on their inaction in many areas of social policy. Gray and Lawrence (2001) noted that in Australia at least, governments have promoted local economic development as a sop to disenfranchised and disadvantaged rural communities. The funding provided by governments to these initiatives is often insufficient for the task at hand (Beer et al., 2003a). A better informed community and network of local development practitioners could potentially pressure governments for greater funding and powers. Once again, governments have a strong disincentive to assist in the development of greater linkages between the theory and practice of developing locally.

A number of researchers (of whom the British-born but US-based Jamie Peck is probably best known) have argued that the practice of local economic development has been very much influenced by neo liberalism, which has involved a 'reworking' of the powers and roles of the state (Peck, 2004; Leitner et al., 2007; Larner, 2005). While it is important to acknowledge that nations have pursued neo liberal agendas in different ways (Larner, 2003; Jessop, 2002) commonalities are evident, especially in the ways governments seek to shape local development efforts. As Beer et al. (2005 p. 51) commented, the state,

> increasingly sets out to determine the regulatory and policy frameworks for others. In short, it seeks to 'steer' not 'row', or it directs rather than directly implements. As such the role of government is in setting the rules of governance. In the case of regional development, for instance, it is the state which decides how much money is to be made available, for which time period, to which types of devolved agency, and what policy remit each agency should be given. In effect the state has retained a disciplinary power over how it allocates funding and responsibilities, a process which has seen the rise of the audit culture and a proliferation of short-term experiments which can be closed, cloned or converted into different approaches.

Critically, while governments have espoused a 'self help' philosophy for communities affected by structural change or other adverse economic conditions, they have sought to maintain a determining influence. The central policy departments of governments in nations such as the UK and Australia look to maintain their role as the final arbiter of what is effective and what is ineffective with respect to local development practice. For example, Haughton (2003, pp. 78–9) noted the frustration expressed by many local development practitioners in England with the 'close central control over local economic development activities'. To draw from an Australian example, in the late 1990s the South Australian Government developed a series of performance indicators for the Regional Development Boards it partly funds. The standing of the Regional Development Board and its Chief Executive Officer with the responsible state government department was included as one of the central performance indicators, essentially awarding the department considerable fiat in any decision to continue or terminate funding (Mack Management Consulting, 1998). From the perspective of this chapter, the central issue is that economic development practitioners who are dependent upon the on-going support of a government department and whose job involves the delivery of programs funded and directed from above, have little incentive or time to consider alternative approaches to economic development. Their role as a conduit for the achievement of program objectives established by central government departments results in limited scope for local innovation in development practice. Information on new or better approaches to economic development is therefore of limited utility.

The nature of economic development practitioners can operate to impede the development of bridges between the theory of regional development and its implementation. In many jurisdictions there is no mandated qualification for economic development practitioners. While there are a number of established university courses in the United States and on-going professional accreditation through the International Economic Development Council and other bodies, other nations have no such programs. Surveys of economic development practitioners undertaken in 1996 and 2001 in Australia (Beer and Maude, 1997; Beer et al., 2003a) found a diverse range of qualifications amongst economic development professionals. While some had qualifications in economics, commerce, accounting or the arts, others had no formal qualifications or had vocational qualifications only. The absence of a shared stock of knowledge – and mutual mechanisms for acquiring information – further impedes the take-up of the insights embedded within academic research, weakening the link between theory and practice.

Overall, the linkages between theory and practice on local or regional economic development are partial because academic efforts are not focussed on disseminating ideas and knowledge to practitioners, while those working 'at the coal face' may have a limited interest in looking beyond the programs they currently deliver. The focus of central governments is limited to the efficient delivery of programs already committed to and they have limited interest – or even hostility – toward spending proposals that originate locally. Even within the US where city governments play a major independent role in promoting local development, the need to keep Mayors and other politicians satisfied shapes economic development activities (Rubin, 1988) and may discourage the take-up of new ideas or the abandonment of discredited approaches (Loveridge, 1996).

From Theory to Practice: Lessons from Porter and Florida

This chapter has argued so far that researchers interested in local or regional economic development and those charged with its implementation are, in large measure, separate communities between whom there is limited dialogue. There are, however, significant exceptions, of which Michael Porter's work on industry clusters and Richard Florida's writings on creative cities are the most outstanding examples. This section briefly reviews the ideas of these two authors and the ways in which the concepts they promoted were adopted globally.

Michael Porter's work on industry clusters (Porter, 1990) gained widespread recognition through the 1990s as governments sought to improve the efficiency and competitiveness of their industries by building 'competitive advantage'. In many ways Porter's insights into economic development processes were not original as they built upon the much earlier Marshallian tradition around the economics and impact of industrial agglomeration. Porter's significant contribution was to transform an academic appreciation that similar businesses that locate together realise economic advantages, into a set of actions that offered the promise of sustained growth to any locality or region with the courage to follow his prescription. Porter's (1990) ideas around competitive, rather than comparative, advantage encouraged some governments to believe that the careful planning of business activities and the explicit formation of 'clusters' would enhance productivity and global competitiveness (Porter et al., 2000). Some governments adopted explicit industry cluster strategies (Roberts and Enright, 2001, 2004) while others were highly influenced by this body of work.

Several factors contributed to the take-up of Michael Porter's ideas on the drivers of local development. First and foremost, industry clustering was an idea whose time had come. In the early 1990s the manufacturing sectors of developed economies were still feeling their way following structural change in the 1970s and industry clusters appeared as a pro-active policy that offered a long term solution to the uncertainties that continued to confront these sectors. Porter's (1990) work on industry clustering was perceived as leading to clearly defined policy interventions. The implementation of his ideas can be contrasted with Robert Putnam's work on social capital, which was equally influential in policy circles, but less easily translated into action. Porter's model was attractive through the 1990s and into this century as it offered the appearance at least of being divorced from the policy prescriptions – including direct subsidies – of the past. Second, Porter was seen to be associated with business studies rather than the more conventional discipline of economics, which added credibility to his ideas. Finally, Porter's ideas on industry clustering were simple and this added to their apparent robustness. The simplicity of these concepts meant that they were taken up by a diverse range of protagonists, including business consultants who have continued to promote business clustering (Ffowcs-Williams, 2004). Indeed, it is worth reflecting on the fact that Porter's ideas first had a policy impact in Australia through the advocacy of a US economic development practitioner who was participating in an OECD conference (Henton and Walesh, 1994). A diverse spectrum of groups promoted and endorsed industry clustering (e.g. US Council on Competitiveness and National Governors Association, 2001; Clusters Builders Australia) thereby extending both its reach and impact. By the late 1990s industry clusters had emerged as the new orthodoxy in local development and while the evidence on their success was mixed, especially in more marginal economies (see, for example, Cloney, 2003) the impact on the practice of developing locally cannot be denied.

The work of Richard Florida on 'creative cities' has had a comparable, but more recent, impact on the practice of local and regional development to that witnessed with the promotion of Michael Porter's ideas in the 1990s. In his most influential work, *The Rise of the Creative Class* (2002) Florida used an analysis of growth rates for cities in the US to argue that metropolitan areas with concentrations of high technology workers, gays, and 'bohemians' working in creative industries experienced higher rates of growth than comparable centres dominated by traditional blue or white collar employees. He referred to these types of workers as the 'creative class' which he further divided into sub groups, including the 'super creatives' and 'creative professionals'. Importantly, Florida (2002) argued that cities that encouraged creativity, were tolerant of different lifestyles – including gays and immigrants – and were attractive to young people, were more likely to reap benefits within the restructuring economies of the developed world. As Florida (2002, 2005) noted, many cities and regions do not attract the creative class, or members of the creative class migrate from those regions to more attractive environments. Florida (2002) set out to measure the attractiveness of individual cities to the creative class through a series of indicies, including a Bohemian index, a gay index and a diversity index.

Florida's (2002) work was presented as directly relevant to the practice of developing locally because he argued that in the 21st century cities and regions need to foster a creative environment or culture. It was argued that instead of adding infrastructure such as highways, cities and regions needed to promote a café culture, introduce social reforms that emphasised tolerance, promote cultural events and reshape their urban environments to make them more attractive to this pivotal group within the labour market. We should acknowledge that in many ways Florida's ideas resonated with the arguments of earlier authors, including Robert Reich's (1991) wrting on the economic importance of 'symbolic analysts', Sharon Zukin's (1995) work on culture and economic development and even Jane Jacobs' (1961) seminal work on the *Death and Life of Great American Cities*. Significantly, however, Florida's (2002) arguments were based on the quantitative analysis of a large scale data set which added to the 'legitimacy' and impact of his arguments.

Florida's (2002) interpretation of contemporary growth processes has been subject to considerable scrutiny within the academic community with some researchers (Nichols Clarke, 2002) challenging his data analysis, while others have questioned its relevance for smaller communities (Rainnie, 2005) or the political context within which his ideas have been adopted (Peck, 2005). Indeed, it could be argued that developing critiques of Richard Florida's work (2002, 2005) has emerged as a new creative industry in English-speaking nations.

Florida's work has had a major influence on the practice of developing locally and it is worthwhile reflecting on the nature of that impact. Florida's (2002) prominence in economic development programs cannot be denied: over the last half decade cities in developed economies around the globe have become convinced that they need to establish themselves as 'creative' cities in order to attract the 'creatives'. Places as diverse as Sheffield in northern England through to Adelaide in South Australia have attempted to establish their 'creativity' or bohemian credentials, while at the same time measuring their performance against one or more of Florida's indicies. Governments have contracted consultants to assess their 'creative city' potential[1] and advise them on strategies to further their credibility as a creative city.

The nature of Florida's (2002) argument, as well as the method for its dissemination, contributed to the impact of his theory on the practice of developing locally. The fact that his arguments were based on a quantitative analysis of data on urban growth rates contributed to the acceptability and impact of his ideas. On the one hand, his analysis was effectively communicated to quantitatively-minded economists employed by central governments, while on the other, his use of case studies and indicies added to the immediacy and poignancy of his arguments for local or regional development practitioners. Florida communicated his ideas through the mass media – including magazine articles – and presented them in symposia and keynote speeches around the globe. In a break with conventional

1 Prof. John Rees who retired from the University of North Carolina in 2007 tells that the city of Charlotte, North Carolina appointed a high profile consulting firm to evaluate their performance as a creative city. The City officials were disappointed when the consultants reported that in their view Charlotte was a 'pleasantly mediocre' city with a limited cosmopolitan footprint.

academic practice, Florida offered his ideas to a wide audience through a single presentation that was repeated time and time again. The repetition of a rehearsed message to large audiences – in the manner of a politician or evangelist – helped generate practitioner acceptance as Florida presented his ideas in a manner that was easily understood by practitioners, thereby adding to their stock of knowledge. The reiteration of one message and a single – carefully scripted – presentation made it possible for practitioners to discuss Florida's ideas with their peers, thereby reinforcing his viewpoint. In addition, Florida's argument was implicitly or explicitly endorsed by the agencies that sponsored his appearance.

There are a number of lessons to be drawn from the translation of Porter and Florida's work into the practice of developing locally. First, in both instances a perspective generated in academia received the widespread endorsement of government departments, which in turn influenced the practices and strategies of economic development agencies. Both sets of ideas received the support of governments because they offered a pro-active policy agenda that did not necessarily rely upon substantial government subsidies. The concepts were also acceptable to governments because they carried with them a legitimacy that derived from their origins in high profile business and economics faculties. Second, Porter and Florida largely communicated their ideas via non-academic media and this made the translation from the theory to the practice of developing locally much more straightforward. Both paradigms of development were presented to development practitioners in unchallenging ways – conference presentations, seminars, magazine articles, public addresses, consultancies – and were offered as a solution to the challenges of local development irrespective of context. In large measure, neither Florida or Porter's work necessarily calls for a finely nuanced approach to the promotion of economic growth in a particular region, or city: all localities can aspire to be a more creative city, region or hamlet, and all communities can seek to develop a 'cluster' of industries based on some notional competitive advantage, whether it is real or imaginary.[2] Significantly, we can conclude from the 'success' of Porter and Florida that conventional academic practice – teaching post graduate or undergraduate programs, the winning of research grants, publication in academic journals et cetera – is very different from the sorts of practices likely to result in the translation of theories of local development into practice.

The Practice of Local and Regional Development: Theoretical Links?

Governments and communities place considerable priority on on-going economic growth and the performance of their region, city or locality relative to their peers.

2 In the 1990s one Australian local government promoted an economic development strategy that featured a 'tourism' cluster based on 15 tourism agencies located in two streets. The same strategy also highlighted the 'X' precinct, which was a cluster of adult entertainment businesses.

Local growth strategies are sometimes explicitly based on a particular theoretical position – such as clusters – but may also reflect the 'accepted wisdom' and practice of the local development fraternity. This section of the chapter considers the local development processes of three cities – San Diego, California; Sheffield, England and Winnipeg, Manitoba – and the role of inward investment programs. Industry attraction programs are commonly dismissed as 'corporate welfare' (Beer et al., 2003b, pp. 159–69; Karmatz et al., 1998) but their inclusion in the armoury of economic development can be justified within regional economic theory, with such firms bringing valuable capital to underdeveloped regions. The case studies focus on the differing growth trajectories of these three cities and the variable role of inward investment programs in achieving (or not achieving) growth. The section then concludes with some observations on how the reality of economic development makes it difficult to draw firm conclusions on the causes of growth and thereby offer robust policy prescriptions.

San Diego, California

San Diego is the ninth largest city in the United States with a population of 1.2 million. It is the seat of San Diego County and is the economic centre of the San Diego–Carlsbad–San Marcos metropolitan area, the 17th largest metro area in the US with a population of 2.9 million as of 2006, and the 21st largest metropolitan area in the Americas when Tijuana is included. It is located on the coast in southern California, adjacent to Mexico. San Diego's development through the 20th century was tied to the expansion of military activities, with the US Navy establishing a presence in 1907. The US Coast Guard and Marines have bases in and around the city. Even today the Navy continues to exert a profound influence on the economy as San Diego hosts the only major submarine and shipbuilding yards on the US West Coast, as well as the largest naval fleet in the world. The city's economy experienced a downturn in the 1990s with the end of the Cold War and the city has established itself as a pre-eminent force in biotechnology and telecommunications. Markers of San Diego's success in transforming its economy include: substantial population growth, rising household incomes and housing affordability problems.

San Diego has emerged as a high technology centre and hosts the headquarters and research facilities for numerous biotechnology companies. Major biotechnology enterprises such as Neurocrine Biosciences and Nventa Biopharmaceuticals have their headquarters in San Diego, while many biotech and pharmaceutical companies, such as BD Biosciences, Biogen Idec, Merck, Pfiser, Élan, Genzyme, Celgene and Vertex, have offices or research facilities in the city. There are also several non-profit biotechnology institutes, such as the Salk Institute for Biological Studies, the Scripps Research Institute and the Burnham Institute. The presence of the University of California, San Diego, and other research institutions has fuelled biotechnology growth. In June 2004, San Diego was ranked the top biotech cluster in the US by the Milken Institute and eight per cent of all biotechnology firms in the US are based there. The city is also home to companies that develop wireless cellular technology. Qualcomm Incorporated was founded in San Diego and is the largest private sector technology employer (excluding hospitals) in the County.

The Economic Development Program

The top four industries in San Diego are manufacturing, defence, tourism and agriculture. In its economic development planning the City of San Diego has a focus on five industry clusters:

- biotechnology/biosciences;
- defence and space manufacturing;
- electronics and manufacturing;
- financial and business services;
- software and telecommunications.

The San Diego Regional Economic Development Corporation (SREDC) seeks to attract and retain companies in the San Diego region by working directly with these companies to assist their relocation and expansion. The SREDC is a private, not for profit corporation, funded by the City of San Diego, the San Diego Port District, the City of Chula Vista and private sector partners, managed by a largely private sector board. The SREDC has a budget of $2.7 million per annum, which is low by US standards because of the presence of eight other organisations in the region that undertake comparable functions. The SREDC offers a range of services, including:

- site selection assistance;
- incentive and business tax information;
- information on key contacts in business and local government;
- demographic, wage and other data provision;
- assistance in navigating local government requirements;
- access to workforce training and recruitment.

A report prepared by KMK Consulting (2006) suggested that the SREDC offered fewer incentives than most comparable organisations because of the lack of incentives at the state and local level. KMK Consulting argued that the SREDC has instead leveraged off existing networks and businesses

> …the bioscience networks between the (SR)EDC, the universities and research institutes have proven to be the most important 'incentive' that the organisation can offer. Despite the lack of any public funding to induce any of the major players who have established significant presence there, the San Diego region is the largest life sciences hub in the US (KMK Consulting, 2006 p. 13).

The University of California, San Diego (UCSD) is an active participant in encouraging innovation and new firm formation within the region. The SREDC works in partnership with the UCSD's CONNECT program that seeks to nurture high technology entrepreneurship and facilitate interaction with the University. The program is funded through the University's Extended Studies and Public Programs area. Other agencies that seek to foster the growth of high technology companies in the region include:

- BioCom San Diego – a regional association for biotechnology, medical device and bio-agriculture companies;
- Center for Applied Technologies – one of 12 state-funded advanced technology centres designed to help manufacturers modernise their manufacturing and production technologies;
- San Diego Technology Fund – supported by the City and County of San Diego;
- Front Door – a University of Southern California (UCSD) program that assists emerging companies gain access to information and resources;
- San Diego MIT Forum – a monthly meeting to address business challenges facing San Diego entrepreneurs;
- San Diego Technology incubator;
- San Diego Software and Internet Council – fosters networking between its members;
- Southwest Regional Technology Transfer Center – assists businesses in using new technologies developed for defence and space programs.

The Inward Investment Strategy

The City of San Diego promotes itself as a centre for investment on the back of a pro-business, anti-regulation agenda. It has lower sales tax, business tax and hotel occupancy taxes than its competitor cities. It also charges lower business licence fees and has no utility user taxes. The City's Economic Development Division includes a Business Expansion, Attraction and Retention (BEAR) team that works directly with key businesses in targeted industries to provide assistance and incentives that will result in the retention and attraction of businesses. It assists with site selection, due diligence processes, permit assistance, fee reductions, financing and other programs. The City also guarantees water supply to firms that locate in nominated zones within the metropolitan area.

San Diego hosts two of the 39 Enterprise Zones within California and firms locating into one of the zones receive tax credits on up to half the wages to qualified new employees; tax credits on sales tax for manufacturing or production equipment; the capacity to carry forward net operating losses to future tax years; accelerated business depreciation; tax credits for low income employees; priority access to Industrial Development Bond applications; deductibility of net interest on loans.

Economic Development Outcomes

In preparing advice for Tucson, Arizona KMK Consulting (2006, p. 18) concluded

> San Diego is a league of its own…San Diego has economic development momentum because it has reached a critical mass in one of the most dynamic industries in the new economy – biosciences. Further, Greater San Diego is working hard to build critical mass in other sectors as well, and given its track record it is likely to succeed.

Wu (2005) concluded that San Diego is a leader in biotechnology and that the growth of this industry over the last decade led the city's economy out of recession. Wu (2005) attributes much of the success to academics, local business and political interests coming together to create a productive environment. The University of Southern California, San Diego, and its CONNECT program is seen as central to this growth, though the Scripps Institute and the Salk Institute have been important also. Other research (Walcott, 2002) has argued that San Diego's growth as a bioscience centre is a function of outstanding research at USCSD and the links between that institution's own spin-off companies and other firms working in the life sciences. On at least one scale, the UCSD is ranked in the top 20 universities in the US and most biotechnology firms are clustered around the university. Government investment in appropriate real estate – i.e. laboratories – has also been critical. Several commentators have noted that biotechnology companies need access to specialist laboratories that are very different from conventional commercial office space. The provision of appropriate facilities has assisted new firm formation and the growth of small enterprises into larger businesses. The Milken Institute (De Vol et al., 2004) nominated San Diego as its first ranked Metropolitan Statistical Area for biosciences for the entire US and specifically noted the importance of research and development inputs – access to risk capital and the impact of current research – in coming to this judgement.

Conclusions on San Diego's Development

San Diego restructured its economy from the early 1990s and has emerged from a major recession. Much of this growth can be attributed to the rapid expansion of the biotechnology sector and it is clear that the City of San Diego is active in economic development, both through the SDREDC and through its own efforts. The examination of local efforts to develop San Diego's economy leads to two apparently contradictory conclusions: first, there are a large number of initiatives directed at helping the city grow and this includes the provision of a raft of incentives and subsidies. As noted above, there are Enterprise Zones, Free Trade Zones, as well as a Redevelopment Agency, all working to enhance the economic standing of the city. Despite these efforts, KMK Consulting (2006) concluded that there were relatively few incentives available to firms entering San Diego because the level of subsidy was small in comparison with the inducements available in other centres. From the perspective of an economic development practitioner, San Diego's growth has been a consequence of endogenous processes rather than a successful inward investment strategy. Walcott (2006) suggests that the critical investment by the public sector has been the expenditure of funds on purpose-built laboratories suitable for biotechnology businesses ranging in size from start-ups to multi national corporations. Second, we can conclude that San Diego's emergence as the premier bioscience hub in the US in the 1990s was somewhat fortuitous. Biotechnology emerged as an important sector in that decade and the USCSD served as a lightning rod for growth because it was already pre-eminent in basic research in that field. USCSD adopted an innovative mindset to the commercial development of its technologies and this resulted in considerable benefits to the city economy.

What then can we conclude from the experience of San Diego about inward investment strategies? At one level, we can note that inward investment instruments have not contributed to the city's success over the last 15 years. The mechanisms it has applied are considered to be somewhat 'ordinary' when compared with the strategies and approaches used by other US cities (KMK Consulting, 2006). However, at another level, we should note that San Diego hosts many initiatives aimed at attracting investment and that, on a global stage, such effort is simply the starting point for cities anxious to attract capital.

Sheffield, England

Sheffield is located in South Yorkshire and in 2005 the City of Sheffield had an estimated population of 520,700 people. It is one of the eight largest English cities outside London. The wider Sheffield Urban Area has a population of 640,720. Like many English cities, Sheffield has been steadily losing population since the end of the Second World War: in 1941 Sheffield had a population of 569,884; in 1971 it was 572,794, but by 1981 it had a population of 530,844. Population loss has been an outcome of multiple causes. In the 1980s the steel making and other manufacturing industries which formed the backbone of Sheffield's economy entered recession as the sector relocated to more competitive locations. More recently population loss has been associated with a prosperous economy and the on-going movement of some households to the countryside. While Sheffield is a relatively small city, it sits within a much larger urban conglomerate with approximately 2,000,000 people living within an hour's drive of the CBD.

In the recent past Sheffield has had to deal with an economy in decline through the restructuring of mature industries such as steel making, as well as the closure of coal mining. Sheffield has needed to reshape its economy and appears to have been successful in this ambition. Some 84 per cent of employment in Sheffield is now tied to the services sector; with manufacturing accounting for only 12 per cent of employment; and transport and communication 5.5 per cent. Sheffield has emerged as a major retailing centre. It is worth noting, however, that Sheffield's prosperity came much later than other northern urban centres such as Manchester and Leeds, who had restructured their economies by the mid-1990s.

Key strategies in the remaking of Sheffield's economy have been:

- The promotion of Advanced Manufacturing/Technology Development. Sheffield hosts an Advanced Manufacturing Park and organisations currently located there include: the Advanced Manufacturing Research Centre (AMRC, a research partnership between Boeing and the University of Sheffield); Castings Technology International (Cti) and TWI Technology Centre;
- The growth of the education sector, with the University of Sheffield and Sheffield Hallam University expanding to attract 55,000 students a year;
- Rebranding the city and changing its image through redevelopment, the remaking of public spaces (e.g. through public art), and the promotion of the arts;
- Formal regeneration activities have been an important part of Sheffield's success in reshaping its economy. A recent independent evaluation of Sheffield One, an Urban Regeneration Corporation established in 2000 and subsequently replaced by Creative Sheffield in 2007, concluded that the organsation has been 'a great success' (Evans et al., 2007).

The Economic Development Program

From the beginning of 2007 the main agency promoting the economic development of Sheffield has been Creative Sheffield. Creative Sheffield was established as a new 'city regeneration company' to spearhead efforts in transforming the city's economy and to lead the implementation of the Economic Masterplan established by the Sheffield City Council. Creative Sheffield has a city-wide mandate and a high level board drawing upon national and international expertise. Creative Sheffield has been charged with focusing on four key areas:

- accelerating the growth of knowledge based businesses, capitalising on the research facilities of the universities, as well as the intrinsic innovation capacities of business;
- strategic physical development ensuring that what Sheffield can offer businesses is fit for the transformation of the economy, including in four nominated strategic regeneration areas: the city centre, Upper Don Valley, Central River and the Lower Don Valley;
- the marketing of the city and the development of its role – through cultural and environmental assets – as a destination;
- inward investment 'in particular taking our success in attracting inward investment to the levels required for economic transformation' (Creative Sheffield, 2007).

Investment attraction is part of the broader economic development program for the city, which promotes seven areas of sector strength:

- advanced manufacturing and materials technology;
- biomedical and healthcare technology;
- business and financial services;
- public sector operations and support services;
- creative and digital industries;
- energy and environmental technology;
- sports science and technology.

Importantly, Sheffield has an active program to attract new enterprises, including public sector organisations. It promotes itself as a cost effective location in the UK because of relatively low employment costs, and inexpensive office rentals. It also promotes itself as being close to untapped pools of labour.

The Inward Investment Strategy

Creative Sheffield includes a Business Investment Team that is organised around the key sectors discussed above and provides a range of assistance for incoming firms. Support includes finding commercial premises; gaining access to grants; recruiting staff through a free-of-charge service (JobMatch); relocation support for incoming employees – including assistance in finding employment for the partners of key personnel; and business expansion assistance for firms already within the city.

A number of grant schemes are available through the UK Government via the Department for Trade and Industry (DTI), including the Selective Finance for Investment (SFI) scheme; the High Growth Start Up scheme; and the Support for Growth Scheme. The SFI scheme is the most significant program and is targeted at businesses investing in manufacturing, as well as service industries that supply a national rather than a local market. Assistance can be provided to establish a new business; expand/modernise/rationalise business; upgrade or introduce technological improvements into business processes; enable businesses to take the next step from development to production. In addition, funding is available from the regional development agency, Yorkshire Forward. As with many inward investment strategies, assistance is tailored for/negotiated with each business. Examples of inward investment/business retention assistance include:

- The Nationwide Building Society was attracted to Sheffield as the location for one of its call handling facilities through a grant of £488,000 from Yorkshire Forward. In addition the JobMatch service supplied the labour for the call centre. The project was expected to generate 180 jobs in total;
- Bolton Surgical Instruments of Sheffield received a SFI grant of £242,000 in 2004 to build new premises within the Sheffield region. This investment retained an advanced manufacturing firm within the region;

- LoadHog has produced a new way of securing loads to pallets and received financial support both to progress the product from concept to production stage (via the Department of Trade and Industry) as well as construct a £14.7 million production facility in the Don Valley. The company received support from Sheffield First for Investment, Yorkshire Forward and Business Link South Yorkshire. In addition, Sheffield First supported the business in achieving planning consent.

Significantly, firms already located in Sheffield and those considering the city as the location for its business potentially have access to thousands of assistance programs sourced from UK Government Departments, the European Union, Yorkshire Forward and other sources. Sheffield and its region has had special status within the SFI scheme – as part of an Assisted Area – though parts of the region have now lost that status.

Economic Development Outcomes

In 1996 the UK unemployment rate stood at just under eight per cent while Sheffield's rate was three percentage points higher at 11 per cent. By 2005 the unemployment rate in both the UK and Sheffield stood at just over two per cent. The city has also recorded rates of new firm formation per capita in excess of the UK average; rents in the city have increased 20 per cent since the year 2000; there have been productivity increases that match the best performing cities in the UK; inward investor inquiries are reported to have increased by 30 per cent over five years; and Sheffield is the only English city to expand its workforce since 1999. A report by the Office of the Deputy Prime Minister concluded in 2004 that inward investment was attracting 2,000 jobs per annum into Sheffield.

A review of Sheffield One noted that there has been considerable employment growth in Sheffield since the year 2000 but cautioned that much of that growth could be attributed to a buoyant national economy. It also noted that while there had been growth in service sector employment, manufacturing employment continued to decline and observed that 'The Sheffield economy is improving. But is running fast up a down escalator' (Evans et al., 2007, p. iv). It concluded that the on-going challenge was to transform Sheffield into an 'innovative, high value added, private sector driven city' (Evans et al., 2007, p. ix).

Clearly there has been significant economic revitalisation in Sheffield and employment growth, but the processes driving this growth are more complex than might appear at first blush. It has been suggested by Dabinett (2005) that by 1999 there had been 20 years of regeneration activity in Sheffield without any appreciable restructuring of the regional economy. The driver for significant change in Sheffield's fortunes was the election of the Blair Labour Government which was committed to new policies of urban and regional regeneration. This resulted in the establishment of the regional development agency Yorkshire Forward; contributed to the in-flow of European Union funding and resulted in

Sheffield One and a new masterplan for the city. Dabinett (2005) observed that Sheffield's growth has been a matter of economic prosperity on a rising tide of national economic growth. Sheffield has not established a dominant position in a strategic sector such as Information and Communication Technologies, instead it has attracted the back office functions of some businesses – such as call centres – on the basis of plentiful access to labour. Critically, Sheffield's growth in service sector employment has coincided with the restructuring of national and regional businesses that have sought out cities with a strong supply of qualified labour to manage customer relations.

Conclusions on Sheffield's Development

By any objective measure the story of Sheffield since 2000 must be viewed as a success and the role of inward investment activities cannot be ignored. In many ways Sheffield's success has been the story of a northern city catching up with its neighbours. Its growth over this period has been helped along by a prosperous British economy, a public sector committed to investing in cities and the restructuring of major enterprises within the UK. That said, Sheffield has made the most of the opportunities presented to it and has grown because of its willingness to collaborate across sectors and with other regions. Importantly, economic development efforts have been focused on key sectors and strategies that have improved the physical fabric of the city. Inward investment strategies have been an important component of the economic development 'mix' and substantial sums have been offered to firms to relocate to Sheffield or to expand within the city. Much of this funding has come from the deep pockets of the UK Government, either directly through the Department of Trade and Industry or indirectly via Yorkshire Forward. The grant provided to the Nationwide Building Society discussed above cost $AUS27,100 per employee.

Winnipeg, Manitoba

Winnipeg is the capital and largest urban centre in the Canadian province of Manitoba, the easternmost of the three prairie provinces. Winnipeg has a population of just over 630,000 people and dominates the population distribution within the province, accommodating 55 per cent of all Manitoba residents. Public sector employment accounts for 14 per cent of all jobs in the city and other major employers – including the University of Manitoba, the University of Winnipeg, the National Microbiology Laboratories and several defence force bases – are publicly funded. Manufacturing accounts for 12 per cent of the labour force and there are more than 70,000 post secondary school students within the higher education sector. Winnipeg is the centre of the grains industry in Canada and accommodates the headquarters of a number of major participants in the industry. The challenge for Winnipeg is that the private sector is not strong – especially in services – and to a certain extent, Winnipeg has remained trapped in the role of an administrative/service centre meeting the needs of its province alone.

One of the key problems for Winnipeg is that while it has grown, its growth has not kept pace with larger high-profile cities such as Vancouver and Toronto and, as several researchers have pointed out, this is seen to constitute 'failure' within the North American scene (Leo and Brown, 2000; Leo and Anderson, 2006; Mayer and Knox, 2006). Winnipeg grew by 0.53 per cent per annum over the decade 1985–1996 and its growth rate has not exceeded one per cent per annum for the last quarter of a century. However, economic growth has outpaced population growth in Winnipeg and over the last decade unemployment in Winnipeg has tended to be lower than in Vancouver.

The Economic Development Program

The main agency promoting the economic development of Winnipeg is Destination Winnipeg 'Winnipeg's economic and tourism services agency, an arm's length organisation and public-private partnership led by an independent board, with core funding from the City of Winnipeg and the Province of Manitoba' (Destination Winnipeg, 2007). Destination Winnipeg was established in 2003 and commentators have suggested that previously Winnipeg's economic development efforts 'were undertaken in a mood akin to that of an addicted gambler, simultaneously desperate and hopeful' and included strategies to attract firms in aerospace, to make Winnipeg the world's grain centre, and attempts to lure high technology firms (Leo and Anderson, 2006). In this period Winnipeg also provided substantial but ineffectual subsidies to sporting teams.

Destination Winnipeg has a focus on five strategic sectors of the economy: aerospace; transportation and distribution; information, communications and the media; biotechnology and health research; tourism – arts, culture, sports and entertainment. Destination Winnipeg claims that it 'works in collaboration with a broad network of partners to drive economic growth for Winnipeg' (Destination Winnipeg, 2007). Destination Winnipeg seeks to provide the following key services:

1. Information – timely and relevant information on Winnipeg's economy, community and strategic services;
2. Marketing – quality marketing materials and promotion of Winnipeg to business, industries and visitors;
3. Brokering – coordination with appropriate City and Provincial departments to facilitate economic development and tourism projects and to leverage investment in targeted projects and sectors;
4. Partnering – mobilising resources and coordination of efforts among key players in strategic sectors;
5. Project management and support – helping to expand and attract business opportunities in Winnipeg.

The Inward Investment Strategy

Destination Winnipeg highlights information provision, marketing and sector development in its economic development plan, but it also makes use of established inward investment levers. Its web site notes that financial assistance packages are available on a client-by-client basis, with each custom tailored to the circumstances of the project, the size of the business and the need. The financial vehicles on offer include:

- Recruitment and Training Grants that are not repaid and help businesses recruit, retain, train and assess employees;
- Strategic Infrastructure Assistance that is focused on the 'downtown' and inner city areas and which build community capacity;
- Repayable loans through the Manitoba Industrial Opportunities Program, a flexible support package tailored to meet the needs of each project;
- The College Expansion Initiative that expands training programs to meet the needs of a business;
- The Provincial Nominee Program that facilitates the migration of key staff;
- Wage subsidies from the Manitoba Provincial Government to cover part of the cost of wages while staff receive training;
- R&D tax credits provided by the Manitoba Provincial Government that can reduce the cost of R&D by almost 60 per cent.

No information is available on the value of inward investment expenditure by Destination Winnipeg but the organisation overall had a budget in 2006 of $CAN3.7 million, of which $CAN 1.6 million could be considered operational expenses. Many of the subsidies available for inward investment come from the provincial government.

Destination Winnipeg's achievements in inward investment are – by their own admission – modest: the 2006 report shows that in 2004 Destination Winnipeg was involved in two announced relocations, in 2005 they were involved in the successful relocation of two businesses, and in 2006 they were involved in three announced relocations. Moreover they were involved in the management of only five business projects in 2004, six in 2005 and eight in 2008.

Economic Development Outcomes

The 2007–2009 Business Plan for Destination Winnipeg is remarkable for the absence of concrete targets in all of its areas of activity – including business attraction. Destination Winnipeg had very modest success over the period 2004 to 2006 in assisting with the relocation of businesses (seven relocations for the three year period), and the agency appears to be more successful in attracting conventions and other tourism related activities. It is worth noting also that Destination Winnipeg's efforts in inward investment are largely facilitative, with most funding for such initiatives coming from other sources, such as the provincial government. The City of Winnipeg has made provision of approximately $CAN0.6 million in financial incentives to business with a further $CAN460,000 in business liaison expenditures and $CAN5.7 million in grants to Economic Development Agencies.

Independent researchers have noted that Winnipeg has struggled in the past to attract businesses. Leo and Brown (2000, p. 2005) observed that:

> The primary focus of many economic development efforts is the attempt to attract new businesses or to lure businesses to relocate. Such a strategy is more likely to prove successful in a rapidly growing center. If a city such as Toronto, Boston, San Francisco, or Vancouver can offer an attractive environment, good facilities, a favourable tax regime and predictable regulations, large companies will consider locating major facilities there…Slowly growing centers are usually not in a position to match such attractions…When it comes to compete for major firms Winnipeg generally finds itself having to offer free land, interest-free loans, and a variety of other incentives – incentives that reduce the net economic benefit obtained.

Conclusions on Winnipeg's Development

Winnipeg has been unsuccessful in its inward investment activities. Independent observers suggest that past efforts were profligate and unsuccessful. Current economic development strategies appear to place their faith in other strategies, especially the development of specific sectors and the promotion of tourism/conventions. However, inward investment remains on the agenda for Winnipeg and there is a range of incentives/subsidies that are available to incoming firms. Many of these incentives are accessed via Destination Winnipeg but funded by the City of Winnipeg or the Manitoba Government. Importantly, Winnipeg's failure in attracting inward investment does not appear to be an outcome of insufficient resources. As noted above, the City of Winnipeg commits substantial amounts in grants and subsidies to firms, and while robust data are not available on the incentives offered by the provincial government, the breadth of programs on offer suggests a significant financial commitment.

Winnipeg has not been successful in attracting inward investment because the incentives offered by Winnipeg to firms potentially interested in relocation are of lesser importance than factors such as access to markets, access to services and access to skilled labour that drive site location decisions; Winnipeg is specialised in only a few sectors – such as grains and transport – but as these industries are already based in the city there are few firms ready to be 'recruited' to Winnipeg. Sector development appears to be pivotal, that is, inward investment needs to target firms working within sectors where the city already has a concentration of expertise; in any bidding war, Winnipeg is liable to be outbid by a larger, more strongly growing rival. In such a competition, a city with better intrinsic growth prospects will be the more attractive location.

In conclusion, it is worth acknowledging that several authors (Leo and Brown, 2006; Leo and Brown, 2000) question whether Winnipeg's slow growth is a fundamental problem. They note the city's advantages with respect to affordable housing, real GDP growth, and incomes that are converging with those in Vancouver and Toronto. They suggest that more appropriate economic development strategies focus on the quality of employment generated (with respect to wages paid) and the stimulation of small and medium sized enterprises, especially within sectors where there is an already identified competitive advantage. However, while we can conclude that Winnipeg may – or may not – be an unsuccessful city, it has clearly been unsuccessful in its industrial recruitment/inward investment efforts.

Reflections on Inward Investment in Three Cities

The three case studies serve to illustrate the complexity of local economic development and the ways in which the impact of otherwise comparable programs varies with context. In some key respects Winnipeg, Sheffield, and San Diego have much in common: each has been confronted by the need to restructure their economies, they are not a national capital, physically they are outside the core regions within their respective national territories and each is part of an advanced national economy. All three cities have used, and continue to use, inward investment strategies as part of their suite of programs aimed at developing locally. The available evidence suggests that while investment attraction was successful in Sheffield, it was irrelevant to the restructuring and subsequent growth of San Diego's economy from the early 1990s and failed miserably in Winnipeg. The differing circumstances and opportunities in each city – national policy frameworks, industry mix, relationship with universities, the skills of the labour force etc. – determined the degree to which investment attraction programs were able to achieve their goals. The context and circumstances of local and regional development initiatives are clearly very important, but as the earlier discussion has shown, the academic theories that are most likely to be adopted by policy makers and implemented by local economic development practitioners are those that are presented as being universal in their applicability.

In many ways, local and regional development remains an art, not a science, with the recommendations for policy or practice of researchers working in the area heavily qualified with respect to the magnitude of any program, the impact of other government policy interventions, changing national economic circumstances *et cetera*. It is unfortunate, however, that the intellectual honesty of researchers in qualifying their findings serves as an impediment to the take-up of their ideas by those charged with developing locally. Time poor practitioners who are challenged to deliver growth as quickly as possible have little scope to consider actions that may – or may not – deliver success, instead they are attracted to programs and interventions that are believed to be successful in all circumstances, especially those that receive the support of relevant government departments. In a sense then, the very nature of local or regional development – where context exerts a pivotal influence – impedes the translation of theory into practice.

Conclusion

This chapter has argued that there are substantial impediments to the translation of theoretical perspectives on regional development into the practice of developing locally. To a certain extent, researchers and practitioners constitute separate communities who more often talk past each other rather than engage in meaningful dialogue. In large measure this is driven by the institutional settings within which each group operates: researchers are encouraged – if not required – to publish in academic journals that emphasise the peer-review process and the development of theory. Economic development professionals, by contrast, are under considerable pressure to achieve growth targets and in many jurisdictions, implement the programs mandated by central governments. They often lack the time and the background to consider alternative approaches to the practice of developing locally. The chapter has shown that the ideas most likely to be accepted by economic development professionals and translated into practice are those that secure the support of high profile institutions and governments; that present themselves as a 'fresh' approach that is universal in its applicability, and which do not overly challenge the budgets of governments or their influence on economic development.

The latter part of the chapter has demonstrated the important influence context plays in determining the success or failure of economic development programs. The inward investment strategies of three broadly comparable cities were reviewed and while investment attraction was significant in the growth of Sheffield, it was irrelevant to San Diego's growth from the early 1990s and may have held Winnipeg back. The case studies illustrate the point that not all local growth strategies work in all circumstances and this observation applies to both conventional policy instruments such as investment attraction, but also more 'fashionable' strategies, such as business clusters and the generation of 'creative cities'. What is needed by both practitioners and researchers is a solid evidence base on local and regional development strategies and policies that are effective and the circumstances that determine whether they have a positive impact. Such research needs to eschew the complex and highly nuanced arguments of much scholarship on regional policy because at best such debates are seen to be irrelevant to the 'real world' of economic development, at worst they are perceived to be alienating to practitioners and misplaced in their policy prescriptions. Academics and economic development professionals need to work together to identify priorities and then undertake the investigations necessary to produce a much stronger knowledge base on effective local and regional development. Inaction in this area would see practitioners and researchers drift further apart and contribute to the continuing weakness of this sector.

References

Armstrong, H. and Taylor, J. (2000), *Regional Economics and Policy*, Blackwell, London.

Australian National Audit Office (2007), *Performance Review of the Regional Partnerships Programme*, ANAO, Canberra.

Beer, A., Haughton, G. and Maude, A. (eds) (2003a), *Developing Locally: An International Comparison of Local and Regional Economic Development*, Policy Press, Bristol.

Beer, A. and Maude, A. (1997), *Effectiveness of State Frameworks for Local Economic Development*, Local Government Association of South Australia, Adelaide.

Beer, A., Maude, A. and Pritchard, B. (2003b), *Developing Australia's Regions: Theory and Practice*, UNSW Press, Kensington.

Beer, A., Clower, T., Haughton, G. and Maude, A. (2005), 'Neoliberalism and the Institutions for Regional Development in Australia', *Geographical Research* 43:1, pp. 49–58.

Blakely, E. (1994), *Planning Local Economic Development*, Thousand Oaks, Sage.

Cloney, M. (2003), 'Regional development policy for Australia', Unpublished PhD thesis, Department of Political Economy, University of Sydney.

Cooke, P. and Morgan, K. (2000), *The Associational Economy: Firms, regions and Innovation*, Oxford University Press, Oxford.

Creative Sheffield (2007), 'Invest in Sheffield', www.creativesheffield.co.uk/InvestInSheffield.

Dabinett, G. (2005), 'Competing in the information age: Urban regeneration and economic development practices in the city of Sheffield, United Kingdom', *Journal of Urban Technology* 12, pp. 19–38.

Destination Winnipeg (2007), wwww.destinationwinnipeg.ca/work_db_os.php.

De Vol, R., Wong, P. Ki, J., Bedrousssian, A. and Koepp, R. (2004), *America's biotech and life science clusters*, Milken Institute, Santa Monica.

Dixon, R. and Thirwell, A. (1975), 'A Model of Regional Growth Rate Differentials Along Kaldorian Lines', *Oxford Economic Papers* 27, pp. 201–14.

Evans, R., Hutchins, M., Meegan, R. and Parkinson, M. (2007), *Sheffield One Evaluation: Final Report*, European Institute for Urban Affairs, Liverpool.

Ffocs-Williams, I. (2004), 'Cluster Development: Red Lights and Green Lights', *Sustaining Regions* 4:2, pp. 24–33.

Florida, R. (2002), *The Rise of the Creative Class. And How It's Transforming Work, Leisure and Everyday Life*, Basic Books, New York.

Florida, R. (2005), *The Flight of the Creative Class. The New Global Competition for Talent*, HarperCollins, New York.

Freebairn, J. (1998), 'Where and Why Government Should be Involved – A Perspective from Economics', *Australian Journal of Public Administration* 57, pp. 66–74.

Freebairn, J. (2003), 'Economic Policy for Rural and Regional Australia', *The Australian Journal of Agricultural and Resource Economics* 47, pp. 389–414.

Goodwin, M. and Painter, J. (1996), 'Local Governance, Local Partnership the Crisis of Fordism and the Changing Geographies of Regulation', *Transactions of the Institute of British Geographers* 21, pp. 635–48.

Gray, I. and Lawrence, G. (2001), *A Future for Regional Australia? Escaping Global Misfortune*, University of New South Wales Press, Kensington.

Halkier, H., Danson, M. and Damborg, C. (1998), *Regional Development Agencies in Europe*, Jessica Kingsley, London.

Harrison, J. (2007), 'From Competitive Regions to Competitive City Regions: A New Orthodoxy, But Some Old Mistakes', *Journal of Economic Geography* 7, pp. 311–32.

Haughton, G. (ed.) (1999), *Community Economic Development*, Jessica Kingsley, London.

Haughton, G. (2003), 'Local and Regional Economic Development in England', pp. 61–83 in Beer, A., Haughton, G. and Maude, A. (eds) (2003a), *Developing Locally: An International Comparison of Local and Regional Economic Development*, Policy Press, Bristol.

Henton, D. and Walesh, K. (1994), 'Reinventing Silicon Valley: A Total Quality Community', pp. 310–316 in *Cities and the New Global Economy: An International Conference presented by the OECD and the Australian Government, Proceedings*, Vol 1, AGPS, Canberra.

Isserman, A. (1994), 'State economic development policy and practice in the United States, a survey article', *International Regional Science Review* 16, 1 and 2, pp. 49–100.

Jacobs, J. (1961), *The Death and Life of Great American Cities*, Random House, New York.

Jacobs, K. (2007), 'Territorial Modes of Governance and the Discourses of Community Reaction in the State of Tasmania', *Space and Polity* 11:3, pp. 263–79.

Jessop, B. (1990), *State Theory: Putting the Capitalist State in its Place*, Polity Press, Cambridge.

Jessop, B. (1997), 'The entrepreneurial city: Re-imaging localities, redesigning economic governance, or restructuring capital?' in Jewson, N. and MacGregor, S. (eds) *Transforming Cities: Contested Governance and New Spatial Divisions*, Routledge, London.

Jessop, B. (2002), 'Liberalism, neoliberalism and urban governance: A state theoretical perspective', *Antipode* 34:2, pp. 452–72.

Jones, M. (1997), 'Spatial selectivity of the state? The regulationist enigma and local struggles over economic governance', *Environment and Planning A*, 29, pp. 831–64.

Jones, M. (2001), 'The rise of the regional state in economic governance: Partnerships for prosperity; or new scales of state power?', *Environment and Planning A* 33, pp. 1185–211.

Kaldor, N. (1970), 'The Case for Regional Policies', *Scottish Journal of Political Economy* pp. 337–48.

Karmatz, L., Labi, A. and Leveinstein, J. (1998), 'Corporate Welfare', *Time*, pp. 29–47, Nov 9.

KMK Consulting (2006), *Tucson Economic Blueprint, Strategic Analysis Report*, Tucson Regional Economic Opportunities, Tucson.

Larner, W. (2003), 'Neoliberalism?', *Environment and Planning D* 12, pp. 509–12.

Larner, W. (2005), 'Neoliberalism in (Regional) Theory and Practice: The Stronger Communities Action Fund in New Zealand', *Geographical Research* 41:1, pp. 9–18.

Leitner, H., Peck, J. and Sheppard, E. (eds) (2007), *Contesting Urban Frontiers: Neoliberalism*, Guilford, New York.

Leo, C. and Anderson, K. (2006), 'Being Realistic About Urban Growth', *Journal of Urban Affairs* 28:2, pp. 169–89.

Leo, C. and Brown, W. (2000), 'Slow Growth and Urban Development Policy', *Journal of Urban Affairs* 22:2, pp. 193–213.

Loveridge, S. (1996), 'On the continuing popularity of industrial recruitment', *Economic Development Quarterly* 10:2, pp. 151–8.

Lovering, J. (1999), 'Theory led by policy: The inadequacies of the new regionalism', *International Journal of Urban and Regional Research* 23, pp. 379–95.

Mack Management Consulting (1998), 'Key performance indicators for regional development boards', Report prepared for the Local Government Association of South Australia and the South Australian Regional Development Association, Adelaide, unpublished.

MacLeod, G. (2001), 'New regionalism reconsidered: globalisation and the remaking of political economic space', *International Journal of Urban and Regional Research* 25:4, pp. 804–29.

Mayer, H. and Knox, P. (2006), Slow Cities: Sustainable Places in a Fast World, *Journal of Urban Affairs* 28:4, pp. 321–34.

Nichols Clarke, T. (2002), *Urban Amenities: Lakes, Opera, and Juice Bars*, Available at http://www.coolcities.com/cm/attach/ACFAEF2D-708B-4861-96D4-CA6FD5B87436/UrbanAmenitiesandGrowthUC.pdf.

North, D. (1990), *Institutions, Institutional Change and Economic Performance*, Cambridge University Press, Cambridge.

O'Dwyer, L. (2004), *A Critical Review of Evidence Based Policy Making*, Final Report, Australian Housing and Urban Research Institute, Melbourne.

OECD (1997), *Trends in regional policies in OECD countries*, OECD, Paris.

OECD (2001), *Best practices in local development*, OECD, Paris.

OECD (2005), *Building Competitive Regions: Strategies and Governance*, OECD, Paris.

Peck, J. (2004), 'Geography and Public Policy: Constructions of Neoliberalism', *Progress in Human Geography* 28:3, pp. 392–405.

Peck, J. (2005), 'Struggling with the Creative Class', *International Journal of Urban and Rural Research* 29, 4: 740–70.

Peck, J. and Tickell, A. (1992), 'Local Social Modes of Regulation? Regulation Theory, Thatcherism and Uneven Development', *Geoforum* 23:3, pp. 347–63.

Peck, J. and Tickell, A. (1995), 'Jungle Law Breaks Out: Neoliberalism and Global-Local Disorder', *Area* 26:4, pp. 317–26.

Peck, J. and Tickell, A. (2002), 'Neoliberalizing space', *Antipode* 34, pp. 380–404.

Porter, M. (1990), *The Competitive Advantage of Nations*, Macmillan, London.

Porter, M., Takeuchi, H. and Sakakibara, M. (2000), *Can Japan Compete?*, Macmillan, Basingstoke.

Rainnie, A. (2005), 'Hurricane Florida: The False Allure of the Creative Class', *Sustaining Regions* 4:3, pp. 4–10.

Rainnie, A. and Grobelaar, M. (2005), *New Regionalism in Australia: Limits and Possiblities*, Ashgate, Aldershot.

Reich, R. (1991), *The Work of Nations: Preparing Ourselves for 21st Century Capitalism*, AA Knopf, New York.

Roberts, B. and Enright, M. (2001), 'Regional clustering in Australia', *Australian Journal of Management* 26(special issue), pp. 65–86.

Roberts, B. and Enright, M. (2004), 'The Emergence of Regional Industry Clusters in Australia: Recent Trends and Evidence', *European Planning Studies* 12:1.

Rubin, H. (1988), 'Shoot Anything that Flies, Claim Anything that Falls: Conversations with Economic Development Practitioners', *Economic Development Quarterly* 2:3, pp. 236–51.

Statskontoret (2007), *Joining Up for Regional Development*, Statskontoret, Stockholm.

Stimson, R., Stough, R. and Roberts, B. (2006), *Regional Economic Development, Analysis and Planning Strategy*, Springer, Berlin, Second Edition.

US Council on Competitiveness and National Governor's Association (2001), *Clusters of Innovation: Regional Foundations of US Competitiveness*, www.isc.hbs.edu.

Walcott, S.M. (2002), 'Analyzing an innovative environment: San Diego as a bioscience beachhead', *Economic Development Quarterly* 16, pp. 99–114.

Wu, W. (2005), *Dynamic cities and creative clusters*, World Bank Policy Research Working Paper 3509.

Zukin, S. (1995), *The Cultures of Cities*, Oxford University Press, Oxford.

PART 3
Theoretical Concepts

Chapter 5
'Globalisation' and 'Local Economic Development' in a Globalising World: Critical Reflections on the Theory–Practice Relation

Richard Le Heron

Introduction

The chapter's title is deliberately provocative. First, it sets 'theory' about globalisation in relation to a field of 'practice' known as local (or regional) economic development[1] and so highlights learning as much as we can about globalisation and local economic development *together*. Second, it positions globalisation and local economic development in relation to *other processes* – especially earlier trends and trajectories when state intervention was a hallmark of *capitalist economic development* and the contemporary conditions of a globalising world where governing capitalist economic development involves far more than the state. The *conditions* under which ideas about globalisation and local economic development are developed must be taken seriously. This view challenges the idea that local economic development is a pre-given, homogeneous and timeless set of practices. The practices of local economic development are likely to alter, according to context and conditions. Pressures to promote local economic development come from at least two main sources: on the one hand they are expressions of uneven and inequitable outcomes in the economic landscape and on the other hand they reflect variability in the aspirations and concerns of actors about the pace and extent of local investment. Both sources are arguably heavily influenced by capitalist dynamics. Third, the title acknowledges that there will be many encounters with globalisation and local economic development. Where one lives and works (and reads this chapter) will make a difference to experiences of

1 It is difficult to separate the notions of local and regional economic development as they are often elided in the literature. A genealogy of these co-constructed fields of theoretical and practical knowledge would show differing trajectories in their development, from context to context. I use these notions interchangeably in the chapter because much writing on local economic development has been heavily influenced by that of regional economic development where there has been much formal development of ideas and because in geographic scale terms both local and regional denote a distinctive sub-national focus.

globalisation and local economic development and interpretations that are placed on the particulars of developments. What the main title does not readily capture is that *local economic development constantly involves the local grounding of capital, labour and land.* This trilogy is central to local economic development, regardless of how it is approached and understood. Finally, the subtitle indicates that in attempting to comprehend our situations and acting locally we need to be open to re-assessing and re-developing our frameworks. Indeed Appadurai (1999, p. 230) forcefully reminds us of the unstable character of knowledge formation when he drew attention to the interdependencies now arising between 'knowledge about globalisation and the globalisation of knowledge'. How do we deal with this situation of complexity and all change as we approach globalisation and local economic development?

The chapter is organised into sections that help reveal conceptual and contextual changes that bear upon understandings of local economic development. The sections show how what are thought to be very important ideas about local economic development in any context at a given time are assigned their significance by actors who are investing[2] on the basis of particular understandings of their conditions. The chapter emphasises these contextual dimensions, recognising that actors are constrained by their circumstances and resources that they have to commit to investment – aspects of which are often not of their choosing[3]. By highlighting changes in contextual conditions it is then possible to explore what issues were perceived and acted upon by actors whose capacities and capabilities are changing differentially, over time and in space. The chapter argues that the heritage of ideas from earlier eras can be shown to be inadequate, insufficient and even misconceived when viewed in contemporary conditions. Moreover, while the inherited ideas co-exist with new ideas, they are only occasionally considered in relation to each other. It concludes with reflections on knowledge formation strategies pertaining to local economic development in a globalising world, contending that to make progress on re-visioning local economic development the accumulated theoretical knowledge of half a century needs to be re-thought.

The opening section conceptualises local economic development as an integral part of changes in economic and institutional processes. These dimensions are then examined by looking at the expansion of (mainly) capitalist processes through the lens of relevant literatures written in developed countries since World War II. The second half of the 20th century featured three eras, a long boom associated with the rise of the interventionist state that fuelled the economy through fiscal management, a phase of restructuring in response to crisis conditions that opened up protected economies to wider influences, and more recently, a period

2 The centrality of investment can not be over emphasised. Too frequently this aspect is overlooked.

3 The focus on globalising processes in the chapter means discussion on the development of local economic development perspectives per se and specific local economic development initiatives is minimal.

characterised by globalising (and neo-liberalising) tendencies designed to re-establish conditions for capitalist profitability. The central concern of discussion in each section is the kind of knowledge produced about geographical, especially local unevenness, and the manner in which this has or may have impacted on thinking about local economic development.

Conceptualising Economic and Institutional Processes

The title invites the creation of a conceptual space in which the obviously multiple and differing notions about globalisation and local economic development might be explored. This section frames such a conceptual space. A major advantage of this strategy is that a conceptual space allows discussion about phenomena without having to immediately resolve competing definitions and understandings. Rather than squeezing the world into a priori definitions, relationships and interactions of interest, in this case those making up globalisation and local economic development, can be examined to show how the world is constantly in-the-making - through changes in relationships and interactions. A second advantage is that what we might consider to be globalisation and local economic development can be set in spatial and temporal terms, as emerging from the variety and dynamics of economic and institutional processes and patterns found around the world. This gives scope for those whose work in many parts of the world is local and about local economic development, but whose ideas are not visible in the present international literature, to shape fresh dimensions to their local understandings through engagement in the conceptual space.

The conceptual space can be activated by viewing economic processes as set in institutional processes. I take economic processes to mean the diverse range of activities undertaken to provide the basis for life and livelihood. Institutional processes are those arrangements developed to shape the direction and content of activities in the economic sphere. I stress *processes* because this wording focuses on *relationships and interactions* that result in outcomes and patterns. All this can be made more concrete. We are, at the same time as conceptualising a broad relational field involving economic and institutional processes, able to identify and position *actors*. A slightly more elaborate statement is that behaviours of economic actors are intertwined with the behaviours of other actors putting in place institutional arrangements designed to change the behaviours of economic actors. Importantly, this wording is very specific, especially with respect to institutions. When I use the term institutions I am referring to the range of rules, procedures, regulations, legislation, norms, conventions, habits, agreements, practices, and so on that form the investment environment and so help constitute the decision processes of investors. In particular I am not reducing institutions to just organisations but instead am emphasising the conduct of conduct relating to activities. This is not to dismiss organisations – they are vital, important and everyday sites in and through which institutional arrangements are developed.

What sort of directionality can we expect in this relational field? Are economic processes influenced and shaped by institutions? Are institutional processes influenced and shaped by economic actors? To phrase such questions is to open up conceptual space. We know of course that the answers to these questions are both 'yes' and 'it depends'. At the most concrete, local economic development practitioners are caught up in the developmental and operational sides of *both* economic processes and institutional arrangements.

In this relational field actors are likely to be vying to achieve their objectives. Tensions can arise. Will personal and organisational goals and behaviours to achieve goals be the same as or consistent with collective, social, community and territorial goals? Are goals espoused as collective, social, community and territorial comparable to personal and organisational goals? These are challenging and much debated questions. The particular configurations of economic-institutional relationships and interactions of the three eras considered in the chapter can be thought of as 'settlements', temporary system-wide arrangements intended to facilitate relatively ordered investment by actors, in both the economic and institutional spheres. Importantly 'settlements' amongst economic and institutional actors usually spring from conflict and negotiation. As a result the investment environment is unlikely to be a level playing field (advantages and disadvantages for different actors appear or disappear with any change). Efforts to make changes will elicit negative reactions from existing investors who are currently advantaged, or be applauded by those standing to gain from change. Capitalist and other processes generate continuing pressures to accumulate through expanded investment. This makes it hard for economic and institutional actors to reach agreements on goals and develop governing (regulatory and governance) frameworks. Local economic development can not escape such dimensions, though the dimensions do not in themselves determine investment decision making.

Each of the following sections is a short and illustrative discussion of developments impinging on the concept of local economic development. The sections sketch out broad dimensions rather than probing detail. The main objective is to highlight the interdependence of knowledge systems and material and discursive conditions and growing awareness of the significance of such interdependence and how this influences the basis on which we know local economic development. Rather than extensively reference the ideas discussed, I cite examples of work that provides assessments of where understandings are moving and studies that helped alter the directions and strategies of theoretical inquiry.

The Interventionist State and Investing for National Development: A Literature about Local Economic Development Emerges

In the post-World War II period national development by nations became the dominant political project. This led to the creation of techniques for guiding investment (the actions of actors) in the private and public domain. The national development project gradually incorporated and re-positioned the local (areas, territories within the nation-state) as part of the national space economy[4]. Regional development (the more used phrase at this time) and local economic development were gradually seen as subsets of national economic development (Le Heron, 1987, Roweiss, 1981, Scott, 1982). The framing provided a distinctive and increasingly dominant guide to action, at various spatial scales, about local economic development. It identified goals that made sense and were acceptable, named what strategies would get endorsement and funding support and facilitated the development in the academy of practices and expertise to deal with the information required by national policy makers and planners. Within the academy the distinction between growth and development was often blurred, the former being favoured by analysts because it was measurable and the latter by those concerned with explicating the nature of changes in economic and institutional relations.

Principles relating to local economic development sprang from powerful intellectual trajectories in the literature; one trajectory was inspired by both neoclassical and Keynesian economics, the other by political economy (Peet and Thrift, 1989). The neoclassical and Keynesian traditions dominated in the 1950 –1970s while the 1980s were the heyday of political economy contributions. This section deals with early knowledge production that used the neoclassical and Keynesian approaches to conceptualise and theorise regional and local economic development, and the implications the knowledge produced had for the emergence of practices relating to local economic development.

The nation-state formed the macro context around which intellectual efforts focused. For those interested in the economy this world was shaped by massive state-led investment in general economic and social infrastructure and standard of living oriented programmes, with investment over long time periods. A distinctive economic landscape was fashioned through this investment. This included: transportation infrastructure (interstate systems, airports, ports, local roads), defence infrastructure, housing developments, education complexes, medical and health systems, subsidies frameworks for agriculture, forestry, fisheries and so on.

In this principally national investment environment both economic actors and industries evolved. A number of characteristics of the evolving space economy began to take on special significance for regional and local economic development. They were:

- the growing concentration of largely national firms in industries (leading to large firms dominated by particular products and branch plants in a number of areas and firms that in particular areas were large relative when compared to the majority of firms present);

4 In federal and commonwealth-type political systems this was and still remains complicated by another layer of government involvement, states and provinces, with the regional and local scale being constructed in relation to each administrative system.

- the rise of diversified firms with activities across industries and regions;
- consolidation of vertically integrated operations at one sites (with extensive supplier and sales links throughout the nation);
- an increasing proportion of firms operating in more than one country (the nature of functional organisation accompanying this internationalisation varied, ranging from a multi-domestic presence of branch plants to linked production facilities in several countries).

The main propositions that were embodied in regional growth and development theory were stimulated from several directions: recognition that national development investments had major regional and local effects, national scoping of regional problems (e.g. regions with declining industries, population out-migration, low incomes) in response to popular and political pressures, cascading to the regional and local levels principles from understandings of national development processes, and insights of analyses using census and national accounting information. It should be noted that without these influences or with different sets of influences, the nature of the propositions might have been different.

Criteria relating to local economic development arose in tandem, being refined as new regional and local issues surfaced. The criteria were wide ranging and embraced: regional growth understood and as measured in terms of employment (this was easy because of excellent data collection procedures in many countries and few confidentiality constraints on the use of employment data), regional growth measured by income from taxation returns, changes in regional income differentials, spatial balance in the nation (measured in a variety of ways through population change across regions, the diversity of regional economic activities, the shape of the distribution of city sises, and so on).

Based on the challenges of experience and intervention funding frameworks researchers began to reformulate national economic development models in regional terms. These formulations aimed to identify and explain how the broad structure of economies changed over time, how the growth of individual regions could be promoted by targeting particular portions of the economy, identifying whether the main contributions to individual regional growth were from outside or inside the region, and pinpointing the main mechanisms of growth that could be sought. A core of propositions cohered (Rees et al., 1981). These included:

- regions underwent stages of development (like nations);
- the export base of a region was crucial to regional growth (like nations);
- the success of the economic base had a big influence on non-economic activities;
- growth poles arising from industrial sectors propel economic growth processes;
- economies of scale, increasing returns and agglomeration economies underpin regional economic growth and development;

- industrial districts and territorial production complexes are engines of regional and national economic growth;
- growth centres, either of a spontaneous or of a planned kind, can lead to trickle down effects;
- cities of particular sizes offered different potential for regional growth (e.g. intermediate-sized cities).

Professionals in the field were greatly assisted by the availability of official statistics on population, industrial production, expenditure patterns on economic activities and so on. The data matrix form of the statistics (by industries and regions) encouraged the rise of analytical techniques to compare the performance of regions in a nation. Among the more widely used and enduring techniques from this era we see location quotients; shift and share analysis; coefficients of localisation, specialisation and diversification; regional input-output analyses, to calibrate regional/local direct, indirect and induced effects in regions; and a variety of procedures for choosing or justifying locations (countries, regions, cities, local sites) for investment.

These procedures, however, gave limited guidance about how to implement local economic development. What were some of the flaws and failures of the nation-centric neoclassical and Keynesian accounts and toolkits? The list is lengthy:

- narrow conception of investment (e.g. a manufacturing bias);
- imports were largely overlooked (e.g. given the preoccupation with exports, although this was counterbalanced by input-output analyses at the state and regional levels especially in the US);
- frequent reduction of investment decisions to location decisions (e.g. minimising analysis of companies and industry developments);
- failure to recognise economic actors (e.g. an absence of a tradition to track enterprise investment paths);
- absence of the state as an actor, despite the state at every level being the prime recipient of knowledge produced;
- role of prime movers or significant organisational actors in regions and in local economic development was often overlooked;
- the capitalist dynamics of industries and the consequences this might have in regions were typically side stepped;
- reliance of aggregate and statistical summaries of outcomes, the causal origins of which had been decoupled in the measurement procedures;
- urban land development was considered independently of regional and local economic development questions under the rubric of urban rent theory.

Probably the most telling of all was that the knowledge generated missed the fact that, with the adoption of similar strategies in most developed countries and the modernisation push in developing countries that replicated thinking in a similar manner, competitive pressures mounted. The very knowledge used to alleviate the outcomes of competitive processes intensified those processes.

What did this very incomplete and under conceptualised framing mean for those actors who were the end users of the knowledge produced? Unwittingly practitioners were badly exposed to the risks of under conceptualised understandings. Two concepts effectively disabled the theoretical contributions of this era. First, the neoclassical belief in equilibrium took investigating the processes of geographical unevenness off the research agenda. Equilibrium relates to how an idealised abstract 'model' world works. Applying this notion to multi-regional-systems deflected attention away from underlying causes of geographical unevenness as this patterning was assumed to be temporary or not relevant. Second, government intervention was reduced through Keynesian fiscal management to simple stimulus-response propositions (i.e. if a steel industry could be created (having spotted the gap in an input-output table), then multipliers effects (which could be calculated) will follow). This aggregate thinking hobbled the investigation of economic processes.

Summary

The neoclassical and Keynesian strategy involved modelling an idealised world independent and detached from processes. Changes in the nature of competition were ignored. Rather the belief was that so long as growth models for individual regions and firms were developed, industrial and regional decline and firm failures could be set aside. Structural change was interpreted statistically, through analyses of industry and regional economic structures. This limited conceptual foundation enshrined a view that geographic unevenness could be managed by selective government or government incentivised investment. Most effort went into identifying unevenness and not exploring the nature of processes generating unevenness. Local economic development had a place, but was mis-placed because regions and the local were poorly conceptualised.

Capitalist Crises, Restructuring Processes: Challenges to the Orthodoxy

The slow down in economic growth in many countries by the early 1970s was exacerbated by geo-economic and geo-political conditions; the end of the Bretton Woods agreement, the oil crisis, the Middle East conflict and so on. On the ground this appeared, for instance, as plant closures and declining industries on such a scale that new words were needed – de-industrialisation, rust belt and so forth. Different questions were prompted in this context and were motivated by concern over the inability of the existing theory and practice to provide answers to wider political-economic questions. The political economy put a whole new set of relationships and interactions onto the stage (Scott 2000, 2004). The interpretation of the nature of regional and local economies and their fortunes was fundamentally altered[5].

The first target was location theory which provided little or no purchase on the socio-economic relationships in which location decisions were embedded (Scott and Storper, 1984; Peet and Thrift, 1989). Attention quickly turned to opening the black box of the region. A pivotal article was that by Massey (1978) 'In what sense a regional problem?' She socialised the region, not in the manner of the multi-region framework of regional science, but in a manner that made visible the theorisable interconnections of any region with other regions – through the competitive process. Regions should not be seen as problems in their own right (epitomised in the idea of the regional problem, reinforced by regional growth theory's emphasis on atomistic models such as export base or growth pole theory). This prompted supportive critiques, including Gore (1984) *Regions in question*, which systematically laid down the internal logical flaws in different facets of regional growth and development theory.

Political economy was initially used to re-approach traditional problems relating to local economic development. The result was a recasting of the economic world's gain/loss, profits/wages, employment/unemployment realities as socially constructed in its geographic patterning and particular location opportunities. Perhaps the exemplar of this epistemological break was Massey and Meegan (1982) *The Anatomy of Job Loss*. This methodologically innovative book (it combined data analysis with graphs, excerpts from press coverage, quotations from interviews, theoretical discussion and empirical analytics) contains a figure that should be on the wall of every local economic development practitioner. Table 6.1 (Massey and Meegan, 1982, p. 127) shows how growth initiatives in one setting are conditional upon what is happening elsewhere. The wider context of a regional unit (a firm, an establishment in a firm) is no longer hidden.

The initial concern with instating the field around a re-visioning of region rapidly turned into major research agenda. A series of thought experiments in geographic political economy were implied by the directions explored. Not unexpectedly these unpicked what was happening *in* specific countries. It was only once restructuring processes had begun to gather momentum that the international dimensions began to be discerned. Some of the more significant lines of research were:

- Examination of the underlying spatiality that both enabled and resulted from capitalist development at different times and over long periods of time. These included the processes of industrialisation, urbanisation and suburbanisation. Local economic development had to be viewed more widely as profoundly conditioned and shaped by quite systemic (capitalist) processes.

5 It must also be noted that Keynesian fiscal management was rejected in favour of monetarist policies. It was not until the mid-1990s that a new impulse occurred in neoclassical research, with Krugman's contributions.

- The study of restructuring processes in different national contexts from a range of perspectives. Pioneering research in New Zealand and Australia revealed that state-led restructuring was not about de-regulation but re-regulation, with the state taking on different roles, and that actors in the economy were finding they needed to develop strategies of governance in order to direct and protect investment trajectories. The unevenness of geographical impacts of restructuring, both in how and where dis-investment occurred and where and how new investment trajectories began to emerge, dramatically re-configured the economic and institutional landscape in which local economic development practitioners were working.
- The contributions of prime movers, organisations whose investment strategies in particular regions were especially critical to regional fortunes received scrutiny. The plight of the US automobile industry and Detroit in particular received much attention (Holmes and Kumar 1995). The industry became the focus of labour/union perspectives on economic restructuring and also showed the difficulties of re-activating local economic development in areas affected by shifts in the spatial division of labour of economic activity.
- What, it was asked, if the dynamic of industries were traced territorially? The pioneering work in this regard has strong roots in two rather different (nearby) locals, the Silicon Valley (more accurately Santa Clara County and environs) and the Salinas Valley, both of Northern California. More than two decades of contribution has come from Saxenian's (2002) theoretically informed research on the microelectronics industry dynamics, at first US centred, then incorporating offshore assembly, overseas state-assisted competitor start ups, increasingly with interlinked labour mobility and intellectual capital dimensions with Taiwan, China and India. The Salinas Valley formed the focus of FitzSimmon's (1986) investigation of the continental reach and ramifications of an emerging increasingly capitalist agricultural region. Such re-mappings of relationships and interactions, started to place local economic development circumstances, and gradually thinking about local economic development, in national and international circuits and networks of capital accumulation.
- In an ambitious project Storper and Walker (1989) formulated a California-like model of geographical industrialisation. Their strategy visualised some of the futility of competition. The diagrams used in *The Capitalist Imperative* depicted geographies of industry emergence (heavily influenced by the microelectronics industry) demonstrated how success is spatially contingent – a great deal depends on what is going on elsewhere in the world!
- A contrasting agenda characterised the UK scene. This work was premised on the question, 'Would fruitful exchanges come from setting side by side conventional economic geography and political economy approaches?' Massey and Meegan's (1984) *Politics and Method* does just this, effectively

demonstrating that when the disciplinary and wider social politics of research questions are opened to scrutiny, it takes some effort to design and align methodologies that actually provide answers to questions posed.
- Early political economy research struggled to incorporate international dimensions in spite of Harvey's (1982) lead. Fagan and Le Heron (1994) provided a lens on restructuring that portrayed how capital is now likely to circulate through production, trade, finance and land in globalising circuits and networks.

Although significant progress was made by geography of political economy researchers in examining the breakdown of existing and the formation of new capitalist relationships and interactions some intractable difficulties remained around knowledge production. The difficulties stemmed in part from the implicit emphasis on capital, despite labour issues (especially union issues) being brought to the fore. The research reflected the unwitting stress on representing how the world works, thereby being in a position to critique and challenge existing knowledge frameworks and their claims, but was unable to show ways to imagine new directions. This was heightened by the failure to fully recognise that as the role of central government was transformed via restructuring processes the intervention powers of government were being stripped away. In place of these new strategies of governance such as supply chain management, led by private sector actors, demanded new institutional arrangements. It was often assumed that policy and planning expertise still existed and could utilise the new knowledge from political economy. Difficulties were compounded by the under-recognition of the geo-economic and geo-political context as a source of sudden and severe shocks and how competitive processes would emerge under globalising conditions. A reluctance to engage with land development processes (urban and rural) left a major gap in the literature. Finally, the scope of political economy (like the neo-classical/Keynesian tradition) was narrow, rarely confronting the interplay of human-biophysical processes. The spotlight on restructuring per se and not on the emergence of unprecedented conditions on the planet distances much of this research from the contemporary scene.

Nonetheless, what the theoretical and empirical work of this trajectory established was that in competitive processes it made a lot of sense to track how and why local actors were behaving. But trying to get a fix on local economic development in conditions where competitive pressures were arriving from all directions was a formidable challenge – with few if any obvious answers – even when considered through a political economy lens.

Summary

The political economy strategy attempted to represent the real world by focusing on abstractions of the actual structures of relationships and interactions that characterised investment trajectories of industries, nations and regions. This theoretical thrust gave different content to the wording, structural change. It took the goals of national development and showed the inescapable contradictions of capitalist processes. Despite efforts to incorporate actors the approach made little progress on the political dimensions of political economy. While neoclassical/ Keynesian economics had not prepared us for capitalist restructuring crises of the kinds experienced in the second half of the 20th century, geographical political economy could only explain how we had got into difficulties and who was being affected and in what ways. Meanwhile national economies were being opened through state-led restructuring. These territories formed new environments for the expanded circulation of capital. Local economic development was again *re*-placed, increasingly framed by globalising processes as well as national processes.

Globalisation and Local Economic Development – Emerging Understandings

The previous sections showed the changing conditions under which the contours of local economic development were first drawn and then re-drawn. This section explores changes in material and discursive conditions that are appearing with globalising processes and situates the local, and local economic development, in the globalising conceptual space that is resulting.

The section's argument is twofold: that while the contemporary context and conditions facing investors differs from the past, the accumulated insights available from the literature and the capacities and capabilities of investors are also different. As a result local economic development is at a watershed. The representational knowledge of earlier eras is now being supplemented by efforts to consciously enact local worlds in new ways. Local economic development with its overt focus on the trilogy of capital:labour:land could be at the vanguard of this new direction. Why my guardedly optimistic prognosis about the field?

Globalisation is a concept of an emerging context. Paradoxically globalisation is often associated with the notion that somehow geography no longer matters. In fact, quite the opposite is the case. A common early image of globalisation was of a process that was giving a sameness to the world of economic, social and cultural relations, leading to a McDonaldesque landscape, where boundaries disappear and the effects of distance diminish. This was often summarised in terms of a shrinking world. Research has since shown that the relative distances between some places and some people may have become greater or lesser and that globalisation may be facilitated and influenced by technology but this is not the same as technology driving globalising processes. Furthermore the inherited message of the political economy literature is that competitive capitalist pressures are far more important to outcomes than technology.

By the mid-1990s the landscape of comprehension about globalisation was being actively clarified. In an attempt to capture the interconnections of global-local interactions that were becoming very obvious as globalisation intensified Swyngedouw (1992) merged these ideas into a new concept, *glocalisation*. This refers to '(a) the contested restructuring of the institutional, regulatory level from the national scale both upwards to supranational and/or global scales and downwards to the individual body, the local, the urban or regional configurations... and (b) the strategies of global localisation of key forms of industrial, service and financial capital' (Swyngedouw, 1997, p. 170). He goes on to say, 'these 'glocalising production processes and inter-firm networks cannot be separated from 'glocalising' levels of governance' capital' (Swyngedouw, 1997, p. 171), noting that 'perhaps the most pervasive process of 'glocalisation and redefinition of scales operates through the financial system'. According to Dicken (2000, p. 459) glocalisation is a term that 'helps us to appreciate the interrelatedness of the geographical scales and in part, the idea that while the "local" exists within the "global" the "global" also exists with the local'.

A set of principles outlined by Dicken et al. (1997, p. 165) gives the flavour of understandings at the time. They identified the following:

- globalisation is a complex of processes, not an end-state or a new order;
- globalisation is a contradictory process, not an unbending force or uni-directional in character;
- globalisation will proceed hand in hand with uneven spatial development, it is not the opposite to it;
- globalisation processes, just like any other, do not float in the air, but are realised in institutionally, historically and geographically specific sites;
- globalisation implies qualitative as well as quantitative changes in the relationships between scales, social structures and agents;
- globalisation dynamics are worked out through a range of sites and channels, not just TNCs and the state;
- globalisation involves the complex diffusion, re-articulation and re-constitution of power relationships, and not simply a zero-sum redistribution among nation-states and TNCs.

Their principles situate globalisation into the conceptual space of the chapter, thereby providing fresh framing of local economic development.

By the time Murray (2006) was writing *Geographies of Globalisation* researchers were explicitly focusing on the generative qualities of interactions implied by the new relationships that characterised a globalising world. Using Gibson-Graham (2002) he specifies six ways of conceptualising interaction (Murray, 2006, p. 56).

- the global and the local do not exist – they are just ways of 'framing' things;
- the global and local each get their meanings from what they are not; that is, their opposition to the other;
- the global and the local offer different points of view concerning social networks;

- the global is the local – all global things have local expression. Multinational firms are actually multi-local;
- the local is the global – the local is where global processes interact with the surface of the earth;
- all spaces are global – the global is constituted by the local and vice versa.

The wording used in the above list is infused with poststructural insights and opens new avenues for thought about local economic development in a globalising world.

A few remarks on the poststructural turn of the 1990s are now appropriate. This new wave of philosophical ideas swung the spotlight away from pre-occupations with structural conditions to the importance of circulating knowledge discourses amd the contributions of actors in shaping the directions and content of change. The availability of the poststructural literature meant the changing material and discursive dimensions and interactions of a globalising era were interpreted very differently to what would have been the case had only the neoclassical/Keynesian and political economy traditions been on hand (Gibson-Graham, 2005). One notable outcome was that understandings of globalisation quickly moved from naïve and simplistic 'big bang' assertions to nuanced accounts of processes that were continuing to develop and recognition that the accounts were framings. The double empowering from structural and poststructural writing is resulting in re-visioning of economic and institutional processes, giving depth in addition to breadth to process-based understandings.

A number of implications for knowledge production are increasingly apparent from the poststructural contributions. Foremost, is the need to abandon the word 'theory', replacing it with the word theorising because the content of theoretical framings, relationships and interactions, keep emerging. An immediate consequence of a switch to theorising is that explanation is a word applicable to representational knowledge and not to performative knowledge. This is not to suggest that representational knowledge is unnecessary. Indeed, it would be a mistake to ignore the earlier geographic political economy literature for instance. Second, the meanings that might be assigned to place, local, locale, locality and region (all those notions pertaining to small areas) have been sharpened up. Crang (1999) identified three: place as an empirical domain (differences can be spotted thereby facilitating the attachment of significance to the differences); place as a normative concept (the local is thought to stand for 'good', 'innovation' and so on); and place as an epistemological domain (where the local is important to knowledge formation processes such as the buzz from proximity of activities and people). To this must be added another domain, the ontological, where the relations constitutive of place constitute differing conditions of possibility for development. This is a re-statement of one of the basic ideas that has been examined throughout the chapter – the importance of mixes of relationships and the interactions that differing mixes of relationships make possible. Third, these are huge steps forward from thinking that an explanation (which is ex-post and detached) can scope, identify and explore the nature of possibilities for action. Local economic development with its real time engagement with investment processes is therefore a highly strategic site for the development of performative knowledge.

Amin and Thrift (1997, p. 155) sound a warning, however, about the difficulties ahead when attempting to explicate local economic development. They point out that 'to recognise the significance of territorial assets is not in any way to argue that all places can flourish equally in the global economy. Globalisation represents a tying in of nations and regions' to a more common set of global forces'

Materially then, what is the globalising world beginning to look like? Key sources include Peck and Yeung (2003) and Dicken (2007). The expanded circulation of capital through the three circuits is leading to deeper geographic integration of economic activities. Thus, national production linkages are now demonstrably part of global production networks, trade patterns are dominated by intra- and inter-corporate flows and not country-country links, and financialisation has spawned a vast transactional web using complex forms of property rights and financial instruments. Concentration in globalising industries is accompanied by segmentation and oligopolistic behaviours. This involves extensions in both the size and nature of operating features of TNCs as well as new relationships with SMEs. Exporting and importing arrangements have morphed into supply and value chains. Consumption-facilitating infrastructure has been added to that considered basic to product ion competitiveness. A myriad of new actors have appeared e.g. NGOs, supra-national governance organisations, public-private partnerships. Waves of large scale investment characterise the economic landscape e.g. inner city, waterfronts, airports and ports with shopping arcades and associated logistic centres, shopping centres, recreational complexes, medical complexes, retirement complexes, theme parks etc. Developments of this kind are simply entangling much local economic development in increasingly complex processes, the dimensions of which continue to be poorly understood. New economic spaces are being constituted involving the complex interactions of big and small economic and institutional actors. Foci such as primate cities, metropolitan centres in nations, conurbation and the peri-urban fringe tensions and so forth have been supplanted by interest in world and global cities.

As these dimensions are more fully grasped for their structural qualities and informed by poststructural insights, the focus is swinging to what it means to knowingly inhabit globalising processes (Neill et al. 2005). Initial directions suggest a roll-over of much earlier knowledge into notions of learning regions, regional innovation systems and city-regions. At-a-distance technologies of governance such as standards, benchmarks and audit frameworks are leading to new metrics to evaluate performance, largely conceived in terms of growth and development. However, these traditional goal sets are being challenged by calls for sustainable development, ethical consumption and sustainable consumption. These alternative framings of how to invest are straining the appeal and credibility of conventional wisdom about the returns from growth and development.

Dani (2006, p. 411) writes 'Globalisation is here to stay. It consists of several globalising flows – finance, commodities (trade), people, ideas, and services – some of which are welcomed, while others are considered problematic by different people'. Massey (2006, p. 322), recasts this, 'local places (local territories) are always in part a product of wider flows - the real question should be what *kinds* of wider flows we want to be open to' (Massey, (italics in original)...the argument is over the *way* in which the world is globalised (italics in original). These correctives move us towards developing practices for a differently conceived local economic development. How do we develop expertise, embracing the theoretical and practical, in a globalising world? The challenges voiced by Massey can and are being addressed through combinations of poststructural and structural strategies (Le Heron, 2007)

The intention of the section has been to expose some of the issues and pressures associated with the geographical unevenness of globalising capitalist processes. Hart (2001, p. 655) conceptualises the contemporary dynamics as 'multiple non-linear interconnected trajectories'. This suggests any conceptions of local economic development need to embed actors in the processes of context. Openness towards diversity and difference in local economic development experience must therefore be an integral part of strategies of practice.

Summary

Globalisation as a concept exposes the dilemmas and tensions that arise as the people of any local area attempt to valorise (achieve adequate valuation) their labour in wider circuits and networks. Concerns behind the rise of many globalising networks and circuits are giving new content and meaning to what values should be valorised. Understandings about ways of investigating who is involve, how, under what conditions and constraints, with what outcomes, where, and for what duration, have accelerated with poststructural thinking. This points to developing situated understandings of the processes constitutive of the discursive and material worlds of local economic development. The big unresolved conceptual issue is finding ways to put *processes* relating to capital, labour and land into easily grasped framings.

Conclusions: Connections, Responsibilities and Commitments in a Globalising World

Murray (2006, p. 89) goes to the heart of contemporary local economic development when he observed 'Although globalisation to date has been driven by capitalism, to move to a post-capitalist globalising world would require new 'globalised imaginations' that are only now beginning to form'. Globalisation has forced dramatic re-thinking of what relationships and interactions should be bundled together when referring to local economic development. The use of globalisation as a lens with which to centre and explore local economic development has, paradoxically, led to a re-appraisal of globalisation as a concept. The wording 'in a globalising world' acknowledges the ongoing or in-the-making nature of flows, practices and concepts.

In the 21st century we have the capacities and capabilities to connect to other places, peoples, economies and ecologies. We are beginning to sense the detail of what the responsibilities individually and collectively of engaging might imply. We are slowly recognising that a condition of long run planetary life and livelihood is commitment to others (all animals and plants). Organising on the principles of the past offers only problems like the present. Will those working in the local economic development field confront such issues and engage to fashion far sighted and fair investment principles and practices for living for the new conditions we all face?

References

Amin, A. and Thrift, N. (1997), 'Globalization, socio-economics, and territoriality'. In Lee, R. and Wills, J. (eds) (1997) *Geographies of Economies*. London, Arnold, 147–57.

Appadurai, A. (1999), 'Globalisation and the research imagination', *International Social Science Journal*, 51, 160, 229–38.

Crang, P. (1999), 'Local-global'. In Cloke, P., Crang, P. and Goodwin, M. (eds) *Introducing Human Geographies*. London, Arnold, 24–34.

Dani, A. (2007), 'Social sciences, globalisation and regionalism: Reflections on Alain Touraine's keynote speech', *International Social Sciences Journal*, 58, 189, 409–412.

Dicken, P. (2000), 'Localization'. In Johnston, R., Gregory, D., Taylor, P. and Watts, M. (eds) *The Dictionary of Human Geography*. Blackwell, London.

Dicken, P. (2007), *Global Shift: Mapping the Changing Contours of the World Economy*. London, Sage Publications.

Dicken, P., Peck, J. and Tickell, A. (1997), 'Unpacking the global'. In Lee, R. and Wills, J. (eds) *Geographies of Economies*. Arnold, London, 158–66.

Fagan, R. and Le Heron, R. (1994), 'Reinterpreting the geography of accumulation: The global shift and local restructuring', *Environment and Planning D: Society and Space*, 12, 265–85.

FitzSimmons, M. (1986), 'The new industrial agriculture: The regional integration of specialty crop production', *Economic Geography*, 62, 334–53.

Gibson-Graham, J.K. (2002), 'Beyond global vs. local: Economic politics outside the binary frame'. In Herod, A. and Wright, M. (eds) *Geographies of Power: Placing Scale*. Oxford, Blackwell.

Gibson-Graham, J.K. (2005), *A Postcapitalist Politics*. University of Minnesota Press, Minneapolis.

Gore, C. (1984), *Regions in Question: Space, Development Theory and Regional Policy*. London, Methuen.

Hart, G. (2001), 'Development critiques in the 1990s: Culs de sac and promising paths', *Progress in Human Geography*, 25, 649–58.

Harvey, D. (1982), *The Limits to Capital*. Oxford: Blackwell.

Holmes, J. and Kumar, P. (1995), 'Harmonisation or diversity? North American economic integration and industrial relations in the automobile industry'. In Van der Knaap, B. and Le Heron, R. (eds) *Human Resources and Industrial Spaces. A Perspective on Globalization and Localisation*. Wiley, Chichester, 31–64.

Le Heron, R. (1987), 'Rethinking regional development'. In Holland, P. and Johnston, W. (eds) *Southern Approaches. Geography in New Zealand*. New Zealand Geographical Society, Christchurch, 261–82.

Le Heron, R. (2007), 'Globalisation, governance and post-structural political economy: Perspectives from Australasia'. *Asia Pacific Viewpoint* 48, 1, 26–40.

Massey, D. (1979), 'In what sense a regional problem?', *Regional Studies*, 13, 233–43.

Massey, D. and Meegan, R. (1982), *The Anatomy of Job Loss: The How, Why and Where of Employment Decline*. London, Methuen.

Massey, D. and Meegan, R. (eds) (1985), *Politics and Method*. London, Methuen.

Massey, D. (2006), 'Geographies of solidarities'. In Clark, N., Massey, D. and Sarre, P. (eds) *A World in the Making*. The Open University, Milton Keynes, 311–53.

Murray, W. (2006), 'Globalization across space – Contesting theories'. In Murray, W. *Geographies of Globalization*. Routledge, Oxford, 30–58.

Neill, D., Dowling, R. and Fagan, B. (2005), 'Sydney/global/city: An exploration', *International Journal of Urban and Regional Research*, 29, 4, 935–44.

Peck, J. and Yeung, H. (eds) (2003), *Remaking the Global Economy*. Sage, London.

Peet, R. and Thrift, N. (1999), 'Political economy and human geography'. In Thrift, N. and Peet, R. (eds) *New Models in Human Geography*. Oxford, Blackwell, 3–29.

Rees, J., Hewings, G. and Stafford, H. (eds) (1981), *Industrial Location and Regional Systems: Spatial Organization in the Economic Sector*. Brooklyn, NY, Bergin Press.

Roweiss, S. (1981), 'Urban planning in early and late capitalist societies: Outline of theoretical perspective'. In Dear, M. and Scott, A. (eds) *Urbanization and Urban Planning in Capitalist Societies*. New York, Methuen, 159–77.

Saxenian, A. (2002), 'Transnational Communities and the Evolution of Global Production Networks: Taiwan, China and India', *Industry and Innovation*, 9, 3, 183–202.

Scott, A. (1982), 'The meaning and social origins of discourse on the spatial foundations of society'. In Gould, P. and Olsson, G. (eds) *A Search for Common Ground*. London, Pion, 141–56.

Scott, A. (2000), 'Economic geography: the great half-century'. In Clark, G., Feldman, M. and Gertler, M. (eds) *The Oxford Handbook of Economic Geography.* Oxford, 18–44.

Scott, A. (2004) 'A perspective of economic geography'. *Journal of Economic Geography* 4, 479–99.

Scott, A. and Storper, M. (eds) (1984), *Production, Work, Territory. The Geographical Anatomy of Industrial Capitalism.* Boston, Allen and Unwin.

Storper, M. and Walker, R. (1989), *The Capitalist Imperative: Territory, Technology and Industrial Growth.* New York, Basil Blackwell.

Swyngedouw, E. (1997), 'Excluding the other: The production of scale and scaled politics', In Lee, R. and Wills, J. (eds) (1997) *Geographies of Economies.* London, Arnold, 167–76.

Chapter 6
Configuring to be Globally Competitive

Michael I. Luger

The powers that be within the world's regions are coming to terms with one of the realities of the 21st century, namely, that they cannot expect to bring economic prosperity to their citizens by looking inward. Isolation is no longer an option. Nor is it enough to compete only with other regions in the same state (prefect, Länder, etc.) or country. National borders are becoming less important. We are in the age of global competition. It is as important for Manchester (my current home town, for example) to compare itself with Frankfort, Osaka, and Philadelphia, than with Birmingham and Leeds, and for the Research Triangle in North Carolina (my immediate past home) to compare itself with Taejon, Helsinki, and Cambridge, than with Charlotte, Greensboro, or Nashville. The businesses these regions seek to grow, attract and retain look at many locations across state and national borders, and the human knowledge resources so critical for success today are similarly globally footloose.

Scholars have understood this reality for generations. The geography and regional science and economics literatures long have discussed comparative/competitive advantage, typically without regard to political boundaries. Distance to inputs and to markets, the local cost and productivity of factors of production, access to natural resources and amenities, all were used to explain the growth and development of city-regions[1]. The dry economic analysis of advantage was made more accessible by Michael Porter, in *Competitive Advantage of Nations*. Paul Krugman explicated the notion of competitiveness in an open economy (which more and more characterises the world) in his *Geography and Trade*, and Annalee Saxenian and others popularised the notion of regional advantage in a planning context in such books as *Regional Advantage: Culture and Competition in Silicon Valley and Route 128* and *The New Argonauts Regional Advantage in a Global Context*. (Porter, 1990; Krugman, 1991; Saxenian, 1996, 2006).

My intention here is not to provide a literature review, but rather, distil from this long and deep history some lessons about what global competitiveness means in practical terms and to focus on one of the critical success factors. The

1 Of the many references, see the following, somewhat randomly drawn from different eras: Ricardo (1821), Samuelson (1938, 1948), Robinson (1948), MacDougal (1951), Bellasi (1963), Bhagwati (1964), Thompson (1965), Maroney and Walker (1966), Kaldor (1970), Rosen and Resnick (1980), Krugman and Venables (1995), and Venables and Limao (2002).

powers that be, to whom I referred above (the elected and appointed decision-makers within regions, influencers, and operatives) now appreciate the importance of global competitiveness, but typically do not know how to operationalise the concept. They turn to high-priced consultants to show them the way. This also is not the place to provide a critique of that sector (I do elsewhere; see Luger and Bae, 2007). Suffice it to say that many consultants provide a good service. But the very nature of their business is to provide guidance and then move on to other opportunities, often leaving the client still confused about their direction. It is not easy to make the gems of wisdom passed down from the consultants on high part of the region's policy fabric. It requires built-up local expertise and the proper institutional infrastructure.

Indeed, in place after place that has the will to become globally competitive there is often an in-built handicap that works against both good intentions and good policy. That handicap is the configuration of the economic development apparatus that can mobilise to meet the global challenge. That is so important today because most jurisdictions cannot become global leaders by themselves; unless they join forces with other nearby jurisdictions and work to coordinate amongst themselves, they will not have the resources or visibility to compete effectively on the global stage.

In this chapter I do three things that relate to the global competitiveness challenge: I provide a working definition of global competitiveness and a stylised set of requirements for any place to prosper economically. Then I provide a case study of how an illustrative region has struggled to overcome the internal challenges of unproductive competition stemming from the configuration of the economic development landscape. The case study is drawn from a recently completed report to the North Carolina legislature, whose members were concerned about the erosion of global competitiveness due to configuration issues.

Defining Global Competitiveness

Regions throughout the world are asking: "what are our unique advantages around which we can build an economic future, and what opportunities can we pursue that will pay off economically?" I call the two prongs of this question "capacity" and "ambition."

One lesson from Porter's (and related) work is that almost every place has some competitive advantage it can exploit. The challenge is to identify it and then to use it as leverage to grow the economy. Classic competitive advantage comes from strategic location, proximity to vital natural resources, the presence of good weather and other natural amenities. These factors explain the growth of almost all prominent cities in Europe and many in the United States and elsewhere. For those places, competitive/comparative advantage was a necessary, but not sufficient condition for development. Those strategic advantages had to be recognised and exploited, and then agglomeration economies had to take effect. In many cases, growth begot growth in a phenomenon referred to as the "ratchet effect" and rank-size growth (Thompson, 1965). A related theme in the literature is that the economy overall is better off if local/regional economies specialise in the production of those goods and services in which they have an advantage, and then trade with others that have different specialisations.

Competitive/comparative advantage is not just a fact of nature. It can be created as a matter of policy. In history, cities grew up around military outposts that may have been strategically located only in the sense of being at the frontier (and not also at the confluence of rivers or on a harbour). Other cities grew up around church or university centres (Salt Lake City, Oxford, and more recently many state universities in the United States). Some cities were built to be centrally located capitals (the most prominent being Brasilia). If one looks at time-lapsed satellite images of North America, s/he would see major development along rail lines (Kansas City and Omaha), interstate highways (Phoenix, Columbus (Ohio)), and near major airports (Atlanta and Dallas)[2]. And there are examples of thriving cities built in what previously was "nowhere," around recreation themes: Orlando (Disney World) and Las Vegas being the best cases. Las Vegas did not even have water until the federal government build Hoover Dam and created Lake Meade.

The language of competitive/comparative advantage for regions is not unlike that used for marketing in the retail sector. Companies ask: "what brands can we create and promote that will bring in the most consumers?" Some companies can exploit an invention and have first-mover advantage (IBM and the first PCs). Others create products that become valuable only via marketing (the "pet rock"). Those companies that recognise their market position, create a product that the market will value, and then promote it effectively, will succeed.

Regional competitive/comparative advantage is proving to be somewhat different in the 21st century than it was earlier. First, similar to the retail sector, immediate and inexpensive global communications shrinks protected markets. In the past, a consumer seeking to buy a camera (for example) would shop in local stores for the best deal. Prices may have been higher in that market than elsewhere (though that fact could not easily be known) because of limited competition (or even collusion, but higher margins in either case), higher costs of getting the goods from the manufacturer to the retailer, or higher local production costs (if there was not an open economy). Now, that consumer can shop on the internet for the best price for a wider variety of products, with very low transaction costs. The local camera seller is now part of the global retail community. Adapt or perish. Similarly, communities seeking to appeal as locations for businesses and residents operate in a global market more than in the past.

2 Indeed, airports have become important hubs of commerce and economic development in the 21st century. John Kasarda writes about the importance of such airposrts as Schiphol, Atlanta. Incheon, Frankfurt, Chicago, Dallas-Ft.Worth, and others, to their regions and nations. http://www.aerotropolis.com/articles.html provides a list of Kasarda's citations on the topic.

The second reason global competitiveness is different today than in the past is that competitive/comparative advantage can more easily be created as a matter of policy. The "traditional" location factors are less important because of changes in technology. Heavy intermediate and final goods have had to be, and still need to be near seaports, rail lines, and major highways. But more and more of the value produced by the industrial sector is lighter in weight (computer chips, pharmaceuticals), and they can be transported quickly and cheaply by air. And an increasing amount of value is in software that can be shipped electronically, rendering location irrelevant. Similarly, a higher percent of the value of all goods produced today is in the knowledge component (R&D and design) that went into them, and in their service component (financing, maintenance, technical assistance, ordering). Those activities can be separated geographically from production, and placed in locations in which knowledge and service workers want to live – places with affordable and attractive housing, good weather, recreation and culture, etc. The separation of the knowledge/service component from manufacturing also makes universities and other knowledge institutions an important attraction for business location, and indeed, we see that as a common feature of many of the growing regions in North America and elsewhere.[3]

These new realities have consequences for economic development policy. More than ever before, competitive/comparative advantage can be created: build golf courses and other recreation, develop and market attractive science parks, move and/or expand colleges and universities and research facilities, work with airlines to expand air services, and so on.

Planning and Operationalising Global Competitiveness

Consultants like the Monitor Group (Michael Porter's company), KPMG/ Bearing Point, New Economic Strategies, Market Street Consulting, Angelou Economics, and others[4] have what could be criticised as a formulaic approach to client regions' competitiveness: assessment, SWOT, and recommendations. The assessment consists of an inventory of the region's assets in quality and quantity terms. The SWOT, or analysis of strengths, weaknesses, opportunities, and threats, overlays judgment on the inventory, thus putting the assets in the perspective of benchmark regions and time, and factoring in realities of the external environment. Recommendations come from stakeholder analysis and negotiation, ascertaining the value tradeoffs of key groups in the region, given the existing and likely future resources.

---

3 This topic also has developed a sizable literature. For example, see (Goldstein and Luger (1994) and Feldman and Desrochers (2003).

4 www.angeloueconomics.com, www.marletstreetservices.com, www.bearingpoint.com, www.new-econ.com, www.monitor.com.

The inventory of assets illustratively includes the following categories. Obviously, the list can be expanded and refined:

- Physical capital: traditional infrastructure
  - developable land
  - availability and cost of electricity, gas, water
  - national, international, regional, municipal airports
  - miles of roads, railway in county
  - military bases
- Physical capital: knowledge infrastructure
  - Information and communications technology and connectedness
  - Research institutes, training facilities, higher education
- Financial capital
  - Debt
  - Equity
  - Venture funds
  - Taxes (-) and subsidies, etc. (+)
- Human capital
  - Workers (by age, occupation/skills, experience, education etc.)
  - Non-working population (by age, skills, gender, income, etc.)
  - Leaders

The asset inventory also typically includes what might be called "mediating mechanisms" that are used to translate assets into outcomes. Among these are:

- External connectedness
  - Trade: value of goods exported outside region
  - Number of air travelers originating in/destined for region
  - Number of train travelers originating in/destined for region
  - Number of international visitors
  - Migration
  - Number of cities served by air directly from local airport
- Internal connectedness
  - Private/public partnerships
  - Intergovernmental cooperation/coordination
  - Private/public university consortia
  - Industry/university collaboration
  - Government/voluntary sector relationships

- Policy-making effectiveness
  - Effective government structure
  - Consistency of policy within/between local governments
  - Leveraging external government resources
  - Bipartisanship

There are countless variations of the inventory list, differing because of the consultants' style/approach, the appetite of the client for detail, and the availability of data in different places.

Along with the inventory data, consultants typically will review past reports and other descriptive materials that are available and assess other more qualitative data (for example, from interviews, focus groups, and/or surveys). Then, to make normative judgments about the region's strengths, weaknesses, opportunities, and threats, the consultant considers the region's assets in the context of: (1) the region's own ambitions, (2) the likely trajectory of the assets over time, (3) the relative position of the region vis-à-vis other comparison regions, and (4) the likely path of the external environment (interest rates, GDP growth, etc.). Clearly, this is more an art than a science, and no one seriously regards the SWOT as anything more than suggestive.

In addition, or instead of this approach, regions undertake cluster-based analysis as a way to judge their competitiveness. In short, this entails a detailed assessment of existing and emerging business cluster strength and potential, where business cluster is defined as a group of businesses related by trading, common technology, common markets, or common labour needs (see Luger, 2005). The cluster-based analysis helps the client region decide on which types of businesses to try to maintain or develop more, which types to allow to decline, and which types to create from almost no presence at all (see Feser and Luger, 2003).

However one conducts the global competitiveness analysis a few general requirements emerge as necessary, if not sufficient, for a region's success:

- Several of the region's assets are better in quantitative and qualitative terms than other regions with similar ambitions
- Whether or not the region has relative asset strength, it should minimise its asset weaknesses and threats
- Regions choose outcome targets (for example, attracting certain types of people or businesses) consistent with the relative asset strengths they have
- Any interventions the region plans to maintain or build asset strength are likely to be productive and appropriate given the region's resources and ambitions

There are many examples of regions for which the first bullet did not apply: they did not have any relative asset strengths. Some succeeded anyway because they:

- reduced their weaknesses and threats more than others, and/or
- invested strategically to build relative asset strength.

That is the story of the Asian Tigers and Dragons over the past 50 years, of the Celtic Tiger, and a few other places that have risen dramatically along the development curve.[5]

Among the assets delineated above are what I referred to as "mediating mechanisms." Regions with the strongest relative physical, financial, and human capital assets still will not succeed if those mediating mechanisms are not well developed. This argument is made, as well, by social scientists writing about "social capital"[6]. In the next section I discuss a mediating mechanism that falls between the categories of internal connectedness and policy effectiveness: the configuration of the economic development apparatus necessary to translate public sector actions into private sector outcomes. I focus on that because I have found that to be a problem in many regions around the world. Some regions have managed to enjoy success anyway, though one could argue that there would have been greater success if that problem were solved. But many regions with all the right intentions, strong physical assets, and good policy tools have been thwarted in their ability to compete globally because they "did not have their act together," to use the common vernacular.

Configuring for Global Competitiveness: A Case Study of North Carolina

After WWII, North Carolina was dominated by traditional manufacturing industries (textiles and apparel, tobacco products, and furniture) and agriculture. Wages were relatively low. The education system was below average. The state was in the bottom quartile in many socio-economic indicators. Prospects were grim since the dominant industries were all vulnerable to foreign competition and changes in demand.

Strong and moderate political leadership, strategic investments in education, other innovative policy-making (including development of the nation's second research park), and favourable location and climate all contributed to North Carolina's turnaround. It became the 11th largest state by population (with approximately 9 million residents). Charlotte grew into North America's second largest banking centre and the Raleigh-Durham-Chapel Hill region (Research Triangle) emerged as one of the world's elite science and technology hubs.

However, North Carolina's generally robust economy slowed down considerably in the period 1997–2002. New announcements fell off, as did resident firms' expansions. Population growth remained strong, including unprecedented levels

5 Of the large literature on this topic, see Vogel (1991); Kim 1998); and Garran (1998).

6 Most notable is Robert Putnam (for example, 2000, 2002).

of migration from Mexico. The loss of traditional manufacturing jobs, slower rates of new job formation, and continued in-migration of workers together resulted in rising unemployment, even higher than in neighbouring states, and lower real wages for many workers. The consequences were felt most acutely in the already poor, rural parts of the state.

Some critics attributed the slowdown in announcements to the way North Carolina approached business recruitment. Associated with that was the belief that there was unnecessary duplication of effort among the various economic development actors, poor accountability, and lack of performance-based rewards. Some even claimed that North Carolina's approach to economic development was outdated, with too much focus on "buffalo hunting" and too little focus on "growing its own."

To understand these issues more fully, the North Carolina General Assembly commissioned a study (in S.L. 2002–2126) to assess the effectiveness of the state's economic development delivery system – specifically, to address how the N.C. Department of Commerce (NCDOC) and the seven regional economic development partnerships could improve coordination and communication in their activities, and on how appropriate measures could be developed and implemented to track and improve the effectiveness of economic development activities in the state.[7]

The Major Problems

Economic development is a "feel good" activity. Prospects shopping for a business location ultimately have to feel good about a place, in order to choose it. That is one way to think of "business climate." And those working in the trenches, trying to attract new business and help existing companies stay competitive, have to feel good about their products in order to sell them effectively. That is "morale."

Through a series of interviews and surveys, we found that the economic development community did not feel terribly good, and not just because the recession had slowed down economic activity. The malaise reflected problems related to structure, communication, and leadership – the "mediating mechanisms" listed above under policy-making effectiveness and connectedness. The structure issues arose because of the decentralised system of economic development in North Carolina, which included a cabinet department (Commerce) with personnel in Raleigh and in field locations, an economic development board, seven different regional partnerships, and other actors, such as the North Carolina Rural Center, the Small Business Technology Development Center, and the university and community college systems. Those actors had separate but overlapping roles.

Some decentralisation is unavoidable. No state is able to dictate a strict top-down model of economic development. They can, however, ensure good communication and coordination among the players, a clear understanding of

7 The material that follows is from Luger and Stewart (2003).

different groups' primary roles, and strong leadership to ensure that the various actors pull together toward the same end. Strong leadership sends signals to the professional community about the relative importance of their work. The lack of strong leadership in North Carolina affected morale within the state more than it affected he external perception of North Carolina initially, but there was concern and some indications that the external community (site location specialists, the business community) soon would become disaffected.

Three Keys: Coordination, Communication, and Leadership

Our study concluded that the configuration of economic development would be improved if the regional economic development partnerships and the North Carolina Department of Commerce (NCDOC):

- Jointly developed a statewide marketing plan
- Better delineated roles, both for the partnerships and NCDOC, as well as the many other state-funded economic development actors
- Strengthened the strategic planning process, under the Economic Development Board, to give the strategic plan it develops more relevance and traction to the many economic development professionals who need to commit to the plan's implementation
- Measured according to well-delineated and differentiated roles

Our message to the General Assembly was that communications would be improved by the improved coordination discussed above. We also stressed the importance of building teamwork and improving trust, which are so important around an activity (industrial recruitment and development) that requires the sharing of various types of relevant but often confidential information about clients.

There was a shared sense among state, regional and local economic development professionals of the importance of creating a more competitive economy and business climate in North Carolina. The common desire for improvement served as a good foundation. Economic development is a relationship business. Trust hinges in part on a belief in the competence and good judgment of one's partners. Good performance at all levels must be rewarded in both quantitative ways (for instance, tied to organisational funding or individual pay) and qualitative ways, including pats on the back from high-level public and private leaders.

Developing Measures that are Useful

Appropriate measurement is important to assure accountability. But measurement should be a useful exercise – helping those measured improve their performance and those requiring the measurement to understand better the value of the enterprises being measured. We found that measurement contributed to in-fighting over who gets the credit for certain outcomes, was regarded as a burden to those required to report, and was not widely used by policy-makers. We argued that better measurement was needed by and for both Commerce and the partnerships.

Measuring NCDOC

NCDOC was measured on the volume of jobs and investment generated in the state. It was not measured on progress toward stated goals in a marketing plan, because there wasn't one. It was not measured on teamwork with its many partners, yet that was important since they all help achieve the jobs and investment reported. It was not measured on individual or unit performance, because as a state agency NCDOC was governed by the State Personnel Act, and thus lacked effective mechanisms for sanctioning poor performance or rewarding excellence of individuals or business units.

We recommended the following:

- NCDOC should develop a marketing plan, with the help of the Economic Development Board, its own staff, the seven regional partnerships, and other key partners. The marketing budget needed to be increased substantially. NCDOC must be held accountable for progress against plan goals.
- Client and partner satisfaction measures should be incorporated routinely – at least annually – into the NCDOC evaluation.
- Benchmarking against other states with which North Carolina competes – not just South Carolina and Virginia, but the knowledge economy leaders including California, Massachusetts, Colorado and Maryland – should be standard practice.
- A system of merit-based pay and individual performance contracts should be instituted for the economic development staff at NCDOC.

Measuring the Partnerships

The partnerships were accountable to their boards, most of which included strong, if not demanding, private sector leadership. Each had a program of work that was tailored to the needs of its sub-region. The partnerships also were required to report annually to the North Carolina General Assembly. Unfortunately, the measures required by the legislature did not capture the real value of what the partnerships did. It focused on direct job creation rather than on competitive product development and regional branding, and it did not capture the diversity among the partnerships, which was inevitable given the diversity among the regions in which they were located. The legislature did not ask for evidence about partnerships' teamwork or customer satisfaction. Based on the above, we recommended the following:

- The partnerships should be held accountable for their defined roles and contributions in implementing the state-wide strategic plan for economic development and (when developed) the marketing plan, including good teamwork with NCDOC staff.
- The partnerships should delineate their roles in ways that did not create competition with what local developers, NCDOC staff or other economic development professionals were doing in their regions.
- All board should be reconstituted to include CEO-level private leadership.
- Client and partner satisfaction measures should be incorporated into the partnerships' annual reports.

A Continuing Role for State Government

All large regions (or in the case of the US, all states) need to have a central coordinating policy unit to ensure consistency and complementarity among sub-units (the regional partnerships in the case of NC). We recommended that the Economic Development Board be recognised as the lead policymaking organisation for economic development in North Carolina. It should set challenging but realistic action plans for each year that specify lead organisations and timelines, and it should convene an annual economic development summit to report to the legislature and the public on economic development outcomes for the state and its regions.

We also recommended that the General Assembly 1) work with the Economic Development Board to establish and monitor economic development performance measures that are specific to the defined roles of the various actors; 2) provide stable funding that is realistic for the outcomes it demands; and 3) develop tax and regulatory policies that foster a strong and innovative business climate. Then it should leave the day-to-day work to the impressive array of committed and experienced economic development professionals state-wide.

Summary and Conclusions

I began by underscoring the growing interest in the concept of "global competitiveness" by regions all over the world that recognise they cannot succeed in isolation, but rather, are part of a worldwide network of interrelated economies competing for many of the same businesses and talented people. I then provided a sample framework used to assess the competitive/comparative advantage of regions, including an asset inventory, SWOT analysis (and/or cluster-based analysis), and strategic actions. The assets typically include human, physical, and financial capital and "mediating mechanisms" used to translate those assets into successful outcomes. Among the mediating mechanisms are efficient government operation and inter-connectedness – or, in short, the way the economic development apparatus is configured.

The central message of the chapter is that regions can have a strong asset base and considerable will to succeed, but can falter if their economic development apparatus is poorly configured. Conversely, regions that have their act together can overcome the disadvantage of being uncompetitive in some of the asset areas. Competitiveness in some part (but not all) of the asset base, and strong mediating mechanisms are individually necessary for success, but neither is sufficient.

I illustrated the importance of the configuration of the economic development apparatus with a case study of North Carolina, which established a strong competitive position through the 1990s, and then found its competitive advantage eroding. A major study commissioned by the legislature found that there was duplication of effort, unnecessary in-fighting, inappropriate incentives and rewards, and general confusion among the economic development stakeholders in the state. The report recommended improvements in the configuration of the apparatus. Some of those recommendations have been followed, and the state has regained some momentum.

This story seems to be generalisable to other parts of the world. It is not uncommon for turf battles, mixed messages, and a lack of clearly articulated roles to be present in multi-jurisdictional regions. Those places that get their act together and act in unison will have an additional advantage in the competitive 21st century.

References

Bellasi, Bela (1963), "An Empirical Demonstration of Classical Comparative Cost Theory." *The Review of Economics and Statistics 45*, 3, August: 231–8.

Bhagwati, J. (1964), "The Pure Theory of International Trade: A Survey." *The Economic Journal 74*, 293: 1–84.

Feldman, Maryann and Pierre Desrochers (2003), "Research Universities and Local Economic Development: Lessons from the History of the Johns Hopkins University." *Industry and Innovation 10*.1.

Feser, Edward and Michael Luger (2003), "Cluster Analysis as a Mode of Inquiry," *European Planning Journal 11*, 1: 11–24.

Garran, Robert (1998), *Tigers Tamed: The End of the Asian Miracle*. New York: Allen and Unwin.

Goldstein, Harvey A. and Michael I. Luger (1994), "Universities as Engines of Economic Development: What Role Can They Effectively Play?" *Economic Development Commentary 18*, 1.

Isard, Walter (1960), *Methods of Regional Analysis*. Cambridge, MA: M.I.T. Press.

Kaldor, Nicholas (1970), "The Case for Regional Policies." *Scottish Journal of Political Economy 17*: 331–48.

Kim, Eun Mee (1998), *The Four Asian Tigers*. New York: Academic Press.

Krugman, Paul R. and Anthony J. Venables (1995), "Globalization and the Inequality of Nations." *The Quarterly Journal of Economics 110*, 4, November: 857–80.
Krugman, Paul (1991), *Geography and Trade*. Cambridge, MA: MIT Press.
Luger, Michael and Suho Bae (2006), "Speaking Falsehoods to Power: The Misguided Use of 'Cost-of-Doing-Business' Studies in Economic Development." *Review of Regional Studies 36*, 1: 15–43.
Luger, Michael I. (2005), "Smart Places for Smart People: Using Cluster-based Planning in the 21st Century." In Scott Shane, (ed.), *Economic Development Through Entrepreneurship: Government, University and Business Linkages*. Northampton, MA: Edward Elgar.
Luger, Michael I. and Leslie Stewart (2003), *Assessing the Economic Development Delivery System in North Carolina*, Prepared for the N.C. General Assembly, March.
MacDougall, G.D.A. (1951), "British and American Exports: A Study Suggested by the Theory of Comparative Costs." *Economic Journal 61*, 244: 687–724.
Moroney, J.R and J.M. Walker (1966), "A Regional Test of the Heckscher-Ohlin Hypothesis." *Journal of Political Economy 74*: 573–86.
Porter, Michael (1990), *The Competititve Advantage of Nations*. New York: Free Press.
Putnam, Robert D. (2000), *Bowling Alone*. New York: Simon and Schuster.
Putnam, Robert D. (ed.) (2002), *Democracies in Flux: The Evolution of Social Capital in Contemporary Society*. Oxford: Oxford University Press.
Ricardo, David (1821), *On the Principles of Political Economy and Taxation*. London: John Murray.
Robinson, Joan (1946), "The Pure Theory of International Trade." *Review of Economic Studies xiv*, 2: 98–112.
Rosen, Kenneth T. and Michael Resnick (1980), "The Size Distribution of Cities: An Examination of the Pareto Law and Primacy." *Journal of Urban Economics 8*, 2, September: 165–86.
Samuelson, Paul A. (1938), "Welfare Economics and International Trade." *American Economic Review xxviii*: January: 262.
Samuelson, Paul A. (1948), "International Trade and the Equalisation of Factor Prices." *Economic Journal lviii*, June: 163–85.
Saxenian, Annalee (1996), *Regional Advantage: Culture and Competitition in Silicon Valley and Route 128*. Cambridge, MA: Harvard University Press.
Saxenian, Annalee. (2006), *New Argonauts Regional Advantage in a Global Economy*. Cambridge, MA: Harvard University Press.
Thompson, Wilbur. (1965), *Preface to Urban Economics*. Baltimore, MD: Johns Hopkins University Press.
Venables, Anthony J. and Nuno Limao. (2002), "Geographical Disadvantage: A Heckscher-Ohlin-von Thunen Model of International Specialisation." *Journal of International Economics 58*, 2, December: 239–63.
Vogel, Ezr. (1991), *The Four Little Dragons: The Spread of Industrialization in East Asia*. Cambridge, MA: Harvard University Press.

Websites

http://www.aerotropolis.com/articles.htm.
www.angeloueconomics.com.
www.marletstreetservices.com.
www.bearingpoint.com.
www.new-econ.com.
www.monitor.com.

Chapter 7
Location Theory

Philip McCann

Introduction

Over the last two decades there has been an enormous increase in interest in the analysis of firm location behaviour. For scholars working in this field this is obviously an extremely welcome development, as increasing numbers of scholars from a range of disciplines participate in the debates. While this increase in interest leads to new breakthroughs in our understanding of location phenomena, on the other hand, however, much of the research in these areas often leads to a certain amount of confusion as analytical terminology is used in different, and sometimes conflicting, ways. These confusions are sometimes exacerbated by the fact that the authors are unaware that analytical terminology they employ has a very specific meaning and logic, which has been developed on the basis of a long research tradition.

The field of location theory has three major stream of research, each of which derives from rather different analytical traditions. The first stream of location theory was developed out of what might be termed the *regional science and urban economics* tradition, the second stream emerged out of a fusion of traditional *economic geography* and the *business and management* theory, and the third steam developed out of *trade theory*. These various strands of location theory literature for many years remained largely unconnected, largely because they were initially designed in order to answer apparently rather different types of questions. Today, however, many different aspects these three strands of literature are rapidly converging as new data sources and new understandings of the relationships between the various characteristics of location behaviour are developed. This has lead to the emergence of a rather more holistic approach to describing and explaining location behaviour in which cross-disciplinary research is now commonplace. Huge quantities of material have been published on each of these four location theory literature streams, so our literature review of each stream is necessarily brief and succinct. Instead, our aim here is to identify what are the salient features underpinning each approach and to identify they key insights attained. These insights will then help us to understand how each stream of location theory relates to each of the other streams, and therefore will allow us to identify commonalities across theoretical approaches.

This chapter will argue that the continuing fusion of these three streams of literature will entail a deeper understanding of the nature of organisational relations, and in particular the transactions-costs associated with knowledge spillovers. There are two major reasons for this. Firstly, understanding the links between knowledge and location behaviour provide the means by which the insights of these three traditions can be linked and related to each other. As such, this is the analytical rationale for focusing on knowledge issues as the focal point of modern location theory. Secondly, as the economy is increasingly orientated towards knowledge activities, the management of knowledge flows, knowledge exchanges, and knowledge spillovers will become an increasingly central feature of firm decision-making, and this will be as true for location decisions as for any other forms of firm investment decisions. This is therefore the empirical rationale for focusing on knowledge issues as the focal point of modern location theory.

The chapter is organised as follows. The next section provides a brief overview of each of these three location theory streams of literature, in which we explain the basic concepts underpinning each of the various streams of location theory. On the basis of these explanations in section three we then focus on the question of industrial clustering, a topic which has become of major interest across a range of disciplines over the last two decades. Our rationale for focusing on industrial clustering is not simply because it is interesting topic in its own right, but rather that it highlights the theoretical and conceptual differences between the different location theory literature streams, and helps us to unravel many of the current confusions regarding locational analysis. In order to do this, in section 4 we adopt a transactions-costs framework in order to identify the relationships between firms and industry organisational issues, knowledge issues, and locational issues. This approach allows us to demonstrate that the various streams of location theory not only ask rather different questions, but more fundamentally, they are actually appropriate for analysing very different types of locational phenomena. Identifying which phenomena are related to which location theory approaches helps us to better understand the relationships between the theory and empirics of locational behaviour, and to points towards a more coherent overall approach to the analysis of industrial location phenomena. Section five then identifies some theoretical empirical issues associated with the empirical interpretation of location behaviour, and section six provides some brief conclusions.

Differing Traditions in Location Theory

The first steam of theoretical literature in locational analysis, and indeed the most longstanding tradition, comes from the field of regional science. Here there are actually three different sub-streams of literature. The first sub-stream of location theory within the regional science tradition comes from regional economics, and was based on the original insights of Alfred Weber (1909) and Leon Moses (1958), and subsequently developed by numerous authors (Miller and Jensen, 1978; Eswaran et al., 1981). These models were mathematical location-production optimisation models set explicitly in geographical space, and the focus of these models was to identify the relationships between the properties of the firm's production function, the transport costs it faces, and its optimal locational behaviour under conditions where factor prices are invariant with location. Although Weber (1909) was one of the very earliest scholars to discuss the issues of local factor price variations and agglomeration effects on location, following the work of Moses (1958) variations and local factor costs were not part of these location-production optimisation frameworks. The general conclusion to emerge from these types of models is that the optimal location of the firm is invariant with the output as long as the firm's production function is homogeneous of degree one, and that the cost minimisation and profit maximising locations are the same. The locational solution to the fixed-coefficients model of Weber therefore coincides with the solution to the Moses model of varying coefficients. Other analogous approaches have also set these location-production models in one-dimensional space, and have demonstrated that for a range of very general production function properties, no intermediate optimum location exists.

A range of extensions have since been proposed to these types of location-optimisation frameworks. For example, instead of focusing on the impacts of transport costs on location behaviour, it is possible to re-specify these models using total logistics costs, which include all of the inventory costs and inventory handling costs associated with moving goods across space (McCann, 1993). In this case, all of the locational conclusions become much richer than in the earlier models. For example, the optimal location of the firm is found to move towards the market as the value-added at the production location increases and this is true for either a fixed coefficients production function or a production function which is homogeneous of degree one (McCann, 1993, 1998). As such, if we consider this broader notion of distance costs, there is no Weber-Moses optimum, unless the firm has no value-adding capacity at its production location, in which case the 'firm' is simply a warehouse. Furthermore, these arguments become even more complicated when we try move from theory to reality because applying a microeconomic location-production function methodology to even the most basic notion of the firm in the real-world is actually far more complex than at first it appears (McCann, 1999). The reason is that, if we employ input-substitution arguments with locational changes, as is typical in neo-classical production-location models, then severe problems of interpretation and observation arise if we then apply these models to the real world. The reason for this is that the relationship between the inputs and the outputs, in terms of product characteristics, becomes indefinable (McCann, 1999). These models only work empirically where all factors have fixed coefficients, such that no factor substitution is allowed. Multi-facility location modeling which attempts to optimally allocate different types of functions and facilities across different types of locations therefore adopts only works where production functions are specified ex ante (ReVelle, 1987).

The second sub-steam of theoretical location analysis which emerged from the field of regional science is the spatial competition literature, based primarily on one-dimensional spatial models. This stream of location theory within the regional science tradition was based on the original insights of Hotelling (1929), and focuses on the interactions between location and competition. The basic insights arrived at in the spatial competition literature are that if there is no price competition operating, then a stable clustered optimal outcome is possible, whereas if prices are also variable, then no stable clustered optimal market structure is possible (d'Aspremont et al., 1979). Subsequent to the regional science tradition, these models nowadays have a direct parallel in oligopolistic and monopolistic competition models set in product-space.

The third sub-steam of theoretical location analysis which emerged from the field of regional science is based on land use models. This stream of location theory within the regional science tradition was based on the original insights of Von Thunen (1826) which were then re-specified within a formal utility-maximisation framework by Alonso (1964). These models have since been extended in numerous ways, most notably by Mills (1970) and Fujita (1989). The basic insights generated by these models are that with homogeneous amenities, land prices are convex with distance from the city centre, as are population densities and capital-land ratios (McCann, 2001). There are also other alternative explanations of land price-distance convexity derived from similar framework, most notably associated with Wheaton (DiPasquale and Wheaton, 1996), and these various models nowadays underpin modern urban and real estate economics. These arguments can also be extended to analyzing the impacts of heterogeneous amenities, problems associated with externalities, and poly-centric urban systems.

As well as providing fundamental analytical insights into real-world locational phenomena, with all social science constructs, each of the three sub-streams of location theories which emerged from the regional science and urban economics tradition also suffers from some problems of interpretation when applied to the real world. The most important issue here is that these models all treat a firm as a single point in space whereas many firms are very different in nature to this assumption. In particular, these models are largely inappropriate for analysing the location behaviour of multi-plant and multi-national firms, which make a very significant contribution to the spatial structure of the economy. For example, much of the geographical relocation of activities within multi-plant and multi-national firms consists of the reallocation of activities and resources within an existing spatial configuration of establishments, with little or no discernable external changes (Healey and Watts, 1987) of a type which can be modeled by microeconomic location theory. Indeed, the largest component of geographical changes in foreign direct investment is via mergers and acquisitions rather than 'greenfield' investments. Therefore many of these geographical investment changes are largely opaque. This is particularly important in the case of financial service industries (Cohen, 1998; Leyshon and Thrift, 1997; Coleman, 1996), whose firm and industry characteristics are largely unsuitable for modelling by orthodox microeconomic location theory.

In direct response to the problems of dealing theoretically with multiplant and multinational firms, the second stream of location theory which has been developed has emerged from a hybrid mixture of international business and management theory and traditional case-study based economic geography. This location theory literature has developed as part of attempts to analyse at the level of the firm, the rationale for, and nature of, international foreign direct investment. As such, this literature attempts to deal directly with the critiques of the microeconomic location theories discussed above. In the international business and management literature, the explanation for the existence of multiplant and multinational firms is based on the assumed existence of firm-specific intangible assets which give the multiplant and multinational firms firm major cost advantages over other, and in particular, foreign, producers (Caves, 1982). Within this broad theme, the strategic behaviour of the multiplant and multinational firms has traditionally been analysed within the framework of Dunning's (1977) 'eclectic' or 'OLI' paradigm' which posits that multinational activities are driven by three sets of advantages, namely ownership (O), location (L) and internalisation (I) advantages. According to this approach, it is the particular configuration of these sets of advantages that either encourage or discourage a firm from undertaking foreign activities and becoming a multiplant and multinational firm.

In this schema, ownership (O) advantages are perceived to be the firm-specific advantages that emanate directly from resources or assets owned or controlled by a firm, such as economies of scale or product diversification; the management of organisational expertise; the ability to acquire and upgrade resources; product differentiation; marketing economies; and access to domestic markets and to capital. Location-specific (L) advantages are assumed to be based on the resources, networks and institutional structures that are specific to a country. Examples here are low wages and the availability of cheap natural resources; labour productivity; the size and character of markets; transport costs; and the psychic distance from key markets to the home country of the MNE, the tariff and tax structures, attitudes toward FDI, and the structure of competition.

Note that none of these potential ownership (O) features or advantages are specific to the multinational firm or to international business research, as each of these individual elements is already contained within the standard industrial economics literature. Nor are any of the potential location (L) features specific to the multinational firm or to international business research, as each of these elements is already contained within the standard urban, regional geographical economics literatures. Rather, what is different in the international business literature from these other fields is the particular way in which these features are combined with a third hypothesised advantageous feature of the multinational firm, namely the internalisation (I) advantages of multiplant and multinational firms.

For analysts who posit this theoretical approach, the most crucial perceived advantage of the multiplant and multinational firms are known as internalisation (I) advantages. These are the hypothesised advantages that accrue to a firm when it eliminates the transaction costs associated with market interactions, and internalises these activities by bringing them inside the hierarchy of the firm (Buckley and Casson, 1976). As such, the firm is perceived to gain an advantage from being able to better coordinate a complex set of interrelated activities by moving from a market system, in which the firm would be forced to rely on imperfect or non-existent markets, to a planned and organised system of internal markets. In particular, the key imperfect market which multiplant and multinational firms seek to replace is that of the pricing of crucial proprietary knowledge across geographical boundaries. On one hand, knowledge can be regarded an asset that is generated by a firm, but at the same time knowledge also often has many of the attributes of a public good. Therefore, in order to profit from investment in knowledge development, in some cases it will be more efficient for the firm to use an internal hierarchy to internalise knowledge production and to monitor and control its use in a way that the market is unable to do. In these situations, knowledge is being treated as an intermediate product, and the firm accrues profits from the sale of the resulting final product or service produced on the basis of this knowledge. In cases where there are imperfections across international markets, this approach argues that a hierarchically organised multiplant and multinational firm can often be the most efficient means of production. As such, market failure may therefore often be the primary rationale for the existence of the multiplant and multinational firms.

Each of these three aspects of Dunning's (1977) eclectic paradigm are perceived to interact and to explain the location decision of the MNE. As becomes immediately clear, however, in this approach location problems are therefore perceived simply one aspect of a tri-dimensional organisational problem, in which a firm seeks to optimise its particular arrangement of ownership, location and internalisation features. As such, location behaviour can only be understood in the context of the ownership and internalisation issues simultaneously faced by the firm. Therefore, while location advantages are only the direct component, the ownership and internalisation advantages also influence the actual decision that is taken. As such, the location decision is a complex one, since it subsumes within it decisions regarding the mode of entry and the industry of entry (Mudambi and Mudambi, 2002) as well as the location of entry into a market. This level of organisational complexity is therefore fundamentally different to the microeconomic location theory approaches discussed above which emerged from regional science and urban economics, in which all aspects of the firm are reduced to production function properties and all behavioural features of the firm governed by profit maximisation.

Dunning's (1977) eclectic paradigm which underpins these lines of argument has tended to suffer from the limitation that location decisions in this framework are rarely analysed theoretically at anything less than the level of an individual country. As such, in their most basic form, these arguments still exhibit a level of generality which limits our analytical progress. Therefore, in order to provide a more explicit spatial nature to these argument, analysts of multiplant and multinational firms have developed several stylised models of the geographical behaviour, the most important of which is the product cycle model of Vernon (1966). According to the product cycle model, multiplant and multinational firms operate primarily by creating new products and processes in their home markets and then, as a secondary activity, subsequently adapt these for use in other markets, in order to exploit their home market strengths. The subsequent setting-up of any subsidiaries would involve the setting-up of rather routine activities required in order to ensure the local assembly and provision of the goods or services designed and developed in the home market regions. The home market would therefore generally be characterised by outputs at earlier stages in the product cycle and the other market locations by products in the later stages. The major rationale for this pattern is that the home market is assumed to be the location where the key information generation of the firm took place. The original simple product cycle model was subsequently adapted into the 'stage theory' of multinational evolution (Johanson and Vahlne, 1977), which perceives the multinational firm as a mature divisionalised company that often grows large in its domestic markets before turning to international activity beginning with exports. Subsequently, as the volume of foreign sales grows, the multinational firm responds by increasing the scope of its activities in the foreign market, eventually replacing exports with local value creation like manufacture (Hood and Young, 1979). This shift is often accompanied by the multinational firm moving to take tighter control of activities in the foreign market by, for example, the setting up of wholly-owned subsidiaries. On the basis of this theory, it has been argued that even secondary adaptive manufacturing activities in foreign markets occur at a later stage of foreign operations.

These international product cycle arguments were subsequently adapted from international space to explicitly geographical space by Marksuen (1985), by assuming that the theoretical rationale for the existence of the multiplant firm is more or less analogous to that of the multinational firm, in that it is the internalisation advantages which are assumed to dominate the location or ownership advantages. As such, she argues that such location behaviour can only be understood in a geographical setting by assuming that the headquarter functions of the mutiplant firm represent the home market location, and more peripheral lower-wage areas constitute the other regions. In the economic geography versions of the product cycle model (Hayter, 1997) the general stylised argument is therefore that the multiplant firms will tend to locate their knowledge-intensive activities and facilities in knowledge regions, such as dominant and dynamic cities, while locating more routine and standardised activities in more geographically peripheral regions, in order to take account of lower local factor costs. As such, the interregional product cycle geography of the multiplant firm within an individual country should exhibit a similar pattern to the international geography of the multinational firm. Similarly, in the case of inward investment by foreign-owned multinational firms, the simple logic here also suggests that investment locations will be driven by analogous considerations. In other words, knowledge-intensive activities will tend to be located in urban or regional centres of knowledge and information generation, while more routine activities will tend be located in more peripheral lower wage regions.

It is interesting to note that the product cycle model was actually initially developed within an urban and regional setting (Vernon, 1960). However, from the 1960s onwards, the urban and regional economics and international business traditions diverged into rather separate fields. The urban and regional aspects of the product cycle arguments therefore largely disappeared from the regional science research agenda, because they were not suited to mathematical analysis, and only re-emerged with the work of Markusen (1985). Meanwhile, in the international business literature, the analytical focus was on international locations, rather than domestic or internal locational issues. For this reason, many of the geographical subtleties of Vernon's original regional and urban economic insights disappeared.

The third stream of locational analysis to have been developed has emerged from trade theory. In early neo-classical trade theory there was neither any explicit economic geography nor any multiplant nor multinational firms as such. This was because traditional neo-classical trade theory was based on the twin assumptions of constant returns to scale and perfect competition in production. New trade theory (Helpman and Krugman, 1985; Krugman, 1990) theory extended the analysis of international trade by incorporating both economies of scale and product differentiation into trade models, both of which are features of multiplant and multinational firms. As such, many of the issues raised by the international business literature are now being slowly and progressively incorporated in general equilibrium trade-industrial organisation model. These include issues such as the internalisation and pricing of knowledge assets (Markusen, 1984, 2002), the advantages of horizontal (Horstmann and Markusen, 1992; Markusen and Venables, 2000) and vertical integration (Grossman and Hart,1986; Aghion and Tirole, 1997), and the advantages of sub-contracting and licensing versus FDI (Horstmann and Markusen, 1987; Ethier and Markusen, 1996; Helpman and Grossman, 2002; Markusen, 2002). However, even allowing for these recent developments in trade theory, and also allowing for the focus on multi-product firms in the new industrial economics literature (Tirole, 1988), Markusen (2002) contends that most trade-industrial organisation models are still generally of a type which assumes a single firm is associated with producing a single good at a single location, thereby still largely excluding a role for multiplant and multinational firms.

An even more important development regarding location theory issues which has emerged indirectly from the new trade literature is the new economic geography literature. This field is originally associated with the work Paul Krugman (1991a,b) but also subsequently includes the ground-breaking insights of Masahisa Fujita and Anthony Venables amongst many others. These models, which are based on monopolistic models of product variety, ascribe a central role for agglomeration economies as a source of increasing returns to scale in the economy, and the interaction between agglomeration effects and transport costs is seen to play a crucial role in determining the nature and level of trade patterns (Fujita et al. 1999). The new economy geography field has subsequently spawned a very large, and rapidly expanding, research literature, and an excellent review of this can be found in Fujita and Mori (2005). The basic insights from this literature are that under conditions of localised agglomeration economies, economic development tends to be very spatially concentrated either for very high transport costs or for very low transport costs, whereas for intermediate level transport costs, various alternative outcomes are possible, depending on the relationship between the localised economies of scale and the transport costs.

In new trade theory and also in new economic geography each individual firm is associated with an individual differentiated product. In both new trade-location models and also new economic geography models each firm is also still identified with a single establishment at a single location. As such, there is still no multiplant or multinational production (Markusen, 2002) in either schema. However, the strength of new economic geography models is their ability to demonstrate within a general equilibrium framework that a self-organising economy produces clustered locations and areas with little development as a natural process of agglomeration economies and spatial transactions costs. Moreover, these models have shown to work in both two-dimensional (Stelder, 2002) as well as one-dimensional (Fujita et al. 1999) space.

Industrial Clustering

A challenge posed by each of the various streams of location theory described above is that while each of these theoretical schema allows us to analyse particular aspects of industrial location behaviour, linking these different approaches and the insights gained into a cohesive theory is proving to be extremely difficult. Yet, there is one major feature which is common to all of these different theoretical approaches, and that is the concept of industrial *cluster*ing. Microeconomic approaches to location-production theory which emerged from the regional economics and regional science literature have discussed the effects of clustered agglomeration locations in terms of their cost and supply-side impacts for altering optimum firm location behaviour; models of spatial competition analyse the competitive processes by which industrial clustering may emerge; urban economic models assume as their starting point that clustered locations exist as the focal points of economic activity; multiplant and multinational models of location also assume that the firms will locate different activities in different locations, with some activities being focused towards areas of industrial clustering; new economic geography assumes that clustering generates agglomeration economies, which provide the key mechanism which drives the spatial organisation of the economy. Yet, each of these approaches is based on subtly different sets of assumptions regarding the nature and role of industrial clustering. The result of this is that in their necessarily partial and incomplete analyses, many different commentators often use terminology is rather inconsistent ways. In particular, commentators often move from one stylised theoretical construct to another when using terminology whose various meanings and assumptions are overlapping, without necessarily making clear the parsimonious analytical underpinnings of the concept. This is particularly problematic in the case of the concept of an industrial cluster (Porter 1990) because as just mentioned, potentially the concept of clusters can provide the link between the various different strands of location theory.

The concept of an industrial cluster is perceived to be its potential for enhancing the competitive advantage (Porter, 1985) of the firm (Porter, 1990; 1998, a,b). This can occur if an industrial cluster provides the individual firm with valuable local resources, inputs, infrastructure and opportunities for learning from other local firms and institutions. In particular, Porter emphasises the role played by local knowledge acting as a spur to local innovation and consequently local competitiveness. In some situations these potentially favorable aspects of a location can reinforce each other, thereby leading to a virtuous cycle in which there appear to be continuing advantages to investing in particular areas over other alternative locations. The implication of this analysis is that clusters, once formed, have a strong element of irreversibility, and firms therefore have much to gain from locating in such clusters. However, exactly how this concept relates to the various strands of location theory is not as straightforward as many observers assume. The reason is that each of these different location theory frameworks discussed above is based on a different set of assumptions regarding the transactions-costs underpinnings of the cluster.

In order to see this we can adopt a transactions-costs perspective. This allows us to define three distinct types of industrial clusters which exist in all of the research into industrial location theory, and these three types of industrial clusters are defined according to the nature of firms in the clusters, and the nature of their relations and transactions within the cluster (Gordon and McCann, 2000; McCann and Sheppard, 2003). These three distinct types of industrial clusters are the *pure agglomeration,* the *industrial complex*, and the *social network*. The key feature which distinguishes each of these different ideal types of spatial industrial cluster, is the nature of the relations between the firms within the cluster. The characteristics of each of the cluster types are listed in Table 7.1, and as we see, the three ideal types of clusters are all quite different.

In the model of *pure agglomeration*, inter-firm relations are inherently transient. Firms are essentially monopolistically atomistic, in the sense of having almost no market power, and they will continuously change their relations with other firms and customers in response to market arbitrage opportunities, thereby leading to intense local competition. As such, there is no loyalty between firms, nor are any particular relations long-term. The external benefits of clustering accrue to all local firms simply by reason of their local presence. The cost of membership of this cluster is simply the local real estate market rent. There are no free riders, access to the cluster is open, and consequently it is the growth in the local real estate rents which is the indicator of the cluster's performance. This idealised type is best represented by the Marshall (1890) model of agglomeration, and is the notion of clustering underlying models of new economic geography (Krugman, 1991a,b; Fujita et al., 1999). The notion of space in these models is essentially urban space in that this type of clustering only exists within individual cities.

Table 7.1 Industrial clusters: A transaction costs perspective

Characteristics	Pure Agglomeration	Industrial Complex	Social Network
firm size	atomistic	some firms are large	variable
characteristics of relations	non-identifiable fragmented unstable	identifiable stable trading	trust loyalty joint lobbying joint ventures non-opportunistic
membership	open	closed	partially open
access to cluster	rental payments location necessary	internal investment location necessary	history experience location necessary but not sufficient
space outcomes	rent appreciation	no effect on rents	partial rental capitalisation
notion of space	urban	local but not urban	local but not urban
example of cluster	competitive urban economy	steel or chemicals production complex	new industrial areas
analytical approaches	models of pure agglomeration	location-production theory input-output analysis	social network theory (Granovetter)

The *industrial complex* is characterised primarily by long-term stable and predictable relations between the firms in the cluster. This type of cluster is most commonly observed in industries such a steel and chemicals, and is the type of spatial cluster typically discussed by classical (Weber, 1909) and neo-classical (Moses 1958) location-production models, representing a fusion of locational analysis with input-output analysis (Isard and Kuenne, 1953). Component firms within the spatial grouping each undertake significant long term investments, particularly in terms of physical capital and local real estate, in order to become part of the grouping. Access to the group is therefore severely restricted both by high entry and exit costs, and the rationale for spatial clustering in these types of industries is that proximity is required primarily in order to minimise inter-firm transport transactions costs. Rental appreciation is not a feature of the cluster, because the land which has already been purchased by the firms is not for sale. The notion of space in the industrial complex is local, but not necessarily urban, in that these types of complexes can exist either within or outside of an individual city. This complex model is actually the single explicitly spatial element in the transactions costs approach of Williamson (1975), where the focus is on the types of flow-process scale economies which firms can realise by being part of vertically-integrated production complexes.

The third type of spatial industrial cluster is the *social network* model, although this has become extremely popular in research, it is not directly related to the previous research traditions of location theory. This cluster type is associated primarily with the work of Granovetter (1973), and is a response to the hierarchies model of Williamson (1975). The social network model argues that mutual trust relations between key decision making agents in different organisations may be at least as important as decision-making hierarchies within individual organisations. These trust relations will be manifested by a variety of features, such as joint lobbying, joint ventures, informal alliances, and reciprocal arrangements regarding trading relationships. However, the key feature of such trust relations is an absence of opportunism, in that individual firms will not fear reprisals after any reorganisation of inter-firm relations. Inter-firm cooperative relations may therefore differ significantly from the organisational boundaries associated with individual firms, and these relations may be continually reconstituted. All of these behavioural features rely on a common culture of mutual trust, the development of which depends largely on a shared history and experience of the decision-making agents. This social network model is essentially aspatial, but from the point of view of geography, it can be argued that spatial proximity will tend to foster such trust relations, thereby leading to a local business environment of confidence, risk-taking and cooperation. Spatial proximity is necessary but not sufficient to acquire access to the network. As such, membership of the network is only partially open, in that local rental payments will not guarantee access, although they will improve the chances of access. The geographical manifestation of the social network is the so-called 'new industrial areas' model (Scott, 1988), which has been used to describe the characteristics and performance of areas such as Silicon Valley and the Emilia-Romagna region of Italy. In this model space is once again local, but not necessarily urban.

Future Directions

In reality, all spatial clusters will contain characteristics of one or more of the ideal types described above, although one type will tend to be dominant in each observed cluster. Therefore, in order to understand the advantages to the firm of being located in any particular cluster, it is first necessary to determine which of these ideal cluster types most accurately reflects the overall characteristics and behaviour of the firms in the cluster. However, simply observing the clustering of economic activity is not sufficient evidence for the existence of a cluster, if we are considering a cluster in terms of local knowledge-related or transactions-related agglomeration effects and there are two reasons for this. One reason is that the distribution of activities across space is random (Ellison and Glaeser, 1997) and the result of this randomness is that some activities will appear clustered while other activities will appear dispersed, even though there are no differences in the interactions between firms. Observations of spatial industrial concentration are not necessarily evidence of Porter-type clusters. Secondly, localised clustering may simply be a rational response to the spatial organisation of industrial hierarchies, without any recourse to local interactions between the apparently-clustered firms (McCann, 1995). Therefore, understanding the mechanics of a cluster requires a more detailed analysis.

The common central element in each of these cluster types is that knowledge is localised, while the differences between the cluster types relate to how that knowledge is locally transmitted and appropriated and the spatial extent over which this operates. In the agglomeration model knowledge flows as tacit informal spillovers within an explicitly urban setting; in the industrial complex knowledge is a asset which is transferred via formal long-term contracts within a local regional setting; in the social network model, knowledge is transmitted via informal social network ties over a local regional spatial scale. In the simple Porter (1990) model, the critical geographical dimension over which any such (information) competitive advantage is assumed to operate is never specified. This is problematic, because there is much empirical evidence to suggest that information spillovers in the some dynamic sectors extend well beyond the dimensions of the individual metropolitan areas, and may well extend beyond a state, regional or even national level (Iammarino and McCann, 2006; McCann, 2007). Therefore, how important it is for a particular type of firm to be located either within, or immediately adjacent to, a particular type of industrial cluster or metropolitan area is entirely unclear. It will depend on a careful evaluation of the knowledge and transactions-costs relations within the cluster and how these relate to the locational and organisational optimisation problems faced by the firm. While the vast majority of papers on the subject of clustering have discussed the advantages of clustering, very few papers have discussed the disadvantages of clustering. Where the disadvantages of clustering are discussed it is almost always in the context of increasing local land costs, labour costs or congestion. As such, these are all pecuniary effects. Almost nowhere is the issue of knowledge costs discussed in relation to clustering, except in a very few instances (Iammarino and McCann, 2006). The issues here concerns the problems of unintended outward knowledge spillovers, first discussed by Grindley and Teece (1997) in a non-spatial context, although this argument translates directly to problems of industrial clustering (Iammarino and McCann, 2006). The central problem is that geographical clustering increases the likelihood of unintended outward knowledge spillovers occurring. As such, the firm has to try to balance the benefits of unintended inward and outward knowledge spillovers associated with industrial clustering. The seriousness of the effects of unintended outward knowledge spillovers on the firm's proprietary knowledge and profitability will determine, and also be determined by, the organisational structure of the firm and its industry. Therefore, the particular means by which the firm will attempt to avoid such spillovers will underpin the extent to which it engages in long-term formal contracts governing all aspects of knowledge exchanges. This will also determine which type of industrial cluster is attractive to the firm. However, once this has been identified, it is still necessary to decide whether locating in such a cluster, rather than locating at any other clustered or non-clustered location, is optimal. Clues as to how this might be analysed come from the various strands of location theory discussed above.

In terms of our various strands location theory discussed in the earlier sections of this chapter, it is clear that the urban economics model of land use, the models of spatial competition, and new economic geography models all assume and reflect the pure agglomeration type of cluster. Meanwhile, both the location-production models from the regional science tradition and also the multiplant and multinational models location from the international business and economic geography literatures generally assume and reflect the industrial complex, because they assume relatively stable input-output linkages, which can be either internal to, or external to, individual corporate and organisational hierarchies (McCann and Mudambi, 2004, 2005).

On the other hand, as mentioned above, the social network model does not relate directly to any of the previous strands of location theory, and this is largely because it is not based on any economic model or framework. Rather, the social network theories and their application to 'industrial districts' within economic geography have emerged from sociological responses to the original insights regarding industrial clustering of Marshall (1890). These theoretical approaches have become very popular in recent years in both economic geography research and also management research on location, and there are good reasons for this. In particular, as mentioned at the beginning of this chapter, the acquisition and development of knowledge is becoming ever more crucial as a determinant of location behaviour, and models which allow for knowledge flows whose network patterns differ from organisation structures provide possibilities for explaining many of the new organisation forms which are starting to emerge. In particular, over the last two decades there have been fundamental changes which have taken place in modern multiplant organisational structures and strategic behaviour, and these organisational changes have changed the ways in which multiplant firms operate geographically. Of particular importance here are the changes in the ways in which information technology allows such firms to develop, employ and communicate knowledge and information at both a local and global scale simultaneously. The earlier generations of economic geography approaches had adapted fairly static and stylised geographical versions of the product cycle model to sub-national regional or international space. However, evidence from social network models suggested that these models were increasingly out of step with many of the newly-emerging forms of spatial and organisational behaviour. Finding ways of integrating these social network notions of knowledge spillovers within an optimisation setting reminiscent of the regional science and urban economics models, and which also allows for organisational and transactions-costs issues raised by the analysis of multiplant firm structures, is now the major theoretical challenge for the coming decades. Three recent papers (Storper and Venables, 2004; Iammarino and McCann, 2006; McCann 2007) have attempted to develop models in this spirit. Two of these papers (Storper and Venables, 2004; McCann, 2007) adopt optimisation approaches and one of these papers (Iammarino and McCann, 2006) extends the clusters taxonomy discussed above to the issues of knowledge and innovation. Each of these papers suggests that more cohesive integration between the different location theory approaches is indeed possible, although much remains to be done.

References

Aghion, P. and Tirole, J. (1997), "Formal and Real Authority in Organizations", *Journal of Political Economy*, 105, 1–29.

Alonso, W. (1964), *Location and Land Use*, Harvard University Press, Cambridge, Mass.

Audrestch, D. and Feldman, M.P. (1996), "R&D Spillovers and the geography of innovation and production", *American Economic Review*, 86.3, 630–40.

Buckley, P.J. and Casson, M.C. (1976), *The Future of Multinational Enterprise*, London: Macmillan.

Caves, R.E. (1982), *Multinational Enterprise and Economic Analysis*, Cambridge, Cambridge University Press.

Cohen, B.J. (1998), *The Geography of Money*, Cornell University Press, Ithaca, NY.

Coleman, W.D. (1996), *Financial Services, Globalization and Domestic Policy Change*, Macmillan, Basingstoke.

d'Aspremont, C., Gabszewicz, J.J., and Thisse, J.F. (1979), "On Hotelling's Stability in Competition", *Econometrica*, 47.5, 1145–50.

Dunning, J.H. (1977), "Trade, location of economic activity and the multinational enterprise: A search for an eclectic approach", in Ohlin, B., Hesselborn, P.O., and Wijkman, P.M. (eds), *The International Allocation of Economic Activity*, Macmillan, London.

Ellison, G. and Glaeser, E.L. (1997), "Geographic Concentration in US Manufacturing Industries: A Dartboard Approach", *Journal of Political Economy*, 105, 889–927.

Ethier, W. and Markusen, J.R. (1996), "Multinational Firms, Technology Diffusion and Trade", *Journal of International Economics*, 41, 1–28.

Eswaran, M., Kanemoto, Y., and Ryan, D., (1981), "A Dual Approach to the Location Decision of the Firm", *Journal of Regional Science*, 21.4, 469–89.

Fujita, M., Krugman, P., and Venables, A.J., (1999), *The Spatial Economy*, MIT Press, Cambridge Mass.

Gordon, I.R., and McCann, P. (2000), "Industrial Clusters: Complexes, Agglomeration and/or Social Networks?", *Urban Studies*, 37.3, 513–32.

Granovetter, M. (1973), "The strength of weak ties", *American Journal of Sociology*, 78, 1360–80.

Grindley, P.C. and Teece, D.J. (1997), "Managing Intellectual Capital: Licensing and Cross-Licensing in Semiconductors and Electronics". *California Management Review*, 39.2, 8–41.

Grossman, G.M. and Hart, O. (1986), "Costs and Benefits of Ownership: A Theory of Vertical and Lateral Integration", *Journal of Political Economy*, 94, 691–719.

Hayter, R. (1997), *The Dynamics of Industrial Location: The Factory, The Firm and the Production System*, John Wiley and Sons, Chichester.

Healey, M. and Watts, H.D. (1987), "The Multiplant Enterprise", in Lever, W.F. (ed.), *Industrial Change in the United Kingdom*, Longman, Harlow.

Helpman, E. and Krugman, P.R. (1985), *Market Structure and Foreign Trade*, Cambridge MA, MIT Press.

Helpman, E. and Grossman, G.E. (2002), "Integration versus Outsourcing in Industry Equilibrium", *Quarterly Journal of Economics*, 117, 85–120.

Hood, N. and Young, S. (1979), *The Economics of Multinational Enterprise*, Longman, London.

Horstmann, I.J. and Markusen, J.R. (1987), "Strategic Investments and the Development of Multinationals", *International Economic Review*, 28, 109–121.

Horstmann, I.J. and Markusen, J.R. (1992), "Endogenous Market Structure in International Trade (natura facit saltum)", *Journal of International Economics*, 32, 109–129.

Hotelling, H. (1929), "Stability in Competition", *Economic Journal*, 39, 41–57.

Iammarino, S. and McCann, P. (2006), "The Structure and Evolution of Industrial Clusters: Transactions, Technology and Knowledge Spillovers", *Research Policy*, 35, 1018–1036.

Isard, W. and Kuenne, R.E. (1953), "The Impact of steel upon the greater New York–Philadelphia industrial region", *Review of Economics and Statistics*, 35, 289–301.

Johanson, J. and Vahlne, J. (1977), "The Internationalization Process of the Firm: A Model of Knowledge Development and Increasing Foreign Market Commitments", *Journal of International Business Studies*, 7, 22–32.

Krugman, P.R. (1990), *Rethinking International Trade*, MIT Press, Cambridge MA.

Krugman, P. (1991a), *Geography and Trade*, MIT Press, Cambridge, MA.

Krugman, P. (1991b), "Increasing Returns and Economic Geography", *Journal of Political Economy*, 99, 483–9.

Leyshon, A. and Thrift, N. (1997), *Money Space*, Routledge, London.

Markusen, J. (1984), "Multinationals, Multi-Plant Economies, and the Gains from Trade", *Journal of International Economics*, 11, 531–6.

Markusen, A. (1985), *Profit Cycles, Oligopoly and Regional Development*, MIT Press, Cambridge, Mass.

Markusen, J. (2002), *Multinational Firms and the Theory of International Trade*, Cambridge MA, MIT Press.

Markusen, J.R. and Venables, A.J. (2000), "The Theory of Endowment, Intra-Industry and Multinational Trade", *Journal of International Economics*, 52, 209–235.

Marshall, A. (1890), *Principles of Economics*, Macmillan, London.

McCann, P. (1993), "The Logistics-Costs Location-Production Problem", *Journal of Regional Science*, 33.4, 503–516.

McCann, P. (1998), *The Economics of Industrial Location: A Logistics-Costs Approach*, Springer, Heidelberg.

McCann, P. (1995), "Rethinking the Economics of Location and Agglomeration", *Urban Studies*, 32.3, 563–77.

McCann, P. (1999), "A Note on the Meaning of Neo-Classical Location Theory and its Usefulness as a Basis of Applied Research", *Papers in Regional Science*, 78.3, 323–31.

McCann, P. (2007), "Sketching out a Model of Innovation, Face-to-Face Interaction and Economic Geography", *Spatial Economic Analysis*, 2.2, 117–34.

McCann, P. and Mudambi, R. (2004), "The Location Decision of the Multinational Enterprise: Some Theoretical and Empirical Issues", *Growth and Change*, 35.4, 491–524.

McCann, P. and Mudambi, R. (2005), "Analytical Differences in the Economics of Geography: The Case of the Multinational Firm", *Environment and Planning A*, 37.10, 1857–76.

McCann, P. and Sheppard, S.C. (2003), "The Rise, fall and Rise Again of Industrial Location Theory", *Regional Studies*, 37, 6–7, 649–63.

Miller, S.M. and Jensen, O.W. (1978), "Location and the Theory of Production", *Regional Science and Urban Economics*, 8, 117–28.

Mills, E.S. (1970), *Urban Economics*, Scott, Foresman and Co., Glenview, Illinois.

Moses, L. (1958), "Location and the Theory of Production", *Quarterly Journal of Economics*, 78, 259–72.

Mudambi, R. and Mudambi, S.M. (2002), "Diversification and Market Entry Choices in the Context of Foreign Direct Investment", *International Business Review*, 11.1, 35–55.

Porter, M.E. (1985), *Competitive Advantage,* The Free Press, New York.

Porter, M.E. (1990), *The Competitive Advantage of Nations*. New York: The Free Press.

Porter, M.E. (1998a), "Clusters and the New Economics of Competition", *Harvard Business Review*, 76.6, 77–90.

Porter, M.E. (1998b), "Competing Across Locations" in *On Competition*, Harvard Business School Press, Cambridge Mass.

Revelle, C. (1987), "Urban Public Facility Location", in *Handbook of Urban and Regional Economics, Vol. 2: Urban Economics*, North Holland, Amsterdam.

Scott, A.J. (1988), *New Industrial Spaces*, Pion, London.

Stelder, D. (2002), "Geographical Grids in New Economic Geography Models", in McCann, P. (ed.), *Industrial Location Economics*, Edward Elgar, Cheltenham.

Storper, M. and Venables, A.J. (2004), "Buzz: Face-to-Face Contact and the Urban Economy", *Journal of Economic Geography*, 4, 351–70.

Tirole, J. (1988), *The Theory of Industrial Organization*, Cambridge MA, MIT Press.

Vernon, R. (1960), *Metropolis 1985*, Harvard University Press, Cambridge Mass.

Vernon, R. (1966), "International Investment and International Trade in the Product Cycle". *Quarterly Journal of Economics*, 80, 190–207.

von Thunen, J.H. (1826), *Der Isolierte Staat in Beziehung auf Landtschaft und Nationalokonomie*, Hamburg, translated by Wartenberg, C.M. (1966), *von Thunen's Isolated State*, Pergamon Press, Oxford.
Weber, A. (1909), *Uber den Standort der Industrien*, translated by Friedrich, C.J. (1929), *Alfred Weber's Theory of the Location of Industries*, University of Chicago Press, Chicago.
Williamson, O.E. (1975), *Markets and Hierarchies*, Free Press, New York.

Chapter 8
The Theory Behind Business Clusters

Martin Perry

Introduction

The theory behind clusters is potentially vast. The term cluster has been applied to geographical scales ranging from part of a single urban economy to a group of neighbouring economies. The 'new economic geography', for example, relates clustering to the tendency for economic activity to concentrate in extensive metropolitan regions rather than to diffuse evenly across national economies (see Brakman et al., 2001). 'Old' economic geographers, on the other hand, are most likely to reserve the term for pockets of economic specialisation within a city or shared among neighbouring settlements (see May et al., 2001). In the context of a book that is concerned with the policy applications of theory, this chapter is most aligned with the old geography interpretation of a business cluster. While new economic geography has played a significant role in convincing policy makers that enterprise policy should include a spatial dimension, new economic geographers recognise that their methods are still too abstract to yield policy guidance. As one prominent economic geographer has put it, this branch of economics is still in the Wright Brothers' phase of learning to fly (Fujita cited in Stelder, 2002). In contrast, the old economic geography conception of clusters has been extensively promoted and highly influential within the field of local economic policy. Indeed, it can be claimed that encouraging business clusters has been one of the biggest ideas in local economic development of the last few decades (Martin and Sunley, 2003). This is seen the efforts of public agencies to increase awareness of the existence of business clusters (Department of Trade and Industry, 2001) and in many industry-based projects to promote membership-based cluster groups (Sölvell et al., 2003).

The popularity of clusters among local economic policy makers can be explained in two ways. For people in the local development business, enterprise clusters can appear to be something under their influence (Benneworth, 2002; Raines, 2002; Pinch et al., 2003; Rosenfeld, 2005). They are associated with fostering local economic communities and leveraging development by building on local institutions and capabilities. A second reason is the appeal of the case that underlines business cluster promotion. Cluster advocates see an optimal balance of competitive pressures and cooperative opportunities being created as business communities agglomerate with a consequent substantial gain in competitive advantage (Porter, 2000). In contrast to such optimism, there is evidence that clusters have no necessary impact on business performance (Malmberg et al.,

2000; Beaudry and Breschi, 2003; Braunerhjelm and Johansson, 2003; Cingano, 2003) or that they have significance for independent firms only (Beardsell and Henderson, 1999) or that they encourage enterprise start up but not survival (Sorenson and Audia, 2000; Stuart and Sorenson, 2003). Equally, it is apparent that many of the public agency efforts to enhance business and local economic growth through clusters have failed (Kotval and Mullin, 1998; Schmitz, 1999; Huggins, 2000; Perry, 2004; Tambunan, 2005).

This chapter provides an overview of the theory that should be considered before encouraging the promotion of clusters and reflection on the contradictory claims being made about their significance. An appropriate starting point is to consider how industrial location trends may have influenced the formation of clusters. The discussion then shifts to the identification of enterprise clusters and the contrast between 'top down' and 'bottom up' approaches. The centrality of agglomeration theory in the explanation of cluster advantage can then be explained. Agglomeration economies offer a mechanism that may create business advantage but this depends on specific characteristics of the local economy affected. From this it is important to have some means of differentiating business clusters and appraising their prospective ability to sustain competitive advantage. Once this theory has been reflected upon, policy makers can be informed of the priority they should give to cluster promotion in their individual local economic strategies.

Industrial Location Trends

Two accounts of the major trend in industrial location and regional specialisation exist with sharply contrasting implications for cluster formation.

A long view of regional specialisation has been presented for the USA (Kim 1995). It finds a modest decline occurred from 1860 to 1890, then rose substantially and flattened out during the interwar years. Regional specialisation then fell substantially and continuously from the 1930s to 1987. The net outcome was that regions were less specialised at the end of the 20th century than they were in 1860. Alongside the increased diversity in regional economic structure, industries became more dispersed than originally. These trends were interpreted as showing that the geography of business activity is driven by patterns of resource usage and the pursuit of economies of scale. Typically resource availability has become less constraining on where industry locates, although it can still help explain the relative dispersion of individual industries. Average plant size (measured by employment) in most industries peaked in the 1930s or 1940s and subsequent falls have assisted the dispersion of activity.

From this long term perspective, any advantage of being located near to like firms appears to be a minor influence on the distribution of activity. If important industry knowledge 'spills over' from one firm to its neighbour, it might be expected the activities most dependent on knowledge would have a greater propensity to concentrate than less knowledge sensitive activities. Kim (1995) does not identify this impact. Over time, most industries have seen an increase in their proportion of non production workers and an increase in research and development expenditure. This has not been associated with more spatial concentration or regional specialisation. Looking at contemporary industry, activity regarded as high tech tends to be more dispersed than low tech activity.

The distribution of structural materials used in manufacturing story illustrates how industrial location choices have expanded. Initially wood was the main structural material used by industry and this was available throughout the USA. As markets expanded and structural materials diversified to iron and steel, transport cost and logistics encouraged use close to the source of these manufactured inputs. As a consequence, industry activity tended to concentrate and regional specialisation tended to increase. More recently, many substitutes for wood and steel have been developed including light metals, alloys, plastics, plywood and particle board. Diversification of the sources of supply and reduced transport costs allowed industry to disperse and regional specialisation tended to decline as a result of this.

A two stage model of cluster development proposed by Schmitz (1995) and Schmitz and Nadvi (1999) can be applied to reconcile this long view of industrial location with some contemporary occurrences of business clustering. In the Schmitz model, clusters commence on the basis of unplanned advantages that are available to any business locating in the cluster. Responding to the resource constraints at the outset of industrialisation, enabling smaller amounts of investment than where production commences in isolation or among dissimilar activities is the key unplanned advantage obtained (Schmitz 1995). For example, producers can concentrate on a specific task and leave others to complete the process. Specialised workshops to repair and upgrade equipment further reduce the barriers to entry. In effect:

> …the enterprise of one creates a foothold for the other, that ladders are constructed which enable small enterprise to climb and grow. It is a process in which enterprises create for each other – often unwillingly, sometimes intentionally – possibilities for accumulating capital and skill. (Schmitz and Nadvi, 1999: 1506)

Being unplanned, clusters are easy to form but while there is equality of access to cluster benefits they are unlikely to stimulate significant business growth (Schmitz and Nadvi, 1999). Open access implies that no business can sustain an advantage over any other and the cluster as a whole has limited capacity to withstand competitive shocks. The main impact of stage one clustering is to reduce the scale of investment required to gain entry to the cluster.

A second stage of cluster development is needed to realise significant outcomes for business growth. In the second stage, dominant enterprises emerge with greater entrepreneurial capacity and ambition than 'ordinary' cluster firms (Schmitz, 1995). Dominant enterprises make deliberate decisions about the use of cluster resources and selectively work with other cluster firms. According to these decisions, differences emerge between enterprises with respect to their sise, resources, markets and pursuit of growth. Business heterogeneity has the potential to change the character of the cluster. Leading enterprises may, for example, start to build business networks beyond the cluster and lessen the opportunities for the original cluster enterprises left outside these networks.

This two stage model was developed from the evaluation of clusters in developing countries but it has also been applied to Italy's industrial districts (Rabellotti and Schmitz, 1999). These districts, which are widely seen as the exemplars of business clustering, emerged during the 1950s with a new wave of industrialisation based on small scale, family enterprise (Bamford, 1987). With market expanding rapidly for the products specialised in, firms could operate without entering rigid relations with other enterprises and on the basis of opportunistic marketing strategies (Nuti and Cainelli, 1996). Post 1980, the districts entered a second stage of development as market growth slowed and informal ways of working were replaced by more selective and structured inter-firm relationships (Brusco et al., 1996; Cossentino et al., 1996). Typical outcomes for individual districts included the internationalisation of leading cluster enterprises, more reliance on non cluster businesses and the increased concentration of production within fewer, larger enterprises compared with the earlier phases the district's development. The 'classical' district comprising many independent small enterprises and supporting agencies is now a minority among the local economies still recognised as industrial district (Paniccia, 2002). Consistent with Kim's long view, therefore, there is a parallel in the industrial geography of the 'third Italy'.

The alternative pro cluster view of industrial location trends tends to rely on the flexible specialisation thesis (Scott, 2006). According to this thesis, economic activity has entered a period of increased market uncertainty and high rates of technological change. This environment reduces the advantages of internal economies of scale and scope and favours business strategies based on horizontal and vertical disintegration. Consequently, enterprises are expected to replace their ownership of production capacity with a network of linkages to suppliers, supporting services and business partners as well as developing close relations with their customers. It is not simply a case of using subcontractors. External relationships must be configured to cope with market instability, meet customer expectations for distinctive products and services and be adaptable to shifts in technology. This means cooperative partnerships rather than the 'arms length' relationships that characterised outsourcing in the past.

In turn, spatial agglomeration is encouraged as it is easier to form and maintain cooperative linkages with enterprises that are geographically as well as functionally close to your own (see Scott, 1988; Scott and Storper, 1992). The specialisation of local economies is a further outcome as it makes economic sense for activities that do not generate mutual linkages to avoid each other (Henderson, 1974; 1988). So, for example, if film production and automobile assembly generate few mutual external linkages they should locate in different places. This way they avoid generating congestion and high land rents for each other.

A growth in outsourcing has been viewed as the stimulus to a new industrial geography. Even where the outsourcing of comparatively low value services is involved, the idea of supply-chain partnering has become influential. The essential proposition is that developing close, long term working relationships with a limited number of suppliers reduces the risks associated with 'arm's length' contracting. It relies on both parties expecting a long-term relationship, developing complementary capabilities, sharing information and engaging in more joint planning than was customary. The commitment to a long term relationship is the essential prerequisite. Cooperation is based on the expectation of reciprocal actions; for example, a supplier's willingness to share information on the true costs of production or invest in dedicated production capacity is based on the expectation that this will be rewarded with future work orders. In turn, for the purchaser to make a long term commitment, it implies that their outsourcing is concentrated with a comparatively small number of suppliers.

The flexible specialisation thesis has been influential but there are detractors who see it as too sweeping and simplistic (Harrison, 1992; Martin and Sunley, 1996). It tends to imply a return to small scale enterprise whereas most industries are now controlled by large enterprises with an increasingly global reach (Dicken, 1998; Humphrey and Schmitz, 2002). Against that reality, the supply-chain partnership model is only one way that buyer-supplier relations may have been changing. Alongside interest in the nature of the relationship with individual suppliers, buyers have frequently given priority to standardising the inputs that they buy (Phelps, 1993; Perry, 1999). This strategy widens the pool of suppliers that can be selected from and reduces the concern a buyer may have about their proprietary technology diffusing to competitors via their outsourcing partners. Standardisation counteracts the influence of supply partnering as it facilitates 'off the peg' sourcing rather than the need to rely on customised supply (Perry and Tan, 2000: 46). This is a preferable outcome for many organisations as it reduces the risk of buyers have an obligation to support suppliers during market downturns (Miles and Snow, 1992). Similar evaluation exists about the recommendation for business to concentrate on their 'core competencies' (Hamel and Prahalad, 1994). As well as this focus businesses need to retain capacity for frequent renewal of their core competencies (Christensen, 1997). This means maintaining a broad conception of the unique expertise held otherwise the ability to test and protect new innovations is reduced (Miles and Snow, 1992). In practice, many organisations have nominated general skills such as technology or their market position ('being number one or two in the industry') as their core competency (Micklethwait and Wooldridge, 1997). At this level, clear competence-based rationalisation of activity between internal and external production tends to be limited to services such as property management, transportation, selected human resource functions, IT management and standardised component manufacture.

Counting Clusters

Acceptance of the long view of industrial location does not immediately reduce the significance of business clusters. The long view is a challenge to the importance of business clustering if it is thought to imply the development of specialised local economies. Some cluster advocacy is not predicated on this outcome but on a more general interest in recognising the interdependence of business activity. The two perspectives can result in opposing assessments of the significance of enterprise clustering (Perry, 2005). A failure to distinguish between them has caused much confusion and it is, therefore, important to be clear whether a 'top down' or 'bottom up' evaluation of clusters is taking place.

The top down or 'mode of inquiry perspective' makes use of input-output data to trace the linkages between industries (Feser and Bergman, 2000; Feser and Luger, 2003). By identifying groups of industries with high amounts of inter industry trade, it is possible to divide an economy into groupings of inter-connected activity. On this basis using 1992 data, the manufacturing sector in the USA has been reduced to 23 'clusters' (Feser and Bergman, 2000). These clusters comprise various major final market producing sectors with their key first, second and third tier supplier sectors. Close to 90 per cent of manufacturing was attached to the 23 national clusters. They vary in composition from 116 separate industries (defined at the 3 or 4 digit SIC level) in the case of metalworking to 4 in the case of tobacco. The researchers present these national clusters as templates that may be compared with the industry profiles of regions or local economies. Such comparison reveals the relative strengths of sub national economies as well as the gaps in their industry structure in terms of missing cluster components.

Guidance from national templates is judged better than investigating actual input–output linkages in the locality of interest. Local data reveal existing connections. They do not suggest gaps in supplier chains that may point to development opportunities. Applied to North Carolina, industries that form part of the vehicle manufacturing template cluster are discovered to account for 15 percent of the state's employment. As the state did not currently have a vehicle assembly industry, Feser and Bergman (2000) argue that the presence of potentially linked activity reveals gaps in the existing range of activity compared with the national template. These gaps might represent specialisations to be filled to help attract final assembly as well, although fuller investigation is needed to establish this. In this way, the top down approach provides a tool for cluster promotion by local economic policy makers.

The bottom up approach starts with the assumption that business clusters are a locality with an unusual concentration of a particular type of economic activity that is not explained simply by the presence of a single, large establishment. Among other applications, this perspective has influenced the identification of Italy's industrial districts (Sforzi, 1990; Burroni and Trigilia, 2001; Paniccia, 2002). The national statistics agency – *Istituto Nazionale di Statistica* (ISTAT) – uses two main indicators to count an industrial district. First, the locality (identified by travel to work area boundaries) must have an above national average employment dependency on manufacturing. Second, geographically concentrated sectors must be comprised of an above average proportion of small and medium sised enterprises (defined as firms with fewer than 250 employees). These criteria capture what some see as the minimum conditions for a business cluster: geographical concentration of an industry in a local economy based on the presence of a large number of independent enterprises.

Compared with the top down approach, the bottom up perspective is more selective as specified criteria must be met to count as a cluster. Indeed when the Italian criteria are applied to other economies the incidence of clusters is low. In the case of the UK, for example, it was necessary to drop the requirement for an industry to be disproportionately present in a travel to work area and reduce the industry participation to 20 separate establishments before large numbers of 'clusters' were identified (Crouch and Farell, 2001). When a bottom up approach was applied in Germany, no clusters were identified in one study (Glassmann and Voelzkow, 2001). The German researchers concluded that resources supporting competitive advantage were distributed evenly across the economy so that no one location offered a particular location inducement over another. In contrast, the top down approach can attach the label cluster to any geographical scale, from a single city to a group of neighbouring countries as ultimately all economic activity is inter connected to some degree (see Porter, 2000; 2003). For those who start from the belief that a cluster is a unique geographical phenomenon based on local specialisation, the interdependence perspectives make clusters an infinitely elastic concept and a reason for doubting the claimed importance of business clusters (Martin and Sunley, 2003).

Agglomeration Economies

The distinction between the top down and bottom up approaches reduces when agglomeration economies are brought into the equation. Agglomeration economies are the cost savings to a firm that result from the concentration of production at a given location (Parr, 2002). Agglomeration economies are ultimately what gives rise to the advantages obtained by a business cluster and thus are at the heart of most accounts of clustering whatever the starting point for analysis. Nonetheless, as with other aspects of cluster theory there is much debate the precise role played by agglomeration. To understand the sources of controversy it is first important to recognise that agglomeration benefits may accrue to firms, industries or cities (Ohlin, 1933; Hoover, 1937; 1948; Parr, 2002).

1. *Internal scale economies*: these arise from the expansion of a single establishment. In detail, they may be of three types: (i) economies of horizontal integration (the form usually thought of and arising from the fall in the unit cost of production with increased output); (ii) economies of lateral integration (or internal economies of scope and occurring when a firm's joint output of two or more products involves less cost than the

same product range produced by single-product firms); (iii) economies of vertical integration (or internal economies of complexity and obtained by integrating steps in the production chain in a single operation). The ability to purchase in bulk, use specialised equipment, optimise the deployment of worker skills and equipment are all potential sources of internal economies. In many cases, organisations can realise these economies without consolidating activities on a single location (in which case, these agglomeration advantages do not lead to geographical agglomeration). Recent literature on the agglomeration advantages of business clusters, at least that produced by non economists, has tended to have a clear bias against recognising the advantages of increased firm size because it challenges the importance of clustering. For individual firms, any additional advantage from consolidation at a single location will be balanced by the loss of flexibility associated with multi-site operations.

2. *Localisation economies*: these refer to the cost savings that accrue to a group of firms within the same or related industry, located in the same place. Strictly, localisation advantages are those external economies that are immobile and are a function of the scale of the industry at a particular location (Parr, 2002: 719). The first identification of localisation advantage is generally accredited to Marshall (1923; 1927). Reduced information transaction costs are the key feature of Marshall's economies (McCann, 2001: 57). If firms are located together, it suggests that there is relatively easy access to representatives of other firms of interest. In contemporary terms, this is equated with the sharing of tacit knowledge between organisations. These *information spillovers* may be realised through the ease of arranging formal, face-to-face meetings or through informal contact. The incentive for *specialist suppliers* to join the cluster is a separate benefit. Equivalent specialist support may take longer to emerge for a dispersed industry than a concentrated one, partly due to the effort in ascertaining demand or identifying the market opportunity. Marshall's classification included *non traded local inputs* as a further advantage, such as where a group of clustered firms invested in some form of testing or certifying agency for their own, exclusive joint use. Labour cost savings from the development of a *local skilled-labour pool* are a further potential economy. Greater use of the external labour market may be possible than for isolated employers. For example, it may be easier to lay off workers when business is slack: employees move willingly to better performing employers in the cluster and employers have the assurance that skilled workers will remain in the locality. As well, on-the-job experience gained across several employers may reduce an employer's need to invest in training. Collectively, Marshall's economies are frequently identified as external economies because they are beyond the control of individual firms. Some degree of external economy is obtained from the scale of an industry to which an enterprise belongs, but their full realisation is generally thought to arise where the industry or a significant part of it is spatially concentrated.

3. *Urbanisation economies*: these economies arise where benefits are external to both individual establishments and the industry, being sometimes referred to as external economies of scope. Sharing of infrastructure and services among diverse firms are examples. Their magnitude is a function of the size and diversity of an urban concentration. Traditionally, it has been thought that small and new firms have obtained most benefit from urbanisation economies, as with the so-called incubator hypothesis (Vernon and Hoover, 1959), and evidence from the computer industry suggests that this continues to be the case (Beardsell and Henderson, 1999). Activity-complex economies are a specific variety of urbanisation economy. Mutual proximity of the members of a production-chain sequence can save transport costs and the need for inventory as well as improve the efficiency of material flows between stages of production.

Based on this classification, claiming advantage for business clusters is also claiming that localisation economies offer superior benefits to business than internal or urbanisation economies. One study to attempt the measurement of their relative importance examined the impact on the export performance of manufacturing firms in Sweden (Malmberg et al., 2000). It estimated that the gain from localisation was from 40 to 80 times smaller than the gain from urbanisation and from 50 to 100 times smaller than the effect of internal economies depending on the sectors examined. The conclusion was, therefore, that the clustering of similar firms in individual labour markets had little impact on export activity.

Evidence about the relative impacts of localisation and urbanisation economies has been searched for by examining how the same activity performs when located in a city that is specialised in that activity compared with the performance of the same activity in a diversified economy (Duranton and Puga, 2002). This evidence has many problems associated with it but it generally points away from any universal advantage residing in favour of either localisation or urbanisation economies. One widely quoted study based on USA data found that employment growth in a city industry is positively correlated with the initial diversity of industry employment in the city but not with initial own-industry employment in the city (Glaeser et al., 1992). The study concluded that geographical specialisation reduces growth ('specialisation hurts') while city diversity helps employment growth. The example of the steel industry was used to illustrate the story favoured by this study (Glaeser et al., 1992: 1140). Steel declined in the United States through the impact of foreign competition and through displacement by new construction materials. The steel industry located away from the specialised centres of the industry adapted best to the changing business environment. This may reflect the greater opportunity for ideas to cross fertilise between industries in diversified cities than in specialised cities. The study does not confirm this but the story is consistent with ones told about heavy industry districts in other countries (Checkland, 1981; Grabher, 1993).

The distribution of innovative activity between specialised and diversified economies has been the subject of separate investigation reflecting the alleged importance of information spillovers among the other sources of localisation advantage. Using a database of new product introductions in the USA as an indicator of information spillovers, once again there is more support for the importance of urbanisation over localisation economies (Feldman and Audretsch, 1999). A slightly different picture emerged from a study of UK and Italian patent registration data. It is based on a database of 26,055 UK-based firms (6 per cent with patents) and 37,724 Italian-based firms (6.2 per cent with patents) that were allocated to broadly defined regions. The frequency of patent registrations among firms in the same industry was found to be affected by the regional concentration of same industry employment in firms with patent registrations but not by the concentration of same industry employment alone (Beaudry and Breschi, 2003). The researchers took this to show that clustering stimulates innovation only where the cluster is densely populated by innovative firms. No general advantage to belonging to a cluster is found. Indeed, a high concentration of own industry employment in non innovative enterprise appears to depress innovation.

Perhaps the most direct source of evidence about the operation of agglomeration economies has come from studies by Sorenson and Audia (2000) and Stuart and Sorenson (2003). These studies are based on data for the USA that indicates the location of each establishment relative to all other establishment in the same industry and other details of each establishment. These databases have been used to test how the performance of plants is affected by the density of same industry plants around its location. The database shows annual establishment openings and closures allowing changes in industry geography to be linked to the density of establishments. The findings are of particular interest in covering two contrasting industries: footwear and biotechnology.

In both industries, it is found that establishments located among a high density of own industry establishments are more likely to close down than are relatively isolated establishments. In contrast, openings are most likely to occur in locations with an existing high density of establishments. These observations are used to propose an interpretation of agglomeration that views it as helpful for new entrants but as disadvantageous to incumbents. This interpretation is built upon three claims.

1. The current distribution of production determines the opportunity structure for new entrants. Dense clusters of like industry maximise the ability of individuals to accumulate the knowledge, social ties and confidence needed to form a new venture. Potential employees, investors, customers and collaborators assume greater risk in dealing with a new enterprise compared with an established enterprise with a known track record. Social capital helps would-be entrepreneurs overcome the advantage held by established organisations. It is built through personal relationships and tends to be concentrated among geographically localised contacts.

2. Organisations located among other industry affiliates face stronger competitive pressures than isolated organisations. The pressure is intensified by a tendency for the business strategies of clustered firms to converge. Increased similarity between enterprises is considered especially likely where there is a high level of labour migration between firms and where enterprises occupy structurally equivalent positions within buyer–supplier networks (meaning identical ties to identical actors).
3. The benefits to an individual enterprise of being in a cluster dissipate over time as managers' networks expand geographically. Market growth, participation in industry associations and industry-centred conferences facilitate the formation of ties among dispersed industry participants.

In brief, clusters arise as a consequence of the social structure of opportunity: agglomeration promotes new firm formation but detracts from the performance of established organisations. The test of this proposition is that high founding rates rather than low failure rates sustain clusters, which is found to be the case for the footwear and biotechnology industries.

The Context for Agglomeration Economies

Aggregate evidence indicating that agglomeration economies are of limited advantage does not mean that they may not be important in individual cases. It does mean that the particular context of a cluster needs to be examined and related to its capacity to gain from localisation economies. In this regard it has tended to be overlooked that Marshall's interest in agglomeration economies was stimulated by the need to explain how some activities survived in industrial districts during a time when most industry was dispersing across increasingly diversified urban economies. He judged that industrial districts associated with two types of goods had most chance of survival: goods in general use that were 'not very changeful in character' and goods that could be represented effectively in illustrated catalogues or samples distributed to wholesale and retail dealers (Marshall, 1923: 288). Market stability meant that there was 'no particular time at which strong incitement is offered to open up the industry elsewhere' (Marshall, 1923: 227). Even then Marshall thought that district survival relied on the attraction of 'new shrewd energy to supplement that of native origin' so as to avoid the risk of 'obstinacy and inertia' among established entrepreneurs (Marshall, 1923: 227). In modern day terms, following the interpretation of Pawson and Tilley (1997), it might be argued that Marshall had a realist assessment of cluster survival. Agglomeration advantages provided a mechanism to offset the disadvantages of small scale enterprise but they worked only under conditions of relative industrial stability and open business populations.

The dated nature of Marshall's conditions for agglomeration advantage may partly justify overlooking this aspect of his work. Less defensible has been the tendency to assume that widely experienced changes in markets and technological instability has caused a universal drift to flexibly specialised business populations. Around the industrial world, organisations may have faced similar changes in the economic, political and social environment in which they operate but this does not mean that business behaviour has coalesced around the globe (Whitley, 1999). Pressures for change include reducing trade barriers between countries, the internationalisation of economic activity, rapid technological change associated with the information revolution, the deregulation of markets, privatisation and the ending of state monopolies, broadening conceptions of organisational stakeholders, demographic transitions such as ageing populations and changes in consumer demand (Holman and Wood, 2003). These diverse pressures are experienced with varying degrees of intensity between countries, industries and businesses. Organisations are being pushed in various directions and only modestly toward increasing homogeneity in organisational practice (Djelic, 1998; Zeitlin and Herrigel, 2000). Moreover, common organisational responses are encouraged by social pressures to conform to prevailing business fads (Burke, 2002). The growth in mergers and acquisitions and the frequency of corporate downsizing and outsourcing does not necessarily reflect organisational strategies that are not later reversed by a change in fashion.

The semiconductor manufacturing equipment industry is a good example of how the advantages accruing to different location and industry structures continue to change (Chon, 1997). Originally close integration of the production of semiconductor manufacturing equipment with the manufacture of semiconductors was a source of strength to Japan's electronics sector. The direct transfer of knowledge about trends in the market for semiconductors helped equipment producers innovate more quickly than their competitors in the United States where equipment manufacturers were independent of users. The balance of competitive advantage changed when North American equipment manufactures reorganised through strategic alliances. Working in cooperation with competitors, high tech manufacturers combined resources, shared risks and learned to better link their knowledge of production processes with research and development. Firms in the United States became leading suppliers of equipment to Japan and in Japan ties between equipment users and suppliers have been cut. Today, equipment makers have shifted to prioritise economies of scale with the increase in development cost associated with the sophistication of production equipment now needed to manufacture small semiconductor devices.

Accepting that considerable diversity remains between industries and business environments within industries, more attention needs to be given to the contingencies affecting the significance of agglomeration advantages. A starting point for this is the distinction between physical and functional clustering, as explained by Oakey (1995) and Oakey et al. (2001). Physical clustering exists where businesses locate in proximity to each other without any functional linkages between them and without deriving any special benefit from their location. Functional clustering arises where firms gain some benefit from being close to each other and these benefits explain why the co-location occurs. Application of the distinction has highlighted some of the reasons firms have for rejecting localised cooperation giving some guidance to the circumstances where clustering may bring advantage. For example, a case study of the opto-electronics or photonics industry (based on computer, laser and optic fibre technologies) involving interviews with company representatives in three of the four countries where activity is clustered (Germany, Japan, UK and USA) identified five reasons why companies might eschew local relationships (Hendry et al., 1999; 2000).

- *Strong internal labour markets*: partly as there is a reliance on developing skills through in-house experience there is little mobility of scientists and engineers between work places.
- *Market diversification*: technological breakthroughs require firms to seek out collaborations wherever the relevant expertise is located rather sticking with their original partners.
- *Complex firms*: even relatively small firms in a high tech industry engage in merger and acquisition activity, partly as it is necessary to assemble a range of expertise to develop a complete product or service.
- *Hub and spoke networks*: business networks are largely controlled by the activities of large or otherwise powerful firms rather than through the collective action of small firms.
- *Spin offs merely indicate inertia*: new firms frequently set up close to their former employer but this does not mean that functional linkages to the parent organisation remain.

Among this list of impediments, the existence of hub and spoke networks as a constraint on the advantages obtained by a cluster has been most researched. The hub and spoke network comprises a central coordinating institution and a series of separate linked satellites connected to each other through the hub. This may be contrasted with a cluster based on populations of many independent enterprises that may interact with other cluster participants in less structured ways than in a hub and spoke cluster. Apart from the importance of one or a few organisations hub and spoke clusters may differ from small-firm networks in five main ways (Gray et al., 1996).

1. The spokes from the hub firm to suppliers and subcontractors may extend far beyond the local economy. This can assist local development by facilitating access to ideas or techniques that are new to the region, but it can also act to raise the pressure on local linkages where performance is now judged across a wider range of potential suppliers.
2. The economic growth of hub and spoke districts is regulated by the position and success of hub organisations and their continued commitment to production and procurement within the district. This contrasts with the small-firm district where cooperation to share risk, spread the cost of

innovation and stabilise markets may act to reduce the vulnerability of the locality to economic change.

3. There may be little cooperation within the hub and spoke network, especially if the hub enjoys dominance in an oligopolistic industry as this suggests its suppliers will have a high dependence on its custom. In this context communication between firms may not extend beyond product specification, quality standards and delivery schedules.
4. Labour markets in the hub and spoke district are primarily controlled by the hub. Where the hub offers better pay and more stable employment, labour turnover will tend to be low with workers strongly inclined to stay within the dominant organisation. This differs from the situation envisaged in small-firm networks where labour is committed first and foremost to the district rather than an individual firm, partly through the setting of wages and conditions through regional agreements. Commitment to the hub can encourage a drain on labour skills where staff are transferred to branches outside the locality or where they pursue independent careers by moving away from the locality to other branches of the hub organisation. Similarly the hub can act as a magnet to migrants in search of its superior employment. This potentially fragments the social structure of the community and the uniformity of values that are said to be important in the cohesion of industrial districts.
5. Business and financial services in the hub and spoke district may not provide the specialisations and interests that support local entrepreneurship. Dominant firms, for example, may have ties to national trade associations and frustrate the ambitions of local companies that are perhaps more likely to provide support for small firms through joint training and marketing or technical and financial assistance. Similarly local government may centre its promotion and regulation on the dominant employer.

The hub and spoke district can provide an environment that is conducive for local enterprise and promote business expansion amongst satellites independent of the hub. Other characteristics can disadvantage the locality compared with the successful small-firm industrial district.

A small example of the conflicts potentially arising in hub and spoke type clusters arose in the context of an investigation of four regional clusters in the New Zealand forest processing industry (Perry, 2007). These clusters had all been supported under a government cluster promotion scheme through financial support to formalise the cluster enterprises in a network association with an independent facilitator. Of the four groups, only one sustained participation and a significant programme of activity. It was distinguished by a business population that had a relatively high level of internal transactions as well as comprising businesses of broadly similar size and activity. One of the other cluster groups had some of the characteristics of a hub and spoke cluster in that there was a single dominant business although other cluster business differed in their relationship to it.

Firms with business relationships, directly or indirectly, with the large firm but predominantly dependent on their own marketing capacity were the most likely to report positively on the cluster. These firms can be working in a synergistic relationship with the dominant enterprise, purchasing services or material from it and selling material or services of its own back to the company. This offers mutual advantages and provides a context in which the opportunity provided by the cluster group to discuss business issues informally is valued. Smaller firms have benefited from the success of the large firm as well as retaining their own business development capacity. As well, the cluster has addressed shared issues such as promoting the industry as a source of employment to job entrants and seeking to encourage a positive attitude toward the industry among local politicians.

Firms that relied predominantly on the large firm for their main business activity and had limited capacity to seek additional markets viewed the cluster project as something that reinforces their present dependency. Activity pursued by the cluster tends to rely on it fitting the priorities of all members but with particular influence exerted by the large firm given its influence over business opportunities for small firms. Consequently, an enterprise seeking to reduce its dependence on the large firm can perceive the cluster as something that adds to its difficulty breaking away.

Firms with no business connection to other cluster participants varied in their perception of the cluster. Some have reacted against what they see as a group dominated by big business concerns and have withdrawn from participation. Some value the opportunity to participate in a group where there is the possibility of gaining industry insight from its most successful participant as well as other companies. Others are uncommitted; they see potential benefits in the initiative, especially if it is able to attract activities such as engineering support to the region. At the same time, to date they see little direct outcome from the cluster.

Theory Informed Practice

Cluster advocacy tends to assume that the capacity of firms to benefit from concentration is sufficiently general as to make its promotion a desirable policy goal whatever the activity and wherever the context (Glasmeier, 2000). This is reflected in efforts made by local economic policy agencies to replicate the experience of Silicon Valley or other exemplar clusters. One immediate problem in seeking policy inspiration from established clusters is their tendency to be located in economically advantaged regions, as with England's Motor Sport Valley, the Öresund medical cluster spanning Denmark and Sweden and biotechnology in Rhône-Alpes (Lagendijk, 1999). Such clusters are associated with investment in public institutions sustained over many decades and on a scale that has capacity to influence the location of economic activity (Benneworth, 2002). For this reason, exemplar clusters centred on public institutions are necessarily exceptions. As pointed out from the experience of Sophia-Antipolis, it is simply not possible to reproduce the benefit of accumulated exceptional levels of public funding over many locations (Longhi, 1999).

It has been argued that even if the whole experience cannot be replicated elements of the experience can be applied elsewhere (Benneworth et al., 2003). In practice, even among other IT clusters experiencing high growth a large gap tends to remain between them and Silicon Valley (Bresnahan et al., 2001). The second wave of 'Silicon Valleys' (such as the clusters of IT activity in England, Finland, Ireland and Taiwan as well as other regions within the USA) have experienced spectacular rates of growth of information and communications technology businesses but without catching up to the original valley. Bresnahan et al. (2001) judge that newer clusters remain confined to technology and market gaps that have not already been exploited by any other cluster and this leaves them at a disadvantage to Silicon Valley.

As well as questioning the extent to which exemplar clusters such as Silicon Valley provide a model of regional development, the comparison of IT clusters drew attention to how many of the advantages thought to accrue to cluster participants are not able to exist at the outset of a concentration (Bresnahan et al., 2001). There are not, for example, other firms around in sufficient numbers to generate external economies. Rather than 'new economy' attributes such as agglomeration economies, 'old economy' attributes such as the sustained investment in education and research explained the emergence of second tier clusters. Getting to the point where a cluster stakes a claim on a new technology depends on years of firm and market building effort and long term investment in education and skill development. Even then, identifying a technology able to support a new concentration of business activity was seen to involve luck as well as foresight.

Learning from Silicon Valley is further challenged by the competing claims over the attributes that have contributed most to the locality's advantage. These include the impact of military expenditure (Prevezer, 1998); social and professional networks (Saxenian, 1994); labour market intermediaries (Cappelli, 1999; Benner, 2002); venture capital (Kenney and Florida, 2000); legal entrepreneurialism (Suchman, 2000: 94). Distinctive features of semiconductor technology, the core innovation associated with Silicon Valley's emergence, further constrain the ability to replicate its experiences. The basic technology was invented at the birth of the industry, allowing diffusion to new enterprises at a reasonable price (Freeman, 1982). In the early phases of the semiconductor industry, university basic research lagged behind the work by industry. This was an inducement to concentration. University expertise tends to be highly dispersed whereas business investment in the early phases of a new industry is comparatively mobile, facilitating clustering around an initial centre of expertise (Sharp, 1990). The significance of such influences is seen through comparison with biotechnology (Oakey et al., 1990).

In computing, the key links and information flows were between engineers in different companies; in biotechnology, the important relationships have been between the science base and companies (Prevezer, 1998: 128). In the case of biotechnology, partly because of the need for regulatory approval, a long time frame from scientific discovery to commercial application results in a particular relationship between established companies and new start ups. Incumbents with activity potentially affected by biotechnology innovations could maintain a 'watching brief' over prospective competitors knowing that breakthrough companies would need the assistance of a large-firm partner to bring their innovation to market (Oakey et al., 1990). Thus it was not until the 1990s that commercial products started to emerge from the new biotechnology discoveries arising from scientific advances in genetics and molecular biology of the early 1970s (Audretsch, 2001). Commercialisation proceeded as large pharmaceutical companies selectively took up the products of biotechnology start ups and began to make strategic choices about their own investment (Sharp, 1999).

The comparative development of computing and biotechnology makes it hard to know what policy lessons might be taken from clusters in either sector. The full context of Silicon Valley's emergence and growth draws attention to its uniqueness and dangers of viewing it as a model that can be cloned (Kenney, 2000: 12). Equally, the ability to find biotechnology clusters in many regions reflects features particular to this activity rather than incipient concentrations that public policy can grow into new Silicon Valleys. In contrast, a feature of much policy discussion is the assumption that cluster development can be applied to any concentration of activity.

The perceived universality of cluster development is reflected in the tendency to design policy around a uniform evolution in cluster development characteristics (Ecotech Research and Consulting, 2004). The implicit assumption is that there is always scope to generate benefit from inter-firm collaboration. The challenge is merely to identify a starting point and business champions to drive a change in business behaviour. Italy's industrial districts are frequently given as justification for the optimism in building collaboration, partly as they cover a range of manufacturing activities and partly because they are claimed to show how cooperation can exist alongside intense competitiveness. In reality, opportunities for combining competition and cooperation are sensitive to the precise production and marketing environment operated in. For example, a comparison of two shoemaking districts in Emilia-Romagna, San Mauro Pascoli and Fusignano shows how opportunities to combine cooperation and competition can vary (Nuti and Cainelli, 1996).

Ultimately, much of the case for clusters assumes that firms more easily learn from firms with whom they are in close proximity and that localised learning can be highly effective for business growth. The availability, circulation and absorption of information are certainly critical to the long term survival and adaptability of business. Glasmeier (2000: 566) sees no reason to believe that firms located in a cluster should gain a learning advantage over firms that operate in isolation of their industry peers. Firms wherever they are located have limited capacity to learn, being organisations built around routine and action legitimised more by past experiences than anticipations of the future. Indeed, to the extent that clustering produces uniformity in the sources of knowledge and a lack of attention to developments going on elsewhere, it may even be detrimental to learning. This assessment is a reminder to consider the actual behaviour of firms. Experiences such as Silicon Valley are not created by firms suddenly becoming quick learners but rather rely on conditions and resources accumulated over a long time.

Conclusion

Whatever cluster theory is adhered to there tends to be a strong assumption of universal advantage. There has been relatively little consideration given to how particular industry, technology or market conditions affect the opportunity for clusters to upgrade business performance. This omission can make sense where industry is affected by some overriding challenge. As discussed at the outset of the chapter, much academic inquiry is motivated by the attempt to simplify changing economic conditions to a single uniform transition. There is, of course, much merit in seeking to identify the common forces behind economic and social change but equally there is a need to recognise that organisations will be affected by change with varying degrees of intensity. Equally, any new ways of organising business are likely to be of varying assistance to firms of different type, in different industries and in different economic contexts.

Most explanations of clustering start with a list of advantages that firms can enjoy from a location among their industry peers and supporters. The presence of these advantages is simultaneously the explanation for clustering. Such an approach has three problems. First, it leaves a gap in explaining how the activity accumulated to the point where the advantages emerged. Presumably up to the time when an activity started to assume importance, future cluster members were small in number and part of a diversified economy. Second, the advantages ascribed to clusters are numerous and partly in competition with each other. A cluster that offers a gain through the sharing of tacit knowledge is unlikely to be simultaneously one that gains from the stimulus of intensified competition. If there is intensified competition it suggests a high degree of similarity between businesses and consequently not much new information to be gained from neighbours. Similarly, heightened competition is likely to reduce the likelihood of cluster firms benefiting from a shared labour market. Employers that 'hire and fire' their workers rather than invest in their human capital have less to gain and more to loose from employee turnover than firms which are differentiated from each other. Third, it suggests that all activity should be located in clusters. If clusters are simply about the pursuit of advantages, it would seem that organisations not availing themselves of them will fall behind those that do. For the present at least, clusters are a minority phenomenon and present evidence suggests this is likely to continue to be the case. Instead of the focus on advantages, policy should be guided by knowledge of the mechanisms that can advantage clusters and the contexts in which those mechanisms operate.

References

Audretsch, D. (2001), 'The role of small firms in U.S. biotechnology clusters', *Small Business Economics* 17: 3–15.

Bamford, J. (1987), 'The development of small firms, the traditional family and agrarian patterns in Italy', in R. Goffee and R. Scase (eds) *Entrepreneurship in Europe*, London: Croom Helm.

Beardsell, M. and Henderson, V. (1999), 'Spatial evolution of the computer industry in the USA', *European Economic Review*, 43: 431–56.

Beaudry, C. and Breschi, S. (2003), 'Are firms in clusters really more innovative?', *Economics of Innovation and New Technology* 12(4): 325–42.

Benner, C. (2002), *Work in the New Economy: Flexible Labour Markets in Silicon Valley*, Oxford: Blackwell.

Benneworth, P. (2002), 'Creating new industries and service clusters on Tyneside', *Local Economy* 17(4): 313–27.

Benneworth, P., Danson, M., Raines, P. and Whittam, G. (2003), 'Confusing clusters: Making sense of the cluster approach in theory and practice', *European Planning Studies* 11(5): 511–20.

Bresnahan, T., Gambardella, A. and Saxenian, A. (2001), '"Old economy" inputs for "new economy" outcomes: Cluster formation in the new Silicon Valleys' *Industrial and Corporate Change* 10(4): 835–60.

Brakman, S., Garretsen, H. and van Marrewijk, C. (2001), *An Introduction to Geographical Economics*, Cambridge: Cambridge University Press.

Braunerhjelm, P. and Johansson, D. (2003), 'The determinants of spatial concentration: The manufacturing and service sectors in an international perspective', *Industry and Innovation* 10(1): 41–63.

Brusco, S., Cainelli, G., Forni, F., Franchi, M., Malusardi, A. and Righetti R.(1996), 'The evolution of industrial districts in Emilia-Romagna'. In F. Cossentino, F. Pyke and W. Sengenberger (eds), *Local and Regional Response to Global Pressure: The Case of Italy and its Industrial Districts*, Geneva: International Institute for Labour Studies.

Burke, R. (2002), 'Organizational transitions', in C. Cooper and R. Burke (eds) *The New World of Work – Challenges and Opportunities*, Oxford: Blackwell.

Burroni, L. and Trigilia, C. (2001), 'Italy: Economic development through local economies'. In C. Crouch, P. Le Galés, C. Trogilia and H. Voelzkow (eds), *Local Production Systems in Europe: Rise or Demise?*, Oxford: Oxford University Press.

Cappelli, P. (1999), *The New Deal at Work: Managing the Market Driven Workforce*, Boston: Harvard Business School Press.

Cossentino, F., Pyke, F. and Sengenberger, W. (1996), *Local and Regional Response to Global Pressure: The Case of Italy and its Industrial Districts*, Geneva: International Institute for Labour Studies.

Chon, S. (1997), 'Destroying the myth of vertical integration in the Japanese electronics industry: Rrestructuring in the semiconductor manufacturing equipment industry', *Regional Studies* 31(1): 25–39.

Christensen, C. (1997), *The Innovator's Dilemma, Boston*: Harvard Business School Press.

Checkland, S.G. (1981), *The Upas Tree: Glasgow 1875–1975: A Study in Growth and Contraction*, Glasgow: University of Glasgow Press.

Cingano, F. (2003), 'Returns to specific skills in industrial districts', *Labour Economics*, 10: 149–64.

Crouch, C. and Farrell, H. (2001), 'Great Britain: Falling through the holes in the network concept', in C. Crouch, P. Le Galés, C. Trogilia and H. Voelzkow (eds) *Local Production Systems in Europe: Rise or Demise?*, Oxford: Oxford University Press.

Department of Trade and Industry (2001), *Business Clusters in the UK – A First Assessment*, London: Department of Trade and Industry.

Dicken, P. (1998), *Global Shift: The Internationalization of Economic Activity*, 4th edn, London: Paul Chapman.

Duranton, G. and Puga, D. (2002), 'Diversity and specialization in cities: Why, where and when does it matter?', in P. McCann (ed.), *Industrial Location Economics*, Cheltenham: Edward Elgar.

Ecotech Research and Consulting (2004), *A Practical Guide to Cluster Development*, London: Department of Trade and Industry.

Feldman, M. and Audretsch, D. (1999), 'Innovation in cities: Science-based diversity, specialization and localized competition', *European Economic Review*, 43: 409–29.

Feser, E. and Bergman, E. (2000), 'National industry cluster templates: A framework for regional cluster analysis', *Regional Studies* 34(1): 1–20.

Feser, E. and Luger, M. (2003), 'Cluster analysis as a mode of inquiry: Its use in science and technology policymaking in North Carolina', *European Planning Studies* 11(1): 11–24.

Freeman, C. (1982), *The Economics of Innovation* 2nd edn, London: Pinter.

Glaeser, E., Kallal, H., Scheinkman, J. and Schleifer, A. (1992), 'Growth in cities', *Journal of Political Economy*, 100(6): 1126–52.

Glasmeier, A. (2000), 'Local economic development policy', in G. Clark, M. Feldman and M. Gertler (eds), *The Oxford Handbook of Economic Geography*, Oxford: Oxford University Press.

Glassman, U. and Voelzkow, H. (2001), 'The governance of local economies in Germany' in C. Crouch, P. Le Galés, C. Trogilia and H. Voelzkow (eds), *Local Production Systems in Europe: Rise or Demise?*, Oxford: Oxford University Press.

Grabher, G. (1993), 'The weakness of strong ties: The lock-in of regional development in the Ruhr area', in G. Grabher (ed.), *The Embedded Firm: On the Socioeconomics of Industrial Networks*, London: Routledge.

Gray, M., Golob, E. and Markusen, A. (1996), 'Big firms, long arms, wide shoulders: The "hub and spoke" industrial district in the Seatle region', *Regional Studies* 30,7: 651–66.

Hamel, G. and Prahald, C. (1994), *Competing for the Future*, Boston: Harvard Business School Press.

Harrison, B. (1992), 'Industrial districts: Old wine in new bottles', *Regional Studies* 26,5: 469–O83.

Henderson, V. (1974), 'The sizes and types of cities', *American Economic Review*, 64(4): 640–56.

Henderson, V. (1988), *Urban Development: Theory, Fact and Illusion*, Oxford: Oxford University Press.

Hendry, C., Brown, J. and Defillip, R. (2000), 'Regional clustering of high technology-based firms: Opto-electronics in three countries', *Regional Studies* 34(2): 129–44.

Hendry, C., Brown, J., Defillip, R. and Hassink, R. (1999), 'Industry clusters as commercial, knowledge and institutional networks: Opto-electronics in six regions in the UK, USA and Germany', in A. Grandori (ed.), *Interform Networks: Organization and Industrial Competitiveness*, London: Routledge.

Holmann, D. and Wood, S. (2003), 'The new workplace: An introduction', in D. Holman, T. Wall, C. Clegg, P. Sparrow and A. Howard (eds), *The New Workplace: A Guide to the Human Impact of Modern Working Practices*, Chichester: John Wiley and Sons.

Hoover, E. (1937), *Location Theory and the Shoe and Leather Industry*, Cambridge MA: Harvard University Press.

Hoover, E. (1948), *The Location of Economic Activity*, New York: McGraw Hill.

Huggins, R. (1996), 'Technology policy, networks and small firms in Denmark', *Regional Studies* 30(5): 523–52.

Humphrey, J. and Schmitz, H. 'How does insertion in global value chains affect upgrading in industrial clusters?', *Regional Studies* 36(9): 1017–1027.

Kenney, M. (2000), *Understanding Silicon Valley: The Anatomy of an Entrepreneurial Region*, Stanford: Stanford University Press.

Kenney, M. and Florida, R. (2000), 'Introduction'. In M. Kenney (ed.), *Understanding Silicon Valley: The Anatomy of an Entrepreneurial Region*, Stanford: Stanford University Press.

Kim, S. (1995), 'Expansion of markets and the geographic distribution of economic activities: The trends in US regional manufacturing structure, 1860–1987', *The Quarterly Journal of Economics* 110: 881–908.

Kotval, Z. and Mullin, J. (1998), 'The potential for planning an industrial cluster', in Barre, Vermont: 'A case of "hard rock" resistance in the granite industry', *Planning Practice and Research* 13(3): 311–18.

Lagendijk, A. (1999), 'Learning in non-core regions: Towards intelligent clusters addressing business and regional needs', in R. Rutten, S. Bakkers, K. Morgan and F. Boekem (eds), *Learning Regions: Theory, Policy and Practice*, Cheltenham: Edward Elgar.

Longhi, C. (1999), 'Networks, collective learning and technology development in innovative high technology regions: The case of Sophia-Antipolis', *Regional Studies* 33(4): 333–42.

Malmberg, A., Malmberg, B. and Lundequist, P. (2000), 'Agglomeration and firm performance: Economies of scale, localisation, and urbanisation among Swedish export firms', *Environment and Planning A*, 32: 305–21.

Marshall, A. (1923), *Industry and Trade*, 4th edn, London: Macmillan and Co.

Marshall, A. (1927), *Principles of economics*, 8th edn, London: Macmillan and Co.

Martin, R. and Sunley, P. (1996), 'Paul Krugman's geographical economics and its implications for regional development theory: A critical assessment', *Economic Geography*, 72: 259–92.

Martin, R. and Sunley, P. (2003), 'Deconstructing clusters: Chaotic concept or policy panacea?', *Journal of Economic Geography* 3: 5–35.

May, W., Mason, C. and Pinch, S. (2001), 'Explaining industrial agglomeration: The case of the British high-fidelity industry', *Geoforum* 32(3): 363–76.

McCann, P. (2001), *Urban and Regional Economics*, Oxford: Oxford University Press.

Micklethwait, J. and Wooldridge, A. (1997), *The Witch Doctors*, London: Mandarin.

Miles, R. and Snow, C. (1993), 'Causes of failure in network organizations', *California Management Review* 34(4): 53–72.

Nuti, F. and Cainelli, G. (1996), 'Changing directions in Italy's manufacturing industrial districts: The case of the Emilian footwear districts of Fusignano and San Mauro Pascoli', *Journal of Industry Studies* 3(2): 105–118.

Oakey, R. (1995), *High Technology Small Firms: Innovation and Regional Development in Britain and the United States*, London: Pinter.

Oakey, R., Faulkner, W., Cooper, S. and Walsh, V. (1990), *New Firms in the Biotechnology Industry: Their Contribution to Innovation and Growth*, London: Pinter.

Oakey, R., Kipling, M. and Wildgust, S. (2001), 'Clustering among firms in the non-broadcast visual communications (NBVC) sector', *Regional Studies* 35(5): 401–414.

Ohlin, B. (1933), *Interregional and Internal Trade*, Cambridge MA: Harvard University Press.

Paniccia, I. (2002), *Industrial Districts Evolution and Competitiveness in Italian Firms*, Cheltenham: Edward Elgar.

Parr, J. (2002), 'Agglomeration economies: Ambiguities and confusions', *Environment and Planning A*, 34: 717–31.

Pawson, R. and Tilley, N. (1997), *Realistic Evaluation*, London: Sage.

Perry, M. (1999), *Small Firms and Network Economies*, London: Routledge.

Perry, M. (2004), 'Business cluster promotion in New Zealand and the limits of exemplar clusters', *Policy and Society* 23(4): 82–103.

Perry, M. (2005), *Business Clusters: An International Perspective*, Abingdon, Oxon: Routledge.

Perry, M. (2007), 'Business environments and cluster attractiveness to managers', *Entrepreneurship and Regional Development*, 19, 1: 1–24.

Perry, M. and Tan, B.H. (1998), 'Global manufacturing and local linkage in Singapore', *Environment and Planning A*, 30: 1603–24.

Phelps, N. (1993), 'Contemporary industrial restructuring and linkage change in an older industrial region: Examples from the northeast of England', *Environment and Planning A*, 25: 863–82.

Pinch, S., Henry, N., Jenkins, M. and Tallman, S. (2003), 'From "industrial districts" to "knowledge clusters": A model of knowledge dissemination and competitive advantage in industrial agglomerations', *Journal of Economic Geography*, 3: 373–88.

Porter, M. (2000), 'Locations, clusters and company strategy', in G. Clark, M. Feldman and M. Gertler (eds), *The Oxford Handbook of Economic Geography*, Oxford: Oxford University Press.

Porter, M. (2003), 'The economic performance of regions', *Regional Studies* 37(6–7): 549–78.

Prevezer (1998), 'Clustering in biotechnology in the USA', in G. Swann, M. Prevezer and D. Stout (eds), *The Dynamics of Industrial Clustering: International Comparisons in Computing and Biotechnology*, Oxford: Oxford University Press.

Rabellotti, R. and Schmitz, H. (1999), 'The internal heterogeneity of industrial districts in Italy, Brazil and Mexico', *Regional Studies* 33, 97–108.

Raines, P. (2002), *Cluster Development and Policy*, Aldershot: Ashgate.

Rosenfeld, S. (2005), 'Industry clusters: Business choice, policy outcome, or branding strategy?', *Journal of New Business Ideas and Trends* 3(2): 4–13.

Saxenian, A. (1994), *Regional Advantage: Culture and Competition in Silicon Valley and Route 128*, Cambridge, MA: Harvard University Press.

Schmitz, H. (1995), 'Collective efficiency: Growth path for small-scale industry', *Journal of Development Studies* 31: 529–66.

Schmitz, H. (1999), 'Global competition and local cooperation: Success and failure in the Sinos Valley, Brazil', *World Development* 27: 1627–50.

Schmitz, H. and Nadvi, K. (1999), 'Clustering and industrialization: Introduction', *World Development* 27: 1503–14.

Scott, A. (1988), *New Industrial Spaces: Flexible Production, Organization and Regional Development in North America and Western Europe*, London: Pion.

Scott, A. (2006), 'Entrepreneurship, innovation and industrial development: Geography and the creative field revisited', *Small Business Economics* 26 (1), 1–24.

Scott, A. and Storper, M. (1992), 'Industrialization and regional development', in M. Storper and A. Scott (eds), *Pathways to Industrialization and Regional Development*, London: Routledge.

Sforzi, F. (1990), 'The quantitative importance of Marshallian industrial districts in the Italian economy', in F. Pyke, G. Becattini and W. Sengenberger (eds), *Industrial Districts and Inter-Firm Co-operation in Italy*, Geneva: International Institute for Labour Studies.

Sharp, M. (1990), 'European countries in science-based competition: The case of biotechnology', in D. Hague (ed.), *The Management of Science*, Basingstoke: Macmillan.

Sharp, M. (1999), 'The science of nations: European multinationals and American biotechnology', *Biotechnology* 1(1): 132–62.

Sölvell, Ö., Lindquist, G. and Ketels, C. (2003), *The Cluster Initiative Greenbook*, Stockholm: Ivory Tower AB.

Sorenson, O. and Audia, P. (2000), 'The social structure of entrepreneurial activity: Geographic concentration of footwear production in the United States, 1940–1989', *American Journal of Sociology* 106(2): 424–62.

Stuart, T. and Sorenson, O. (2003), 'The geography of opportunity: Spatial heterogeneity in founding rates and the performance of biotechnology firms', *Research Policy* 32: 229–53.

Suchman, M. (2000), 'Dealmakers and counselors: Law firms as intermediaries in the development of Silicon Valley', in M. Kenney (ed.), *Understanding Silicon Valley: The Anatomy of an Entrepreneurial Region*, Stanford: Stanford University Press.

Tambunan, T.T.H. (2005), 'Promoting small and medium enterprises with a clustering approach: A policy experience from Indonesia', *Journal of Small Business Management* 43(2), 138–54.

Vernon, R. and Hoover, E. (1959), *Anatomy of a Metropolis*, Cambridge MA: Harvard University Press.

Whitley, R. (1999), *Divergent Capitalisms: The Social Structuring and Change of Business Systems*, Oxford: Oxford University Press.

Chapter 9

Regional Economic Development Methods and Analysis: Linking Theory to Practice

Robert Stimson and Roger R. Stough

Introduction

Over the past two decades or so the emphasis in regional economic development theory shifted from *exogenous* to *endogenous* factors. Traditional regional economic development approaches were erected on neo-classical economic growth theory, based largely on the Solow growth model (1956, 2000). New approaches while recognizing that development is framed by exogenous factors recognizes a much more significant role for endogenous forces. In this context, a suite of models and arguments that broadly convey the *new growth theory* are directed towards *endogenous* factors and processes (see, for example, Johansson, Karlsson and Stough, 2001). Those factors are seen as fundamental drivers of regional economic development arising from the resource endowments and knowledge base of a region. *Endogenous* factors include entrepreneurship, innovation, the adoption of new technologies, leadership, institutional capacity and capability, and learning.

These developments are of great interest to regional economic development analysts for several reasons including the recognition of the importance of regions in the development process and also because they introduce an explicit spatial variable into economic growth theory, a mostly ignored element in neo-classical thinking. This evolutionary development is particularly significant as the importance of regions in national economies has changed considerably since the 1970s as a result of globalization, structural change and adjustment. Understanding these newly recognized processes of change is crucial for analyzing and understanding different patterns of regional economic performance and in formulating and implementing regional economic development planning strategy.

Stimson, Stough and Roberts (2006) observe that it is often difficult in regional economic development planning strategy formulation and implementation to match desired *outcomes* of regional economic development with the *processes* that create them. This gap in understanding the relationship between the apparent causes and effects of development pose a dilemma for those responsible for managing regional economic development in the making of policies and strategies, and their implementation of plans. The dilemma they face is how to achieve some form of congruence between desired outcomes and appropriate and acceptable economic development tools and processes. This dilemma is further compounded by the frequently unstable and changing nature of economic environments, where 'externalities' or *exogenous* factors (such as exchange rates, new technologies, foreign competition) increasingly impact the decision-making processes that influence economic policy and strategy in regions.

The Nature of Regional Economic Development

Regional economic development may be viewed as both a *product* and a *process* but often not by the same groups or actors in the development milieu. For example, economic agents that live, work and invest in regions are those most concerned with economic development outputs or products such as job and wealth creation, investment, quality of life or standards of living and conditions of the work environment. Contrary to this is the more process orientation of regional scientists, development planners and practitioners where concern focuses on the creation of infrastructure, labor force preparation, human capital and market development. So it is important when considering regional economic development to maintain an awareness of its *product* and *process* aspects.

Regional economic development also is known in terms of *quantitative* and *qualitative* attributes. In this context, with respect to the benefits it creates, concern is with the quantitative measurement of such factors as increasing/decreasing wealth and income levels, job creation or employment levels, the availability of goods and services and improving financial security. At the same time, concern also lies with such qualitative considerations as creating greater social and financial equity, in achieving sustainable development, in creating a spread in the range of employment and gaining improvements in the quality of life in a region. Thus regional economic development process needs to be informed by both quantitative and qualitative information.

This multi-dimensional aspect of economic development led Stimson, Stough and Roberts (2006) to propose the following definition of regional economic development:

> …Regional economic development is the application of economic processes and resources available to a region that result in the sustainable development of, and desired economic outcomes for a region and that meet the values and expectations of business, of residents and of visitors (p. 6).

Evolving Paradigms for Economic Policy and Regional Economic Development Planning Strategy

Policy for economic development and regional planning strategy has undergone a series of evolutionary changes since World War II, driven by different paradigms of economic thought as shown in Figure 9.1. Those paradigms have shaped the way regional and local communities and people think and plan for the future. But much thinking on regional economic development still remains embedded in the paradigms of the 1970s, because of an inherent reluctance of many regions and local communities to pro-actively embrace change. Subsequently, as suggested by Stimson, Stough and Roberts (2006):

> ....many regions are not re-equipping themselves fast enough to compete effectively in the global age of business and technology of the post-industrial economy. To compete successfully in the global economy, regional organizations and businesses need to understand the implications of the paradigm shifts occurring in economic policy and strategy, and to build the flexible strategic infrastructure to do so (p. 11).

A summary of the changing paradigms that have shaped regional economic development theory and planning strategy is presented in Figure 9.1. It is, however, important to realize that time overlaps between the economic policy and the economic planning strategy paradigms reflected in Figure 9.1 are both deliberate and pragmatic, reflecting the reality of evolutionary changes in the paradigm approaches.

The discussion that follows draws on and elaborates on the discussion in Stimson Stough and Roberts (2006: chapter 1). It focuses on a set of important issues all of which are evident in the context of those paradigmatic evolutions:

- First is the ability of neoclassical economic theory to serve as the basis of regional economic development theory.
- Second is the evolution of economic policy from Keynesian thought and associated master planning paradigms to monetarism or economic rationalism and associated goals and objectives, and strategic planning paradigms.
- Third is the shift over time from a focus on comparative advantage to competitive advantage and more recently an extension of the focus to the notion of collaborative advantage.
- Fourth is the processes of globalization and the emergence of concern for achieving sustainable development, and the focus on regional self-help in the pursuit of endogenous growth.
- And fifth is the evolution of the 'new growth theory'.

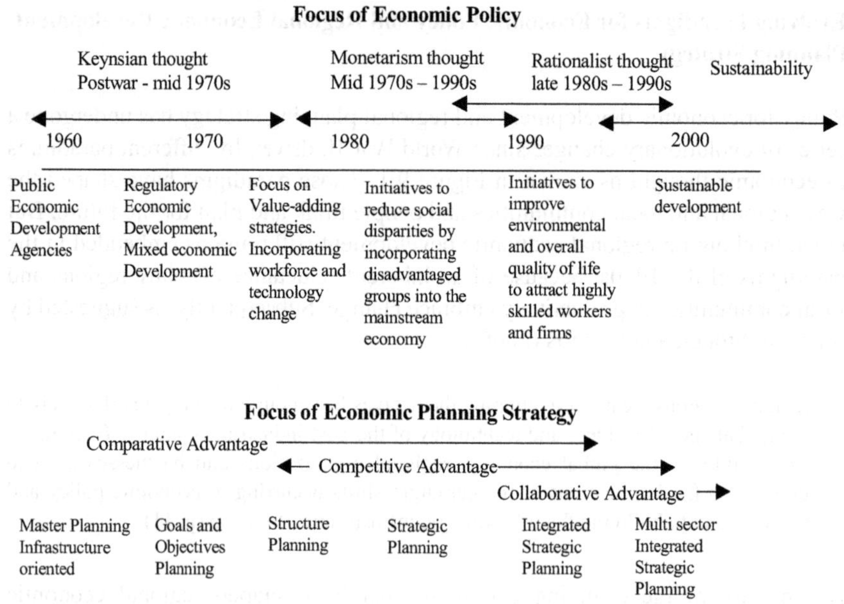

Figure 9.1 Changing focus for economic development policy and planning strategy

From a Neo-classical Base to Theory

Neo-classical economic theory and *Keynesian theory* provided the foundation on which most post-World War II economic policies were grounded. At that time conventional theories and policies for regional economic development tended to focus in one way or another on the *capital-labor production function* and on responses by the state with a range of economic and non-economic policies. In this framework, production (Q) is seen as a function of two inputs capital (K) and labor (L):

$$Q = f(K,L)$$

This simple two-factor model has been used to measure productivity of capital and labor output in regional economies. The model has been expanded to include other functions or factors, such as technology (T), and other variables, including learning and entrepreneurship to equate as:

$$Q = f(K,L,T,\ldots e)$$

Traditional neo-classical growth theory models:

- assume homogeneity of production factors,
- see the price mechanism as the underlying adjustment mechanism of the model,
- emphasize capital accumulation as the net product,

all of which lead to convergence thus eliminating inter-regional, inter-group and inter-sectoral differences over time in the long run.

Neo-classical models provided a useful rationale for understanding the implications of labor and capital changes on the economic performance of nations and also regions (Richardson, 1973). However, they did not adequately explain how productivity, performance, and other attributes related to the application of labor, capital and technology impacted economic development especially in the development of regional economies (Malecki, 1991: p.111). Thus, neo-classical theories have not adequately identified or explained the behavior of factors that give expression to regional economic development and the related economic development processes.

As a result, counter arguments to the traditional neo-classical growth theory emerged (see Stough, Salazar and Haynes, 2005 for a detailed description of these). These approaches include *polarization theory*, as represented early on by the work of Perroux (1950), Myrdal (1957) and Hirschman (1958), and more recently by work that focuses on industrial districts (see, for example, Scott, 1988) and business clusters (see, for example, Porter, 1990; Feser, 1998; and Karlsson, Johansson and Stough, 2005).

Advocates of polarization theory argued that:

- production factors are non-homogenous
- markets are imperfect
- the price mechanism is disturbed by *externalities* and *economies of scale*.

The argument is that deviations from an equilibrium are *not* corrected by counter effects, but rather that they set off a circular *cumulative process* of growth or decline, with a complex set of positive and negative feedback loops accumulating to a growth process whose direction is fundamentally undetermined. In a *spatial* context, those feedback processes generated what are called *spread* and *backwash* effects, transferring impulses from one region to another. *Spatial structure* could be an important element in that growth process, generating *leading* and *lagging* regions that are highly interdependent. The advocates of polarization theory argued that it was not only economic, but also social, cultural, and institutional factors that explain why some regions prosper while others lag.

From Keynesian Thought to 'Monetarism' and 'Economic Rationalism' in Policy

As seen in the top half of Figure 9.1, a number of phases in the evolution of economic thought have had a significant impact on paradigms driving economic development policy over the latter part of the 20th century. The following discussion is an interpretive description of the changes that are outlined in Figure 9.1. This discussion is important because it explains how the current approach to policy and implementation of regional economic development programs is underpinned by the evolution of thought from a the rather mechanical neo classical model to a more flexible approach that relies in a major way on local initiative and effort.

Keynesian and then *monetarist* thought were the most influencial policy paradigms in the post World War II period through to the 1980s. These views subsequently evolved into *economic rationalism.*

Keynesian thought evolved in response to the Great Depression of the 1930s and influenced government approaches from World War II up to the middle 1970s. The Keynesian model envisaged a greatly increased role for governments in balancing (managing) demand and the interests of suppliers the earlier more classical economic thinking. During the 1950s and 1960s, economic processes were driven by a heavy focus on *regulation* and by strong *government directives and initiatives* in the US but even more so in other countries. It was a time when national governments played an exceptionally active role in establishing national industries. Governments played a central role in the provision of infrastructure, planning, industry promotion and marketing systems.

Figure 9.1 shows that there was a focus on *comparative advantage*, through strategies such as promoting cheap land, reduced utility charges, and local tax breaks for new businesses relocating or expanding in a region. Those approaches to economic policy were, by and large, positive in developing national and regional economies.

The lower half of Figure 9.1 shows how, in the 1950s and 1960s, regional economic development and planning strategy tended to be guided by *master planning* and *structure planning*, and was aimed at industry production, infrastructure, and market development. *Master planning* for regions tended to be controlled by government policy agendas designed to address shortages in housing, construction materials, consumer goods, and to create employment. There was a strong focus in regional economic development planning on the formation of industrial estates, many of which were used to support the development of state-owned enterprises as part of a policy of national and regional self-reliance. *Structure planning*, largely concerned with the geography of economic activities, was incorporated into economic development planning in the 1970s and provided a more flexible framework for decision-making.

However, from the late 1960s, regional economic planning strategy moved from master planning to a focus on *goals and objectives* to achieve *strategic outcomes*. Governments played major roles in setting goals and objectives for regional economic development plans, but involvement and support from industry was also increasingly sought and considered important in the creation of expected outcomes. This *goals and objectives* planning paradigm was less deterministic than master planning, the intent being to establish direction and targets for economic development. The role of regions in meeting national goals and objectives became important, but the relative autonomy of regions to shape the future economy was still, in most countries, largely determined by central–national or state–government economic policy agendas. Goals and objectives were determined through various analytical approaches, and economic visions were set based largely on a view of the future being a linear extension of the past.

But these economic policy and planning policy paradigms were challenged severely following the first OPEC oil shock of 1973. From the late 1970s, the advocates of *monetarism* argued that changes in the level of aggregate money were due essentially to prior money stock changes. Economic activities in the economy could be stimulated or slowed by manipulating the flow of money supply (M1–M6) in response to desired economic outcomes, such as reducing inflation, increasing consumption, and reducing unemployment. The Bretton-Woods agreement in 1973 removed gold as a standard for most currencies, marking the floating of national currencies, and the emergence of the contemporary era of globalization of finance and capital and production systems.

There was a shift in economic thought away from heavy public intervention into industry policy towards a focus on *value-adding* and the application and development of *technologies* to enhance production processes.

From the 1980s, there was an increasing recognition of the importance of technology-led regional economic development in the evolving post-industrial era of the information economy which had spawned a large number of technology based industries, and there was a focus on building technology, science and innovation parks as catalysts for 'new age' industrial development.

By the mid-1970s, *strategic planning* in business began to influence planning in other sectors of the economy, including planning strategy for regional economic development. *Strategic planning* involved the preparation of goals, objectives and strategies for organizations, for businesses, and for regions to gain a position of advantage in the broader context within which they operated. In most cases, those environments were still considered to be relatively stable, as the full effects of globalization and the opening of national and regional economies to competition were not yet felt. However, strategic planning continued to provide a valuable tool for economic development after the effects of globalization became more noticeable. Strategic planning for economic development began to evolve in the late 1980s to address broader social and environmental issues.

In the 1980s monetarism evolved into *economic rationalism*, following the lead of the Chicago economist Milton Friedman. Economic rationalism was accompanied by the increasing transfer of traditional public functions to private ownership or management, and the breaking up of public monopolies through full or partial divestiture to private or corporate bodies. There was also an increasing emphasis on the importance of *competitive advantage* in regional economic development planning strategy that was spurred by the writings of Michael Porter (1985; 1966; 1990), with the principles of *competitive advantage* being embedded within the *strategic planning* paradigm that had become so pervasive by the 1990s.

From 'Comparative Advantage' to 'Competitive Advantage' and 'Collaborative Advantage'

As shown in Figure 9.1, and as discussed by Stimson, Stough and Roberts (2006: pp. 30–34), over the four to five decades that represented the transformation from the 'industrial' or 'Fordist' era to the 'post-industrial' or 'post-Fordist' era of the new knowledge economy, there was a shift from a focus on comparative advantage to a focus on competitive advantage as monetarism began to influence macro economic policy, and more recently on collaborative advantage. That shift is reflected in the evolution of regional development planning strategy (Huxam, 1996). The evolution of advantage type thinking from the classical comparative advantage to competitive and collaborative advantage is described here in an effort to illustrate how one of the instruments of regional economic development strategy emerged and thus to futher illustrate the broader evolution of strategy making process.

The older notion of *comparative advantage* was derived from economic theory on international trade, which suggested that a nation or region would or should specialize in an industry in which it had an advantage related to its particular resource endowments thus providing a factor cost advantage in producing a particular good. Until the mid-1970s, the focus of the *master planning, goals and objectives*, and *structure planning* paradigms in planning policy embraced the principles of comparative advantage. Planning policies primarily were directed towards achieving the lowest production costs (labor, materials, energy, taxes and infrastructure) relative to competitors. *Comparative advantage* was heavily entrenched in supply side economics, where goods and services were produced and surpluses sold (often with the support of subsidies and incentives) in international and domestic markets.

Later on during the 1980s, through the influence of authors like Michael Porter (1985; 1986; 1990), the focus of regional economic planning strategy began to move towards *competitive advantage*, which put the focus on less tangible or 'value factors', including efficiencies, performance, and qualitative attributes such as quality of life, and human and social capital, and trust (Putnam, 1993; Fukuyama, 1995), rather than just on factor cost differentials that defined the concept of *comparative advantage*.

The emphasis thus changed towards the notion that regions would need to develop policies and implement strategies that sought to develop and promote their *competitive advantage*. That necessitated not only a factor cost advantage, particularly related to productivity and quality of goods and services that are traded, but also a competitive advantage with respect to other factors that enhance business development and operation, and that minimize risk. However, many governments continued to promote comparative differences and provided incentives to attract industries to regions, policies that do not dismiss the strategy of comparative advantage.

Both *comparative advantage* and *competitive advantage* strategies were and are heavily entrenched in a *win/lose* scenario. More recently, economic development and planning has promoted strategies that seek to develop and promote *collaborative advantage*, where firms and regions are encouraged to 'collaborate in competition' for strategic advantage, particularly through partnerships and alliances. That reflects a change in business attitudes, in which businesses and organizations that might once have considered themselves rivals, are now actively seeking strategic alliances, partnerships, and other forms of collaboration to explore opportunities and synergistically induced benefits for winning, creating and expanding business and business opportunities.

There also emerged in the search for sustainability and economic growth a *win/win* scenario as a strategy to achieve economic development. This strategy is loosely referred to as *collaborative advantage*. It represents a more recent paradigm that has been emerging in regional economic development strategy planning, and it is one that is dependent on a greater integration, cooperation and collaboration among business, governments and communities. It is this new thrust toward collaborative advantage and how to achieve it that has become a common element in the new and emerging approaches to regional economic development strategy formulation, planning and implementation since the mid-1990s.

Globalization, Concerns about Sustainable Development, and the Notion of Regional Self-help

The extravagances of the capital markets splurge in the 1980s, followed by the 1987 stock market crash and a 1989 recession, led to a significant paradigm shift with an increasing focus on the principles of *sustainable development*.

During the 1980s and into the early 1990s, parallel events were occurring that would have a significant impact on economic thought and the evolution of best practice in regional development planning strategy. These included globalization, sustainable development and economic rationalism. We now first turn to explaining the impact of these joint interacting forces and then to offering an interpretive analysis of their influence on strategic development planning and related efforts,

First, *globalization* was continuing to have a major impact on the economic restructuring of regions, which could be both positive and detrimental to their performance and possible futures. By the early 1990s, the impact of globalization had changed the nature and location of production, resulting in greater specialization or clustering (Dicken, 1992). Globalization had resulted in the emergence of an increasingly borderless society with greater unrestricted movement of information, travel and currency between countries. Greater levels of transparency and standardization were occurring in both business and government processes.

Those changes reduced the importance of the nation state and increasingly directed the focus upon major cities and regions as the centers and engines of economic growth (Knight and Gappert, 1989; Ohmae, 1995). In particular, some of the world's larger metropolitan regions were viewed as being the dominant focus of the forces driving the growth of employment, investment, and distribution networks in the newly emerged global market place. With these changes there emerged a new focus on regions rather than just a focus on national economies, as governments placed emphasis on the skill requirements of labor (that is, on labor quality) and on technology-driven investment. In addition, with globalization, trans-national corporations exploited regional differences created by both *comparative advantage* and competitive *advantage strategies*, as governments withdrew from protection and interventionist policies.

Second, issues relating to *sustainable development* and *quality of life* began to have a significant influence on local economic development and planning policy. Growing concerns about the environment, social issues, and sustainable economic growth led to the emergence of *integrated strategic planning* for economic development in the 1990s, as shown in the bottom half of Figure 9.1.

During the 1990s and into the first decade of the new millennium, there emerged a clash between globalization and increasing community concerns about issues to do with sustainability and quality of life. That led to the emergence of a new paradigm in economic development thinking, namely the question of *how to achieve sustainable development*? Achieving sustainability is now posing formidable challenges for regional economic policymakers as they seek to formulate strategy in a new environment of rapid change and uncertainty as well as a concern for achieving continuous maintenance and renewal of their economic and related social and environmental systems or sustainability.

Third, the 1980s and 1990s were also the age of *economic rationalism* with an emphasis in public policy on the corporatization and privatization of public assets and functions. The *neo-liberalism* ideology that became the cornerstone of regional economic development policy and planning strategy in many nations focused on the notion that central or national policies should primarily seek to facilitate conditions that would enhance the building of local capacity and capability in regions with a reliance on strategies of *self-help*. That represents the marked shift to an emphasis on *endogenous* processes of regional growth and development.

Thus, from the 1990s, the increasing focus on *integrated strategic planning* as a pervasive paradigm for economic development led to a renewed interest in industry clusters and the role of smart and soft infrastructure in regional economic development planning strategy processes. As discussed by Stimson, Stough and Roberts (2006: pp. 40–42), the emerging concern with *sustainability* has led to the evolution of a new paradigm for viewing growth and development.

The *traditional growth models* were based on premises such as:

- the goal of profit maximization
- community production and consumption that was resource intensive and concentrated in large urban-industrial centers
- fossil fuel-based energy using energy consumptive technologies
- large scale production systems that were centralized
- the assumption that humans dominate the environment which was seen as abundant and limitless
- a goal of maximizing social benefits.

The *new sustainable development paradigm*, however, is based on premises such as:

- the goal of viable or sustained long-term growth
- conserving resources in production through energy efficient technologies and dispersed production centers of lesser scale
- a shift towards alternative energy sources, recycling and conservation of resources
- the assumption that humans and the environment are mutually interdependent, acknowledgment that resources are exhaustible and often irreplaceable, and that conservation is a principle for long-term viability.

Thus, improvements in regional performance may not necessarily be defined or viewed in terms of economic growth as typically defined in terms of increasing per capita gross regional/domestic product. Further, no-growth is not the same as no-development. Rather, what is seen as being important by the advocates of sustainable development is the acknowledgment that the need for economic progress goes hand-in-hand with development, although such development should minimize costs (economic, social and environmental) and negative externalities, and maximize benefits. This presents a challenging trade-off issue.

The 'New Growth Theory'

As shown in Figure 9.1, during the 1980s – by which time the focus in economic policy paradigms had shifted to monetarism and economic rationalism – there had been a shift from concerns about developing a regional *comparative advantage* to developing a regional *competitive advantage*, and there had been a shift in regional development planning strategy from *master planning* and *structural planning* to *strategic planning* paradigms and thus a new way of conceptualizing regional economic growth and development had begun to emerge which today is known as the '*new growth theory*'.

As early as the late 1970s, Rees (1979) had proposed that *technology* was a prime driver in regional economic development, and since then over the ensuing two to three decades the regional science literature has shown how technology is directly related to traditional concepts of *agglomeration economies* in regional economic development, and more recently to new or re-packaged older concepts of *entrepreneurship*, *institutions*, and *leadership* (Stimson, Stough and Roberts, 2006).

Theorists such as Romer (1986, 1990), Barro (1990), Rebelo (1991), Grossman and Helpman (1991), and Arthur (1994) sought to explain technical progress in its role as a generator of economic development as an *endogenous* effect rather than accepting the neo-classical view of long term growth being due to only to *exogenous* factors.

Thomas (1975) and later Erickson (1994), among others, showed how technological change is related to the competitiveness of regions. And Norton and Rees (1979) and Erickson and Leinbach (1979) showed how the *product cycle*, when incorporated into a spatial setting, may impact differentially on regions through three stages, namely:

- an innovation stage
- a growth stage
- a standardization stage.

Over the course of this transition, production is seen to shift from the original high cost home region to a lower cost location, often off-shore, which has been hastened through the evolution of the internationalization of the production process. Thus some regions are the innovators, while others become the branch plants or recipients of the innovation, and these might even then become innovators via endogenous growth.

Markusen (1985) extended the *product cycle theory* of regional development by articulating how profit cycles and oligopoly in various types of industrial organization and corporate development can magnify regional development differentials.

The concept of *innovative milieu* was formulated to explain the 'how, when and why' of new technology generation. That notion linked back to the importance of agglomeration economies and localization economies that had been viewed as leading to the development of new industrial spaces (Scott 1988; Porter 1990; Krugman, 1991).

Some theorists, such as Fukuyama (1995), have suggested that it is not just economic but also value and cultural factors – including social capital and trust – that are important in the rise of technology agglomerations as seen in the Silicon Valley phenomenon, where collaboration among small- and medium-sized enterprises through networks and alliances and links with universities forge a powerful R&D and entrepreneurial business climate. But Castells and Hall (1994), in discussing innovative industrial milieus, note the following:

> …despite all this activity…most of the world's actual high-technology production and innovation still comes from areas that are not usually heralded as innovative milieus… the great metropolitan areas of the industrial world (p. 11).

However, as Rees (2001) points out, technology based theories of regional economic development need to incorporate the role of entrepreneurship and leadership, particularly as factors in the endogenous growth of regions, and it is the

> …link between the role of technology change and leadership that can lead to the growth of new industrial regions and to the regeneration of older ones (p. 107).

Thus, the *new growth theory* models allow and imply that importance of both:

- agglomeration effects (economies of scale and externalities); and
- market imperfections, with the price mechanism not necessarily generating an optimal outcome through efficient allocation of resources.

Also, the processes of capital accumulation and free trade do *not* necessarily lead to convergence of wage and price levels between regions, with positive agglomeration effects concentrating activity in one or a few regions through self-enforcing effects that attract new investment. Most importantly, the *new growth theory'* allows for both *concentration* and *divergence*.

Implications

As discussed by Stimson, Stough and Roberts (2006), the challenge facing economic development planners in contemporary times is how to formulate economic policy that will respond to:

- global dynamics; and
- sometimes (or often) a national vacuum in adoption of an regionally oriented macro policy in many countries.

At one time regions were protected from outside competition, and to some extent their economies could be manipulated by national governments. But that ability is overwhelmingly compromised as the economic rationalism pursued by many national governments left many regions to fend for themselves. Regions still continue to look to higher levels of government for support and resources to provide economic direction and investment to stimulate economic development. But, unfortunately, many regions fail to understand that globalization has left these higher levels of governments relatively weak when it comes to using their inherent power to apply economic and policy mechanisms to enhance the competitiveness of regional economies.

Thus, as discussed by Stimson, Stough and Roberts (2006), in the contemporary policy era it would seem that it is more and more up to regions to develop and use their own devices to compete internationally in order to survive. Thus, today a reliance on endogenous processes is typically espoused in regional economic development policy, and to do that a region would need first to understand what the factors are that set the dynamics of the new economic age that emerged the late 20th century.

A number of key themes have emerged regarding what constitutes regional growth and development and regional competitiveness. Not surprisingly, however, there are differences of views among regional economic development scholars, and some of those differences relate to the relative focus given to the roles of *exogenous* forces on the one hand and the roles of *endogenous* processes and factors on the other. But there does now seem to be an almost universal realization of what Garlick, Taylor and Plumber (2006) refer to as the '*institutional embeddedness*' of *endogenous* processes and factors in regional development.

Of course *exogenous* factors are important to a region's economic performance and how it develops over time; but increasing importance is being placed on *endogenous* forces as determinants of a region's competitiveness. However, regional economic development policy initiatives now tend to be more oriented towards measures that enhance local capacity and capability for a city or region to develop and cope with rapid change in an increasingly competitive global environment. While endogenous growth theory makes mention of leadership, entrepreneurship, and institutional factors, little systematic analysis has occurred to thoroughly conceptualize or, even more, measure their roles as endogenous factors in the development process.

A New Model Framework for Regional Economic Development

Stimson, Stough and Salazar (2003; 2005) have proposed a new model framework depicted in Figure 9.2. Operationally, that model may be represented as:

$$RED = f\,[RE, M\, ..\ \textit{mediated by}\ ..\ (L, I, E)]$$

The *outcome* of the *regional economic development process* (*RED*) is the degree to which a region has achieved competitive performance, displays entrepreneurship, and has achieved sustainable development. Those *outcome states* are defined as the *dependent variable(s)* in the model.

An outcome state is conceptualized as being dependent on a set of *quasi-independent variables* relating to a city or region's resource endowments (*RE*) and its 'fit' with market conditions (*M*), that are mediated through interaction among sets of *intervening variables* that include factors defined as leadership (*L*) and institutions (*I*) which may interact to facilitate or suppress entrepreneurship (*E*).

The framework proposed (Figure 9.2) incorporates both *direct* and *indirect* effects in the interactions between *RE, M* (the quasi-independent variables) and *L, I* and *E* (the intervening or mediating variables). Also, the interactions between the intervening or mediating variables *L, I* and *E* may be both direct and indirect.

Stimson, Stough and Salazar (2005) have proposed the following possible sets of variables that may be used to operationalize this model of endogenous regional growth and development.

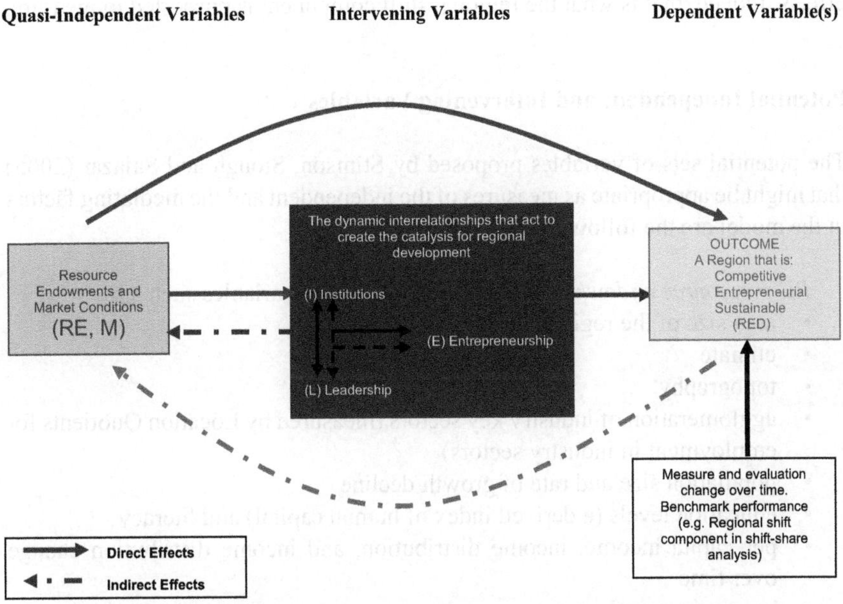

Figure 9.2 A new model framework for the regional economic development process

The Dependent Variable: Measuring Endogenous Growth

One feasible approach proposed by Stimson, Stough and Salazar (2005) to measure the *RED* dependent variable performance across the regions of a state or a nation as the *dependent variable* in the above model is to take a simple surrogate measure of *endogenous growth*, namely the *regional* or *differential shift component* derived from a *shift share analysis* of regional employment change over time by summing the regional or differential employment shift across all industry sectors standardized or weighted by the size of the regional labour force. Thus, *RED* = *endogenous growth* in region may be measured as:

- the aggregate regional differential shift component value in a shift share analysis; or
- an employment scale weighted location quotient change over time.

Secondary data tends to be readily available to do that in most countries, and typically it may be achieved using census data for industry employment in regions. That regional shift component is a reasonable surrogate measure of the degree to which employment growth or decline in a region is due to endogenous or within-region processes and factors against changes due to national and industry-mix shift effects. Indeed, that is what the regional shift component is purported to measure.

Potential Independent and Intervening Variables

The potential sets of variables proposed by Stimson, Stough and Salazar (2005) that might be appropriate as measures of the independent and the mediating factors in the model are the following:

RE = *resource endowments*, measured by a set of variables such as:

- area size of the region
- climate
- topography
- agglomeration of industry key sectors (measured by Location Quotients for employment in industry sectors)
- population size and rate of growth/decline
- education levels (a derived index of human capital) and literacy
- per capita income, income distribution, and income distribution change over time
- housing ownership
- investment in industrial and commercial construction, benchmarked to the region's national share vis a vis its national share of population
- infrastructure investment (per capita), such as on roads, schools, hospitals, etc.
- industrial structure and change in industrial structure (measured by an industrial diversity index)
- regional organizational slack resources.

M = *market fit,* measured by a set of variables such as:

- basic economic activity in major industry sectors (measured by Location Quotients for employment in industry sectors)
- airline connections with other regions/cities
- road freight in/out movements
- volume and value of exports in key products and services.

It would also be useful to use variables that measure the degree to which the region's products fit with changing demand and related markets, to ascertain the degree to which supply fits the local market, and to evaluate the extent to which the local infrastructure provides the necessary linkages to export markets. These are of course thorny issues when one is faced with the decision of measuring them.

L = leadership, measured by a set of variables such as:

- the degree of change/stability in local political leadership
- expert assessment of leadership quality
- relative level of corporate headquaters located in the region
- density (number, budget and/or employment) of region wide business and community organizations (or economic development organizations) per 10,000 population.

I = institutions, measured by a set of variables such as:

- institutional thickness (corporate and community organizations per 10,000 population
- layers of government/government fragmentation
- formal institutions of governance, measured by number of public agencies per 10,000 population
- number of headquarters of major corporations (e.g. Fortune 1000 firms)
- value foundation capitalization per 10,000 population
- government fragmentation
- level of regional organizations (number and budget level)
- index of social capital.

E = entrepreneurship, measured by sets of variables such as:

- churn rate (ratio of start-up to deaths of firms) or business start-up rate
- venture capital activity
- corporate venturing activity
- patents issued per 10,000 workers
- Location Quotient of employment in 'symbolic analyst' occupations.

Stimson, Stough and Salazar (2005) argue that *RED* is positively related to *RE, M, L, I,* and *E*, but that there are likely to be lead and lag and interaction effects in the short to intermediate run, and perhaps cyclical effects in the longer run. Thus,

$$RED_t = RE_{t-1} + M_{t-1} + (I_{t-1} \text{ to } I_{t-10}/10) + L_{t-2} + E_{t-2} + e$$

This modeling approach proposed by Stimson, Stough and Salazar (2003, 2005) to examine the processes of endogenous growth and how regional development may be influenced by, and facilitated through, leadership, entrepreneurship, and institutional factors as intervening or mediating variables which, it is hypothesized, may have a catalytic effect on the endogenous growth processes, but which also accounts for local resource endowments and factors relating to the 'market fit' of a region, represents a potential operational model to measure and examine the impacts of endogenous factors on regional economic growth and development. It is important to note, in keeping with our argument that regional economic development strategy has become more endogenous in nature recently, that the model framework was developed explicitly to conceptualize the interaction of endogenous processes. The authors are currently seeking to empirically test the model.

Towards a New Paradigm for Endogenous Regional Growth and Development Planning Strategy

As stated by Stimson, Stough and Roberts (2006):

> ...Because of the changing role of regional economies within nations and the impacts of globalisation, and given the context of contemporary concerns about how to achieve sustainable development, a set of new considerations are thus now being taken into account in formulating and implementing economic development strategies for regions. (p.46)

The following general points might be made:

1. While traditional models of regional economic growth and development and traditional modes of regional analysis remain important and useful as means of addressing regional economic change, the emergence of the *'new growth theory'* and the emphasis now being placed on the importance of endogenous processes in regional growth, along with increasing concerns over sustainability in regional development strategy planning, have resulted in the emergence of new and more integrated thinking about regional development policy and planning.
2. Many of the traditional approaches to strategy for regional economic development and the implementation of plans have been deficient – or at least appear to be inadequate – to deal with the dynamics of regions having to both compete in the global economy and address issues of sustainability.
3. Following the influence of Porter (1985; 1986), increasingly it has become essential for regions to fully understand what factors (broadly defined compared to traditional thinking on development) constitute their regional competitiveness and how they might maintain and enhance that competitive position.
4. Authors such as Imbroscio (1995) advocate strategies of greater self-reliance, while McGee (1995) and Ohmae (1995) advocate the pursuit of regional economic development strategies based on strategic alliances and inter- and intra-regional network structures, including digital networks (Tapscott, 1996).

5. As indicated in the work of authors such as Henton (1995), Hall (1995), Waites (1995), Sternburg (1991), and Stough (1995), many regional analysts are advocating the need to base regional economic development on the growth of clusters of industries.
6. The concern over sustainability increasingly is evident in regional economic development and is being reflected in regional plans that seek to integrate environmental, economic and social facators to create urban and regional environments that enhance quality of life, meet environmental quality goals, and achieve economic growth and employment diversification.
7. And in the contemporary era of globalization and an age of rapid change and uncertainty, procedures to identify and strategies to manage both exogenous and endogenous regional risks are crucial.

Thus, thinking is diverse on how to plan for and how to facilitate regional economic development in an environment of global competition, rapid change, and a concern over sustainability.

All of this means that regions and regional economic development agencies need to give explicit attention not only to *exogenous* factors but importantly to *endogenous* factors in formulating regional development policy, in framing strategy and implementing plans to achieve regional economic growth and development, and to enhance regional economic performance. In arguing the need for an emerging paradigm of regional economic development planning, and to assist regions to undertake the processes involved in regional economic development strategy, it is important to identify the key elements for regional economic development strategy building and implementation, and to place those in a process that draws together resources, infrastructure, social capital and technology to facilitate the economic development of a region in a dynamic globally competitive environment.

Stimson, Stough and Roberts (2006: pp. 46–27) suggest that giving explicit consideration to the following factors is necessary to achieve these economic development outcomes:

- the identification of regional core competencies, how to maintain them, and how to accumulate new core competencies
- developing social capital
- building and maintaining strategic leadership
- the continuous rejuvenation or re-engineering of the processes of governance and the structure and functions of institutions
- the more effective and efficient exploitation and management of resources
- building market intelligence
- providing strategic and smart infrastructure
- identifying regional risks, and developing a risk management capability
- incorporating the principles of sustainability into regional economic development strategies.

There is, however, no universal model or framework guaranteeing success for regional economic development. Stimson, Stough and Roberts (2006) provide a simple representation of contemporary best practice approach to regional economic development. That approach suggests that the intent of regional economic development strategy may be to:

- establish a platform for change to guide the development of a region and to facilitate its competitiveness in a global environment in the pursuit of a sustainable future
- mobilize key actors or facilitators and agents of change, through partnership approaches encompassing strategic alliances and partnerships between business, markets, government and community.

The framework suggested by Stimson, Stough and Roberts proposes the following:

1. The identification, description, analysis and evaluation of core competencies, resource endowments, infrastructure competitiveness, market intelligence, and regional risk through the combination of qualitative and quantitative methods encompassed in industry cluster analysis (ICA) (see, for example, Bergman and Fesser, 2000; Stough, Kulkarni, Riggle and Haynes, 2000) and multi sector analysis (MSA) (see Roberts and Stimson, 1998).
2. The identification and evaluation of economic possibilities for the future leading to the statement of strategic intent.
3. The evaluation of alternative development futures or scenarios through the participation of stakeholders within the region and, most importantly, external to it to encompass the assessments of key decision-makers controlling capital, trade and other flows to the region. If the assessments of the feasibility of the alternative scenarios by the internal and external stakeholders are incongruent, then there is the potential that inappropriate or unfeasible strategies will be pursued. Thus strategic directions might need to be redefined before formulating an economic development strategy which focuses on industry cluster development and the provision of strategic architecture.
4. Implementation plans and mechanisms need to be developed and put in place by appropriate agencies in the region.
5. The progress made towards achieving the desired development future needs to be monitored, requiring agreement on indicators and benchmarks set to measure and evaluate the performance of the region over time in order to assess the degree of success of the strategy and progress towards achievement of the strategic intent. Inevitably this involves building enhanced regional infrastructure systems along with strengthening existing and building new partnerships, networks and alliances.

6. Finally, in the contemporary era of the global economy, increasingly the pursuit of regional economic development also needs to take place within the context of principles for achieving a sustainable future.

Stimson, Stough and Roberts (2006, pp. 222–35) propose that the implementation of this approach to regional economic development planning strategy might involve the 14 steps set out in Figure 9.3. This new approach to the process of formulating a regional economic development planning strategy framework is firmly embedded in the principles of promoting conditions to enhance *endogenous* growth and development.

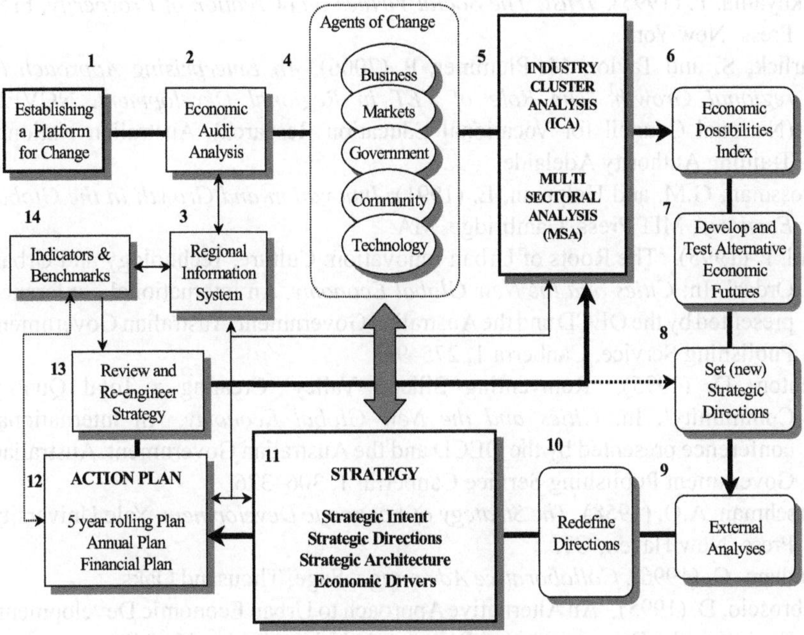

Figure 9.3 The steps involved in implementing the new framework for regional economic development planning strategy

References

Arthur, W.B. (1994), *Increasing Returns and Path Dependency in the Economy*, Ann Arbor: University of Michigan Press.

Barro, R.J. (1990), 'Government Spending in a Simple Model of Endogenous Growth', *Journal of Political Economy* 98, S103–S125.

Bergman, E.M. and Fesser, E.J. (2000), 'National industry cluster templates: A framework for applied regional cluster analysis', *Regional Studies* 34(1), 1–19.

Castells, M., Hall, P. (1994), *Technopoles of the World: The Making of 21st Century Industrial Complexes,* Routledge, London.
Dicken, P. (1992), *Global Shift: The Internationalisation of Economic Activity*, 2nd Edition. Guilford Press, New York.
Erickson, R.A. (1994), 'Technology, Industrial Restructuring and Regional Development', *Growth and Change*, 25, 353–79.
Erickson, R.A. and Leinbach, T. (1979), 'Characteristics of Branch Plants Attracted to Non metropolitan Areas'. In: Lonsdale, R. and Seyter, H.L. (eds), *Non Metropolitan Industrialisation*, Winston, Washington, DC.
Feser, E.J. (1998), 'Enterprises, External Economics and Economic Development', *Journal of Planning Literature* 12, 282–302.
Fukuyama, F. (1995), *Trust: The Social Virtues and Creation of Prosperity*, Free Press, New York.
Garlick, S. and Taylor, M. Plummer, P. (2006), *An Enterprising Approach to regional Growth: The Role of VET in Regional Development*, NCVER (National Council for Vocational Education Research), Australian National Training Authority Adelaide.
Grossman, G.M. and Helpman, E. (1991), *Innovation and Growth in the Global Economy*, MIT Press, Cambridge, MA.
Hall, P. (1995), 'The Roots of Urban Innovation: Culture, Technology and Urban Order'. In: *Cities and the New Global Economy*, An international conference presented by the OECD and the Australian Government. Australian Government Publishing Service, Canberra 1, 275–93.
Henton, D. (1995), 'Reinventing Silicon Valley: Creating a Total Quality Community'. In: *Cities and the New Global Economy*, An international conference presented by the OECD and the Australian Government. Australian Government Publishing Service Canberra, 1, 306–326.
Hirschman, A.O. (1958), *The Strategy of Economic Development*, Yale University Press, New Haven, CT.
Huxham, C. (1996), *Collaborative Advantage*, Sage, Thousand Oaks.
Imbroscio, D. (1995), 'An Alternative Approach to Urban Economic Development: Exploring the Dimensions and Prospects', *Urban Affairs*, 30, 840.
Johansson, B., C. Karlsson and R.R. Stough (eds) (2001), *Theories of Endogenous Regional Growth*, Berlin, Springer.
Karlson, C., Johaansson, B. and Stough, R.R. (eds) (2005), *Industrial Clusters and Inter-firm Networks*, Cheltenham, UK, Edward Elgar.
Knight, R.V. and Gappert, G. (eds) (1989), *Cities in a Global Society*, Sage Publications, Newbury Park.
Krugman, P. (1991), *Geography and Trade*, Cambridge, Mass., MIT Press.
Malecki, E. (1991), *Technology and Economic Development: The Dynamics of Local, Regional and National Competitiveness*, Longman Scientific and Technical, Harlow.
Markusen, A. (1985), *Profit Cycles, Oligopoly and Regional Development*, MIT Press, Cambridge, MA.

McGee, T.G. (1995), 'System of Cities and Networked Landscapes: New Cultural Formations and Urban Built Environments in the Asia-Pacific Region', *Pacific Rim Council on Urban Development*, Conference Proceedings, Brisbane.

Myrdal, G. (1957), *Economic Theory and Underdeveloped Regions*, Duckworth Press, London.

Norton, R.D. and Rees, J. (1979), 'The Product Cycle and the Decentralization of North American Manufacturing', *Regional Studies* 13, 141–51.

Ohmae, K. (1995), *The End of the Nation State: The Rise of Regional Economics*, Free Press, New York.

Perroux, F. (1950), 'Economic Space: Theory and Application', *Journal of Economics* 4, 90–97.

Porter, M.E. (1985), *Competitive Advantage: Creating and Sustaining Superior Performance*, New York Free Press, New York.

Porter, M.E. (1986), *Competition in Global Industries*, Cambridge, Harvard Business School Press.

Porter, M.E. (1990), *The Competitive Advantage of Nations*, Macmillan, New York.

Putnam, R. (1993), 'The Prosperous Community: Social Capital and Public Life', *The American Prospect* Spring, 35–42.

Rebelo, S. (1991), 'Long Run Policy Analysis and Long Run Growth', *Journal of Political Economy* 98, S71–S102.

Rees, J. (1979), 'State Technology Programs and Industry Experience in the USA', *Review of Urban and Regional Development Studies* 3, 39–59.

Rees, J. (2001), 'Technology and Regional Development: Theory Revisited'. In: Johansson, B., Karlsson, C. and Stough, R.R. (eds) *Theories of Endogenous Regional Growth*, Springer-Verlag, Heidelberg, 94–110.

Roberts, B.H. and Stimson, R.J. (1998), 'Multi-sectoral Qualitative Analysis: A Tool for Assessing the Competitiveness of Regions and Developing Strategies for Economic Development', *Annals of Regional Science* 32, 4, 459–67.

Romer, P. M. (1986), 'Increasing Returns and Long-run Growth', *Journal of Political Economy* 94(5), 1002–1037.

Romer, P.M. (1990), 'Endogenous Technological Change', *Journal of Political Economy* 98: S71–S102.

Scott, A.J. (1988), *New Industrial Spaces: Flexible Production Organization and Regional Development in North America and Western Europe*, Pion, London.

Solow, R.M. (1956), 'A Contribution to the Theory of Economic Growth', *Quarterly Journal of Economics* 70, 65–94.

Solow, R.M. (2000), *Growth Theory: An Exposition*, Oxford University Press, New York.

Sternburg, E. (1991), 'The Sectoral Clusters in Economic Development Policy: Lessons from Rochester and Buffalo', *Economic Development Quarterly* 4, 342–56.

Stimson, R.J., A. Robson, R.R. Stough and M. Salazar (2003), 'Leadership, Institutions and Regional Economic Development: A New Conceptual Framework', *Pacific Regional Science Conference Organization*, 18th Biennial Meeting, Acapulco, Mexico, July.

Stimson, R.J. and R.R. Stough (2005), 'Regional Endogenous Growth: The Role of Leadership and Institutions', *Western Regional Science Association*, Annual Meeting, San Diego, February.

Stimson, R.J., R.R. Stough and B.H. Roberts (2006), *Regional Economic Development: Analysis and Planning Strategy*, Revised Edition, Berlin, Springer.

Stimson, R.J., R.R. Stough and M. Salazar (2003), 'Leadership and Institutional Factors in Endogenous Regional Economic Development'. *North American Regional Science Association*, 50th Annual Meeting, Philadelphia, November.

Stimson, R.J., Stough, R.R. and M. Salazar (2005), 'Leadership, and institutional factors in endogenous regional economic development', *Investigaciones Regionales* 7, 23–52.

Stough, R.R. (1995), 'Industry sector analysis of the Northern Virginia Economy', *Proceedings of the Second Annual Conference on the Future of the Northern Virginia Economy*, Center for Regional Analysis, The Institute of Public Policy and the Northern Virginia Business Roundtable, George Mason University, Fairfax, VA., 3–37.

Stough, R.R., K.E. Haynes and M.E. Slazar (2005), 'Economic Development Theory and Practice: The Indian Development Experience', In Thatchenkery, T. and R.R. Stough (eds) *Information Communication Technology and Economic Development: Learning from the Indian Experience*. Edward Elgar, Cheltenham, England, 11–28.

Stough, R.R., Kulkarni, R., Riggle, J. and Haynes, K.E. (2000), 'Technology and industrial cluster analysis: Some new methods', paper presented at 1st South African Regional Science Association meeting, January, Port Elizabeth, South Africa.

Tapscott, D. (1996), *The Digital Economy: Promise and Peril in the Age of Networked Intelligence*, McGraw Hill, New York.

Thomas, M.D. (1975), 'Growth Pole Theory, Technological Change and Regional Economic Growth', *Papers of the Regional Science Association* 34, 3–25.

Waites, M. (1995), 'Economic Development: Building and Economic Future', *State Government News* 38. Phoenix, AZ.

Chapter 10

The Role of Universities in Theories of Regional Development

Paul Dalziel, Caroline Saunders and William Kaye-Blake[1]

> Theorisation of the role of universities in regional innovation systems has evolved in the last 20 years, from the innovation systems approach, which highlighted the importance of knowledge spillovers from the educational and research activities performed by universities in regional knowledge spaces, towards the development of a third role performed by universities in animating regional economic and social development (Gunasekara, 2006, p. 102).

James Rowe has described how the pace of change in modern processes of globalization has accentuated the need for regions to market their competitive advantage based on regional fundamentals of production, trade and the provision of service. This led him to argue that 'the most important activity for regional economic development is the creation of competitive advantage' (Rowe, 2005, p. 1). A substantial literature has addressed the way in which regions might strengthen local innovation systems to assist in this task of ongoing enterprise and creativity, as explained in other chapters of this book. The purpose of this chapter is to survey the ways in which universities are able to assist and encourage regional development. As the quotation at the head of this chapter notes, universities make distinctive contributions to regional development through their research, educational and local animation activities. Indeed, Karlsson and Zhang (2001, p. 180) have suggested that 'research-oriented universities are to the knowledge economy what coal and iron mines were to the industrial economy'. This chapter develops that theme under three headings: universities as producers of new knowledge; universities as educators of advanced knowledge; and universities as animators of regions and sectors.

Universities as Producers of New Knowledge

Drucker and Goldstein (2007, pp. 30–34) surveyed ten studies published between 1993 and 2003 that empirically examined the relationship between the knowledge

1 The authors are grateful to Anita Kumar for research assistance in preparing this chapter, and to James Rowe for providing two of the articles used in the review.

Table 10.1 The university as producer of new knowledge

<table>
<tr><th colspan="2" rowspan="2"></th><th colspan="2">Dissemination of New Knowledge</th></tr>
<tr><th>Non-Marketed
Open Science</th><th>Marketed
Intellectual Property</th></tr>
<tr><td rowspan="5">Basic and Applied Research</td><td>Researcher-Inspired</td><td rowspan="3">Conference Presentations
Journal Articles, Books and Other Publications
Media and Other Public Statements
Contributions to the Research Environment
Peer Esteem
Public Science Funds
Tertiary Sector Research Assessment Exercises</td><td>Patents and Licences
Spin-Off Firms
New Start Incubators</td></tr>
<tr><td>Government-Inspired</td><td>Public Science Funds
Contract Research for Policy
University Policy Institutes</td></tr>
<tr><td>Industry-Inspired</td><td>Industry Research Levies
Joint Ventures
University Research Centres</td></tr>
<tr><td>Enterprise-Inspired</td><td>Research Precinct or Technology Park Close to the University</td><td>Research Sponsored by Firms
Staff Consultancy
University Research Offices</td></tr>
<tr><td>Student-Oriented</td><td>Dissertations or Research Projects
Masters or PhD Theses
Publications</td><td>Employment in a Relevant Firm
New Starts by Graduates</td></tr>
</table>

production function of universities and the impact on their region. The main conclusion of their review was that 'external benefits of knowledge production in the form of spatial spillovers lead to increased innovation among other regional firms, though the body of research demonstrates considerable variety in the measured magnitude and significance of this effect' (Drucker and Goldstein, 2007, p. 34). This section presents in Table 10.1 a two-dimensional classification of university research activities in producing new knowledge, and uses it to discuss how these activities can contribute to regional and national economic transformation.

The first dimension in Table 10.1 distinguishes five types of research, depending on whether it is inspired by the researcher, the government, an industry, an enterprise or the requirement for postgraduate students to include research as part of their degree. This dimension brings together and expands two different sets of research categories proposed by Garlick (1998, pp. 37–48) and Cox (2000, pp. 15–16, quoting Stokes, 1997). All of these categories include basic and applied research. The second dimension creates a distinction based on whether new knowledge produced by university research is part of the university's contribution to non-marketed open science or is disseminated in the form of marketed intellectual property.

Researcher-inspired research refers to 'curiosity-driven' research initiated by a university staff member to create new knowledge for its own sake. Although results from a researcher-inspired project may have commercial potential, this is not its primary motivation. Government-inspired research is undertaken in response to announced government policy objectives or requests for research proposals, while industry-inspired research refers to research that has its objectives defined by the perceived needs of a particular industry. There may, of course, be close links between government and industry in determining a country's R&D policy. Enterprise inspired research is a project that is initiated in response to the needs of a particular individual firm. This includes contract research or consultancy projects based on the technical or business expertise of university staff. Student-oriented research refers to research undertaken as part of the requirements for a postgraduate degree. The new knowledge produced by a postgraduate student is typically presented in a dissertation or research project (at the honours level) or in a Masters or PhD thesis, and may be publishable in a suitable academic or industry journal.

The tradition of 'open science', which goes back to the late 16th and early 17th centuries (David, 1998), is based on long-established norms of 'open inquiry' and 'complete disclosure' in what is conceptualized as a social process of producing and verifying new knowledge, with rewards being mediated through reputation effects rather than by direct financial reward (David, 2003, pp. 3–4):

> The core of this rationale is the greater efficacy of open inquiry and complete disclosure as a basis for the cooperative, cumulative generation of predictably reliable additions to the stock of knowledge. In brief, 'openness' abets rapid validation of findings, and reduces excess duplication of research efforts. Wide sharing of information puts knowledge into the hands of those who can put it to uses requiring expertise, imagination and material facilities not possessed by the original discoverers and inventors. This enlarges the domain of complementarity among additions to the stock of reliable knowledge, and promotes beneficial 'spill-overs' among distinct research programs.
>
> …To be rewarded for a novel idea, research technique, or experimental result, one must be seen to have been in the vanguard of its creators. It is the prospect of gaining such rewards – whether in reputational standing and the esteem of colleagues, enhanced access to research resources, formal organizational recognition through promotions accompanied by higher salary, accession to positions of authority and influence within professional bodies and public institutions, the award of prizes and honors – that serves to induce races to establish 'priority,' and hence to secure rapid disclosure of 'significant' findings.

The norms of open science are the same whether the research idea originates with the researcher, the government or industry. The results of the research are expected to be made public through conference presentations, journal articles and books. The researcher is expected to be available for public comment on his or her areas of expertise and to make suitable contributions to the national and international research environment (by acting as a journal referee, for example, or organizing conferences or serving on science committees). The significance of a researcher's published findings brings reputation rewards and peer esteem.

In New Zealand, for example, the Marsden Fund is a public science fund that is targeted to curiosity-driven open science that is researcher inspired, and the six-yearly Quality Assessment of the Tertiary Education Commission's Performance-Based Research Fund (similar to the Research Assessment Exercise in the United Kingdom) is specifically designed to reward and enhance the reputation effect of successful open science research undertaken by the country's tertiary institutions.

Enterprise-inspired research is not a significant part of open science, since new knowledge created for an individual firm is typically subject to commercial considerations. Nevertheless, there are some areas where private firms have allowed their research staff to engage in open science (with open source software being a notable example), and there is also evidence that technologically advanced firms may choose to locate in a research precinct or technology park close to a university in order to interact with researchers engaged in open science (Lindelöf and Löfsten, 2004; Alcácer and Chung, 2007).

The involvement of universities in producing marketed intellectual property is relatively recent (Bercovitz and Feldmann, 2006). In the early and mid-20th century, a small number of universities in the United States began patenting some of their discoveries through a central agency, the Research Corporation (Mowery and Sampat, 2001; Mowery, 2002). In the 1970s, the agency went into decline as more universities created their own in-house patenting and licensing capabilities. This process received a further boost with the passing of the Bayh-Dole Act of 1980 that, among other things, permitted universities to own patents arising from federal research grants (Poyago-Theotoky et al., 2002, p. 11). Universities in the United States accounted for just 0.3 per cent of domestically assigned patents in 1970, but this ratio had risen to 3.6 per cent by 1999 (Mowery, 2002, p. 261).

Income flows to universities from licensing patents to firms have grown over the same period (Mowery, 2002, Figure 9; Sampat, 2006, Figure 4). There remains a significant public good element, however, since Heher (2006, p. 406) suggests that technology transfer offices in British universities typically operate at a loss, and Sampat (2006, p. 782) reports that the majority of American universities are losing money on their patenting and licensing activities. In the universities where profits are made, revenues are dominated by a small number of biomedical inventions (Mowery, 2002, p. 267). Some academics argue that involvement in patenting is incompatible with a university's commitment to the norms of open science (see, for example, the debate at John Hopkins University reported in Feldman and Desrochers, 2003, and also the comments of Nelson, 2001), but there is evidence that academic staff who are engaged in patenting activity are as productive in their open science contributions as their non-patenting peers (see Theotoky et al., 2002, pp. 18–19, and Meyer, 2006b).

An alternative path for an academic who has created marketable intellectual property is to start up a new firm to commercialize the invention (Meyer, 2006a; Niosi, 2006). There are a number of different models for spin-off firms of this nature (Franklin et al., 2001). First, the inventor might remain a member of the university and develop the business as a secondary occupation. Second, the inventor might resign in order to work full-time on the start-up firm. Third, the inventor or university might invite a 'surrogate entrepreneur' to initiate the start-up company (with a suitable compensation package to reflect the entrepreneur's skills and risks) so that the inventor can remain employed as an academic. The university may be involved in a 'new starts incubator' (with associated business advisors, venture capitalists and angel investors) to assist the early stage development of new companies that seek to commercialize an invention produced by university researchers. In some cases, a new start incubator may be part of a university's technology park constructed to attract rent-paying private firms.

Government, industries and individual enterprises have needs for new knowledge that may inspire the creation of marketable intellectual property by university researchers. Government-inspired research originates from two primary sources. First, the government may encourage university researchers to undertake basic or applied research to advance national R&D policy priorities. In New Zealand, the Foundation for Research, Science and Technology annually invests approximately NZ$450 million of public science funds in science and technology research. Much of this research is open science, but contractors are explicitly required to have a set of intellectual property policies and procedures in place before work begins.

The second important source for government-inspired research is the demand for research to support evidence-based policy advice. A government agency may issue a request for proposals to provide research on a specific policy issue and university staff members are among those who can tender for the research contract. In some cases, a university (with or without the financial support of the government) may create a specialist institute to be a national centre of research expertise in a particular area of government policy.

Industry organizations may purchase research to address an identified need or opportunity in their sector. In New Zealand, the Commodities Levy Act 1990 allows an industry to impose a levy on a commodity to finance certain activities such as 'research relating to the commodity or commodities concerned, or in relation to any matter connected with it' (section 10; Greer et al., 1999, surveys industry views on this legislation). Alternatively, a university might enter into a joint venture with an industry organization or major supplier to fund a specialist research capability or to market a sector-wide innovation or trademark. In the United States, joint ventures between universities and firms for research and for production have been encouraged by specific legislation in 1984 and 1993 (Poyago-Theotoky et al., 2002, p. 11). In New Zealand, some of the major regional initiatives funded under the government's Regional Partnerships Programme have involved joint ventures between tertiary education institutions and industry (see www.nzte.govt.nz/section/11962.aspx). A university may create a dedicated research centre to provide new knowledge to a particular industry or sector (Santoro and Gopalakrishnan, 2001; SSTI, 2006, pp. 14–18).

Individual firms sponsor research at a university in a number of ways, including: providing financial support for an endowed chair or specialist research facility;

entering into a joint venture with the university for research or production; contracting to finance a specific research project; participating in the governance of a research centre; or providing opportunities for student-oriented research in their business. University policy might allow or encourage staff to provide technical or business consultancy services to individual firms under a revenue-sharing arrangement between the university and academic, typically overseen by a dedicated research office for managing research sponsored by outside agencies (firms, industries and government). Martin (1998) describes the consulting activities of teachers and star researchers as one of three ways that universities make knowledge available to the national economy, while Cox and Taylor (2006) demonstrate the significant impact that the provision of business advice by a university business school can have on local economic development. Bercovitz and Feldmann (2006, p. 178) argue that a general lack of data about the extent of academic consulting results in the impact of universities in transferring technology being underestimated. Cambridge University in the United Kingdom, for example, advertises that 'the provision of expert advice to external clients by the University's staff is one of the principal mechanisms by which knowledge that has practical application can be disseminated, thereby contributing to the growth of the economy and to the needs of society generally' (www.enterprise.cam.ac.uk/consultancy/consultancy.html).

Student-oriented research creates specific human capital for the postgraduate student that may be valuable in finding employment in a firm requiring those technical skills. In some cases, employment may commence before the research is completed or an employer may release an employee to undertake postgraduate research to acquire specific skills. If the research project produces a marketable innovation, the graduate may choose to set up a new company to commercialize his or her idea. Such a student may be eligible to participate in a new start incubator sponsored by the university.

It is not easy to quantify the economic transformation benefits of university research, since open science is designed to generate and disseminate reliable new knowledge to a vast range of potential users in industry and government. Because new knowledge has the characteristics of an economics 'public good', successful open science gives rise to increasing returns to scale and significant spillovers or externalities (Blakeley et al., 2005), particularly in their region (Drucker and Goldstein, 2007). A public good is: non-rival in consumption, meaning that one person's use of the good does not prevent another person from using the good at the same time; and non-excludable, meaning that the supplier cannot prevent people who do not pay from using the good. These properties mean that a public good (in this case, new knowledge produced by university research) will be under-supplied by private firms in competitive markets, opening the door for welfare-enhancing public provision or subsidy.

In an often-cited paper, Mansfield (1991) estimated the medium-term social rate of return to academic research. Mansfield sampled 76 major American firms in seven manufacturing industries, who reported that 'about 11 per cent of these firms' new products and about 9 per cent of their new processes could not have been developed (without substantial delay) in the absence of recent academic research' (p. 2). A further 8 per cent of new products and 6 per cent of new processes would have been much more expensive and time-consuming to develop without recent academic research (p. 3). The total value of sales and savings amounted to just under US$60 million in 1985 (p. 5), which led to a tentative but conservative estimate of a social rate of return to global academic research of 28 per cent (p. 11). Mansfield (1998) updated his study to cover the period from 1986 to 1994. This confirmed his previous analysis, with an interesting addition: compared to the earlier period, there was a decrease in the average time lag between academic research results and the first commercial introduction of new products and processes based on those results. As Mansfield commented, 'this decrease could be of considerable economic benefit if it represents a quicker utilization of the findings of recent academic research, but it could have quite different implications if it is due to a shift in academic research toward more applied and short-term work' (p. 703).

Another method for measuring the influence of university research on regional and national economic transformation is to trace the reliance of industry patent applications on cited scientific papers produced in universities. In the first study of this type, Narin et al. (1997) documented that references from US patents to US authored research papers had tripled from 17,000 during 1987–1988 to 50,000 during 1993–1994. Hicks et al. (2001) confirmed the importance of public research in citations, but also demonstrated a strong geographical effect, with patent applications far more likely to cite science papers from the same state rather than from a different part of the country.

Salter and Martin (2001) undertook a critical review of studies using econometric methods, surveys and case studies to measure the economic benefits of publicly funded basic research. Their article found 'extensive evidence that basic research does lead to considerable economic benefits, both direct and indirect' (p. 509); their Table 2, for example, cites six studies between 1968 and 1993 that estimated the rate of return to public research and development in agricultural research to be between 28 and 67 per cent. This is consistent with the estimate by Scobie and Eveleens (1987) of a 30 per cent rate of return for New Zealand agriculture investment in research, extension and human capital development. More recently, Hall and Scobie (2006) have suggested that investment in domestic research and development in the agriculture sector has generated a rate of return of 17 per cent per annum.

An offsetting consideration to these benefits of open science has become prominent in public policy debates in recent years. The issue is summarized in a New Zealand context by Blakely et al. (2005, p. 15):

> Clearly the features of open science comprise a package of incentives that encourage the creation, use and dissemination of knowledge. On the downside, open science is generally expensive on the public purse or it requires a high level of private philanthropy. Also, because science is often isolated from market signals, there may be limited incentives on researchers to ensure their work is relevant to the needs of society as a whole.

The suggestion is that while open science taken in its entirety may contribute to economic transformation, the process would be more effective if individual researchers were motivated to align their work more closely to the knowledge needs of the wider community. This has led to considerable work on the so-called 'triple helix model' (see, for example, Etzkowitz and Leydesdorff, 1997; Benner and Sandström, 2000; Gunasekara, 2006; Leydesdorff, 2006; Mayer, 2006). The essence of this model is that the determination of research priorities within a national system of innovation should be a collaborative process involving university, industry and government partners. The role of government funding agencies is particularly important in developing this model, by 'redirecting academic work towards commercial applications and industry-university collaboration…guided by a norm system stressing the importance of techno-economic renewal and market-determined success' (Benner and Sandström, 2000, p. 292). The particular benefit created by this collaborative process involving university, industry and government is explained by Leydesdorff (2006, p. 199):

> A micro-foundation of the model could be proposed by arguing that the knowledge base of an economy is not only agent-based, but also and in important respects communication-based. When information is exchanged among agents, the communication can be provided with meaning, and this meaning can be further codified, for example, by developing knowledge. Knowledge can perhaps be considered as a meaning that makes a difference. Knowledge informs the exchanges and thus selectively reinforces the solutions found hitherto at interfaces. This latter operation potentially reduces the uncertainty, lowers transaction costs, and thus transforms interfaces within the system innovatively.

The gains from communication between university and industry staff has also been emphasized by Bercovitz and Feldmann (2006, p. 178) in their discussion of the benefits of consulting: 'Most pointedly, faculty consulting may complement university technology transfer potential if it opens new research topics and insights into practical problems for the faculty member'.

Universities as Educators of Advanced Knowledge

The second function of universities in contributing to regional and national economic transformation is as an educator of advanced knowledge that produces skilled labour for the local and national workforce. Table 10.2 summarizes five ways that universities achieve this: by providing generic and specialist undergraduate programmes; by providing postgraduate programmes; by offering short technical or business courses; by including business programmes; and through stakeholder communication.

Table 10.2 The university as educator of advanced knowledge

1. Generic undergraduate programmes produce graduates with higher labour productivity than uneducated workers, while specialist undergraduate programmes produce high productivity graduates with industry-specific or occupation-specific skills.
2. Postgraduate programmes produce graduates with research skills capable of contributing to the future generation of new knowledge.
3. Short technical or business courses allow people already in the workforce, or re-entering the workforce, to extend or upgrade their skills.
4. Business programmes produce graduates with management and entrepreneurial skills for commercializing new knowledge.
5. University stakeholder communication, website resources, technical manuals, extension courses, open days and staff participation in industry seminars and conferences contribute to the adoption of new technologies in industry.

A substantial international literature has been produced over the last 40 years estimating the returns to an individual from investing in post-compulsory education; see, for example, the survey by Psacharopoulos and Patrinos (2004). Table 10.3 lists 12 studies of New Zealand data published since 1999. All of these studies reported positive returns to university education. An excellent survey of the New Zealand evidence is provided in Smart (2006) and so attention here is focused on a précis of the table's last three publications.

Le, Gibson and Oxley (2006) measure the stock of human capital in individuals as the net present value of their expected lifetime earnings, based on their current age, gender and qualifications, after making reasonable assumptions about the country's annual economic growth rate and discount rate. Census data are used to calculate average income levels, labour force participation rates, employment rates, enrolment in education rates and survival rates for each cohort defined by age (yearly from 18–64), gender and educational level. The authors note that 'there is a large income gap between university graduates and the less educated, and this gap has widened over time' (p. 599). They concluded that 'overall, the stock of working human capital grew by 54 per cent in the last two decades' and 'the human capital embodied in university graduates almost quadrupled; in relative terms, their share of the total human capital stock increased from 8.8 per cent to 22 per cent' (p. 608).

Maré and Liang (2006) restrict their analysis to 1996 and 2001 Census data, and focus on the income and employment outcomes for 18 to 30 year-olds with a post-school qualification. Their research was able to distinguish 26 fields of study, from creative arts and design (median income in the 2001 sample of $14,350) to medicine ($48,750). They were also able to measure the premium that a young worker received on average for being employed in an occupation that matched their qualification field – around 20 per cent (p. 35).

Nair's (2007) report draws on the Integrated Student Loan Scheme Borrowers (ISLSB) dataset, which brings together information on enrolments, on Student Loan Scheme borrowers and on taxable incomes, loan balances and loan repayments.

Table 10.3 New Zealand estimates of returns to tertiary education

Authors (Date)	Description
Maani (1999)	Analysis of micro level data from the 1981, 1986, 1991 and 1996 Censuses of Population and Dwellings
Maani (2000)	Analysis of a 20% sample of the 1986 and 1996 Censuses of Population and Dwellings
Gibson (2000)	Analysis of the Education and Training Survey attached to the Household Labour Force Survey in September 1996
Maani (2002)	Analysis of a 50% sample of the 1986 and 1996 Censuses of Population and Dwellings
Hyslop, Maré and Timmins (2003)	Analysis of micro level data from the 1986, 1991, 1996 and 2001 Censuses of Population and Dwellings
Maani and Maloney (2004)	Analysis of the Household Labour Force Survey Income Supplements, 1997–2002
Griffin, Scott and Smyth (2005)	Analysis of the Integrated Student Loan Dataset to 2000 (full analysis) or 2002 (partial analysis)
Newell and Perry (2006)	Analysis of micro level data from the 1981, 1986, 1991, 1996 and 2001 Censuses of Population and Dwellings
Hyatt and Smyth (2006)	Analysis of Student Loan Scheme borrowers who left tertiary study in 1997
Le, Gibson and Oxley (2006)	Analysis of micro level data from the 1981, 1986, 1991, 1996 and 2001 Censuses of Population and Dwellings
Maré and Liang (2006)	Analysis of micro level data from the 1996 and 2001 Censuses of Population and Dwellings
Nair (2007)	Analysis of Student Loan Scheme borrowers who left tertiary study between 1997 and 2001

Nair found that having studied for a Bachelors degree results in an earnings premium of 36 per cent relative to having studied for a level 1 to 3 certificate, while having studied at postgraduate level produces a further premium of about 19 per cent after adjusting for other factors. Nair also reported that the premium for those who completed a Bachelors degree, compared to those who studied at the same level but did not complete their studies, is about 28 per cent (p. 16).

It is generally accepted that the existence of significant earnings premiums for university qualifications reflects the higher labour productivity of graduates compared to non-graduates (Vedder, 2004, p. 677). Further, there is evidence that 'skilled people are often more productive when working with other skilled people', so that there are significant positive externalities or spillovers from university education (Lewis, 2002, p. 17). Taken together, these observations imply that university education gives graduates valuable skills, resulting in a more productive workforce and therefore contributing to economic transformation (NZVCC, 2006, p. 14). It has also been long realized that 'highly-educated workers have a comparative advantage with respect to learning and implementing new technologies' (Bartel and Lichtenberg, 1987, p. 1).

This fundamental conclusion still holds even if some of the earnings premium of graduates is not directly attributable to skills learned in education, but reflects higher innate talent and motivation compared to people who do not begin or complete university education (Gibson, 2000; Vedder, 2004). Indeed, one of the reasons people may undertake university education is to use their qualification to signal to potential employers that they will be a hard-working and successful employee, independent of any specific skills they may have learned during their studies. This so-called 'sheepskin effect' is a valuable service to jobseekers and employers, and a well-designed university degree programme can provide important skills to its graduates *and* act as a signalling device for talent.

Goldstein and Drucker (2006) observe that a university's research and education activities can have spillover effects into the local community that raise regional incomes. Their paper included an econometric study of United States data that confirmed this, with a note of caution. Their analysis revealed that too many graduating students can detract from regional incomes, suggesting that 'if maximizing positive economic development impacts is a priority mission for universities, teaching functions should be tailored to meet the skill demands of the local labour market' (p. 37).

University education is no longer confined to traditional degree programmes targeted at youth leaving school. As Garlick (1998, p. 31) notes, 'increasingly, partnerships between universities and key business and government enterprises as well as industry groups are being formed to develop and implement tailored enterprise or industry-specific, management focused accredited degree and non-degree teaching courses'. In some professions, continuing education is considered essential, and perhaps mandatory, to remain up-to-date with evolving technologies and best practices (Eustace, 2001). Universities are also offering certificates and diplomas as credentials for people completing short technical or business courses. These courses can be particularly valuable for people already in the workforce, or who are re-entering the workforce after time spent in full-time family care, and who want to extend or upgrade their skills.

The literature suggests that university education in commerce-related fields can result in measurable positive impacts on regional development. Miller et al. (2002), for example, report on the contribution of a programme on entrepreneurship created by the University of Glamorgan to promote development in depressed regions of Wales. Colombo and Grilli (2005) analysed 506 young firms in the Italian high-tech sector, and found that the number of years spend by the firm's founder in university education in economic and managerial fields, and to a lesser extent in scientific and technical fields, positively affected growth, while education in other fields did not. This is consistent with research in New Zealand that has recorded the importance of providing more people with marketing and product management skills to enable the high-tech sector to grow (Dalziel et al., 2006; Saunders and Dalziel, 2006).

Finally, there are a number of ways in which universities provide education services to their stakeholder communities. This can range from a nation-wide programme in university extension for the agriculture sector (Rasmussen, 1989) to newsletters sent out regularly to the university's alumni. More generally, university stakeholder communication, website resources, technical manuals, extension courses, open days and staff participation in industry seminars and conferences can all contribute to the adoption of new technologies in industry.

Universities as Animators of Regions and Sectors

A university's research and teaching activities make it a unique institution in a region, and can make it a valuable resource for the region as a whole or for particular industry sectors. Table 10.4 summarizes five ways that a university can contribute to economic transformation as an animator of regions and sectors: through its contributions to regional revenue flows; through its specialist skills and facilities; through its position as a creative hub in the broader creative ecosystem of a region or industry; through its role as a magnet for talented people and high-tech firms; and through its contribution to community development projects.

A university is typically a significant employer, and the expenditure flows associated with its operations (including the spending of staff and students) can make an important contribution to the regional economy (Drucker and Goldstein, 2007, pp. 24–29). A number of studies have estimated this effect for New Zealand universities, following the early example of Hughes (1994) for the University of Waikato. More recently, it has been estimated that total spending by the University of Auckland resulted in $3.1 billion of output being added to the Auckland region in 2001 (Duncan, Ballingall and Walton, 2002); that the six public tertiary institutions in Wellington had a combined economic impact of $1.4 billion in 2004 (Gittos,

Table 10.4 The university as animator of regions and sectors

1. A university is typically a significant economic entity in a region, making a measurable contribution to regional revenue flows.
2. A university has specialist skills in information gathering, horizon scanning and problem solving, and specialist facilities, instrumentation and expertise, that may be valuable to regional networks or industry clusters.
3. A university may act as a creative hub in the broader creative ecosystem of a region or industry, especially by mobilizing the creative energy of its staff and network partners and by promoting greater tolerance and innovation in a region by its own example and leadership.
4. A university is a magnet for talented people, including its own staff, employees of high-tech firms attracted by the university to the region, and students who choose to remain in the region after graduation.
5. A university may contribute to community development projects, by participating in the regeneration of an economically depressed region, for example, or by being engaged in the co-production of knowledge with indigenous communities.

2005); that the total contribution of the University of Canterbury to the Canterbury regional economy was $1.5 billion in 2003 (Long and Ballingall, 2003); and that the University of Otago's total economic impact on the New Zealand economy was $1.1 billion in 2004 (Ancell, 2005).

International research networks, specialist facilities and instrumentation and the expertise of its staff all contribute to a university having a strong comparative advantage in information gathering, horizon scanning and problem solving (NZVCC, 2006, p. 16; Costello, 2007). These can be valuable assets in wider regional networks or industry clusters, as long as they are made available outside the university. Weiler et al. (2000) provide a case study of a project in Colorado to determine the feasibility of linking a cluster of microbreweries with local barley growers. The high sunk costs involved in evaluating the economic benefit of such a link, coupled with high risk factors in developing a new market, created an information-related market failure that was overcome through the involvement of academics from Colorado State University. These academics 'were distanced from each group's vested interests yet could harness considerable analytical skills [and so] initiated a cycle of analysis, communication, and workable trust' (Weiler et al., 2000, pp. 371–372). Their study resulted in private sector investment coming into the area to fund a niche micro-malting plant, contributing to the region's economic development.

Another example is the University of North Carolina system, which has 16 campuses, including five rural universities. The UNC system has adopted a strategic goal under the heading of *Economic Transformation*: 'As fundamental to its mission, strengthen and extend the University's contribution to transforming the economy of North Carolina through basic and applied research, innovation and creativity, transfer of new knowledge, application of best practices, and high-quality degree programs' (www.ardisummit.com/about.php). Consistent with this regional animation role, the Appalachian Regional Development Institute and the five rural campuses hosted a state-wide conference in June 2007 of businesspeople, economic developers, educators, media, and public officials to explore the theme of 'Doing our part: The role of North Carolina's rural public universities in economic transformation'.

Examples such as this have led to the concept of an 'engaged university' (Gunasekara, 2006; Florida et al., 2006), describing a university that actively encourages its staff to participate in local networks or initiatives as 'regional animators' (Chatterton and Goddard, 2000, p. 481). Adams (2003) explains the positive meaning of 'regional' in this context, using Stanford University as an exemplar:

> In the second half of the twentieth century, Stanford University rose from a regional school to join the ranks of the world's elite universities. Today, 'regional university' tends to be pejorative, referring to a school that has failed to gain a national reputation. Yet 'regional university' has another meaning, referring to a school that has made a conscious effort to meet the needs of nearby communities. Such was the case with

> Stanford, which set out to prepare its undergraduates for the real world (in contrast to the 'ivory tower' approach of other denominational schools) and sought to serve the needs of the Pacific Coast.

Florida et al. (2006, p. 34) argue: 'In short, the university comprises a potential – and, in some places, actual – *creative hub* that sits at the center of regional development. It is a catalyst for stimulating the spillover of technology, talent and tolerance into the community.' It is not a one-sided process: 'to be successful and prosperous, regions need absorptive capacity – the ability to absorb the science, innovation, and technologies that universities create' (idem; see also Adams, 2003, who argues that Stanford's position in its region was strengthened by the fact that Silicon Valley already had a sense of regional solidarity before systematic attempts were made to turn it into an industry district. Nevertheless, universities are able to be regional creative hubs as a result of the talented people they employ (Florida, 2006, p. 5):

> The strength of the university has always been the ability to mobilize the talent and creative energy of all its participants – faculty members, researchers, administrators, graduate and undergraduate students. When institutions draw upon the collective creative energy of thousands of people, new ideas are generated, and new talent is created on campuses and potentially in their communities, as well.

Andersson et al. (2004) have provided econometric evidence in support of the spillover effect of university staff on regional development. In 1987, Sweden introduced a policy to decentralize higher education, involving a significant increase in resources made available to small and medium-sized colleges of higher education. Andersson et al. (2004) studied the labour productivity over 14 years in Sweden's 285 municipalities, and found strong evidence that the expansion of university presence in a municipality (especially the number of university-based researchers) increased the productivity of communities located near to the university facilities.

Thus, one of the significant benefits to a region from having a university in its midst is that a university acts as a magnet for talented people. This includes the talented people on its own staff, but also includes employees of high-tech firms attracted by the university to the region, the university's students, and the graduates who choose to remain in the region after completing their studies.

As noted in the Colorado case study above, the staff of an engaged university can make important contributions to addressing local community issues such as creating opportunities in an economically depressed region (MacLeod et al., 1997) or addressing shortages of affordable housing (Cox, 2000). Writing more generally in favour of community-university partnerships for research, Savan (2004, p. 382) argues that 'community-based research can be an efficient and effective mechanism for community-directed research and development, combining faculty research expertise with student energy and enthusiasm and community experience of local needs and knowledge gaps'. Kassam and Tettey (2003) argue that universities should reward their staff for non-academic publications that are nevertheless useful for communities and policymakers, emphasizing in particular the value of being engaged in the co-production of knowledge with indigenous communities in a way that acknowledges the proprietary rights of those communities.

Conclusion

This chapter has highlighted three ways in which universities make significant contributions to regional and national economic development. First, a university's research activities not only produce new knowledge that can directly promote economic development, but also have been shown empirically to spill over into increased innovation by other regional enterprises. Second, a university's education activities produce skilled graduates for a region's workforce, and offer opportunities for employees in the region to upgrade or diversify their skills. Third, the interaction of university staff with local government, business enterprises and community organizations contributes to regional animation, turning an engaged university into a creative hub at the centre of regional development.

The most important of these functions is the creation of new knowledge. Without this creativity, the ability of universities to provide quality education of advanced knowledge or to animate their local regions would be severely compromised. Florida (2006), for example, argues that the talent and creative energy of university staff and students is a unique contribution to the local community. Inspiration for creation of new knowledge can come from many sources; indeed diversity of inspiration is important for a university's robustness and resilience, to keep it from becoming irrelevant. Creativity on its own, however, is not enough. Dissemination is also required, to get the created knowledge to where it can make a difference. This is primarily achieved through the education of students, which has the added effect of producing more knowledgeable and creative citizens who therefore become potential consumers of the future production of new knowledge. Dissemination is further enhanced if a university is strongly connected to local government, business and community networks, with regional animation then being the social pay-off. In short, by actively pursuing all three of their core functions, universities sustain a unique contribution in providing private and public benefits for their regional and national communities.

References

Adams, S.B. (2003), 'Regionalism in Stanford's Contribution to the Rise of Silicon Valley.' *Enterprise and Society* 4(3), pp. 521–43.

Alcácer, J. and W. Chung (2007), 'Location Strategies and Knowledge Spillovers.' *Management Science* 53(5), pp. 760–76.

Ancell, S. (2005), 'Otago University Worth Over $1 billion Annually.' Press Release. Dunedin: University of Otago, 12 May.

Andersson, R., J.M. Quigley and M. Wilhelmson (2004), 'University Decentralisation as Regional Policy: The Swedish Experiment.' *Journal of Economic Geography* 4(4), pp. 371–88.

Bartel, A.P. and F.R. Lichtenberg (1987), 'The Comparative Advantage of Educated Workers in Implementing New Technology.' *Review of Economics and Statistics* 69(1), pp. 1–11.

Benner, M. and U. Sandström (2000), 'Institutionalizing the Triple Helix: Research Funding and Norms in the Academic System.' *Research Policy* 29(2), pp. 291–301.

Bercovitz, J. and M. Feldmann (2005), 'Entrepreneurial Universities and Technology Transfer: A Conceptual Framework for Understanding Knowledge-Based Economic Development.' *Journal of Technology Transfer* 31(1), pp. 175–88.

Blakely, N., G. Lewis and D. Mills (2005), 'The Economics of Knowledge: What Makes Ideas Special for Economic Growth.' *Policy Perspectives Paper* 05/05. Wellington: New Zealand Treasury.

Chatterton, P. and J. Goddard (2000), 'The Response of Higher Education Institutions to Regional Needs.' *European Journal of Education* 35(4), pp. 475–96.

Colombo, M.G. and L. Grilli (2005), 'Founders' Human Capital and the Growth of New Technology-Based Firms: A Competence-Based View.' *Research Policy* 34(6), pp. 795–816.

Cox, D.N. (2000), 'Developing a Framework for Understanding University-Community Partnerships.' *Cityscape: A Journal of Policy Development and Research* 5(1), pp. 9–26.

Cox, S. and J. Taylor (2006), 'The Impact of a Business School on Regional Economic Development: A Case Study.' *Local Economy* 21(2), pp. 117–35.

Dalziel, P., C. Saunders and E. Zellman (2006), 'Forecast of Skills Demand in the High-tech Sector in Canterbury: Phase Two.' *AERU Research Report* No. 288. Lincoln University.

David, P.A. (1998), 'Common Agency Contracting and the Emergence of "Open Science" Institutions.' *American Economic Review Papers and Proceedings* 88(2), pp. 15–21.

David, P.A. (2003), 'The Economic Logic of "Open Science" and the Balance between Private Property Rights and the Public Domain in Scientific Data and Information: A Primer.' *Stanford Institute for Economic Policy Research Discussion Paper* No. 02–30. California: Stanford University.

Drucker, J. and H. Goldstein (2007), 'Assessing the Regional Economic Development Impacts of Universities: A Review of Current Approaches.' *International Regional Science Review* 30(1), pp. 20–46.

Duncan, I., J. Ballingall and M. Walton (2002), *The University of Auckland: Economic Contribution to the Auckland Region.* Report to the University of Auckland by the New Zealand Institute of Economic Research, Wellington.

Etzkowitz, H. and L. Leydesdorff (eds) (1997), *Universities and the Global Knowledge Economy: A Triple Helix of University-Industry-Government Relations*. London: Pinter.

Eustace, L. (2001), 'Mandatory Continuing Education: Past, Present and Future Trends and Issues.' *Journal of Continuing Education in Nursing* 32(3), pp. 133–7.

Feldman, M. and P. Desrochers (2003), 'Research Universities and Local Economic Development: Lessons from the History of the Johns Hopkins University.' *Industry and Innovation* 10(1), pp. 5–24.

Florida, R. (2006), 'Regions and Universities Together Can Foster a Creative Economy.' *Chronicle of Higher Education*, 15 September.

Florida, R., G. Gates, B. Knudsen and K. Stolarick (2006), *The University and the Creative Economy*. Washington: Creative Class Group.

Franklin, S.J., M. Wright and A. Lockett (2001), 'Academic and Surrogate Entrepreneurs in University Spin-out Companies.' *Journal of Technology Transfer* 26(1–2), pp. 127–41.

Garlick, S. (1998), *'Creative Associations in Special Places': Enhancing the Partnership Role of Universities in Building Competitive Regional Economies*. Canberra: Department of Employment, Training and Youth Affairs.

Gibson, J. (2000), 'Sheepskin Effects and the Returns to Education in New Zealand: Do They Differ by Ethnic Groups?' *New Zealand Economic Papers* 34(2), pp. 201–220.

Gittos, A. (2005), *Growth of the Wellington Tertiary Education Cluster and Economic Impact 2004*. Wellington: Positively Wellington Business.

Goldstein, H. and J. Drucker (2006), 'The Economic Development Impacts of Universities on Regions: Do Size and Distance Matter?' *Economic Development Quarterly* 21(1), pp. 22–43.

Greer, G., J. Manhire and A. Zwart (1999), 'Industry Views on the Making and Operation of Levy Orders under the Commodity Levies Act 1990.' *MAF Policy Technical Paper*, No. 8. Wellington: Ministry of Agriculture and Forestry.

Griffin, F., D. Scott and R. Smyth (2005), *Living with a Student Loan: A Profile of Student Loan Debt and Repayment, Post-Study Income and Going Overseas*. Wellington: Ministry of Education.

Gunasekara, C. (2006), 'Reframing the Role of Universities in the Development of Regional Innovation Systems.' *Journal of Technology Transfer* 31(1), pp. 101–113.

Hall, J. and G.M. Scobie (2006), 'The Role of R&D in Productivity Growth: The Case of Agriculture in New Zealand: 1927 to 2001.' *Treasury Working Paper* 06/01. Wellington: New Zealand Treasury.

Harrington, A. (2005), 'The Contribution of the Primary Sector to New Zealand's Economic Growth.' *Policy Perspectives Paper* 05/04. Wellington: New Zealand Treasury.

Heher, A.D. (2006), 'Return on Investment in Innovation: Implications for Institutions and National Agencies.' *Journal of Technology Transfer* 31(4), pp. 403–414.

Hicks, D., T. Breitzman, D. Olivastro and K. Hamilton (2001), 'The Changing Composition of Innovative Activity in the US – A Portrait Based on Patent Analysis.' *Research Policy* 30(4), pp. 681–703.

Hughes, W.R. (1994), 'Regional Economic Impacts of the University of Waikato.' *New Zealand Economic Papers* 28(1), pp. 81–7.

Hyatt, J. and R. Smyth (2006), *How do Graduates' Earnings Change Over Time?* Wellington: Ministry of Education.

Hyslop, D., D. Maré and J. Timmins (2003), 'Qualifications, Employment and the Value of Human Capital, 1986–2001.' *Treasury Working Paper* 03/35. Wellington: New Zealand Treasury.

Karlsson, C. and W.-B. Zhang (2001), 'The Role of Universities in Regional Development: Endogenous Human Capital and Growth in a Two-Region Model.' *Annals of Regional Science* 35(2), pp. 179–97.

Kassam, K.-A. and W.J. Tettey (2003), 'Academics as Citizens – Collaborative Applied Interdisciplinary Research in the Service Communities.' *Canadian Journal of Development Studies* 24(1), pp. 155–74.

Le, T., J. Gibson and L. Oxley (2006), 'A Forward-Looking Measure of the Stock of Human Capital in New Zealand.' *The Manchester School* 74(5), pp. 593–609.

Leydesdorff, L. (2006), '"While a Storm is Raging on the Open Sea": Regional Development in a Knowledge-Based Economy.' *Journal of Technology Transfer* 31(1), pp. 189–203.

Lindelöf, P. and H. Löfsten (2004), 'Proximity as a Resource Base for Competitive Advantage: University–Industry Links for Technology Transfer.' *Journal of Technology Transfer* 29(3–4), pp. 311–26.

Long, J. with J. Ballingall (2003), *University of Canterbury: Economic Contribution to the Canterbury Region*. Christchurch: University of Canterbury.

Maani, S.A. (1999), 'Private and Public Returns to Investments in Secondary and Higher Education in New Zealand Over Time: 1981–1996.' *Treasury Working Paper* 99/02. Wellington: New Zealand Treasury.

Maani, S.A. (1999), 'Secondary and Tertiary Education Attainment and Income Levels for Māori and Non-Māori Over Time.' *Treasury Working Paper* 00/18. Wellington: New Zealand Treasury.

Maani, S.A. (2002), 'Education and Māori Relative Income Levels Over Time: The Mediating Effect of Occupation, Industry, Hours of Work and Locality.' *Treasury Working Paper* 02/17. Wellington: New Zealand Treasury.

Maani, S.A. and T. Maloney (2004), 'Returns to Post-School Qualifications: New Evidence Based on the HLFS Income Supplement.' Report to the Labour Market Policy Group. Wellington: Department of Labour.

MacLeod, G., B. McFarlane and C.H. Davis (1997), 'The Knowledge Economy and the Social Economy: University Support for Community Enterprise Development as a Strategy for Economic Regeneration in Distressed Regions in Canada and Mexico.' *International Journal of Social Economics* 24(11), pp. 1302–1324.

Mansfield, E. (1991), 'Academic Research and Industrial Innovation.' *Research Policy* 21(1), pp. 1–12.

Mansfield, E. (1998), 'Academic Research and Industrial Innovation: An Update of Empirical Findings.' *Research Policy* 26(7–8), pp. 773–6.

Maré, D.C. and Y. Liang (2006), 'Labour Market Outcomes for Young Graduates.' *Motu Working Paper* 06–06. Wellington: Motu Economic and Public Policy Research.

Martin, F. (1998), 'The Economic Impact of Canadian University R&D.' *Economic Policy* 27(7), pp. 677–87.

Mayer, H. (2006), 'What is the Role of Universities in High-Tech Economic Development? The Case of Portland, Oregon, and Washington, DC.' *Local Economy* 21(3), pp. 292–315.

Meyer, M. (2006a), 'Are Patenting Scientists the Better Scholars? An Exploratory Comparison of Inventor-Authors with their Non-inventing Peers in Nano-Science and Technology.' *Journal of Technology Transfer* 31(4), pp. 501–510.

Meyer, M. (2006b), 'Academic Inventiveness and Entrepreneurship: On the Importance of Start-up Companies in Commercializing Academic Patents.' *Research Policy* 35(10), pp. 1646–62.

Miller, C., G. Packham and D. Pickernell (2002), 'It's Regional Economic Development Jim, But Not As We Know It: The Reasons for, Structure of and Preliminary Results of Enterprise College Wales.' *Australasian Journal of Regional Studies* 8(3), pp. 275–302.

Mowery, D.C. (2002), 'The Changing Role of Universities in the 21st Century U.S. R&D System.' Chapter 25 in A.H. Teich, S.D. Nelson and S.J. Lita (eds), *AAAS Science and Technology Policy Yearbook 2002*. Anapolis Junction, MD: American Association for the Advancement of Science, pp. 253–71.

Mowery, D.C. and B.N. Sampat (2001), 'Patenting and Licensing University Inventions: Lessons from the History of the Research Corporation." *Industrial and Corporate Change* 10(2), pp. 317–55.

Nair, B. (2007), *Measuring the Returns on Investment in Tertiary Education Three and Five Years After Study*. Wellington: Ministry of Education.

Narin, F., K.S. Hamilton and D. Olivastro (1997), 'The Increasing Linkage Between U.S. Technology and Public Science.' *Research Policy* 26(3), pp. 317–30.

Nelson, R.R. (2001), 'Observations on the Post-Bayh-Dole Rise of Patenting at American Universities.' *Journal of Technology Transfer* 26(1–2), pp. 13–19.

Newell, J. and M. Perry (2006), *Trends in the Contribution of Tertiary Education to the Accumulation of Educational Capital in New Zealand, 1981–2001*. Wellington: Ministry of Education.

Niosi, J. (2006), 'Success Factors in Canadian Spin-Offs.' *Journal of Technology Transfer* 31(4), pp. 451–7.

NZVCC (2006), 'An Investment Approach to Public Support of New Zealand's Universities.' Submission to the New Zealand Government. Wellington: New Zealand Vice-Chancellors' Committee, August.

Psacharopoulos, G. and H.A. Patrinos (2004), 'Returns to Investment in Education: A Further Update.' *Education Economics* 12(2), pp. 111–34.

Poyago-Theotoky, J., J. Beath and D.S. Siegel (2002), 'Universities and Fundamental Research: Reflections on the Growth of University-Industry Partnerships.' *Oxford Review of Economic Policy* 18(1), pp. 10–21.

Rasmussen, W.D. (1989), *Taking the University to the People: Seventy-Five Years of Cooperative Extension*. Ames: Iowa University Press.

Rowe, J. (2005), 'Economic Development: From a New Zealand Perspective.' Chapter 1 in J. Rowe (ed.), *Economic Development in New Zealand*. Aldershot: Ashgate, pp. 1–13.

Salter, A.J. and B.R. Martin (2001), 'The Economic Benefits of Publicly Funded Basic Research: A Critical Review.' *Research Policy* 30(3), pp. 509–532.

Sampat, B.N. (2006), 'Patenting and US Academic Research in the 20th Century: The World Before and After Bayh-Dole.' *Research Policy* 35(6), pp. 772–89.

Santoro, M.D. and S. Gopalakrishnan (2001), 'Relationship Dynamics between University Research Centers and Industrial Firms: Their Impact on Technology Transfer Activities.' *Journal of Technology Transfer* 26(1), pp. 163–71.

Saunders, C. and P. Dalziel (2006), *Identifying the Way Forward for High Growth Firms in the ICT Sector*. Auckland: HiGrowth Project Trust.

Savan, B. (2004), 'Community-University Partnerships: Linking Research and Action for Sustainable Community Development.' *Community Development Journal* 39(4), pp. 372–84.

Scobie, G.M. and W.M. Eveleens (1987), 'The Return to Investment in Agricultural Research in New Zealand, 1926/27 to 1983/84.' *Research Report* 1/87. Ruakura: Ministry of Agriculture and Fisheries.

Smart, W. (2006), *Outcomes of the New Zealand Tertiary Education System – A Synthesis of the Evidence*. Wellington: Ministry of Education.

SSTI (2006), *A Resource Guide for Technology-based Economic Development: Positioning Universities as Drivers, Fostering Entrepreneurship, Increasing Access to Capital*. Westerville, OH: State Science and Technology Institute.

Stokes, D.E. (1997), *Pasteur's Quadrant*. Washington DC: Brookings Institution.

Vedder, R. (2004), 'Private vs. Social Returns to Higher Education: Some New Cross-Sectional Evidence.' *Journal of Labor Research* 25(4), pp. 677–86.

Weiler, S., E. Scorsone and M. Pullman (2000), 'Information Linkages in Local Economic Development.' *Growth and Change* 31(3), pp. 367–84.

Chapter 11
Philosophies in Entrepreneurship: A Focus on Economic Theories[1]

Luke Pittaway

Introduction

The purpose of this chapter is to explore the philosophies underpinning economic approaches to the study of entrepreneurship. Economic theories have made significant contributions and are one of the historical roots of the subject (Bygrave, 1989). Despite these contributions the concept of the 'entrepreneur' and the function of entrepreneurship in society have ranged extensively within theories (Hébert and Link, 1988). Previous categorisations have shown that the 'entrepreneur' has been viewed as a class of economic actor, a capitalist, a manager, an owner, an arbitrageur, an innovator and the bearer of uncertainty (Binks and Vale, 1990). These early theories of entrepreneurship continue to have a profound affect on the meaning of 'entrepreneurship' within contemporary society and consequently influence current debate in the subject (Kirchhoff, 1991). Although previous research has explored many of the differences between economic theories contributing to our understanding there is only limited prior work on the philosophical basis of these differences (Barreto, 1989). The purpose of the chapter is to explore these 'taken for granted' assumptions explaining some of the fundamental differences that exist in key conceptions of the 'entrepreneur'. Understanding these differences is important because it helps us recognise the factors which influence policy interventions designed to promote 'entrepreneurship' and 'enterprise'.

Meta-theory, which can be translated as the philosophical assumptions made by researchers before they construct theories, plays an important role in how theory is developed and the type of 'knowledge' found when research is conducted (Grant and Perren, 2002). Researchers in entrepreneurship have recently begun to recognise that ideology, or the political basis of ideas, meta-theory and other 'taken for granted' assumptions (axioms) have an influence on knowledge construction and they have begun to explore the issue (Bygrave, 1989; Aldrich, 2000; Ogbor, 2000; Grant and Perren, 2002). This chapter makes a contribution to these discussions by exploring the philosophical assumptions that underpin many

---

1 Reprinted by permission of Inderscience Publications. The chapter was originally published in the *International Journal of Entrepreneurship and Small Business*, 11(3), 201–221. Inderscience retains the copyright.

of the key economic theories. A review of meta-theory is carried out by using Burrell and Morgan's (BM's) 1979 paradigms to assess the assumptions made in economic theories, illustrating their contribution to contemporary debate. The study conducted is reported and the implications for future study are highlighted.

Philosophies in Social Science

Discussions about meta-theory have become a key feature of academic inquiry in many social sciences. In organisational studies the publication of Burrell and Morgan's (1979) 'Sociological Paradigms and Organisational Analysis' led to considerable debate throughout the 1980s and 1990s in organisational studies (McCourt, 1999). There are potentially many gains for the study of entrepreneurship if researchers are prepared to learn from the experience of these debates. For example, Burrell and Morgan's work highlighted the role of philosophies in research endeavour; it informed researchers about the complexities of organisational inquiry and raised awareness about the influence of research paradigms on knowledge construction (Burrell and Morgan, 1979). Figure 11.1 highlights BM's paradigms as outlined in their original thesis.

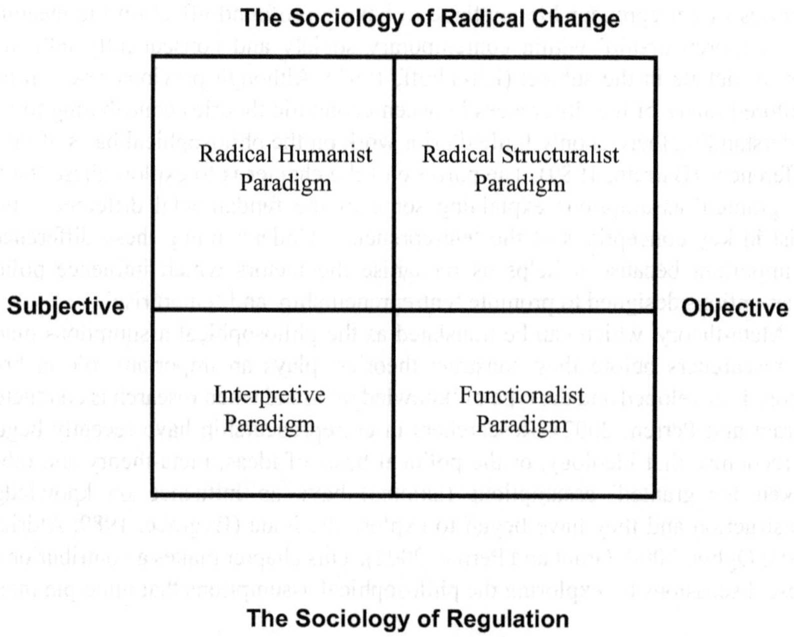

Figure 11.1 Four paradigms of social scientific research

The paradigms were constructed by reviewing organisational research according to certain types of philosophical assumption. These included:

i. Ontological assumptions – ontology is a branch of meta-physics, a part of philosophy that examines the nature of being. Ontological assumptions, therefore, focus on the nature of reality, and are about how reality is constructed and represented in human consciousness.
ii. Epistemological assumptions – epistemology is a branch of philosophy that is concerned with the nature of knowledge, together with its sources and forms. Epistemological assumptions are about how people understand and conceptualise the world around them, making assumptions about what constitutes knowledge, how it might be constructed and appropriately communicated.
iii. Assumptions about human nature – focus on the different assumptions about human activity and behaviour that underlie theory. These typically revolve around a series of debates about human behaviour. For example, one such debate between 'free-will' and 'determinism' concerns the degree to which human beings have the ability to act on their environment or whether circumstances beyond their control determine behaviour.
iv. Assumptions about the nature of society – are assumptions about how society works. The main debate focuses on the sociology of order, assuming that every society is relatively stable, in contrast to the sociology of conflict, which assumes that deep-seated structural conflict occurs within society.

An assessment of these philosophies in organisational studies led Burrell and Morgan (1979) to conclude that there were two dimensions to philosophical debate in social sciences, the subjective versus objective dimension and the regulation versus radical change dimension. These dimensions represented different views about the nature of social science which they constructed into four paradigms. The word 'paradigm' was used to describe different forms of social science demonstrating fundamentally different philosophical orientations. In their view the paradigms are "*contiguous but separate*" (Burrell and Morgan, 1979, p. 22). In this sense the paradigms were originally considered to be incommensurable; if a researcher undertook work in one paradigm they were likely to be unable to appreciate the philosophical basis of study in alternative paradigms. By contiguous they meant each paradigm had shared characteristics but that there was sufficient differentiation for them to be considered as four distinct entities. The four paradigms were described as functionalist, interpretive, radical humanist and radical structuralist. Gioia and Pitre (1990) summarise the theory building approaches of each of the four paradigms (see Table 11.1).

Disagreement surrounding the thesis continues and revolves around a number of themes. The first theme focuses on the nature of paradigms (Weaver and Gioia, 1994), which has included disputes about how paradigms should be viewed. Some researchers have argued that paradigms are ways of bringing unification

Table 11.1 Paradigm differences affecting theory building

Interpretive Paradigm	Radical Humanist Paradigm	Radical Structuralist Paradigm	Functionalist Paradigm
Goals To describe and explain in order to diagnose and understand	Goals To describe and critique in order to change (achieve freedom through revision of consciousness)	Goals To identify sources of domination and prescription in order to guide revolutionary practices. (Achieve freedom through revision of structures)	Goals To search for regularities and test in order to predict and control.
Theoretical Concerns Social construction of reality Reification Process Interpretation	**Theoretical Concerns** Social construction of reality Distortion Interests served	**Theoretical Concerns** Domination Alienation Macro Forces Emancipation	**Theoretical Concerns** Relationships Causation Generalisation
Theory-Building Approaches Discovery through code analysis	**Theory-Building Approaches** Disclosure through critical analysis	**Theory-Building Approaches** Liberation through structural analysis	**Theory-Building Approaches** Refinement through causal analysis

to organisational study (Pfeffer, 1993). Some have reasoned that the research community should protect and foster new paradigms (Willmott, 1993a) and others have argued that paradigms are different ways of understanding social scientific phenomena (Scherer and Steinmann, 1999). The second theme has concentrated on the use and meaning of the word 'paradigm'. For some, the concept of a paradigm has been eroded of its rigour (Holland, 1990) and for others; it continues to represent a valuable means for differentiating between philosophical assumptions (McCourt, 1999). In the third theme researchers have engaged in debates about incommensurability, where views have ranged comprehensively. They have included relatively strict interpretations (Jackson and Carter 1991; 1993) seeing little room for communication across paradigms. There have been approaches seeking to question the concept of incommensurability between paradigms (Hassard, 1998; Holland, 1990; Willmott, 1993a; 1993b), as well as, attempts to build multi-paradigm communication (Gioia, Donnellon and Sims, 1989; Gioia and Pitré, 1990). Other arguments have suggested that the concept of paradigm is itself problematic and have suggested more complex alternatives (Weaver and Gioia 1994; Scherer and Steinmann, 1999). The final theme has centred on the common divisions thought to exist in organisational inquiry that underlie Burrell and Morgan's schema and these researchers question these divisions. Critiquing BM's paradigms as an over simplification of complex philosophical debates they argue that BM's approach overlooked other important philosophical discussions[2]. Such arguments also question the implied duality within the two dimensions outlined, suggesting that these over simplify complex debates in social science and philosophy (Davies, 1998).

Despite these debates, disagreements and complexities the value of this stream of work in organisational studies has been its ability to raise awareness about the importance of meta-theory when constructing research in the social sciences. This chapter seeks to build on these benefits for the subject of entrepreneurship by reporting a historical analysis that used a technique adapted from this stream of work in organisational studies. Consequently, the chapter will explore the usefulness of the paradigms in a different subject domain and build on other approaches that have used them as tools for exploring implicit philosophical assumptions in research. These prior studies include Holland's work on professional education (Holland, 1990), McCourt's (1999) analysis of personnel selection and Grant and Perren's (2002) analysis of contemporary study in entrepreneurship. The main contribution of the chapter is that it applies some of the insights identified in organisational studies to an analysis of the economic theories in entrepreneurship.

Methodology

The purpose of the chapter, as outlined, is to contribute to debate by applying BM's paradigms as a method to explain the philosophical assumptions used in economic studies of entrepreneurship. A number of developments were necessary to use BM's thesis outside organisational studies and these will be outlined, there were two key operational questions:

i. Given the incommensurability debate outlined previously, how are the paradigms viewed in this study?
ii. As the subject of entrepreneurship is wide-reaching how was the analysis reduced, while retaining sufficient depth, and ensuring a representative understanding of the philosophies used?

2 These include structure versus agency, functionalism versus interpretivism, determinism versus voluntarism, causation versus meaning, holism versus individualism, object versus subject and description versus prescription (Astley and Van de Ven, 1983).

Operationalising the Paradigms

The issue of permeability versus incommensurability remains a controversial issue. In order to use BM's paradigms to review another field of study it was necessary to make some decisions about how to view the paradigms boundaries. Researchers supporting incommensurability argue that the boundaries are immutable. By immutable they mean that ideas and concepts cannot easily flow between paradigms because the philosophical basis of knowledge in each paradigm is entirely different (Jackson and Carter, 1991). Those advocating permeability between paradigms, however, accept greater communication suggesting that while the paradigms are clearly at odds there is scope for knowledge to permeate between them at the transition zones (Gioia and Pitre, 1990). When taking a position on the way in which knowledge is constructed, it is evident that this debate is somewhat of a non-starter, in the sense that the paradigms and continua constructed by Burrell and Morgan are themselves social constructions (Parker, 1998; Nightingale and Cromby, 1999). They are useful because they can be used as a tool to explore the underlying meaning of theory but 'exist' only in the sense that they describe current social science research activity. Even as descriptions of underlying philosophical assumptions they are less than perfect depending on dualism[3] (Willig, 1999), as represented by the use of continuums, which tends to be an over-simplification of the debates. Consequently, in this analysis the paradigms and dichotomies[4] were viewed as social constructions[5] that could be used to help describe social science research activity. They are considered useful because they can be used to explore theory (Willmott, 1993a; Parker, 1998; Nightingale and Cromby, 1999). Permeability occurs because the research paradigms represent social processes where communication between research groups can happen (Willmott, 1993b). Incommensurability also exists because philosophical assumptions when made automatically exclude alternatives (Scherer and Steinemann, 1999).

In operational terms problems were encountered when applying BM's paradigms to entrepreneurship. The concept of duality and the use of dichotomies, for example, presented questions when explaining differences of emphasis between meta-theories that derived from the same paradigm. It was also difficult to transfer the original criteria used to interpret study in organisational studies, as these were not reported explicitly. The first issue was resolved by reconceptualising the dichotomies. A metaphor of an elastic band was used at the same time as the concept of continua, individual dualities remain but there are different degrees of emphasis within paradigms (see Figure 11.2).

3 The term 'dualism' or 'duality' is used to explain the view that certain philosophical assumptions must always oppose each other (e.g. determinism versus voluntarism; nature versus nurture).

4 The word dichotomy means here the combination of two opposing philosophies.

5 A 'social construction' means here something that has been abstracted from its context via the use of language to provide order and explanation to something that is complex.

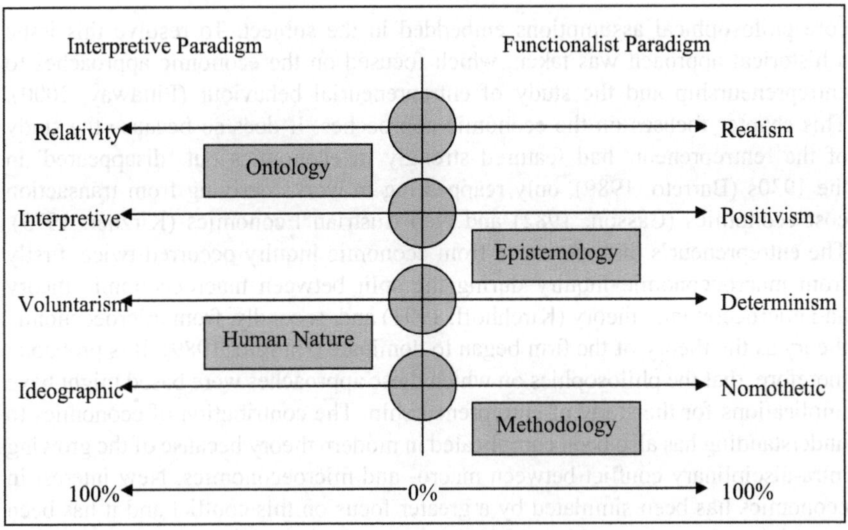

Figure 11.2 The dichotomous nature of the Burrell and Morgan continua

The research followed the approach used by Morgan and Smircich (1980) by allowing for different forms of approach within continua while retaining the dichotomous nature of the assumptions. The second issue meant that there were no clear criteria that could be used to apply BM's paradigms to another research field. This factor initially limited the transferability of the paradigms and their usefulness as tools of explanation. It was resolved for the subjective – objective dimension by building on the work of Morgan and Smircich (1980), which outlined key criteria for six points along each of BM's four dichotomies. It was resolved for the regulation-radical change dimension by undertaking an analysis of the sociology literature with an emphasis on 'Marxism', 'conflict theory' and 'functionalist sociology'. From the source material three core dichotomies were identified and six different forms of philosophical assumption within each were highlighted. The dichotomies represented philosophical assumptions about change, structure and conflict in society. Appendix II and III provide a summary of the criteria used for both dimensions.

Focusing the Paradigms on the Study of Entrepreneurship

The challenge in this study was to capture an understanding of the philosophies guiding study in entrepreneurship while creating a manageable research study. A full analysis of the subject would have been comprehensive but unmanageable and would potentially have lacked sufficient depth, failing to understand the core philosophical assumptions embedded in the subject. To resolve this issue a historical approach was taken, which focused on the economic approaches to entrepreneurship and the study of entrepreneurial behaviour (Pittaway, 2000). This chapter focuses on the economic approaches. It does so because the study of the 'entrepreneur' had featured strongly in economics but 'disappeared' in the 1930s (Barreto, 1989), only reappearing in works deriving from transaction cost economics (Casson, 1982) and Neo-Austrian Economics (Kirzner, 1973). The entrepreneur's disappearance from economic inquiry occurred twice, firstly from macroeconomic inquiry during the split between macroeconomic theory and microeconomic theory (Kirchhoff, 1991) and, secondly, from microeconomic theory as the theory of the firm began to dominate (Barreto, 1989). It is probable; therefore, that the philosophies on which these approaches were based might have implications for the study of entrepreneurship. The contribution of economics to understanding has also been complicated in modern theory because of the growing intra-disciplinary conflict between macro- and microeconomics. New interest in economics has been simulated by a greater focus on this conflict and it has been argued that entrepreneurship could be a catalyst for a paradigm shift in economics (Kirchhoff, 1991).

Economic approaches consequently provide a useful starting point to examine the philosophies underpinning the historical roots of the subject because they provide a context where entrepreneurship was studied but disappeared and where its re-emergence may have unforeseen consequences for the prevailing paradigm (Hébert and Link, 1988; Barreto, 1989). The following research questions were asked:

i. What are the meta-theoretical assumptions underpinning economic study in entrepreneurship?
ii. How can these be categorised according to BM's paradigms?
iii. Are there any philosophical explanations for the decline of 'the entrepreneur' in economic inquiry?
iv. Are there any commonly used philosophies that could limit research in entrepreneurship?

Discussion

These research questions guided the study, which is reported in full in Pittaway (2000). Table 11.2 provides a summary of the findings of this analysis using BM's framework. The study used an in-depth historical review of the economic literature and its contribution to entrepreneurship, starting with the work of Cantillon (1931).

The categorisation of economic theories in entrepreneurship has previously been undertaken by chronological order (Hébert and Link, 1988; Binks and Vale, 1990; Lydall, 1992) or by 'school of thought' (Ricketts, 1987; Chell et al., 1991). Neither

Table 11.2 A summary of philosophical assumptions in economic approaches to entrepreneurship

	Ontological Assumptions	Epistemological Assumptions	Assumptions about Human Nature	Assumptions about Society	Paradigm
Neo-classical Economics[1]	Reality as a concrete structure	To construct a positivist social science	Man as a responder	Social Order	Functionalist
English Classical Theories	Reality as a concrete structure	To construct a positivist social science	Man as a responder	Society as an Organic System	Functionalist
French Classical Theories[2]	Reality as a concrete process	To construct a positivist social science	Man as a responder	Society as an Organic System	Functionalist
Transaction Cost Economics[3]	Reality as a concrete process	To construct a positivist social science	Man as an adapter	Society as an Organic System	Functionalist
Information Based Transaction Cost Economics[4]	Reality as contextual fields of information	To study systems, processes and change	Man as an information processor	Society as an Organic System	Functionalist

1 Including *Micro-economics and the Theory of the Firm* (Barreto, 1989).
2 Excluding Cantillon (1931).
3 Includes Coase (1937) and Williamson (1985).
4 Based principally on Casson's work (1982; 1990; 1998).

of these approaches has captured the underlying differences between theories based on their philosophies. As Barreto (1989) illustrates, however, philosophies may have played an important role in the decline of the 'entrepreneurial concept' in economics. The disappearance of the 'entrepreneur' from neo-classical economics (1930s onwards) was explained in his work by the rise of the theory of the firm and its use of assumptions that derived from a mechanistic[6] philosophy. Given Barreto's argument, it is possible that certain philosophical assumptions may have a pivotal influence on how 'entrepreneurship' is perceived and understood, even to the extent that the concept can effectively disappear from theorising. Kirchhoff

6 'Mechanistic' applies here to theories that view organisational systems as if they were machines.

(1991) illustrates the point when he discusses the axioms[7] that exist within macroeconomic theory:

> With these axioms, macroeconomic theory eliminates the role of individually initiated behaviour. If these axioms apply, then buyers and sellers are "non-decision makers" who follow set rules in carrying out their day-to-day purchasing/producing functions. Entrepreneurship cannot exist because it requires rule-violating behaviour (Kirchhoff, 1991: 97).

In both macroeconomic theory and the theory of the firm the gradual erosion of purposeful behaviour has led to an uncomfortable context for entrepreneurship and this has occurred despite the fact that significant contributions were made to understanding in early economic thought. Economic theories continue to contribute to the field but there are diverse opinions in economics about the nature of 'entrepreneurship' and whether it exists in a dynamic, static or turbulent economic system, as well as, debate about what role it plays in such a system. Within the theories analysed there was considerable difference regarding assumptions about 'human behaviour'. For example, in Kirzner's (1980) work an assumption of human behaviour can be illustrated in his definition of the pure entrepreneur:

> ...a decision-maker whose entire role arises out of his alertness to hitherto unnoticed opportunities (Kirzner, 1980: 38)

In Kirzner's research the role of the 'entrepreneur' derives from an assumption that human behaviour is bounded by its context and entrepreneurial capacity arises from an ability to recognise opportunities and make decisions in an existing set of circumstances. When compared to Schumpeter's (1963) concept of new combinations there is a difference in the presuppositions made. For Schumpeter, the assumption of human behaviour has a greater element of 'agency'[8], indeed the role of the entrepreneur is to create new circumstances rather than to be alert to new opportunities in existing circumstances. Both approaches apply some idea about human action but they differ in degree and nature and some form of determinism[9] remains.

---

7 'Axiom' refers to 'taken for granted assumption', it is often used to mean the base assumptions on which a subject of study begins.

8 'Agency' refers to the philosophical view that human beings are agents of their own destiny, having the ability to change the circumstances of their context.

9 'Determinism' is the philosophical idea that human beings are largely limited by their context and that their behaviour is consequently influenced by factors that are beyond their control.

Within the economic theories major theoretical and practical differences exist regarding the nature of the scientific enterprise, between subjectivity[10] and objectivity[11], on the one hand, and abstract theorising[12] and practical description[13], on the other. Discussion about the nature of economics as a social science featured within many of the classical works. Despite these differences, one can conclude from the research that the majority of economic approaches had used functionalist assumptions. This was a consequence of theorists' desire to explain how 'entrepreneurship' worked in the economic system and what function it had in that system (Binks and Vale, 1990). By trying to explain how entrepreneurship impacts on economic systems these theorists tend to view it as a universal phenomenon[14] and consequently do not apply the individualistic axiom[15] held widely in contemporary study (Ogbor, 2000). Regardless of this presupposition of universality, however, there was little agreement about what the 'entrepreneurial' function actually entailed (Lydall, 1992). For example, it has been used to mean forms of behaviour (Schumpeter, 1963), types of decisions (Knight, 1921) and types of people (Say, 1880). Indeed, many of the ambiguities surrounding the definition of entrepreneurship in contemporary study would appear to have their foundation in the economic domain (Hébert and Link, 1988).

Another common philosophy running across the economic theories was the use of different forms of determinism. For example, 'entrepreneurs' were reduced to relatively powerless figureheads in the extreme determinism of microeconomics (Barreto, 1989) and, despite the use of concepts related to human action in the theory of creative destruction, Schumpeter's (1934) approach returned to psychological determinism[16] to describe the individual entrepreneur. The philosophies linking the economic approaches, therefore, were some form of determinism and a universal philosophy with regard to theories in social scientific research. There

---

10 'Subjectivity' as applied here refers to the idea that social scientific inquiry is embedded within its context and cannot escape being influenced by interaction with the subject of study (unlike natural sciences).

11 'Objectivity' refers to the philosophical view that social scientific research must seek to provide objective conclusions that can be generalised from a specific context (like natural sciences).

12 'Abstract theorising' is used to describe theory and empirical study that seeks to abstract understanding from its context, normally via the use of mathematics.

13 'Practical description' refers to research that assumes that theory must be embedded in its context and that it loses its usefulness once abstracted from its context.

14 'Universal phenomenon' means something that has a widespread impact on social systems across time and space that will not be changed because of context.

15 'Individualistic axiom' is a taken for granted assumption in the entrepreneurship field identified by Ogbor (2000). It refers to the idea that 'entrepreneurship' is carried out by individuals, rather than by groups or organisations.

16 'Psychological determinism' refers to the idea that something about an individual's personal makeup (e.g. personality or cognitive style) has a fundamental influence on the way that they behave.

were, however, some clear differences in study and these have been categorised into three groups: equilibrium, disequilibrium and revolution-equilibrium theorists (Pittaway, 2000).

Equilibrium Theorists

Classical, neo-classical and microeconomic theorists who had made some contribution to the study of entrepreneurship dominated the equilibrium group e.g. Say, Smith, Ricardo, Bentham, Mill, Walras, Marshall, Clark, Dobb and Tuttle (Barreto, 1989). In this group, theorists have sought to identify fundamental 'laws' to explain the economic system. The subsequent models developed tend to be of a mechanistic nature, are mainly prescriptive[17] and tend to assume that there are general principles explaining society, as is evident in general equilibrium theory. In these approaches, individual human action does not play a significant role and even at the collective level human behaviour is explained by general principles. Change within economic systems also tends to be modelled according to stable state or equilibrium philosophies. Marshall's (1961) macroeconomic welfare theory, for example, is now well-known for its introduction of rationality axioms[18] about human behaviour in exchange theory and for creating many of the axioms on which general equilibrium theory is based (Walsh, 1970).

Kirzner (1980), Barreto (1989) and Harper (1996) have criticised these approaches as having neglected the entrepreneurial function because of their disregard for philosophies of human action and their over-application of mechanistic models. The assumptions used in the theory of the firm provide an illustration of the validity of these criticisms. The production function, the concepts of rational choice and perfect information all limit the capacity for 'entrepreneurial' behaviour (Barreto, 1989). These underpinning philosophies explain why the 'entrepreneurial' concept is not addressed directly by microeconomic theory. In these approaches the 'firm', for example, represents its own 'reality', which is abstracted from the motivations, rationality and fallibility, associated with individuals. The calculation of inputs, including intangibles such as quality of decision making, assumes a capacity to measure inputs divorced from specific human capacity, as well as, assuming that unknown events will not dislodge the factors of production. The assumptions of rational choice and perfect information create further abstractions in the theory by assuming that everything is known

17 'Prescriptive' is used to explain approaches to theory building that are designed to predict the behaviour of something and to provide guidance for practical or policy interventions.

18 'Rationality axiom' is the assumption in micro-economic theory that human beings making decisions will behave according to rationale rules (e.g. they always seek to make profit).

either 'deterministically' or 'probabilistically'[19]. In its search for a mechanistic model it has to take out of theorising individuals and groups making and acting on decisions, based on imperfect information, in uncertain conditions, surrounded by unknown future events that can have unforeseen circumstances. For example following his study of contemporary microeconomic empirical research and its contribution to entrepreneurship Kirchhoff (1991) concludes:

> Extensive research effort has been invested in economies of scale, industry concentration, market structures, pricing, technology transfer etc. In all these areas, microeconomists have shredded the axioms of general equilibrium theory to such a degree that few realize that neoclassical theory continues to dominate macroeconomic policy prescriptions...But adoption of general equilibrium theory leaves mainstream macroeconomists with a dilemma. Entrepreneurship is an important component of wealth creation and distribution...American politicians clamor for information and policies to help the entrepreneurs who have become public heroes. Small firms are a sizable portion of the economy and voting public. By one count, they total 19 to 20 million voters. But, mainstream macroeconomists have no answers. Their macro theory fails them. This is widely acknowledged, especially by microeconomists. But all the microeconomic research has not led to the development of a theory even close to the elegance and rigor of general equilibrium theory (Kirchhoff, 1991: 103).

The failure of neoclassical theory to incorporate entrepreneurship can be explained by its axiomatic assumptions on human nature. It is possible to conclude that equilibrium theorists apply extremely determinist, realist[20], positivist[21], mechanistic and ordered views of social science and the social world and that these can create difficulties for the conceptualisation of 'entrepreneurship' despite its many guises (Barreto, 1989; Pittaway, 2000).

Disequilibrium Theorists

Set against these approaches are those that incorporate concepts of entrepreneurship into variations of mainstream economics. These have included two forms of transaction cost economics. The first introduced a theory of regularity in exchange processes based on the cognitive limits of human actors (Coase, 1937; Williamson, 1985), which moved away from assumptions based on human rationality and perfect choice. The second sought to directly link concepts based on theories of information, information exchange and information markets to the process of

---

19 To know something 'deterministically' means that when one can identify the underlying causes of an event it can be predicted. To know something 'probabilistically' means that one has sufficient information to be able to predict the probability that an event will occur.

20 'Realist' refers to the philosophical assumption that social 'reality' exists in a tangible way and that its underpinning rules can be identified.

21 'Positivist' is an epistemological assumption meaning that knowledge can be abstracted, measured and understood via the mathematical method.

entrepreneurship (Casson, 1990; 1998). Unlike these theorists the disequilibrium theorists, who included Austrian and Neo-Austrian economists (Mises, 1949; Kirzner, 1982) as well as the work of Knight (1921) and Cantillon (1931), did not attempt to construct equilibrium models of the economic system based on general principles but sought explanations based on observations of experience. The models created tend to be descriptive rather than prescriptive and tend to observe that equilibrium did not occur in the 'real' economy. Models based on disequilibrium suggested that there are opportunities for profit within economic systems because of inequalities between supply and demand and 'entrepreneurial' actions are designed to exploit these opportunities, driving economic systems toward equilibrium. This orientation is represented in Cantillon's definition of the entrepreneur and Knight's critique of classical theories.

> …set up with a capital to conduct their enterprise, or are undertakers of their own labour without capital, and they may be regarded as living of uncertainty (Cantillon, 1931: 55).

> "…it is a world of change in which we live and a world of uncertainty. We live only by knowing something about the future; while the problems of life, or of conduct at least, arise from the fact we know so little. This is true of business as of other spheres of activity. The essence of the situation is action according to opinion, of greater or less foundation and value, neither entire ignorance nor complete and perfect knowledge, but partial knowledge" (Knight, 1921: 199).

The disequilibrium group applies two philosophical assumptions that differentiate it from the equilibrium theorists. They use more complex assumptions about human action and accept greater uncertainty in social systems. Jones (1998) illustrates this perception of human behaviour when he discusses transaction cost economics.

> Indeed, they explicitly rejected imperfect knowledge and unforeseen circumstances as providing any rationale for the existence and organisation of the 'classical firm'. The new institutional theory of the firm that was to follow turned this position on its head, arguing that in many instances the growth of the firm was designed precisely to overcome market failures, especially the costs and difficulties of transacting in markets under conditions of uncertainty (Jones, 1998: 13).

The move away from perfect knowledge as an axiom in transaction cost economics, while retaining elements of equilibrium theorising allowed for a more sophisticated view of bounded rationality[22] introducing greater uncertainty into exchange relationships. Although it shares elements with Neo-Austrian economics there is clear disagreement about the value of opportunistic (entrepreneurial) behaviour

22 'Bounded rationality' refers to the philosophical stance that human beings can have the ability make choices and to change their environment but that this ability to choose is controlled within a particular context.

within conditions of uncertainty. In early transaction cost economics opportunistic behaviour is viewed quite negatively while in Neo-Austrian economics it has a more positive orientation. In the former it is the consequence of disequilibrium while in the latter it is the equilibrating force. Disequilibrium theorising, therefore, provides a complex disagreement between humans as positive actors and negative abusers of opportunity. At once being the guiding force behind equilibrium and being the exploiters of disequilibrium. Despite these differences, however, both approaches do provide an assumption about human behaviour that is quite different from that applied in equilibrium theories. Within these theories one can see more voluntarism[23] and less determinism than is present in equilibrium theories, as well as, greater evidence of human action, bounded rationality and concepts of information exchange. The nature of society within the disequilibrium group is also viewed to be more unstable and open to unpredictable changes, for example:

> …every action is embedded in the flux of time…In other words the entrepreneurial element cannot be abstracted from the notion of individual human action, because the uncertainty of the future is already implied in the very notion of action. That man acts and that the future is uncertain are by no means two independent matters, they are only two different modes of establishing one thing (Kirzner, 1990: 81).

Uncertainty, not predictability enters as the guiding force behind economic systems. In terms of BM's paradigms these approaches remain functionalist in orientation but apply assumptions that allowed for human influence over economic structures, recognising the limits of knowledge, information and expecting greater unknown disequilibrating forces to impact on economic systems in unexpected ways.

Revolution-equilibrium Theorists

The third group of theorists has been described as the revolution-equilibrium group (e.g. Schumpeter, Cole, Knies, Roscher, Hildeband). The principle philosophies originate from the work of Schumpeter. Within this group three presuppositions exist. Firstly, theorists take the concepts of human action and choice a step further, secondly, they assume economic and social systems experience radical rather than incremental changes and, thirdly, they advocate greater linkage between historical 'facts' and abstract models. Schumpeter (Kilby, 1971) takes the concepts of human action further by arguing that while the entrepreneurial function may be mingled with ownership and management of resources the key function of the 'entrepreneur' was the person who innovates or makes 'new combinations' of production. Human action is conceptualised at the individual rather than the collective level (Shionoya, 1997). For example:

---

23 'Voluntarism' is the philosophical stance that much of human behaviour is open to choice.

> These concepts are at once broader and narrower than the usual. Broader, because in the first place we call entrepreneurs not only those 'independent' businessmen...but all who actually fulfil the function...even if they are...'dependent' employees of a company... On the other hand, our concept is narrower than the traditional one in that it does not include all heads of firms or managers or industrialists who merely operate an established business, but only those who actually perform that function (Schumpeter, 1971: 54).

The difference for the individual is related to behaviour, in the sense that in a static system the individual can become accustomed to his/her own abilities and experience and their usefulness. In a dynamic system, however, the individual must become accustomed to uncertainties and must interact with them. Operating a business in conditions of uncertainty is quite different from operating one where certain knowledge exists.

> Carrying out a new plan and acting according to a customary one are things as different as making a road and walking along it (Schumpeter, 1971: 56).

Assumptions about human action, therefore, differ from those applied by theorists in the disequilibrium group because individuals create new opportunities rather than respond to existing ones. This conception may derive from the second philosophical difference focusing on the nature of social systems, which holds that economic systems go through radical discontinuous changes. Schumpeter moves away from equilibrium theories by arguing that creative destruction involves periods of stability in economic systems followed by periods of transformation, within which he places the entrepreneurial function. This departure illustrates far greater usage within the functionalist paradigm of concepts of social conflict derived from Marxism and BM's radical structuralist paradigm and these are evident when one analyses in detail the concept of creative destruction (MacDonald, 1971). In direct contrast to Ogbor's (2000) critique, therefore, within this perspective the 'entrepreneurial' function involves the destruction of the current social order not its maintenance.

The final philosophies that differentiate this group of theorists derive from their views about social science research and Shionoya (1992; 1997) has examined these in detail. In summary research is viewed as a more inductive process, theories are used as mechanisms to help explain 'reality' and are viewed as abstractions that can be used to interpret observations. Such concepts are embedded in their historical context, are accumulated over time and are socialised within society, for example:

> The kind of data that is missing in entrepreneurial analysis could, in Schumpeter's opinion, best be supplied through qualitative data or by 'economic historians' and not economic mathematicians...According to Schumpeter, it is only through an intimate collaboration between facts and theory that it would be possible to make substantial advances in the study of entrepreneurship (Ogbor, 2000: 623).

> Nobody can hope to understand the economic phenomenon of any, including the present, epoch who has not adequate command of historical facts and an adequate amount of historical sense or of what might be described as historical experience (Schumpeter, 1954: 12–13).

This view of social science is near the boundaries between BM's interpretive and functionalist paradigms as it illustrates the important place of subjectivity and contextualism in research.

Results of the Analysis

The analysis of the economic approaches using BM's paradigms shows three distinct modes of theorising based on different philosophical assumptions about social science and society. As a consequence 'entrepreneurship' within these modes of theorising is quite different and events based on a variety of philosophies about human behaviour, change and social science have led to mutually exclusive concepts. For example, the difference between Schumpeter's and Kirzner's 'entrepreneur' is profound. This review using BM's paradigms also found that any form of purposeful behaviour as implied in most theories of entrepreneurship is obliterated from inquiry if functionalist assumptions are too extreme. The work of Barreto (1989) and Hébert and Link (1988) support this conclusion, it was highlighted historically by Schumpeter (1954) and confirmed by Bygrave (1989) and Kirchhoff (1991). Hébert's and Link's (1988) conclusion captures the point perfectly.

> One lesson to be learned from all of this is that the problem of the place of entrepreneurship in economic theory is actually not a problem of theory. It is a *problem of method.* The history of economic theory clearly demonstrates that the entrepreneur was squeezed from economics when the discipline attempted to emulate the physical sciences by incorporating the mathematical method. Clearly, mathematics brought greater precision to economics, and thereby promised to increase powers of prediction. Yet the introduction of mathematics was a two-edged sword. Its sharp edge cut through a tangled confusion of real world complexity, making economics more tractable, and accelerating its theoretical advance. However, its blunt edge bludgeoned one of the fundamental forces of economic life – the entrepreneur. Since there was not then, and is not now, a satisfactory mathematics to deal with the dynamics of economic life, economic analysis gradually receded into the shadows of comparative statics, and the entrepreneur took on a purely passive, even useless role (Hébert and Link, 1988: 158, added emphasis).

Although this chapter would prefer to substitute the term 'a problem of method' for the term 'a problem of meta-theory'. It is clear from the experience of the theory of the firm that certain assumptions about reality and knowledge, which may have led to the use of the mathematical method, created difficulties for understanding dynamic economic systems that depend upon human endeavour. The essential point that can be drawn is that economic theories that adopted equilibrium models, applying extreme functionalist assumptions, have tended to eradicate meaningful interpretations of entrepreneurship from their inquiry as a consequence of the philosophies used.

Conclusions

Ogbor (2000) described entrepreneurship as being dominated by the theories of social control and Grant and Perren (2002) described it as being dominated by functionalist inquiry. On the one hand, this study agrees with both critiques, it does appear that the economic foundations of entrepreneurship have applied major axioms within their study. It is further evident that the study of entrepreneurship has not explicitly analysed the meta-theoretical assumptions in economic studies and many of these meta-theories do indeed appear to be dominated by functionalist inquiry. On the other hand, both critiques of the subject are somewhat in danger of over simplifying the differences, as this analysis found a range of historical works that used assumptions based on other BM paradigms and found a great deal of diversity within the functionalist paradigm. For example, the core theories derived from Schumpeter applied Marxist concepts and there are significant elements of human action in many theories. In general, therefore, the research found that there was evidence of diversity in the meta-theories used but there was less evidence of philosophies drawn from other BM paradigms, somewhat supporting Grant's and Perren's (2002) conclusions. This deduction can perhaps be viewed both positively and negatively. For those wishing to expand these foundations and draw more widely from other BM paradigms than is currently the case the current diversity indicates a tolerance for alternative views and approaches. For those wishing to create a more 'scientific' paradigm the dominance of functionalist inquiry does provide a foundation for further consolidation.

Based on the analysis conducted in this study it is argued that extreme functionalist assumptions do little to help, and a great deal to restrict, the study of entrepreneurship. The main research objective as outlined was to explore if there were any philosophical reasons why the concept of the entrepreneur disappeared from macro- and micro-economic inquiry. The common thread discovered was the application of extreme functionalist assumptions in a desire to construct a 'scientific' approach to the subject. The problems for such philosophical assumptions are outlined as follows:

i. Extreme realist ontological assumptions tend to hypothesise that the social world represents an external structure, which is tangible and existing of many interrelated parts. Such an 'objective' assumption about social reality has led theorists to consider social behaviour to be somewhat unchanging and immutable, as is evident in the concepts of perfect information and the production function in the theory of the firm. Entrepreneurship, however, appears to be about change to social structures and social reality whether that is the exploitation of opportunities during periods of disequilibrium, via the deliberate creation of new opportunities or indeed through new forms of sensemaking in society. Such realist assumptions as those applied in extreme functionalism provide little opportunity for the 'entrepreneurial' function to change society in unpredictable ways.

ii. Relatively strong forms of positivism appear to be problematic for the study of entrepreneurship because they require greater degrees of mathematical precision that depend on accurate definitions. Problems of definition remain inherent to the subject and where they have been drawn around the firm they appear to lose much of the complexity and dynamism that is incorporated into wider interpretations of entrepreneurship. For example, most recently attempts have been directed at making 'entrepreneurship' synonymous with the behavioural act of venture creation. For a positivist this is inherently attractive, but it risks applying the same philosophical assumptions that led the theory of the firm to cast the 'entrepreneur' as the powerless figurehead of a 'firm', which itself became 'the reality' abstracted from the actions of people (Barreto, 1989). A simplification of the definition can lead to more positivism and can lead to the development of a 'scientific' paradigm. When focusing purely on venture creation, however, one disregards Schumpeter's argument that entrepreneurship, as a function of change in society, occurs in a variety of contexts (Schumpeter, 1934).

iii. Determinism applied in an extreme way also appeared to present difficulties for understanding the subject. Theories can rule out philosophies of human action and choice, which appear to be crucial to understanding entrepreneurship, by suggesting that forces outside of an individual's control are the main influence on their behaviour. Yet observations of 'entrepreneurship' suggest that the 'entrepreneur' takes control of their environment in order to create new things; that they aspire to have independence from the domination of forces outside of their control (Chell, 2000). Philosophies based on human action would appear to be relatively important when conceptualising how 'entrepreneurship' impacts on the development of new economic and social realities.

iv. The use of mechanistic metaphors to explain how social systems work can also have negative consequences. Even within the economic theories where the focus of study is the function of 'entrepreneurship', assumptions about the nature of human behaviour are endemic. It would appear that one of the major philosophical dilemmas for the study of entrepreneurship is that it is intricately tied to philosophies about human nature. Mechanistic assumptions sit uncomfortably with the subject because they tend to rule out behavioural complexity and ascribe law like qualities to social interactions.

These philosophical difficulties illustrate that the subject of 'entrepreneurship' could gain significantly if the meta-theoretical base of study is broadened (Grant and Perren, 2002). Based on this analysis one can certainly argue for expanding work in both BM's interpretive and radical structuralist paradigms. Interpretive approaches would introduce greater voluntarism, human action and be able to accept greater diversity in social meaning, while radical structuralist approaches could build on Schumpeter's application of Marxist concepts explaining how 'entrepreneurship', which can be conceived in this context as purposeful behaviour, creates radical change.

References

Aldrich, H. (2000), 'Learning together: National differences in entrepreneurship research', in *Handbook of Entrepreneurship.* D.L. Sexton and H. Landström (eds), 5–25. Oxford: Blackwell.

Astley, G.W. and Van de Ven, A.H. (1983), 'Central perspectives and debates in organization theory', *Administrative Science Quarterly* 28: 245–73.

Barreto, H. (1989), *The Entrepreneur in Micro-economic Theory: Disappearance and Explanation.* New York: Routledge.

Binks, M. and Vale, P. (1990), *Entrepreneurship and Economic Change.* London: McGraw-Hill.

Burrell, G. and Morgan, G. (1979), *Sociological Paradigms and Organizational Analysis.* London: Heinemann.

Bygrave, W.D. (1989), 'The entrepreneurship paradigm (I): A philosophical look at its research methodologies', *Entrepreneurship Theory and Practice* 14 (1): 7–26.

Cantillon, R. (1931), *Essai sur la nature du commerce en general.* London: MacMillan.

Casson, M. (1982), *The Entrepreneur: An Economic Theory.* Oxford: Robertson.

Casson, M. (1990), *Entrepreneurship.* Aldershot: Elgar.

Casson, M. (1998), 'Institutional economics and business history: A way forward?' in *Institutions and the Evolution of Modern Business.* M. Casson and M.B. Rose (eds), 151–71. London: Frank Cass.

Chell, E. (2000), 'Towards researching the 'opportunistic entrepreneur': A social constructionist approach and research agenda'. *European Journal of Work and Organizational Psychology* 9 (1): 63–80.

Chell, E., Haworth, J. and Brearley, S. (1991), *The Entrepreneurial Personality: Concepts, Cases and Categories.* London: Routledge.

Coase, R.H. (1937), 'The nature of the firm'. *Economica* 4: 390–405.

Davies, B. (1998), 'Psychology's subject: A commentary on the relativism/realism debate', in *Social Constructionism, Discourse and Realism.* I. Parker (ed.), 133–45. London: Sage Publications.

Gioia, D.A., Donnellon, A. and Sims, H.P. (1989), 'Communication and cognition in appraisal: A tale of two paradigms'. *Organization Studies* 10 (4): 503–530.

Gioia, D. and Pitre, E. (1990), 'Multiparadigm perspectives on theory building'. *Academy of Management Review* 15 (4): 584–602.

Grant, P. and Perren, L. (2002), 'Small business and entrepreneurial research: Meta-theories, paradigms and prejudices'. *International Small Business Journal* 20 (2): 185–211.

Harper, D.A. (1996), *'Entrepreneurship and the Market Process: An Enquiry into the Growth of Knowledge'*. London: Routledge.

Harré, R. (1979), *Social Being.* Oxford: Blackwell.

Hassard, J. (1988), 'Overcoming hermeticism in organization theory: An alternative to paradigm incommensurability'. *Human Relations* 41 (3): 247–59.

Hébert, R.F. and Link, A.N. (1988), *The Entrepreneur: Mainstream Views and Radical Critiques* 2nd edn. New York: Praeger.

Holland, R. (1990), 'The paradigm plague: Prevention, cure and inoculation'. *Human Relations* 43 (1): 23–48.

Jackson, N. and Carter, P. (1991), 'In defence of paradigm incommensurability' *Organization Studies* 12 (1): 109–127.

Jackson, N. and Carter, P. (1993), 'Paradigm wars: A response to Hugh Willmott'. *Organization Studies* 14 (5): 721–25.

Jones, S.R.H. (1998), 'Transaction costs and the theory of the firm: The scope and limitations of the new institutional approach', in M. Casson and M.B. Rose (eds), *Institutions and the Evolution of Modern Business*, London: Frank Cass.

Kilby, P. (1971), *Entrepreneurship and Economic Development.* New York: Free Press.

Kirchhoff, B.A. (1991), 'Entrepreneurship's contribution to economics' *Entrepreneurship Theory and Practice* 16: 93–112.

Kirzner, I.M. (1973), *Competition and Entrepreneurship.* Chicago: University of Chicago Press.

Kirzner, I.M. (1980), 'The primacy of entrepreneurial discovery', in A. Seldon (ed.), *Prime Mover of Progress: The Entrepreneur in Capitalism and Socialism* No. 23: 5–29: Institute of Economic Affairs.

Kirzner, I.M. (1982), 'The theory of entrepreneurship in economic growth', in C. A. Kent, D.L. Sexton and K.H. Vesper (eds), *Encyclopaedia of Entrepreneurship* 273–6. NJ: Prentice Hall.

Kirzner, I.M. (1990), 'Uncertainty, discovery, and human action: A study of the entrepreneurial profile in the Misesian system', in M. Casson (ed.), *Entrepreneurship* 81–101. Aldershot: Elgar.

Knight, F.H. (1921), *Risk, Uncertainty and Profit.* New York: Houghton Mifflin.

Lydall, H. (1992), '*The Entrepreneurial Factor in Economic Growth.* London: Macmillan.

McCourt, W. (1999), 'Paradigms and their development: The psychometric paradigm of personnel selection as a case study of paradigm diversity and consensus'. *Organization Studies* 20 (6): 1011–1033.

MacDonald, R. (1971), 'Schumpeter and Max Weber: Central visions and social theories' in P. Kilby (ed.), *Entrepreneurship and Economic Development* 71–94. New York: Free Press.

Marshall, A. (1961), *Principles of Economics.* London: Macmillan.

Mises, L.V. (1949), *'Human Action: A Treatise on Economics'.* London: William Hodge.

Morgan, G. and Smircich, L. (1980), 'The case for qualitative research'. *Academy of Management Science* 5 (4): 491–500.

Nightingale, D.J. and Cromby, J. (1999), *Social Constructionist Psychology: A Critical Analysis of Theory and Practice.* Buckingham: Open University Press.

Ogbor, J.O. (2000), 'Mythicizing and reification in entrepreneurial discourse: Ideology-critique of entrepreneurial studies'. *Journal of Management Studies* 35 (5): 605–635.

Parker, I. (1998), *Social Constructionism, Discourse and Realism.* London: Sage Publications.

Pittaway, L.A. (2000), 'The social construction of entrepreneurial behaviour', PhD Thesis, University Newcastle upon Tyne: Newcastle upon Tyne.

Pfeffer, J. (1993), 'Barriers to the advance of organization science: Paradigm development as a dependent variable'. *Academy of Management Review* 18: 599–620.

Ricketts, M. (1987), *The Economics of Business Enterprise: New Approaches to the Firm.* Sussex: Wheatsheaf.

Say, J.B. (1880), *Treatise on Political Economy.* Philadelphia: John Crigg.

Scherer, G.A. and Steinmann, H. (1999), 'Some remarks on the problem of incommensurability in organization studies'. *Organization Studies* 20 (3): 519–44.

Schumpeter, J.A. (1934), *The Theory of Economic Development.* Cambridge, MA: Harvard University Press.

Schumpeter, J.A. (1954), *History of Economic Analysis.* London: Allen and Unwin.

Schumpeter, J.A. (1963), *History of Economic Analysis*, 5th edn. New York: George Allen.

Schumpeter, J.A. (1971), 'The fundamental phenomenon of economic development', in *Entrepreneurship and Economic Development* P. Kilby (ed.) 43–70. New York: Free Press.

Shionoya, Y. (1992), 'Taking Schumpeter's methodology seriously', in F.M. Scherer and M. Pearlman (eds), *Entrepreneurship and Technological Innovation and Economic Growth* 343–62. Michigan: The University of Michigan Press.

Shionoya, Y. (1997), *Schumpeter and the Idea of Social Science: A Meta-theoretical Study.* Cambridge: Cambridge University Press.

Walsh, L. (1970), *Introduction to Contemporary Microeconomics.* New York: McGraw-Hill.

Weaver, G.R. and Gioia, D.A. (1994), 'Paradigms lost: Incommensurability vs structurationist inquiry'. *Organization Studies* 15 (4): 565–90.

Williamson, O.E. (1985), *The Economic Institutions of Capitalism.* New York: Free Press.

Willig, C. (1999), 'Beyond appearances: A critical realist approach to social constructionist work'. D.J. Nightingale and J. Cromby, (eds), 37–51. Buckingham: Open University Press.

Willmott, H. (1993a), 'Breaking the paradigm mentality'. *Organization Studies* 14 (5): 682–719.

Willmott, H. (1993b), 'Paradigm gridlock: A reply'. *Organization Studies* 14 (5): 727–30.

Chapter 12
Theory and Practice of Technology-based Economic Development

Harvey A. Goldstein

Introduction

In the fifteen years since an earlier vintage of this chapter was published, much has changed that affects both our understanding of how the high tech sectors of regions prosper, or not, and the strategies that cities and regions in fact design and implement to attract, grow, and retain high tech economic activity. Much of this change lies in the dramatically different economic environments regions face then and now. The process of increasing globalization was taking place then, but its reach had not advanced nearly as far as now. The term 'knowledge economy' would have been an unusual one to see in print, and we were only beginning to imagine some of the impacts of the IT revolution on how business would be conducted. In the world of practice, 'high tech', or technology-based economic development, was still seen as a niche area affecting only a relatively small number of sectors in most regions, and thinking about planning for clusters of related industries rather than individual sectors had not yet been adopted.

The realm of theory has also undergone considerable change since the early 1990s. In the 1993 chapter we reviewed and compared neoclassical growth theories, stage/wave/cycle theories, theories of production organization, and theories of entrepreneurship and creative regions to identify the critical factors that purportedly 'determined' the course of regional economic development. Unfortunately, no one of these alternative theories offered explanations that were unambiguously superior to all the others, while the success factors and conditions varied considerably among the competing theories. Since then endogenous growth theory, first formulated by Nelson and Winter (1982) and formalized by Romer (1986, 1990) and Lucas (1988) has gradually emerged as a consensus paradigm in the regional growth/development scholarly literature. In this author's view endogenous growth theory supplies a strong and relevant knowledge base for economic development practice, particularly so in the context of a national economy which is increasingly based on science and technology as inputs and provides the US with comparative advantage in the global economy. Other influential theoretical or conceptual developments have included Porter's (1990) emphasis on institutional infrastructure and capacity – in addition to his more widely recognized emphasis on clusters – and a re-emphasis on creative milieu by Florida (2002, 2004).

We shall begin with a brief review of the definition and measurement of "high tech", and reconsider how we might consider the meaning of high tech with the emergence of the knowledge-based economy. Section 3 will provide a review and explication of endogenous growth theory and several other conceptual frameworks that have become influential to the practice of high tech economic development. We shift in section 4 to a description of the institutional actors in the contemporary practice of technology-based economic development. This is followed in section 5 with a typology of economic development strategic approaches that form the 'legs' for the contemporary practice of technology-based economic development at the state, regional, and local levels. Finally in section 6 we assess the coherence – consistencies and gaps – between theory and practice.

Definitions, Measurement, and Meanings of High Tech

The high tech sector of the economy was first delineated in the early 1980s. Two indicators have been consistently used to demarcate and measure the high tech sector: the relative amount of R&D expenditures of an industry (as a percentage of its total sales) and/or the proportion of scientists and engineers in an industry sector. Using thresholds usually based upon the distribution of these indicators among all industries at a given time, three-digit SIC codes (later four digit NAICS codes) were generated by different analysts and organizations as comprising the high tech economy of the US (OTA, 1984; Marcusen, Hall, and Glasmeier, 1986). Although several of these definitions and subsequent lists of industry sectors were widely adopted by other analysts and state and regional economic development organizations, there was never a strong justification put forward for using any particular threshold, say, above the all-industry average, or 1.5 times above the all industry average. In the end the choice of thresholds has been rather arbitrary.

A second issue that has been repeatedly raised is whether industry sectors are the most appropriate units for defining the high-tech economy. Good arguments have been made to use the *establishment* as the unit since there has always been a high degree of heterogeneity within industries in terms of activities, or functions (Yin, Sottile, Bernstein, 1985; Malecki, 1997). For example, should we count employment in sales offices and distribution centers of establishments in the microelectronics or biotech sectors as high tech? While there was recognition this would be conceptually superior, the paucity of data at the establishment level – and issues of data confidentiality – would make this impractical.

Changes in the size and composition of the high tech portion of the economy since the early 1990s, and the emergence of the knowledge-based economy, call for a reconsideration of how we should think about the label 'high tech', even if we may not provide a more accurate way to measure and demarcate it.

The size of the high tech sector, in employment terms, has grown, though not at a higher rate than total wage and salary employment. The US Bureau of Labor Statistics has estimated that the proportion of total wage and salary employment in the high tech industries actually declined from 12.2 percent in 1992 to 11.0 percent in 2002 (Hecker, 2005). Over this period, the employment growth rate of the high tech sector was 7.5 percent (using the most inclusionary criterion of at least twice the proportion of scientific, engineering, and technician occupations as total, all industries) while total employment grew at a rate of 19.7 percent. But more important than changes in size has the change in industry composition that qualifies as 'high tech'. The most vivid of these changes has been the inclusion of a number of service industries after the NAICS code was adopted. These service industries were also the fastest growing of the industries classified as high tech. But the general point here is, as Porter has observed, "Widely applicable technologies such as microelectronics, advanced materials, and information systems have rendered obsolete the traditional distinction between high and low technology industries." (Porter, 1998, pp.13–14). In addition, some notable older, traditional industries have invested heavily in new technology in order to retain and even increase market share in certain specialized niches (for example in textiles and furniture); if we had more disaggregated industry data or at the individual establishment level, manufacturing modernization would account for additional high tech activity.

There have been several recent contributions to the literature about the high tech economy in which operational definitions are laid out. DeVol wrote an influential monograph, *America's High Tech Economy*, published by the Milken Institute in 1999, that measures the concentration of the high tech sector among US metro areas for purposes of ranking them. DeVol, however, identifies high tech industries using essentially the same two indicators described above – proportion of R&D spending to total sales, and proportion of scientists, engineers, mathematicians, and programmers – and includes those sectors (3-digit SIC) that are above average on *both* indicators. This yields nine high tech manufacturing and five high tech service industries.

Cortright and Mayer (2001) take a more innovative stance in conceptualizing high tech economic activity by thinking about clusters of industries as the relevant units, rather than using the standard individual SIC or NAICS codes. Clusters, for Cortright and Mayer, are groups of firms that share similar labor force demands, technologies, and markets, for which there are likely to be significant buyer-supplier relationships. To the degree that the economic health and viability of regional clusters – by providing significant positive externalities, or spillovers to firms that comprise them – are increasingly being viewed as the preferred target for regional economic development policies, then it may make sense to operationally define and identify whole clusters that are 'high tech' in nature, even though some of the constituent individual industry sectors might not pass the test, or threshold levels, of R&D spending and/or employment in scientific and engineering occupations. Unfortunately though, Cortright and Mayer then somewhat arbitrarily choose the computer, electronics, instruments, and software industries as the high tech component of their metropolitan economies, conspicuously leaving out such sectors as biotechnology, pharmaceuticals, and aero-space.

Florida's work (2002) on the creative class and creative cities offers a potentially new way to conceive of a region's high tech economy. Although he uses a Tech Pole measure borrowed from DeVol (1999) in his Milken Institute study mentioned above, Florida's measure of the creative class itself can be considered as a way to define high tech as a region's set of knowledge workers. This is also a broader conception of knowledge workers because it is not limited to scientists, engineers, and programmers.

Chapple et al. (2004) use a standard set of science and technology occupations as the basis for defining high tech industries – if an industry's share of S&T occupations is 9.0 percent or more – but they also offer a new category of industries labeled I-Tech, comprised of sectors in which a specific set of information technology occupations comprise at least three times the all-industry average share, representing 3.0 percent or greater. The I-Tech category would add a number of advanced services sectors that would not otherwise be included in definitions of high tech.

The changes in the industrial composition, structure, and behavior of regional economies within the last twenty years suggest the traditional definitions are too narrow and at the same time may miss important targets. A good case can be made to conceive of high tech as a region's knowledge-based economy, with a consequent broadening of both occupations and industry sectors – particularly in the services – under the high tech umbrella. And from an economic development strategy point of view, we would also suggest the targets of high tech should include industry clusters, the composition of which may be sectors that would not pass the usual thresholds of 'high tech', but may be important components of high tech clusters.

'New' Theoretical Concepts to Guide Practice

The development of new (endogenous) growth theory in the 1980s and its subsequent diffusion into the economic development literature have provided a major advance in our understanding of the most critical factors and conditions for stimulating and sustaining regional economic development. Other influential contributions have emphasized institutional capacity, a creative milieu, industry clusters, and the concepts of path dependency and 'lock-in'. In this section we summarize, in a nonmathematical way, the essential contribution of endogenous growth theory to our understanding of strategies of high tech economic development and explicate other theoretical frameworks and concepts that add to the repertoire for potentially guiding practice.

Endogenous Growth Theory.

To appreciate endogenous growth theory, it is useful to briefly review neoclassical growth theory, its forerunner, developed principally by Solow (1956). The neoclassical growth model posited that a region's rate of economic growth is a function of the stock of capital and its stock of labor. There is assumed to be some rate of technological progress, but this exogenous, i.e., it can not be affected by any actions or policies within a region. In the short-term a region can grow because of an increase in either its supply of capital or an increase in its labor supply. But a region's supply of capital and labor are determined solely by differences in wage rates and rates of return to capital among regions. The model predicts that there is a steady state growth path applicable to all regions. This is due to the equilibrating tendencies for: (i) labor to migrate to higher wage regions, increasing wage rates in the lower wage region and decreasing the wage rates in the higher wage region, and, (ii) for capital to flow to regions where there is higher expected rates of return, with the effect of decreasing the returns to capital in the region with the initial higher rates of return. A key determinant of the equilibrating behavior of this model is that both labor and capital are subject to decreasing returns.

With endogenous growth theory, this assumption of a "given" and spatially constant rate of technological progress is withdrawn. Specifically, endogenous growth theory is built upon the notion that a region's rate of technological progress is at least partially determined within the model, and specifically by the production of knowledge and by investments in human capital. Indeed, knowledge and technology play the key role in stimulating and sustaining a region's economic growth because these particular inputs display, unlike physical capital and labor, *increasing* returns to scale. The reason for this is that at least some component of knowledge has the attributes of being non-rival and at least partially non-excludable. Non-rival means that individual firm B's ability to make use of an input, say a new idea, is not diminished by firm A's use of that same idea. This attribute leads to the production of positive externalities from the point of view of the individual firm: each firm able to utilize the knowledge input receives a pecuniary benefit it otherwise would not have. In turn, this takes the form of a knowledge spillover effect, since there tends to be a strong negative spatial gradient to knowledge flows, especially of tacit forms of knowledge. So the spatial clustering of knowledge producers and knowledge users leads to increasing positive externalities, and that in turn provides incentives for firms to want to locate within the spatial cluster, up until congestion or other forms of diseconomies of scale occur from non-knowledge inputs. In this sense, endogenous growth theory provides a more elegant and more generalizable explanation of the phenomenon of industrial districts articulated by Marshall (1920) in the early part of the 20th century, and is consistent with theories of agglomeration economies and of cumulative causation such as Myrdal's (1957).

It is precisely because of the existence of these positive externalities and spillovers available within a spatially defined area that lead to unequal rates of technological progress among regions. It is by this factor that endogenous growth theory provides an explanation for why any cumulated advantages a particular region might have do not dissolve as a result of the equilibrating tendencies for capital to flow across regions in search of the highest expected return, and labor to migrate to regions with the highest wage rates. With its focus on raising productivity by realizing potential increasing returns to scale, the model directs the focus of economic development policymakers to those particular investments, incentives, and supporting policies that should lead to the creation of knowledge spillovers captured within the region, resulting in increasing firm productivity.

Cluster Theory

The idea of clusters as the strategic target for regional economic development, although popularized by Porter (1990, 1998), goes back at least to Marshall (1920) with his discussion of the advantages of industrial districts as mentioned earlier. Clusters can be considered as groups of related firms and organizations concentrated in the same geographic area. Firms and organizations can be related by being within the same buyer-supplier chain, by supplying specialized services needed by the producing firms, competitors producing the same products, intermediaries and institutions such as trade associations, training and educational centers, universities, and other R&D producers.

Clusters confer economic advantage to members in terms of positive externalities known as agglomeration economies. That is, firms reduce their out-of-pocket costs as well as transaction costs by being in proximity with other organizations that provide information, services, intermediate goods, R&D, and so on. Firms can organize and act collectively for certain needs and issues such as the regulatory environment or specific government services. Accordingly in a cluster-based strategy, policies would focus on enhancing the competitive advantage of a group of (related) firms and more likely be more comprehensive, rather than target a particular firm or a particular sector, and be limited to addressing only one factor. Porter (1998) argues that membership in a cluster can increase the competitiveness of firms through rivalry and the creation of a dynamic and risk-taking culture. The competitive advantage of a region is not merely the vector sum of the competitiveness of individual companies, but instead can be enhanced by the location of other firms and organizations nearby. In this sense, cluster development is highly consistent with the theory of endogenous growth even if the theory does not explicitly address clusters.

To be sure, there are many different notions of what a cluster is and how it should be measured, as well as how it should be appropriately used in tech-based economic development policymaking. Maskell and Kebir (2005) critically discuss the concept of clusters as a 'theory' while Feser and Luger (2003) assess the usefulness of clusters as a concept in the broader context of regional economic development policy.

Path Dependence and Lock-in

The concept of *path dependence* is that how regional economies develop in the future is dependent upon the historic path they have followed up to the present (David, 2000). It is an idea from evolutionary economic theory (Nelson and Winter, 1982) that in turn came from chaos theory. Seen from the perspective of chaos theory, small chance events such as the initial location of a particular firm in a region – for no obvious reason – occurring at a critical point in time can have persistent long-term effects that are difficult, if not impossible, to reverse. What happens is that the firm might draw other related businesses to concentrate in the same area, say to take advantage of positive externalities in the form of agglomeration and/or localization economies. This network effect builds momentum and becomes self reinforcing.

One of the implications of path dependency is that regional economies are not as malleable as perhaps we wish they were, and thus the attribute of lock-in. Lock-in means that as a result of an area's historical economic base, specific public investment decisions, or institutional arrangements selected, a region's economic development outcomes in the future may become suboptimal and resistant to the equilibrating and self-correcting set of market forces. The tendencies of both path dependence and lock-in are exacerbated by increasing returns to scale that is the prominent driver in exogenous growth theory. The existence of increasing returns may lead collectively many actors adopting a particular technology or co-locating firms in a particular industry sector in a region that at one time may be economically beneficial to the individual firms and the region. Yet at a later time this may mean firms in the region are locked into the same technology that becomes inefficient, or a sectoral specialty that is no longer competitive in that region, but is hard to reverse. Detroit and the US auto industry is an obvious example.

Another implication of path dependence and lock-in is that the equilibrating and self-correcting tendencies of markets that are integral in the neoclassical model generally and neoclassical growth theory in particular can not be assumed. Path dependence and lock-in provide theoretical explanations of why some regions that suffer from chronic economic decline and disinvestment may not necessarily recover by in-flows of capital investment to seize opportunities to get above average rates of return. Obversely, it explains why some regions that initially had favorable endowments or were just plain lucky somewhere in their economic history have been able to sustain high levels of growth and wealth.

Regional Institutional Capacity

While the contributions of endogenous growth theory for helping to fashion more effective technology-based economic development strategies are evident, Malecki (1997) and others have criticized the theory for paying insufficient attention to the institutional context and institutional adaptivity as prerequisites for successful knowledge-based regional economic development. With the focus on increasing firm productivity – consistent with endogenous growth theory – Porter's (1998) diamond model has highlighted a number of institutional conditions that allow firms within certain sectors to be able to gain national (or regional) competitiveness. The diamond – the four sets of interacting determinants of national (or regional) competitiveness – consists of (1) firm strategy, structure, and rivalry; (2) demand conditions; (3) factor (input) conditions; and (4) related and supporting industries. Porter argues that economic development policy and government more generally have important roles to play in each of these four determinants of competitiveness. These roles may be direct, such as timely and responsive investments in physical infrastructure, information technology, K-12 education, and instruction and R&D at public universities. But perhaps just as important are the indirect and 'soft' roles of government in helping to create a (regional) environment that is conducive to innovation and competitiveness. These may include: building social capital and trust; encouraging the participation of stakeholders in shared governance; assisting the formation of collaborative efforts at regional problem-solving; expediting the sharing of information among firms, universities, training institutions, and government agencies; increasing the density of networks and intermediary organizations that enable firms, entrepreneurs, researchers, workers, and educational institutions to connect; coordinated and cooperative intergovernmental relations and policies.

A specific aspect of institutional capacity emphasized by Bellini and Landabaso (2005) in the context of designing and implementing regional innovation systems (RIS) for lagging regions in the EU is the role of government itself. The idea that is central in RIS for creating learning regions and increasing their innovative capacity is that a model of *shared governance* – a government-business-higher education 'policy network' adapted to the potential capacity of organizational actors in the region and shaped around specific policy problems or arenas – might allow for broader participation, greater buy-in by stakeholders, and more innovative policy approaches. Traditional government in this type of shared governance structure may well take the role of facilitator, broker, or catalyst rather than the final decider of policies that support regional innovation.

A region's knowledge infrastructure has been discussed by Goldstein (2006) as an attribute of a regional economy that when developed can increase that region's productivity generally. Using the development of a region's physical infrastructure as an analogy, the knowledge infrastructure – consisting of knowledge producers such as research universities and other R&D organizations, knowledge adopters, training and educational centers, and a range of intermediary organizations and institutions that expedite and manage the flow of knowledge – increases the productivity of actors that utilize it.

Creative Milieu and the Creative Class

The role and importance of a regional environment conducive to regional competitiveness and innovativeness has also been addressed in Florida's extensive writing (2002, 2004) on the 'creative class'. Florida asks what distinguishes metro areas that are thriving and those that are lagging behind in terms of economic growth and competitiveness. His answer is those areas that can attract members of the creative class, defined as people in scientific, computer programming, designing, and artistic occupations. The attributes of cities and metro areas that attract members of the creative class are found in the three T's: talent, tolerance, and technology. Talent refers to the concentration of the population within the creative class already there. Tolerance refers to diversity in terms of foreign born, sexual preference, and artistic types. Technology refers to the concentration of high tech employment and output in the area. Government policies that cater to the needs and interests of the creative class, such as a lively after 5:00 downtown, culturally diverse entertainment venues and neighborhoods, and investment in education and R&D, will be successful. While Florida to a degree emphasizes the high-tech or knowledge-based sectors as one of the means of regional economic development, rather than as a goal, it is clear that Florida assumes there is a two-way causal relationship between the size and health of the knowledge-based sectors and a region's overall economic development prospects. What Florida adds to the factors already discussed that are critical to the region developing its knowledge-based economy is attractiveness of an area as a place to live for arguably the most important scarce factor, the knowledge workers themselves.

The Practice of Knowledge-based Economic Development: Institutional Actors

Because the benefits and beneficiaries of economic development projects and programs often cross over municipal and county boundaries and the front-end investments can be prohibitively large for a single local government, the economic development function has often been pursued as much at the regional and state levels as at the local level. In the practice of knowledge-based economic development, the increasingly key role of institutions of higher education has shifted the center of gravity even closer to state government because most of the higher education institutional actors tend to be part of state-funded university and community college systems.

For these as well as other reasons, in knowledge-based economic development there is a particularly complex web of both public and private actors, and a mix of public-sector organizations at various levels with a division of responsibility that is often blurred. The description below is based on the institutional arrangements in the United States, though there are a number of similarities in other national contexts.

State Government

At the state government level, many states have created boards of science and technology that serve an advisory and coordinative role for governors and legislatures on science- and technology-based economic development initiatives. We also see a number of states creating and funding institutes or centers in particular technology areas, such as the North Carolina Biotechnology Center. These centers provide a key node in the formation of networks among private companies, university research centers, venture capital, other specialized service providers, and would-be entrepreneurs. The lead state economic development organization often has within it industry sector or cluster teams that focus on the recruiting, retention, and expansion needs of firms in that specific sector or cluster. In the high tech sectors in particular these teams often include experts in the particular technology areas from some of the private sector firms in the state.

Higher Education

In the higher education sector, many research universities as well as regional four-year institutions now have vice presidents with 'economic development' in their titles. These officials have responsibility for their institutions' myriad activities that involve conducting research that has commercialization potential, university-industry partnerships, management of intellectual property developed in the university including patenting and licensing, investments in start-ups based on university research, and the operation of research parks and incubators. Community colleges, but also sometimes four year colleges and universities, work cooperatively with state, regional and local economic development organizations involved in recruiting or to assist displaced workers prepare for 'new economy' jobs by planning customized curricula and training programs.

Regional and Local Government

Economic development organizations at the multi-county, or regional level, often have had responsibility for conducting research and providing information about the region's economic assets that can be used to market the region by industry recruiters. But increasingly counties and municipalities are partnering with each other in sharing the funding of facilities such as research parks and incubators and workforce development programs.

Municipal and county governments, as well as chambers of commerce, are engaged in knowledge-based economic development efforts much like traditional economic development – particularly in terms of recruitment and provision of physical infrastructure – but their role in knowledge-based economic development has expanded to include those activities and functions that can make the area attractive for knowledge-based workers, and the 'creative class', to want to live there. Downtown revitalization, neighborhood revitalization, public safety, historic preservation, K-12 education, and the public sponsorship of cultural arts are all functions that local governments have always performed, but which now are elements of economic development plans and strategies requiring coordination with explicit economic development organizations.

The Federal Government

The federal government over the last 25 years has been decreasing its role in regional and local economic development, including technology-based economic development, as the states have increased theirs. The Economic Development Administration (EDA) of the US Department of Commerce is the lead federal agency in support of local and regional economic development efforts. The EDA maintains five programs, including providing funds for infrastructure construction in support of economic development (Public Works and Economic Development Program), funding for regions experiencing significant economic distress to enhance economic competitiveness and to promote entrepreneurial and innovation-based economic development efforts (Economic Adjustment Assistance Program), trade adjustment assistance to affected firms, economic development planning grants, and support of local and regional economic development efforts through provision of technical assistance. The most important of these programs that specifically supports technology-based economic development is the Economic Adjustment Assistance Program. In fiscal year 2006, this program's total funding was $44 million, an increase from $34.3 million in FY 1999. A total of 103 grants were awarded with amounts ranging from $21 thousand to $4 million. The lion's share of EDA grants in FY 2006 – $158 million – were for public works construction, but this was a decrease from $205 million in FY 1999. So while there has been an increase in federal funding of the economic adjustment assistance program, absolutely and relative to other EDA grant programs, the total level of funding is still rather modest.

The US Department of Housing and Urban Development has also had a long tradition of support for urban economic development, and is still active primarily through its Renewal Community/Empowerment/Enterprise Community, the Brownfield Economic Development Initiative,Youthbuild, and Section 108 Loan Guarantee programs. None of these programs focus on knowledge-based economic development, however.

The Office of Technology Assistance (OTA) was an important federal government resource in its brief lifespan between 1972 and 1995 when it was defunded by Congress. OTA's mission was to provide Congress and Congressional staff with "objective and authoritative analyses of the complex scientific and technical issues." It issued hundreds of reports with assessments of competitiveness in key industrial sectors and of the implications of new technologies for the national and regional economies. A small sample of its reports were: "Technology and the American Economic Transition: Choices for the Future"; "Technology and Structural Unemployment: Reemploying Displaced Adults; "Making Things

Better: Competing in Manufacturing"; "Rural America at the Crossroads: Networking the Future; and "The Technological Reshaping of Metropolitan America".

The US Small Business Administration, Office of Technology, operates two programs with the purposes of stimulating and supporting R&D by small businesses. With funds set aside from the overall R&D budgets of eleven large federal agencies, the Small Business Innovation Research Program (SBIR) competitively awards Phase 1 grants of up to $100,000 to small businesses for approximately six months to support the feasibility of an idea for a new technology that has commercialization potential. For those grant awardees whose ideas show substantial promise, additional Phase 2 grants of up to $750,000 may be awarded for the R&D work to be performed and the commercialization potential evaluated. In the fiscal year 2004, over 4,600 Phase 1 awards and over 2000 Phase 2 awards were made together worth $1.87 billion dollars. The second program, the Small Business Technology Transfer Program (STTR), makes competitive awards to small business and non-profit research institution partnerships. The idea is that non-profit research laboratories are often productive in innovation but poor at commercialization. Small businesses often have the entrepreneurial skills and business sense but lack the innovation capacity. The partnership combines the respective strengths of each partner. Structured similarly to SBIR awards, STTR awards are made in two phases with the same maximum amounts and the same contingencies for partnerships receiving Phase 2 awards. In fiscal year 2004 just over 600 STTR Phase 1 awards were made and just under 200 Phase 2 awards were made, totaling about $200 million (www.sba.gov/SBIR/indexwhatwedo.html).

National Support Organizations

There are now several national-level organizations that provide a range of services for knowledge-based economic development practitioners. The State Science and Technology Institute (SSTI) is a membership organization created in 1996 comprised of practitioners and policymakers working primarily at the state level but also at the local level. The organization serves as a network for the distribution of data and articles on trends and descriptions of best practice. A recent SSTI publication, "A Resource Guide for Technology-based Economic Development" was prepared for the EDA. It also conducts an annual conference and commissions publications that serve the educational needs of practitioners.

Other membership organizations include the Association of University Research Parks (AURP) and the National Business Incubation Association (NBIA). The AURP membership consists of universities and other owners of research parks and technology-based incubators, as well as developers of research parks. It performs a networking and educational role through newsletters and conferences of informing members of best practice for the management of research parks and by providing advice and assistance for cities, regions, and universities contemplating initiating research parks. AURP estimates there are now over 400 research parks worldwide, and hundreds of additional technology incubators that either stand alone or are located in research parks. NBIA serves similar functions for incubators as AURP does for research parks, but is not necessarily focused on technology-based incubators.

The Progressive Policy Institute (PPI), an educational and advocacy organizational arm of the Democratic Leadership Council of the national Democratic Party, has regularly published reports that evaluate and score the states and major MSAs on their technology-based economic development performance (Progressive Policy Institute, 2001, 2002). Perhaps the greatest value of PPIs reports has been the data they publish on a range of relevant indicators of participation in the knowledge economy that accompanies the scores. The Milken Institute based in Santa Monica, CA, although not focused on regional economic development specifically, performs a similar educative function with rankings and indicators of the performance of universities in biotechnology transfer and commercialization (DeVol and Bedroussian, 2006).

Local and Regional Networks

Finally, the existence of a dense social network of organizations and actors is now seen as a vital ingredient for interaction, innovation, creativity, synergy, and energy to occur, and that is critical for knowledge-based economic development. Such actors include law firms with IP expertise, equity investment firms, outsourcing specialists, human resource specialists, product development specialists, industrial designers. Networks of these actors might develop serendipitously, but many economic development strategies now explicitly plan for network facilitating organizations. They vary from region to region in organizational form and location; they can be in only one or two, or distributed among multiple organizations; in the public sector, private, sector, universities, or non-profit organizations; coordinated or just loosely connected. The organizations that provide such facilitation, however, have become part of the new 'governance' structure of knowledge-based economic development even if their responsibilities are informal rather than codified.

The Practice of Technology-Based Economic Development: Strategic Approaches

There are a number of prescriptions of the practice of technology-based economic development in the literature. A report written for the Brookings Institution by Sommers (2000), for example, lists the 'ten steps to a high tech future';

1. Understand high tech firms in your region and your city's competitive advantages.
2. Invest in human capital.
3. Create a research and development presence.

4. Invest in physical capital.
5. Invest in quality of life.
6. Streamline permitting, planning, and other public services.
7. Adapt other local laws (such as special tax policies and administrative procedures).
8. Provide venture and seed capital.
9. Create support programs for entrepreneurs.
10. Apply information technology in the public sector.

Reviewing a number of descriptions of economic development practice and planning documents over the last ten years, we can identify four strategic approaches, or legs, used to support technology-based economic development at state, regional and municipal levels:

- Investing in human capital and workforce development.
- Investing in R&D capacity.
- Facilitating university-industry partnerships and commercialization.
- Creating a 'milieu' that will be attractive to knowledge workers and entrepreneurs and conducive to innovative activity.

In practice most technology-based economic development plans include a mix of these approaches, though there is notable variation in the respective mixes in terms of their emphasis and priority in effort and resources.

Investing in Human Capital and Workforce Development

Above all else, globalization and the rise of the knowledge-based economy has brought *human capital* to the fore as the critical ingredient – and often limiting factor – in successful technology-based economic development. Surveys of high tech company executives invariably cite having access to a supply of highly skilled workers in the region as the most important locational factor. Not having enough or the right kind of labor skills, currently or prospectively, will yield low success in recruitment efforts and limit the possibilities of existing firms to expand. Regions have two options for meeting the human capital needs of technology-based firms: be able to attract knowledge workers to relocate in the area, or invest in human capital for existing residents. While the former represents the 'cheaper' option, the most successful and leading technology regions in the US and the world by and large all invest heavily in programs to raise the human capital of its extant workforce and to increase the flow in the educational pipeline of future science and technology workers (Schweke, 2007).

Almost all students of economic development view investment in human capital as a "no-brainer", but there has been historically a functional and institutional separation within government between public education and workforce training, on the one hand, and economic development on the other. There is little doubt this organizational separation led to the loss of opportunities to seamlessly plan and coordinate economic development programs – aimed to increase demand for highly skilled workers – with education and workforce development programs aimed to increase their supply. Fortunately this has begun to change, particularly at the community college and university educational planning levels.

Programmatic efforts in human capital investment in the leading technology regions include improving basic adult literacy, science and math education in K-12, incentives to increase interest in science and engineering fields, lifelong and distance learning for adults, specialized technology training programs targeted to displaced workers, and the planning for expansion of some university educational programs tied to emerging regional high tech industries.

Another major thrust has been investing in IT infrastructure that networks public schools and colleges to each other as well as to private firms and government organizations. This initiative, begun in the 1990s and promoted by the Clinton administration, was to extend internet access to a majority of classrooms in the US, with the goal of educating students to be internet-ready and technologically smart. Some states, however, took the initiative and the lead more than others. North Carolina, for example, developed its Information Superhighway through a cooperative arrangement between the state and several IT providers to extend high capacity fiber optic to every public school in the state – focusing on rural areas – for the transmission of multi-point interactive video, data, and computer programs at a minimum rate of 45 megabites per second. This investment in IT infrastructure, allowed rural high schools to offer Advanced Placement and other college level courses via real-time video transmission when they did not have the resources to offer these themselves. Subsequently a number of other states have followed North Carolina's lead.

Ongoing joint planning and alignment of economic development and workforce development programs is also a relatively new phenomenon. States and regions for many years have included customized training programs provided by community colleges as one element of the incentive package offered to recruited companies, whether high tech or not. But more long-term and proactive coordination, rather than ad-hoc and reactive efforts is becoming the norm in response to the need for state and regional leaders to prepare workers displaced from traditional manufacturing industries for jobs in the 'new economy'. Such coordination also provides evidence to prospective firms of an *existing* pipeline of highly skilled workers for high tech manufacturing jobs in certain strategic sectors or clusters.

One such example is the BioWorks program of North Carolina. BioWorks is an approximately 120 hour curriculum offered at twelve community colleges distributed around the state to prepare individuals to take manufacturing processing jobs in the burgeoning life sciences cluster. Although one of the leading states in biotechnology R&D, North Carolina had lagged in the development of the *production* side in biotech and other life sciences including medical devices and pharmaceuticals. The idea was that workers who were being displaced from the shrinking textiles, furniture, and tobacco industries, could be provided the skills within four months to take bioprocessing jobs in facilities that would locate in the regions of the state hardest hit by the decline of it traditional manufacturing sectors. Several years after BioWorks began to enroll students, the National Center for Biotech Workforce (NCBW) was created and funded by the US Department of Labor to provide a series of national pilots based at community colleges in New Hampshire, Iowa, Washington, California and North Carolina, modeled in part on the experience with BioWorks.

Investing in (and Supporting) R&D Capacity

Investing in a region's research and development represents a more 'mainstream' activity of economic development organizations compared to human capital investment. Economists and others have long noted the chronic under-investment in private R&D investment as a result of its public goods aspects. So there is a clear justification for public sector investment in R&D as a correction for market failure. Endogenous growth theory provides further justification beyond market failure in that R&D activity can lead to increasing returns to scale by creating positive externalities, including knowledge spillovers. Yet the relationship between investment in R&D activity in a region and ensuing commercialization and job growth in the same region is far from clear.

Specific activities and programs that provide support and investment in R&D capacity have a wide range. They include providing subsidies to lower the business costs to firms performing R&D, initiating and funding research centers at universities, including recruiting 'star' scientists, and investing in the area's physical and knowledge infrastructure.

Providing subsidies to lower the cost of doing business to firms, of course, has had a long and controversial history in traditional economic development practice (e.g., Bartik, 1992, 2005). Many have argued that incentives are a form of corporate welfare, with often a low return on investment from the public tax base point of view, or unnecessary since in many cases the firm would have located in the area anyway (Schweke, 2005). In the context of tech-based economic development, however, a stronger justification can be provided for subsidies that serve as incentives to firms to invest in R&D, owing to the tendency for private firms to under-invest. Many states have R&D tax credits for some combination of spending for new equipment, investments in worker education and training, and new job creation. Other programs have included elimination of certain sales taxes on equipment such as computers, subsidized loans and revolving loan funds targeted to smaller firms, small business development and assistance centers to provide consulting services and technical expertise to R&D start-ups, often affiliated with university business and/or engineering schools.

Research universities have become prominent actors in technology-based economic development. Besides human capital creation, their other principal role in stimulating regional economic development is performing research that can lead to innovation with commercialization potential (Goldstein, Maier, and Luger, 1995). States and to some extent cities have been investing in both the physical facilities and the scientists and engineers for new or expanded research centers, institutes, and labs in strategic R&D areas such as genomics, nanotechnology, robotics, that have been identified as existing or potential areas of competitive strength. In best practice, the designation of academic R&D areas for strategic investment also takes into account the strength of private sector R&D in the state or region. The idea here is to generate a critical mass of world-class talent and R&D output in strategic scientific and technology niches that would induce private technology-based firms to locate in the region and to spawn new start-ups by faculty and graduates based upon research developed in the universities. The non-profit Georgia Research Alliance (GRA), established in 1990, perhaps represents perhaps the most successful program of this type in the US.

GRA is a partnership among research universities, business, and state government. Its purpose is to stimulate research in universities that will translate into commercialization opportunities through university-industry partnerships and start-ups. One of the principal program activities for the GRA is to identify the technology areas in which Georgia is believed to have competitive advantages and then distribute substantial funding packages to Georgia's research universities in those research areas by attracting 'eminent' scientists and building world class laboratory facilities and equipment. The GRA also operates several technology incubators and operates a seed capital fund to support new and promising research in small technology-based companies. Since inception, the GRA has invested $400 million which has been used to leverage about $2 billion in federal and private industry research, created and supported 50 eminent scholars and helped to form over 120 new technology-based firms in the state (www.gra.org 10/5/07).

Another well-regarded but different model for investing in R&D capacity has been the Ben Franklin Technology Development Authority in Pennsylvania. It was originally created in the early 1980s as an economic development and jobs program as an antidote to the severe dislocations in the state's traditional durable goods manufacturing sectors. The strategy was to initiate a set of technology centers utilizing the resources and capacities of the state's research universities located in four different regions – Pittsburgh, Bethlehem, Philadelphia, and University Park – that would lead to university-industry partnerships to working on specific technology projects that would yield new products, new businesses, and most importantly, new jobs. When the universities began having difficulty generating the right kind of R&D projects, the primary focus of the four technology centers shifted away from university-industry partnerships to a strategy that emphasized investing and supporting technology-based companies directly utilizing the resources of all institutions of higher education including community colleges. The range of activities includes providing training and curriculum development, technology assistance and transfer, incubators, market development, and staff support for regional and state advanced technology councils. When the Pennsylvania

Technology Development Authority was merged with the Ben Franklin Partnership in 2001, the new entity added a focus of facilitating commercialization of new technologies through equity investments and loans to companies as well as helping to arrange and finance consortia of university R&D centers in strategic technology areas (www.benfranklin.org).

Facilitating University-Industry Partnerships and Commercialization

Investing in R&D capacity in an area does not necessarily lead to growth in jobs, new business start-ups, and innovative products. For R&D investments to yield regional economic returns, technology developed in R&D labs needs to become commercialized and that needs to occur *within* the region. This is now becoming apparent to a number of regions with highly rated research universities but an underdeveloped high tech economy. Achieving a high level of commercialization requires different strategies and programs than for building a high R&D capacity.

Realizing regional economic growth requires companies that will adopt technology developed in university or industry R&D labs. Firms that adopt new technology developed in the region will tend to be either: existing, highly capitalized businesses that will pay for licenses; firms that have gained sufficient tacit knowledge through informal networks or the skill and experience to be able to scan and search the codified scientific and technical literature to scope out commercialization opportunities; or entrepreneurial start-up businesses that emerge from university labs.

From a regional economic development perspective, such a strategy will focus on achieving better 'connections' between R&D activity in universities (and independent industry labs) and potential adopters. Activities and programs include the formation of formal university-industry partnerships, the development of research parks with a mixture of academic labs and established and start-up firms, support and assistance for faculty entrepreneurship, technology transfer office activities aimed at disseminating information on university-based technology development to potential markets within the state or region, and increasing the availability equity funding for seed capital and start-up capital.

Universities play central roles here as well as in building a region's R&D capacity. They form one end of the establishment of university-industry partnerships whose aim is to undertake research projects that will potentially lead to innovation and new products for the private industry partner. Establishing such arrangements is now routine for a number of research universities in the US. New York State's Centers for Advanced Technology (CATs) is one of the best known and most successful programs to support commercialization partnerships. CATs are designated for targeted technology areas – for example, integrated electronics, optics, biotechnology, and imaging – and each is located on a particular university campus in the state that has strong research capacity in the particular technology area. Competitive proposals for funding a partnership are submitted by the CATs after each has successfully demonstrated collaboration with industry partners. Successful proposals are funded for up to ten years and occasionally longer when the partnership can be shown to have generated unusual levels of economic development. As of 2006 there were 15 designated centers funded at a total of 12.5 million dollars for the year. That level of funding yielded approximately $24 million in matching funds and created a net increase of 383 jobs (SSTI, 2006, p. 21). Maryland's Industrial Partnership Program operates somewhat differently. The program provides matching funds for university-based research projects that lead companies to develop new products, after first helping companies find the appropriate faculty member or university lab with whom to partner. This approach actively encourages and provides support for faculty entrepreneurship in terms of actively engaging in those research projects that have high chances of leading to commercialization. As a third example, Utah operates the Utah Centers for Excellence Program. This program annually provides about $2 million in a competitive proposal process. Funds are allocated on the basis of expected direct economic benefit to the state, with a particular focus on generating spin-off businesses from the centers. Since its creation in 1986, more than 120 new businesses have spun-off from funded centers and over 2,000 net new jobs have been created, with an average annual salary of $65,000.

The establishment of research parks and technology incubators is another widespread activity for universities (and other entities) aimed at promoting commercialization of new technology. Research parks have been around since the 1950s in the US when the Stanford Research Park and a few years later the Research Triangle Park were established and began serving as models for the conception of research parks in many other regions of the world (Luger and Goldstein, 1991). Many of the early generation of research parks were built as 'industrial country clubs' with wide expanses of manicured lawns, grass, and trees separating the R&D branch plants of large national and international corporations. The costs of locating in such sites were often prohibitive for small R&D firms and start-ups, while the physical design inhibited informal interaction of scientists and engineers across R&D organizations and between research park tenants and the universities, despite the rhetoric to the contrary. In part because of the high costs of building the infrastructure and the limited market of R&D facilities, research parks were high risk investments with high failure rates. The latest generation of university research parks has been designed to maximize interaction between industry and academic scientists and engineers with higher density buildings and often the mixing of industry and university labs and offices within the same buildings. Providing space for faculty and recent graduates to start their own businesses aimed at the commercialization of technologies developed in university labs has now become a point of emphasis in many universities' research parks. As well, universities are now more likely to make decisions about their research parks taking into account the strengths and weaknesses of the region as a location for R&D facilities in various technology areas, rather than copying models developed elsewhere (Luger and Goldstein, 2006).

Some subset of universities focus on direct commercialization of technology developed in the academy as an alternative to partnering with industry through joint R&D projects or by licensing intellectual property. Because the costs of commercialization projects can not usually be covered by external research grants, universities must be willing to invest their own funds for what amount to relatively high risk ventures, or else be able to attract outside investors such as angels. The in-house expertise required to assess the probability of successful commercialization, the need for a large and flexible supply of capital to fund the development work long before any revenues can be expected, the inherent high risks of such ventures, and the belief by some that this type of activity might not be appropriate for universities, have all limited the instances of this approach of universities towards commercialization. One notable example is MIT's Deshpande Center for Technological Innovations that was infused with a $20 million endowment gift at its inception and has an array of connections with private industry and world-class expertise at its finger tips (SSTI, 2006, p.25–26).

University technology transfer programs through patenting and licensing has broadened significantly from just five research universities having them prior to 1970 and only 20 by 1980, to over 120 universities having tech transfer offices by 2004 (AUTM, 2004; Goldstein, 2008). Spurred by the intellectual property rights given to institutions of higher education in the Bayh-Dole Act of 1980 and the ensuing revenue possibilities, universities have beefed up their staffing and expertise and have become more aggressive in both encouraging faculty entrepreneurship and in marketing technologies and innovations developed in university labs. There has been a dramatic increase in the number of disclosures, patents received, and licenses sold by universities. From a regional economic development perspective, there are, however, several conundrums associated with this approach to technology transfer. First, firms that purchase the rights to use the intellectual property developed in universities are not likely to be located within the same region or state, so the potential regional economic benefits are 'leaked'. Second, some have claimed that the practice of university technology transfer offices of making exclusive license agreements with firms actually *inhibits* the diffusion and adoption of innovation from universities to the private sector and thus retards economic growth and development (Crespi et al., 2006).

Still another mechanism for spurring the commercialization process is providing direct funding in the form of grants to private R&D firms. As mentioned in the earlier section on institutional actors, the US Small Business Administration's SBIR and STTR grants programs provides competitive awards totaling more than $2 billion to small firms whose proposals show ideas with the greatest promise for commercialization and that will contribute to economic growth and new jobs. Both programs award smaller grants to demonstrate *feasibility* of the idea in Phase 1. Phase 1 type-grants are critical because at this proof-of-concept stage it is extremely difficult to attract outside investors. Those firms that demonstrate feasibility are given Phase 2 grants for the actual product development work. This program requires neither repayment nor sacrifice of equity by the firm recipients.

Moreover, the firm retains the intellectual property rights in most cases. Although a federal government program, many states and regional economic development organizations provide support and help for firms to prepare competitive proposals and also provide state matching funds if the firm's SBIR or STTR proposal is successful.

A number of states offer tax credits to firms as incentives for them to engage in R&D activity. The traditional type of tax credit, the firm's tax liability is reduced, using the federal state tax code as the basic model for restrictions and qualifications for the state tax credit program. One major problem with this traditional type of tax credits is that businesses need to have a tax liability, i.e., net income, in order to benefit from the program. But many start-up companies that would benefit the most from the program do not yet have any positive income. So New Jersey pioneered a R&D tax credit program whereby companies may sell their tax credits of which they are unable to take advantage to other companies making a profit and thus who can take advantage of the tax credits (SSTI, 2006, p. 81).

A more relatively recent use of state tax credits has been as an incentive to 'angel investors' to increase the supply of private equity capital, particularly in those places where the venture capital industry has shunned. The tax credit in effect helps to reduce the risk faced by potential individual investors. The amount of the tax credit varies among states – and sometimes within states – as do the qualifications and eligibility of the businesses receiving the investment.

Some states and municipalities, when faced with lack of private capital for R&D investment, use public employee pension funds or other public fund set asides. These programs vary widely among the states and municipalities in terms of restrictions on the type of investments and at which stages on the road to commercialization – conforming to different levels of risk – public funds can be used. Typically, the public sector entity will invest a certain amount into a fund pool as a limited partner. The managing partner of the fund will use these funds to leverage additional private investment, as well as supply the experience and expertise in venture capital investing. The fund will then purchase equity in a number of ventures. One issue, from the point of view of the public sector source of equity, is the amount and proportion of the fund's investments in ventures within the region or state. The more geographical restrictions, the lower the expected return to the fund, but the less leakage of the economic benefits that might accrue.

The Creation of Innovative Milieu

The fourth leg in technology-based economic development is strategies for cities, regions, and states to become places attractive to knowledge workers and stimulating for the innovation process. Although Richard Florida's work (2002, 2004) on the creative class has been an important impetus for putting such strategies in place, the practice has been informed by earlier work on the arts as an economic development stimulant (Marcusen and King, 2003), on creative milieu and learning regions (e.g., Maillat and Kebir, 2001), and on regional innovation systems (Cooke et al., 2004), with the latter two focused on European regions and cities.

This strategy is an eclectic one, with a range of action 'targets' including historical preservation, crime reduction, beautification of shopping districts, public transit, publicly provided arts and performance venues, and support to arts-related businesses and non-profits. In addition, the regional innovation system approach emphasizes the improvement of 'governance', including streamlining permitting, planning and provision of public services; increasing social capital and civic participation; and creating networks and intermediary organizations that link actors within the innovation system.

A number of US, Canadian, and European cities have already embarked upon a 'creative class', arts, or regional innovation systems strategy. The city of Toronto provides a well-articulated and highly comprehensive approach that was designed based upon a best-practice study of other cities including Barcelona, Berlin, New York, and San Francisco, as well as some medium-sized cities.

Toronto 's strategy consists of a five pronged approach: People – supporting knowledge and skill development, but particularly in design and innovation; Place – improving the business climate and stimulating investment; Prosperity –targeting and building competitive clusters and establishing entrepreneurial networks; Positioning – branding Toronto for both local and global markets; and Partnership – creating an 'alignment of strategic intent' (Gertler et al., 2006). The city supports its arts economy at multiple levels: a number of citywide festivals – including the well-known Toronto International Film Festival – that attract international visitors and tourists, neighborhood-based street fairs, funding arts councils, building venues and 'creative spaces', providing support and funding for youth-based arts programs. Toronto also has invested in historical preservation, established 'creative districts' with special zoning and taxing provisions that help increase the attractiveness of such areas and reduce the upward pressure on rents faced by artists, and begun a trust fund of working capital available to arts-related businesses and non-profits.

Within the regional innovation systems approach, Rosenfeld (2002) lists a number of action items for building cluster-based economic development that have been successfully tried in less favored regions of Europe and the US. These actions include:

- Creating associations of businesses within the same cluster
- Fostering inter-firm collaboration
- Establishing one-stop service delivery hubs
- Forming partnerships between educational institutions and clusters
- Supporting regional skills alliances
- Encouraging entrepreneurs' networks
- Creating cluster-based technology hubs
- Forming export networks
- Provide incentives or set aside funds for multi-firm projects only.

While there is substantial variation among regional innovation systems, the commonalities include the use of clusters as economic development building blocks, the creation of networks and a culture of inter-firm collaboration, and willingness to depart from old modes of governance and guidance of the innovation system between public sector actors and the private sector (Cooke et al., 2004).

Reflections on the Theory-Practice Nexus in Technology-based Economic Development

We have reviewed in section 3 some of the most important ideas, concepts, or theories that have emerged to inform the practice of technology-based economic development within the past twenty years or so. These are endogenous growth theory, emphasizing increasing returns and knowledge spillovers, cluster theory, the concepts of path dependence and lock-in, the importance of regional institutional capacity and more generally the productivity of a region's knowledge infrastructure, and the idea of creative milieu. In section 5 we have described the best-practice of tech-based economic development in terms of four strategic approaches, or 'four legs': (1) investing in human capital including workforce development, (2) investing in a region's R&D capacity, (3) facilitating commercialization of new ideas and technologies through university-industry partnerships and related mechanisms, and (4) creating a milieu attractive to knowledge workers and conducive to innovation.

Although there is wide variation in the actual practice of technology-based economic development, it appears in general that a number of the ideas and theories about how regions develop and thrive in the globalized, knowledge-based economy have become embedded and changed the practice, and mostly for the better.

First, economic development for many years has been characterized as 'smokestack chasing' to be nominally replaced by 'chip chasing'. Indeed industry recruitment is still a major mode of organizing economic development practice, and offering incentives is still an important tool in many states and sub-state regions. Yet there seems to be greater discrimination in the use and justification of incentives, i.e., in situations when we could expect positive externalities to occur. This advancement in level of sophistication may be a result of the ideas from endogenous growth theory diffusing to both economic development policy-makers and analysts.

Second, we can see that the *idea* of industry clusters has taken hold as strategic building blocks of competitive regional economies. Indeed, it is getting difficult to find a state that has not yet conducted a cluster analysis to identify which set of industry clusters offer the state its greatest competitive advantages, while recognizing that there is a high level of variation in thoughtfulness and quality in how such analyses are conducted. Many sub-state regions have followed suit. On the other hand, the number of states and sub-state areas that have actually attempted to *implement* a cluster-based strategy is much smaller. Still, at least thinking about designing programs that target not individual firms or industries, but groups of sectors whose individual health and competitiveness are intimately affected by the health and competitiveness of related sectors is a leap forward.

Third, the idea of the importance of a region having a set of intermediary organizations to facilitate interaction between knowledge and technology producers and adopters, and more generally a productive regional knowledge infrastructure, has become embedded in the institutional arrangements for tech-based economic development in a number of places. There are many more organizations that are involved in technology-based economic development compared to, say, twenty years ago. These often crossover traditionally defined public and private sectors, and include universities, community colleges, independent research institutions, equity capital providers, and public-private industry/cluster 'teams'. While it can be argued that having a larger number of actors carries the potential risk of creating confusion about respective roles, the potential increase in flexibility, the ability to combine and complement the strengths of different types of organizations, and the potential to streamline the provision and delivery of both public and private services very likely more than compensates in terms of the perceived attractiveness of regions by technology-based firms.

Fourth, contemporary tech-based economic development practice has recognized that having a supply of knowledge workers is the critical regional competitive factor, not low taxes or low labor costs. Economic development practice has responded in two ways: (1) making workforce development, better alignment of community college programs with labor market needs, and expansion of public universities in technology-related areas as key elements, even though these functions normally are administered in separate agencies; and (2) pursuing and supporting 'creative class' strategies – also often undertaken outside traditional economic development organizations – that are aimed at helping to make the 'place' a more attractive location for highly educated workers and entrepreneurs.

If the four items above describe the glass half full, there is also the glass half empty. First, the extant theory – evaluated in terms of its effectiveness as a guide to practice – still suffers from several deficiencies. Much of it, such as endogenous growth theory and path dependency, retains a high level of abstractness. After all it *is* theory! But by being inadequately equipped to take into account contingencies – idiosyncratic local and regional conditions – the predicted or expected economic development outcomes may be inaccurate. Other new theories such as the creative class have not yet been subjected to rigorous empirical tests. One recent paper has compared the explanatory power of Florida's 3 T's to human capital investment and several other traditional factors of regional economic development for a sample of MSAs in the US (Donegan et al., 2008). The results from this study show relatively low explanatory power for both sets of factors, but that Florida's measures are inferior to the set of traditional factors.

For the most part, theories of tech-based economic development tend to ignore the distributional dimensions. This makes it difficult to offer compelling justifications for certain kinds of investments in, say, R&D capacity, or expansion of university programs in the most competitive regions in a state, when it is not clear how displaced workers from a region's traditional manufacturing sectors, or how rural areas will benefit from such investments.

The second area needing attention is institutional inertia. Although there has been substantial progress in a number of states and regions, economic development practice – including technology-based economic development – is still mired in industry recruitment as its *modus operandi*. Many state and regional economic development organizations have successfully upgraded their analytic capacity and sophistication with young, bright staff in applied research and policy analysis functions. Their abilities to monitor and track the competitiveness of key clusters and sectors, conduct economic development impact studies for estimating costs and benefits of prospective investments, and evaluate the effectiveness of programs and policies is, on average, vastly higher than twenty years ago. Yet this has not necessarily changed how developers go about their daily business of playing the recruitment game out in the field, nor has it changed the attitudes of a sufficient number of state legislators as to what economic development practice should be.

Another dimension of institutional inertia is the gap between the design of policy plans and implementation. It was mentioned earlier, for example, that a large number of states now have spend considerable money to conduct cluster studies to identify and target their most competitive clusters. Yet very few states have gone on to implement their cluster-based strategies. Related to this are the high hopes given to research universities as engines of regional economic development, when the empirical record is spotty at best (Feller, 1990; Goldstein, 2008). While research universities are well-equipped to produce high levels of R&D and to provide students with know-how, they may not be very effective at carrying out other steps in the process of technology-based economic development such as translating research results into products. This may be a case, more than institutional inertia, of a misfit between the organizational structure and traditional academic norms, and the new institutional mission of many public universities.

Finally, there is the resistance to adapting or creating – and then funding – organizations that enable R&D capacity to be translated and transformed into technology commercialization with attendant growth in jobs, wages, and new firms. Developing the necessary organizational infrastructure, especially in regions and states that are starting off with a low level of technology-based economic development, can not be accomplished 'on the cheap'. There must be a willingness to invest substantial amounts of funds, and the patience to wait a number of years before there is a visible return on investment. This requires strong political leadership in addition to deep pockets.

References

Association of University Technology Managers (2004). *AUTM US Licensing Survey, FY 2004.*

Bartik, T. (1992). "The Effects of State and Local Taxes on Economic Development: A Review of Recent Research," *Economic Development Quarterly*, Vol. 6, 1: 102–110.

Bartik, T. (2005). "Solving the Problems of Economic Development Incentives," *Growth and Change*, Vol. 36, 2.

Bellini, N. and M. Landabaso (2005). "Learning about Innovation Policy. Reflections on the State of the Art in Europe's Regions." Paper presented at the Regional; Studies association International Conference, Aalborg, May.

Ben Franklin Partnership (2007). www.benfranklin.org.

Camagni, R. (1995). "The Concept of Innovative Milieu and Its relevance for Public Policies in European Lagging Regions," *Papers in Regional Science* 74 (4), 317–340.

Chapple, K. et al. (2004). "Gauging Metropolitan 'High-Tech' and 'I-Tech' Activity," *Economic Development Quarterly*, Vol. 18 No. 1: 10–29.

Cooke, P., M. Heidenreich, and H.-J. Braczyk (2004). *Regional Innovation Systems*, 2nd edition. London: Routledge.

Cortright, J. (2002). "21st Century Strategy: Prospering in a Knowledge-based Economy," Technical memorandum, Westside Economic Study, Impresa, Inc.

Cortright, J. and H. Mayer (2001). *High-Tech Specialization: A Comparison of High Technology Centers*. Washington, DC: The Brookings Institution.

Crespi, G.A., A.Geuna, and B.Verspagen, 2006. "University IPRs and Knowledge Transfer. Is the IPR Ownership Model More Efficient?" SEWPS Working Paper No. 154, University of Sussex, Science and Technology Policy Research.

David, P. (2000). "Path Dependence, Its Critics and the Quest for Historical Economics" in P. Garrouste and S. Ionnides (eds), *Evolution and Path Dependence in Economic Ideas: Past and Present.* Cheltenham, England: Edward Elgar.

DeVol, R. (1999). *America's High Technology Economy: Growth, Development, and Risks for Metropolitan Areas.* Santa Monica, CA: Milken Institute.

DeVol, R. and A. Bedroussian (2006). *Mind to Market: A Global Analysis of University Biotechnology Transfer and Commercialization.* Santa Monica, CA: Milken Institute.

Donegan, M., J. Drucker, H. Goldstein, N. Lowe, and E. Malizia (2008). "Which Indicators Explain Metropolitan Economic Performance Best?," *Journal of the American Planning Association*, 74,2: 180–95.

Feller, I. (1990). "Universities as Engines of R&D-Based Economic Growth: They Think They Can," *Research Policy*, 19 (4), 335–348.

Feser, E. and M. Luger (2003). "Cluster Analysis as a Mode of Inquiry: Its Use in Science and Technology Policymaking in North Carolina," *European Planning Studies*, Vol. 11, 1: 11–24.

Florida, R. (2002). *The Rise of the Creative Class: And How It's Transforming Work, Leisure, Community and Everyday Life*. New York: Basic Books.

Florida, R. (2004). *Cities and the Creative Class*. New York: Routledge.

Gertler, M., L. Tesolin, and S. Weinstock (2006). "Toronto Case Study". Strategies for Creative Cities Project, Munk Centre for International Studies, Universdity of Toronto, Toronto, Canada.

Goldstein, H. (2008). "What We Know and What We Don't Know About the Regional Economic Impacts of Universities," in A. Varga, ed., *Universities and Regional Economic Development*, forthcoming. Edward Elgar Publishing.

Goldstein, H. (2005). "The Role of Knowledge Infrastructure in Regional Economic Development: The Case of the Research Triangle," *Canadian Journal of Regional Science* XXVIII (Summer), 199–220.

Goldstein, H. and M. Luger (1993). "Theory and Practice in High-Tech Economic Development," in R.D. Bingham and R. Mier, eds, *Theories of Local Economic Developoment*. Newbury Park, CA: Sage Publications.

Goldstein, H., G. Maier, and M.Luger (1995). "The University as an Instrument for Economic and Business Development: US and European Comparisons," in D. Dill and B. Sporn, eds, *Emerging Patterns of Social Demand and University Reform: Through a Glass Darkly*. Pergamon.

Hecker, D.E. (2005). "High Technology Employment: A NAICS-Based Update," *Monthly Labor Review* (July), 57–72.

Koo, J., M. Luger, and L. Stewart (1999). "Best Practices in Science and Technology-Based Economic Development Policy: US and Global." Paper prepared for the North Carolina Board of Science and Technology.

Krugman, P. (1991). "Increasing Returns and Economic Geography," *Journal of Political Economy*, 99 (3), 483–499.

Lucas, R. E. (1988). "On the Mechanism of Economic Development," *Journal of Monetary Economics*, XXII: 3–42.

Luger, M. and H. Goldstein (1991). *Technology in the Garden*. Chapel Hill: University of North Carolina Press.

Luger, M. and H. Goldstein (2006). "Research Parks Redux: The Changing Landscape of the Garden." Final report to the Economic development Administration, US Department of Commerce (Award # 99–07–13827), November 2006.

Maillat, D. and L. Kebir (2001). "The Learning Region and Territorial Production Systems," in B. Johannson, C. Karlsson, and R. Stough, eds, *Theories of Endogenous Regional Growth, Lessons for Regional Policies*. Heidelberg.

Malecki, E. J. (1997). *Technology and Economic Development*, 2nd edition. Essex, England: Addson-Wesley.

Marcusen, A., P. Hall, and A. Glasmeier (1986). *High Tech America*. Boston: Allen and Unwin.

Marcusen, A. and D. King (2003). "The Artistic Dividend: The Arts' Hidden Contribution to regional Development". Project on Regional and Industrial

Economics, Humphrey Institute of Public Affairs, University of Minnesota, Minneapolis, MN.
Marshall, A. (1920). *Principles of Economics*. London: Macmillan.
Maskell, P. and L. Kebir (2005). "What Qualifies as a Cluster Theory?", DRUID Working Paper No. 05–09, Danish Research Unit for Industrial Dynamics, Copenhagen Business School, Copenhagen, DK
Myrdal, G. (1957). *Economic Theory and Underdeveloped Regions*. London: Duckworth & Co.
Nelson, R.R. and S. G. Winter (1982). *An Evolutionary Theory of Economic Change*. Cambridge: Harvard University Press.
Office of Technology Assessment (1984). *Technology, Innovation, and Regional Economic Development*. Washington, DC: US Government Printing Office.
Porter, M.E. (1990). The Competitive Advantage of Nations. New York: The Free Press.
Progressive Policy Institute (2001). The Metropolitan New Economy Index, 2001. Washington, DC: Progressive Policy Institute (www.neweconomyindex.org).
Progressive Policy Institute (2002). *The 2002 State New Economy Index*. Washington, DC: Progressive Policy Institute (www.neweconomyindex.org).
Riche, R.W., D.E. Hecker, and J.U. Burgan (2003). "High Technology Today and Tomorrow: A Small Slice of the Employment Pie," *Monthly Labor Review* (November), 50–58.
Romer, P. (1990). "Endogenous Technical Change," *Journal of Political Economy*, Vol. 98: S71–103.
Romer, P. (1986). "Increasing Returns and Long Run Growth," *Journal of Political Economy*, Vol. 94, 5: 1002–1037.
Schweke, W. (2005). "Curbing Business Subsidy Competition: Does the European Union Have an Answer?" www.cfed.org.
Schweke, W. (2007). *Smart Money – Education and Economic Development*. Economic Policy Institute.
Solow, R. (1957). "Technical Change and the Aggregate Production Function," *Review of Economics and Statistics*, Vol. 39: 312–320.
SSTI (2006). "A Resource Guide for Technology-based Economic Development," Report prepared for the US Department of Commerce, Economic Development Administration.
Summers, P. and D. Carlson (2000). "Ten Steps to a High Tech Future: The New Economy in Metropolitan Seattle". Discussion paper prepared for the Brookings Institution center on Urban and Metropolitan Affairs and for CEOs for Cities, Daniel J. Evans School of Public Affairs, University of Washington, Seattle, WA.
US Small Business Administration www.sba.gov/SBIR/indexwhatwedo.html.
Yin, R. K., S. A. Sottile, and N. K. Bernstein (1985). *Attracting High-technology Firms to Local Areas*. Washington, DC: Cosmos Corporation.

Chapter 13
Social Capital in Local Economic Development

John P. Blair and Michael Carroll

Local economic development practitioners recognize that social relationships and networks shape local economies. Yet academic research is only starting to incorporate social resources into economic development practice. The emerging concept of social capital promises to be useful towards this end. Its integration into local economic development theory has potential to illuminate existing development strategies, suggest new approaches, and bridge the divide between community and economic development. Section I describes the concept of social capital and considers why there has been resistance to it among some scholars. Next, the resonance of social capital in many local economic development strategies is reviewed. Understanding social capital can illuminate how these approaches operate and improve implementation. Section III describes how social capital operates in the social economy. Finally, local management of a community's social capital is discussed.

Social Capital as a Resource

Social capital is the ties that link individuals to groups and groups to each other. These networks can significantly shape the performance of local economies. The literature on social capital has been muddied by definitional ambiguities. Although the concept is intuitively easy to grasp, researchers have tended to create their own, slightly nuanced definitions. It is not our intent to pettifog definitions. However, by any reasonable definition, assimilation of social capital into local economic development theories will strengthen the understanding of local economies and significantly enhance program implementation.

The term "social capital" is newly coined, but the concept is not new. Weber (1930) described how admission to local church group could certify someone as trustworthy and make doing business in that community easier. More recently, trust within a group was described as reducing information and transactions costs (Fukuyama, 1995, p. 27).

Coleman (1990) noted that, "Social capital is defined by its function…It is not a single entity. Like other forms of capital, social capital is productive, making possible the achievement of certain ends that would not be attainable in its absence…" (p. 302). "Social capital is embodied in the relations among persons…" (p. 304) and institutions whose members trust one another "will be able to accomplish more than a comparable group lacking that trustworthiness… (p. 302)." Even before they knew what to call it, local economic development practitioners used social capital regularly in their work as they built economic development partnerships, and secured "buy-ins" from various interests.

Gittel and Vidal (1998) distinguished bonding and bridging social capital. Bonding social capital unites individuals within a group or network. Accordingly, organizations with ample social capital might be able to maintain cohesion as the economic base of the community changes. Organizations with less social capital might atrophy or disintegrate. Social capital also has a bridging function, allowing individuals to work across networks. Bridging capital is reflected in the ability to form coalitions. Social capital can also overcome vertical barriers that make it difficult for individuals and groups with unequal social status or power to work together.

Local and Economic Contexts

The emerging interest in social capital theory and its potential importance to local economic development has lead to attempts to quantify the idea. The CONCISE project (Institute for Health and Social Science Research, 2003) project and the European Values Study (van Schaik, 2002) represents two efforts to formalize and measure local social capital. The research approaches in the two studies were similar. Based on theoretical descriptions of social capital, the study teams determined attitudes that characterized the presence of social capital. They then developed and administered questionnaires that asked people to respond to statements about trust, expectations regarding reciprocity, community norms and so forth. Answers to questions like "do you believe people can be trusted" and "helping others helps yourself in the long run" were indicators of social capital.

The attempts at empirical measurement represent credible "first steps" and also indicate how difficult it will be to quantify social capital. The similarities between the studies suggest that progress towards a common definition and measure of social capital is being made. The Concise study identified three categories that represent social capital: 1) trust, social networks and reciprocity characterize relationships between individuals 2) shared norms or values among a group of people represent cohesion, and 3) effective information channels represent inter group networks or linking ability. The European Values Study used three, similar factors to represent social capital: 1) interpersonal trust, 2) trust in institutions, 3) civic participation.

The terminology in the two studies differs and there are distinctions between "shared social networks" (i.e. friendship networks) and "civic engagement" (i.e. voting). Nevertheless, it is clear that the studies are identifying the same closely related set of characteristics. Also, measurement is indirect since basic concepts such as "trust" or "shared norms" are only inferred based on survey responses. These finding suggest that social capital can be identified independently, and that more rigorous use of the concept will evolve.

The presence of social capital can transform the ubiquitous prisoner's dilemma, free rider, and problem of the commons problems represented in Table 13.1. These structurally similar problems represent numerous, specific problems encountered in local economic development, where pursuit of self interest can lead to suboptimal outcomes.

Table 13.1 A generic cooperation game

↓Other individuals or group ↓	Individual's action	
	a. Cooperate	b. Not Cooperate
a. Cooperate	100	105
b. Not Cooperate	-10	-5

Note: For simplicity only the individual pay-offs are shown in the matrix.

The traditional prisoner's dilemma model supposes outcomes depend on a two party decisions. In the free rider and problem of the commons cases the second party is a group of people. Collusion, communication or the development of joint strategies are disallowed. The model assumes the individual seeks to maximize narrow self interest within the rules of game. The individual's pay-off depends upon whether he or she cooperates and it also depends upon whether others cooperate. For simplicity, Table 13.1 shows only the individual's pay-off. The best outcome for the group is when everyone cooperates. In this case, the individual is always better-off not cooperating. Since the model assumes all individuals see the situation the same way, no one will cooperate and the outcome will be the lower right hand box, a suboptimal result. (A wide range of local problems fit this model, such as maintaining a neighborhood or contributing to a community event.)

The introduction of social capital increases the likelihood of the cooperative outcome. First, an individual making a decision within a social network bound by trust and reciprocity will be more likely to believe that others will cooperate. While the strict maximizing agent would see the advantage of not cooperating regardless of what others do, many people will be willing to make a small sacrifice when they believe it is a part of a shared community effort. Second, when decisions are made within dense social networks, choices are less likely to be anonymous. When others in a group know who cooperates and who does not, the individual may build or lose social capital. Since social capital has value, the pay-off from cooperating will be greater than otherwise. Third, a cooperative outcome is more likely to emerge from repetitive games when individuals believe others will follow a "tit-for-tat" strategy if the game is repeated. In reality, identical games are seldom repeated, but individuals will face similar situations so there is advantage to establishing a cooperative reputation. One time the cooperative strategy might be picking-up litter, the next time it might be refereeing a youth baseball game and so forth. In addition, the model often assumes parties cannot communicate to devise a strategy. Effective social network make cooperation more likely. Finally and most importantly, the relative importance of narrow self interests may be diminished when decisions are made within the context of social capital networks. The fact that individuals learn behavior in social networks may explain why the traditional "rational" solution to the problem is not confirmed by experimental economics.

Grudging and Incomplete Acceptance of Social Capital

Social capital has recently been embraced as a tool for understanding local economic development in some regions, particularly in Europe, and academic interest has exploded since mid-1995, especially among interdisciplinary oriented scholars (Policy Research Initiative, 2005). However, the concept has only been accepted grudgingly if at all by many mainstream economists, possibly because social capital does not fit within traditional economic models.

There are several reasons the inclusion of social capital into local economic development scholarship has been resisted. First, the fact that the effects of social capital are context dependent sets it apart from traditional resources.[1] A group's ability to mobilize social capital may depend upon which other groups bring the issue to the table, how the issue is presented, what other issues face the community at the time and so forth. Likewise, social capital may be effectively employed towards some ends and not others.

Also, it is difficult to predict the amount of social capital needed to achieve an end. In some circumstances, using less than a particular measure of social capital may be useless and using more than that measure may be redundant. As a result of these differences, social capital does not lend itself to the traditional mathematical modeling techniques which are stock in trade for many economists. Interesting attempts to integrate social capital into traditional mathematical models of economic development are notable (Chou, 2006). However, efforts to reduce social capital to a variable in an equation come at the cost of ignoring the qualitative dimensions that give social capital theory its power.

Another reason for resistance to the adoption of social capital into the pantheon of traditional economic resources is due to the myopic belief that resources are primarily a means to other ends. While social capital can help achieve ends, is not a pure production resource. It is also an important consumption good. Dealing with people we trust, share values, believe are part of a reciprocating network is integral to developing a sense of community and valued in and of itself (Williamson, Imbroscio, and Alpervitz, 2002: 1–12). It has also been contended that social capital improves health and longevity (Kelly, 1999). Economic and community

1 Traditional resources are not perfectly adaptable to different tasks, but the degree that social capital is context dependent is distinguishing.

development practitioners are aware of the value placed on a sense of community. The value of the direct benefits from social networks (values as a consumption good) may outweigh its value as a means.

Finally, once created, social capital cannot be easily transferred or exchanged in a market process. For instance, if people have built trust or good will with in a group, they cannot sell it to someone others in the group do not know.

Social capital theory contains elements that are unfamiliar to many traditionally trained economists and the complexity of the concept does not appeal to methodological reductionists. Nevertheless, articles are proliferating and the concept helps explain realities of local economic development practice. While the concept still needs refinement, social capital is often a powerful resource for local economic developers. The next section considers how a more explicit incorporation of social capital can strengthen some popular local economic development strategies.

Emerging Economic Development Theories and Social Capital

Social capital is an important element in many emerging economic development strategies. As these approaches are implemented at the local level, further theoretical interest can be anticipated. This section illuminates the role of social capital in implementing a diverse group of emerging local economic development approaches.

Innovation in Entrepreneurship and Cluster Development Strategies

Regions are pursuing entrepreneurial and cluster based economic development strategies. Both approaches emphasize innovation and innovation is enhanced by social capital. The economic application of new ideas often centers on individual entrepreneurship – risk taking, unique vision, leadership, and so forth. Innovations also can result from within corporate and bureaucratic setting. Strengths of geographically based economic clusters include cross fertilization of ideas that enable firms within a cluster to stay atop the product life-cycle. Serendipitous linkages of ideas from different fields spur some innovations and are more likely when social networks are dense. Accordingly, productive social networks can be an important part of local innovation strategies as they organize markets and allow flexibility (Lorenzen, 2007).

Social capital is discussed prominently in the entrepreneurship literature, although it is often referred to with different terminology. Colman (1990) suggested that social capital is strongest within the family and not by coincidence, entrepreneurship is frequently learned within the family where attitudes of trust, obligation and reciprocity, are strongest. The surrounding culture also contributes to entrepreneurship. The density of social networks explains ethnic differences in entrepreneurship (Raijnan and Marta 2003).

Non-entrepreneurial innovation also depends upon social capital within and between organizations. Local innovation depends on the effectiveness of bridging social capital because many innovations are based on cross fertilization of ideas across technologies and industries. Knowledge transfers among firms also can be improved when a trustful and reciprocal exchange atmosphere exists. The CONCISE project (The Institute of Health and Social Science Research, 2003) found that institutions are linked largely by individuals who have first established social capital on a personal level. Social capital within firms also contributes to sharing ideas and innovation.

With the advent of rapid communications, can the same level of information exchange needed for innovation be achieved electronically? If so, the importance of *localized* social capital in the innovation process would be diminished. However a strong argument can be made that social capital will continue to be community centered. A recent series of surveys found that while modern communications make face-to-face contact less important than in the past, it will continue to be important (GEM City Public Services, 2007). Face-to-face contacts build trust quicker than more indirect communications even when the objective content of the exchanges is the same. People evaluate information based on voice tone and body language. It can be difficult for most people to trust someone they have never met. A second reason for believing that social capital will continue to be localized is that contact with persons in non work environment such as clubs, churches, civic events and so forth builds credibility. Also, denser local networks lead to a greater variety of conversations that can generate innovations. Networks that facilitate information exchange are central to the development of "learning regions". Finally, business relationships are reinforced by strong civic networks since trust can be developed by observing how people relate and regard each other even in non-business settings.

Opportunities to build social capital are important to business innovation. High level executives as well as small business operators devote significant time to developing networks. While social capital may exist between individuals scattered globally, local networks are normally easier to develop and maintain. Current efforts by local economic development officials to create "meet and great" events for local businesses represent efforts to build or strengthen local social capital.

Quality of Life

Many communities have adopted economic development paths that rely on improving the quality of life. Sometimes a high quality of life is a primary driver of economic development strategies although (like social capital) it frequently supports other economic development paths. Florida (2002) popularized the idea that advance technology development strategies will be enhanced when communities attract intelligent, well educated, and creative people. He assumes that people with top talent can be selective about where they live so high quality of life can be integral to attracting them and attracting the companies that need the talent. Having a high quality of life is also important to less creative people. Retired people for instance seek high quality of life locations. Judging from the advertising for retirement oriented communities, the ability to fit in is a major ingredient in attracting individuals in this market. Many retirement communities employ social directors to build activities for residents in what could be interpreted as a direct attempt to build social capital.

Florida's view is that creative people seek tolerant communities that will accept them. Florida refers to "plug and play" communities where a new resident can fit-in easily to existing social networks without making a substantial effort. However, advocates of "plug and play" communities should recognize that the amount of effort needed to become part of a social network influences the quality of social capital. Social capital that is easily attained may be inadequate to achieve some difficult ends. Policy makers should also recognise that some types of social capital can lock people out as well as solidify a group. Thus some communities with excessive "bonding" social capital could face difficulties in attracting the creative class.

An area's social capital probably exerts a stronger influence towards maintaining existing populations than attracting new residents. The nature of social capital is probably not evident to someone who is considering moving to an area or it only can be roughly inferred from local "ambiance". After someone is in a network (or has been excluded from networks), a more informed judgment can be made about how an individual will be able to build and use social capital.

Neither the quality of civic life nor access to social networks is represented in major quality of life indicators. These popular indexes tend to count only readily measurable variables like temperature, housing costs, or access to hospitals. If a refinement in the measure of local social capital occurs, quality of life indicators will improve. Social capital also contributes indirectly to local quality of life because community cohesion helps mobilize resources to create cultural, recreational and other amenities.

Micro Credit Strategies

Making small, uncollateralized loans to individuals has been a valuable economic development path in poor villages in developing countries and has shown promise in poor neighborhoods within wealthy countries as well. (Micro credit programs lend to individuals who lack traditional collateral.) Repayment by one person allows additional loans to be made to others in the group.

Micro credit systems depend upon social capital. The potential that other members of the group will receive future loans is a primary motive for repayment. The grant of an uncollateralized loan indicates trust that it will be repaid and others in the group depend on the repayment. Repayment is fostered by a since of reciprocity.

Micro credit lenders report low default rates which help make micro loans profitable. However, traditional micro-credit loans are costly to administer compared to traditional, collateralized loans. The high administrative costs are attributed to the difficulty of assessing and monitoring the social capital that secures the loans (Reinke, 1998). As development lenders better understand how to assess social capital, micro credit practices will become more feasible.

Micro credit practices not only depend on social capital, they also build additional social networks that can be used to further local development. As small loans create local cottage activities, the same, probably strengthened social networks can be helpful in modifying the product, developing alternative production techniques, and tapping new markets. Village or neighborhood workers may share skills, contacts and other information in ways similar to what is done in advanced technology clusters (Anthony and Christine, 2003).

Globalization and "New Economy" Approaches

Local planners are seeking policies that will help their communities fit into the emerging global economy. In an increasing interdependent world where resources are highly mobile, local planners are seeking to help their communities fit into these emerging realities. People, things, and ideas all move from place to place more easily. Decisions by large multi-national firms are becoming increasingly important to the fortunes of local economies. These firms are in positions to seek advantageous locations throughout the world. Even friendship networks are becoming less localized and so elements of social capital have also globalized. Social capital, however, appears to be less mobile than other resources. In this increasingly footloose economy, localized social capital can have an anchoring role and help stabilize communities against the vagaries of global competition.

Location advantages based on place specific networks bound by social capital are likely to be more stable than comparative advantages based on many other traditional cost factors. Compare a "new economy", knowledge-based organization with a traditional, routine manufacturing plant. Which will be more strongly place bound? Intuitively, people often suppose the manufacturing plant to be more geographically rooted because of the large capital investment in plant and equipment. Physically the facilities are difficult to relocate. In contrast, the knowledge based industry may have little physical capital and only rent space in an office tower.

In the new economy, rapid changes in product mix, production technology, and other factors may cause the value of the facility to decline rapidly leaving the manufacturing company little incentive to remain in the area. If required work skills are readily available elsewhere, the plant may easily relocate to a lower labor cost area. The knowledge-based company could also be faced with cost changes and might seek a new location. However, new economy firms might find it more difficult to relocate if their employees have specialized knowledge and are therefore difficult to replace. Some employees may not choose to relocate because they like their neighbors, like their children's school, or fit into the community. As people age they tend to develop deeper community roots and they also become more important to their business organizations. Accordingly, the cost to the company of loosing top talent due to relocation will increase.[2] Even the "job skill" might be the ability to navigate place-based social networks.

Might firms avoid the location orientation of social capital by relying on virtual office technologies to retain high value employees who do not relocate? This response itself highlights the stabilizing importance of social capital. It shows that the true comparative advantage is the locally rooted labor force. However, allowing employees to disperse geographically will not work for many enterprises. Some firms may risk diminishing their internal social capital by reducing the number of personal contacts, spontaneous encounters, and face to face exchanges important to intra-firm networks that also have productive consequences. Thus, intra organizational social capital also anchors establishments.

Social Capital Intensive Organizations and Economic Development

The social economy is composed of institutions that combine non-profit-maximizing goals with significant economic functions. The not for profit sector is about ten percent of the total economy in most advanced countries. When non monetary exchanges such as household production and the underground economy are included, the social economy is much larger.

The social economy is prominent in the social capital literature for two reasons. First, the sector requires significant social capital to operate. Also, it is an important generator of local social capital. This section examines how social capital operates in the social economy.

Social Capital in the Context of the Social Economy

Shared values of trust, and reciprocity bound into a network is a necessary condition for the existence and operation of most organizations in the social economy. Often the initial shared values that motivate the creation of an institution in the social economy are not primarily local (Institute of Health and Social Science Research, 2003). However, the ease with which an organization can initially be formed is probably influenced by the nature of local social capital. For instance, non local green values have motivated many local organizations. These groups in turn make local economic contributions in the form of recycling and clean-up efforts. However, even if existing social capital does not motivate the organization, the start of the new groups is made easier by the nature of local social capital. Potential members

2 The position of a person in a company and that person's social capital with community networks are closely related since some influential networks are open only to individuals who have risen in their organizations. Thus, when executives stay behind their companies stand to lose more than if a lower level employee refuses a transfer. When that same person leaves the area, the loss in social capital is likely to be more significant.

may ask themselves questions like: Is it worth the effort? Will I be accepted? Can anything be accomplished? Individual answers to such questions depend upon the nature of the social capital already in the community.

Existing social capital also helps maintain the social economy. As economic conditions change, organizations are stressed. The unifying values, mutual trust, and expectations of reciprocity with in a network as well as the links with other social networks determine the adaptability of organizations When organizational changes are occurring, bridging social capital can also be useful, allowing organizations to take new functions or share functions with other groups without excessive duplication.

The social economy also contributes to the development of localized social capital. The CONCISE project reported empirical evidence of the importance of the social economy in generating social capital (Institute for Health and Social Science Research, 2003). Many organizations that seek to achieve community betterment goals rely upon social capital in place of other resources, usually money. Hence support for local social institutions may strengthen local social capital. While organizations may start with limited localized social capital, social capital will grow as individuals share responsibilities. When efforts are reciprocated, the bond is strengthened, trust develops, and social capital is enhanced. Social capital is enhanced as contacts are made that can be drawn upon in the future.

There are vast areas where social capital contributes to local economies including supporting the safety net, enhancing household production through such activities as community gardens and local currency plans, and building human capital. A discussion of how social capital contributes in each of these important sectors would constitute a book. However, the role of social capital in the context of the informal economy illustrates the operation of social capital in an interesting context.

The Informal Economy

The informal economy includes those activities that are not fully accounted in the formal sector. These activities have less access to traditional legal protections than formal activities in part because operations tend to short cut laws and regulations. Agreements tend to be based on a hand-shake rather than a formal contract. Consequently, values and attitudes of trust and reciprocity (social capital) are important to successful operations. Many businesses in the informal economy are able to operate successfully because of how they use social capital.

Consider child day care services. In the informal economy, day care may be provided in the home of a friend or relative. The provider may need flexibility in terms of fee structure, hours, and services provided. Such arrangements can often be more efficiently agreed when social capital exists between the parties. Social networks may operate to reinforce shared norms. For instance, if the service provider was shirking his or her duty, a mutual acquaintance might say something to either the parent or provider. The contribution to the local economy in this example includes both income for the provider and the opportunity to work for the parent.

Social capital operating in the informal economy contributes to business start-ups. Many small enterprises initially operate based on informal arrangements with customers, employees, or venders. Reputations often spread through a social network (word of mouth). Accordingly, businesses that depend on social capital in initial stages sometimes grow to the point where they need more formal procedures. Many of the fastest growth sectors of modern economies – elder care, home cleaning, pet sitting, lawn services – have historically depended upon social capital in the formative stages.

A business may improve its growth prospectus if it comes more formal. It will have easier access to capital, marketing channels, and other public and private services. However, the transition to more formal operations will alter business's ability to use social capital. For instance, it may be more difficult to maintain a flexible relationship based on trust with some customers while applying more formal rules to others. Understanding the nature of the transitions will help local developers assist firms in the transition to the formal sector.

Managing Social Capital

Social capital can make positive contributions to local economies by improving performance of both profit maximizing firms and social economy organizations. Therefore, economic and community development officials are challenged to find ways to create, preserve, and use social capital.

The Development of Social Capital

Cultural and historical factors have contributed to the development of social capital. Coleman (1990, p. 313) concluded that, "Most forms of capital are created or destroyed as the by-product of other activities". Coleman's observation could lead to fatalism about the ability of local officials to create social capital because it implies it is not deliberately created. Institutions are held together by bonds of trust, reciprocity, and shared values are both repositories and generators of social capital. Once civic and other networks are formed, social capital can be produced much easier that environments that lacks such organizations. So it is tempting to assume that if a community has few social capital creating organizations, little can be done to create social capital. In addition to the simultaneity problem, social capital builds very slowly. Its genesis often is in the nano-exchanges such as a smile, nod, or pleasant word. There are only a few instances where someone can identify a moment where social capital was produced. Therefore, creating social capital can seldom be credited to a single action or a single person. The persons who helped in the development of social capital may not be recognized for their effort.

Yet, creation of social capital is a legitimate role for government. Social capital has important public goods characteristics. Many or most of the production and "consumption" benefits of social capital can be captured even by persons who do not contribute or who do not share the attitudes that measure the presence of social capital. As in the case of most public goods, economists recognize the need for public intervention to achieve optimal levels of output.

The Canadian Policy Research Initiative research group observed that governments exert indirect as well as direct influence on the creation of social capital (2005). Land use and infrastructure decisions may indirectly influence social networks as they affect everyday interactions. Certainly the construction of a highway through an existing community can weaken or break some existing networks and destroy social capital. Conversely, development of some types of land use patterns can increase individual interactions and build social capital.

Business expansion and retention studies can be used to bring businesses into community networks. An economic development organization may first reach-out to small businesses, asking questions about plans, needs, and concerns. Successful strategies require quick follow-up so that trust is built and the responding businesses do not see themselves as cogs in a bureaucratic process. Eventually networks develop and businesses can be brought into other civic processes.

In concrete terms, there is no formula for producing social capital. Just as in the case of the use of social capital, its production and preservation will depend upon context. Economic development and chambers of commerce officials are often at the center of major networks and can use these positions to create productive networks. These offer the potential for relationships that can build social capital. Economic development officials can also support the actions of other civic groups that contribute to an area's social capital.

Maintaining Social Capital

Social capital does not necessarily get depleted from use. In fact social capital when used under the correct circumstances can increase. Consider a group of people who come together to build a community center. The project will require groups to work together. People will have to trust that if they put forth effort, others will do their share. Organizations within the community will work with each other; information channels will develop; participants will feel part of a group. When a project is completed successfully, networks in the community will likely be enhanced.

While social capital cannot necessarily be depleted, it can be lost or diminished in several ways. First, an organization may undertake a project beyond its ability. In some cases the overwork or lack of success will weaken social bonds. Individuals may be unwilling to commit to future projects with the same people. When the tasks are unrealistically excessive, some parties may feel that others are not doing their share, weakening the bonds of reciprocity and trust. Thus policy makers should match the means of particular networks with the ends when asking organizations to undertake community projects.

Also, an inadequate reward structure can weaken institutions that create and store social capital. Individuals join organizations for a mix of selfish and civic motives. If rewards are not seen as equitable, some participants may believe they were "succors" or taken advantage so the belief that the organization is bound by shared values will diminish.

Third, having too little to do can create a sense of purposelessness and hence the dissipation of social capital. An institution that forms around one pressing issue can survive formally for years as its power and capabilities atrophy.

Changes in the external environment can also break the bonds necessary for effective capital. Williamson and his associates (2002) expressed concerns that economic change was destroying community cohesion. Three particular threats were the increased mobility of capital, suburbanization, and globalization. As individuals leave jobs and neighborhoods, the sense of community also is lost. The sense of community is weakened as everyday nano-exchanges diminish. The loss of individuals with ties to many people within a network or ties to multiple networks can be particularly harmful to the maintenance of social capital.

An individual's position in the community is influenced by his or her position in the economy. As economic roles change, social networks are altered and social capital is diminished. Observers are concerned when independent business owners are displaced by international businesses, significant social capital will be lost.

Tensions between economic changes and the desire to maintain social institutions are not new. What is new is the pace of economic change which may be exceeding the ability of social networks to adapt. Personal relationships generally take much longer to congeal and are slower to change than many strict market oriented relationships. If leaders of community organizations are forced to leave their positions due to relocation, job loss, or other economic change, their social roles in communities will also change. Accordingly, policy makers may be particularly concerned with preserving social capital in periods of rapid change when the threat to social capital is greatest.

Social Capital and Resolution of Development Conflicts

The economic development process generates conflicts between various groups. Sometimes these conflicts harm economic development by creating grid lock, necessitating costly reconciliation processes, or causing missed opportunities. When these conflicts arise, they are sometimes resolved based on "what's good for the community". Often organizations in the social economy and are called upon to help solve these conflicts and represent a community interest.

Social capital can be used to mediate economic development conflicts in at least two ways. First, social capital can be used to provide a forum for compromise. Second, and more subtle, social capital can be used to construct a community vision or "meta-narrative" that can frame unanticipated conflicts that may arise in the future (Lejano and Wessells, 2006). When specific conflicts can be evaluated in terms of a pre existing set of widely shared values, solutions can be considered within the context of community interest in much the way land use plans reduce some conflicts. However, when consensus is struck around abstract meta narratives, there will still be disagreements and the need for compromises.

Nations as well local communities are rethinking the definition and purpose of economic development. The rethinking is motivated by the realization that useful energy and materials are being depleted and the ability of the earth to clean itself is strained. Non polluting and "self actualizing" development paths are being reexamined (Hamilton, 2005). These new models sometimes conflict with traditional growth goals. Local social capital will be an important element in community searches for new models of local economic success.

The concept of social capital can also be used to unify the practice of local economic and community development. Traditionally, economic development focused on a set of variables that are business oriented while community development workers concerned themselves with neighborhoods and service programs for disadvantaged groups. The recognition of social capital as both a consumption good and a contributor to business development will help bridge the gap between these areas. Many local economic development conflicts can be better understood as disagreements between values associated with preserving social networks on the one hand and financial gains on the other. Recognizing the importance of social capital as a consumption good broadens the perspective of winners and losers from economic changes. Social capital has potential to be a central concept in the emerging field of community economic development.

Dysfunctional Social Capital

The majority of the burgeoning literature casts social capital in a very favorable light, perhaps because it represents something missing in modern urban life. Social capital is a tool that can be used to achieve a variety of ends. Some gangs, terrorist organizations, and crime families probably have significant bonding social capital that makes them effective. It is therefore worth asking whose ends social capital serves.

Florida recognized that excessive social capital can result in newcomers being "locked-out" and not accepted into communities (2002). Sometimes social capital may be used to impose standards that result in excessive conformity. The attitude that narrow sets of behaviors are necessary in order to be accepted into local social networks can develop.

Local officials may have difficulty distinguishing between the positive and negative consequences of social capital (Trigilia, 2001). This difficulty is particularly potent when local development officials are themselves members of dominant networks. Officials may feel that the networks they are familiar are the only important ones. Ethnic networks can also become dysfunctional to economic development if other groups feels excluded. Favoring one group can exclude others.

Markets and politics can serve as partial checks on dysfunctional social capital. The costs of sustaining some networks can become excessive and create pressure to change (Trigilia, 2001). Networks of mutual assistance, for instance, can crate moral hazards causing some members to exploit the system by free riding. As the expense of free riders become apparent, intuitional changes will occur. Similarly, excluding members of some groups to hire an incompetent employee who shared social capital may be costly.

Politics is a second constraint preventing social capital from becoming dysfunctional. Bureaucratic (formal, codified rules that apply to everyone) policies for hiring and operating serve as a balance to cronyism and subjectivity. Also, political systems may help prevent inefficient use of social capital. If a dominant political group misuses its power to favor persons within their networks, inefficiencies and moral outrage could make the political faction abusing social capital less popular. Currently there is debate regarding whether faith-based organizations, which are generally rich in social capital, should receive government funds to deliver social services. There is a concern that persons not of that faith might be excluded. Rules generated through the political process or political oversight may guard against such abuse.

Some observers might suggest that local governments should not be concerned with altering system of use and development of social capital. Certainly the ability of government officials to understand how to construct networks is currently derisory. In this regard, the conclusions of the Canadian Research Board (pp. 2–4) seem compelling. "…We have concluded government action could be more effective if, in developing relevant programs and initiatives, the role of social capital were taken into account more systematically. This does not mean, however, that governments could pursue grand strategies…."

Conclusion

Social capital has been part of local economic development ether. Now it is being examined explicitly and moving towards prominence as an important factor shaping communities. The concept of social capital promises to illuminate important aspects of the local economic development process and provide new conceptual tools for community and economic developers. In spite of its promise, there are many ambiguities and uncertainties, regarding the nature of social capital and how it can be managed. The great promise of social capital, coupled with the significant theoretical and practical ambiguities, suggests further refinements is needed and will be forthcoming.

References

Anthony, D and Christine, H. (2003), "Gender cooperation: explaining loan repayment in micro credit groups". *Social Psychology Quarterly* 66(3) 293–302.

Buchanan, J and Tullock, G. (1962), *The Calculus of Consent.* Ann Arbor MI., Ann Arbor Paperbacks.

Canadian Research Board (2005), *Social Capital As a Tool for Public Policy.* September.

Coleman, J. (1990), *Foundations of Social Theory.* Cambridge, MA: Harvard University Press.

Chou, Y. (2006), "Three simple models of social capital and economic growth". *Journal of Socio Economics* 35(5) 889–912.

Evans, M. and Syrett, S. (2007), "Generating social capital? The social economy and local economic development". *European Urban and Regional Studies* 14(1) 55–74.

Florida, R. (2002), "The rise of the creative class: Why cities without gays and rock bands are losing the economic development race". *Washington Monthly*, May, 20–25.

Fukuyama, F. (1995), *Trust*, New York: The Free Press.

Gem Public Services Group (2007), *Ohio Economic Impact Analysis.* Ohio Rail Development Commission, Columbus Ohio.

Gittell, R. and Vidal, A. (1998), *Community Organizing, Building Social Capital as a Development Strategy.* Newbury Park, CA: Sage Publications.

Hamilton, C. (2005), *Growth Fetish.* Pluto Press, London.

Institute of Health and Social Science Research (2003), *The Contribution of Social Capital in the Social Economy to Local Economic Development in Western Europe* (CONCISE). April. Available at www.connscise.info.

Kay, A. (2005), "Social capital, the social economy and community development". *Community Development Journal* 41(2) April, 160–73.

Kelly, M. (1999), "Social Capital—Making the links with community health". *Healthlines.* June, 24–29.

Lejano, R.P and Wessel, A.T. (2006), "Community and economic development: Seeking common ground in discourse and in practice". *Urban Studies* 43(9),1469–89.

Lorenzen, M. (2007), "Social capital and localized learning: Proximity and place in technological institutional dynamics". *Urban Studies* 44(4), 799–817.

Lukkarinen, M. (2005), "Community development, local economic development and the social economy". *Community Development Journal* 40(4). 419–24.

Moulaert, F, and Nussbaumer, J. (2005), "The social region". *Urban and Regional Studies* 12(1), 43–64.

Pisano, V., Ireland D.R., Hitt M.A. and Webb, J.W. (2007), "International entrepreneurship in emerging economies: The role of social capital, knowledge development and entrepreneurial actions". *International Journal of Technology Management* 38(1) 11–28.

Policy Research Initiative, (Jean-PierreVoyer, director) (2005), *Social Capital as a Policy Tool*. Ottawa, Government of Canada.

Raijman, R. and Marts, T. (2003), "Ethic foundations of economic transactions". *Ethnic and Racial Studies* 26(5) 783–99.

Reinke, J. (1998), "How to lend like mad and make a profit". *Journal of Development Studies* 34(3) 44–58.

Trigilia, C. (2001), "Social capital and local development". *European Journal of Social Theory* 4(4) 437–42.

Van Schaik, T. (2002), "Social capital in the European values study surveys". Presented at the International Conference on Social Capital Measurement, September. Available at www.oecd.org/dataoecd/22/22/2381883.pdf.

Weber, M. (1930), *The Protestant Ethic and the Sprit of Capitalism*. New York: Routledge, (First published by Routledge in 1992).

Williamson, T, Imbroscio, D. and Alperovitz, G. (2002), *Making a Place for Community*, New York: Routledge.

PART 4
Theoretical Frameworks

Chapter 14
Imperatives of Enjoyment: Economic Development under Globalisation

Michael Gunder

Introduction

One of the more influential critical articles on the theory of economic development practice can be attributed to the planning theorist Robert Beauregard. In a book chapter in *Theories of Local Economic Development,* Beauregard (1993, 267) sought to 'expose the constitutive rules of economic development as practised in the United States' by governments and not-for-profit organisations. He did so by considering the boundaries and categories of useful ideas, conventions and knowledges then deployed in economic development practice. This chapter suggests that these identified boundaries and categories are insightful as to what they then contained, and some fifteen years on, what they did not then consider, for understanding contemporary economic development policy and practice.

After briefly reviewing the Beauregard article, this work will succinctly summarise the contemporary dimensions of economic development that have emerged over the last fifteen years, perhaps best encapsulated by the expressions 'competitive globalisation' and the 'rise of the knowledge economy'. It will then briefly introduce the reader to the social constructionist theories of Lacan and Zizek prior to considering the role that enjoyment has played in underwriting some of these new discourses of economic development. It will also consider the way that enjoyment and desire produces a requirement for the 'expert that knows' and how this need and desire for the knowing expert underlies, and sometimes blinkers, contemporary orthodox economic development policy formation and approaches.

Beauregard and After

Unsurprisingly, Beauregard found that local economic development in the United States was primarily concerned with generating inward capital investment for an area to achieve efficient and timely growth, principally so that the area did not fall behind other regions and areas in prosperity. Other quantitative and qualitative concerns, such as the actual quality of job created, appropriate democratic processes deployed and equity questions were, at best, secondary political or ideological matters of little consequence to economic development policy and practice. Beauregard (1993, 274–5) concluded that this 'partitioning of reality' by economic development resulted in 'theoretical distinctions' that focussed on 'dominant economic institutions of capital', privileged investors, included but subordinated the state, emphasised 'growth over institutional capacity' and offered 'a linear notion of time mediated by political and economic cycles'. Further, these distinctions failed 'to resolve a variety of spatial contradictions between political territoriality and economic space, local intervention and global influences, and landscapes of production and those of consumption and reproduction.'

Accordingly, economic development practitioners concentrated on marketing their local economies for inward investment. Rather than relying on empirical data and analysis of the local economy, stories of investor success, both local and from other areas, tended to dominate this 'place marketing', particularly when drawn on rhetorically to paint an image of future progress and un-surpassing achievement. Public economic development policy and practice was developed and universalised through attempting to repeat prior stories of accomplishment. Correspondingly, the standard economic development 'response is ideological formulations, the participating of economic development into routine activities and special projects, and a tolerance for [resultant] epistemological conflict' (Beauregard, 1993, 280).

Some fifteen years on, much of what Beauregard observed still rings true in both economic development policy and practice, within both America and elsewhere in the English-speaking world. The greatest change may be in the stories of success used, their context, and how they have come about, not the process itself deployed. In particular, this includes the rise of importance of globalisation, new regionalism, governance rather than government, competitive cities (and city-regions), talented knowledge workers (not to mention bohemian indexes) and the rise of these new, largely, academically derived economic development policy 'success' discourses, themselves (Boland, 1999; 2007).

Moreover, this Chapter wishes to add another consideration to this theorising: the now important role that enjoyment plays in underpinning these new dimensions of local economic development policy and practice[1]. This is an underpinning that both underwrites directly some of the theories deployed – an enjoyable place and 'cool' population corresponds to strong economic growth – and ultimately the desirability of many contemporary economic development initiatives and ideas, themselves, to engender support and enjoyment for economic development decision-makers, policy drafters and practitioners in their deployment, as exemplified by their near universal acceptance.

1 There is another significant dimension to economic development that has arisen in the last 15 years, that is the importance of sustainable development. This chapter will not address sustainable development. The reader is directed to Gunder (2006) where the author documents how in city-regional policy discourses in Australia, Canada and the UK, sustainable development is deployed to privilege economic development over environmental and the social issues and maintain 'business as usual'.

Contemporary Dimensions of Competitive Globalisation

While Beauregard (1993, 274) did made reference to globalisation, it was in regard to the contradictions inherent in attempting to mimic the global economy locally. Globalisation and the transformations that this has subsequently induced on the nation state and local governance was not then a significant consideration, particularly in relationship to competitiveness between city-regions. As well, in 1993, the importance of the knowledge economy was yet to come into view as a key concern of economic development. These considerations emerged as 'foundational concepts in economic development theory' in the second half of that decade (Amin, 1999; 2002; 2004; Boland, 2007, 1022; Brenner, 1999; Duffy, 1995; Jessop, 1999; 2000; Lever and Turok, 1999). In particular, competitive advantage and the fostering and development of competitive industrial knowledge clusters have become important economic development tools at the regional and local level, with Michael Porter's work being especially influential in this area (Amin, 2002; Porter, 1995; 2000; 2003; Turok, 2004). The use of place rankings regarding competitiveness (Huggins, 2003), or as 'world cities' (Beaverstock et al., 1999), as well as rankings of local quality of life (McCann, 2004; 2007), have also all gained in importance. Although these rote rankings are often criticised for missing the mark and tending to compare apples with oranges. In this regard, Cortright and Mayer (2004, 36) observe, economic development related rankings 'conceal more than reveal when they conflate a disparate set of industrial sectors into a single amorphus category'.

A key component of this competitiveness that has materialised, often concomitant with quality of life, has been the knowledge base, or knowledge clusters, of an area and the ability of this knowledge economy to induce innovation, creativity, or even be resurgent for declining areas (Florida, 2003; Landry, 2006; Porter, 2003; Storper and Manville, 2006). Now it is argued that economic development 'is driven by cities' ability to attract creative people, rather than traditional factor endowments, which will, in turn, attract investment and stimulate economic growth' (Boland, 2007, 1022).

Richard Florida (2002a, 743; 2003; 2004) suggests that local innovation, entrepreneurialism and economic growth are dependant on talented knowledge workers – human capital – which in turn is 'associated with regional openness to creativity and diversity.' Beyond traditional employment and investment opportunities, the quality of life available, including amenity, lifestyle and range of leisure opportunities are necessary elements for city-regions to attract both businesses and talented people. Particularly, Florida (2002a, 744) asserts that 'talent is a key intermediate variable in attracting high-technology industries and generating higher regional incomes.' Like firms, regions also compete with each other to attract largely foot-loose highly skilled talent. Key to maximising this city-region success for Florida is the provision of a perceived high quality of life and the willingness to readily accommodate personal diversity of orientation, lifestyle, nationality and ethnicity.

As Florida (2002a, 754) states: 'talent does not simply show up in a region; rather, certain regional factors appear to play a role in creating an environment or habitat that can attract and retain talent, or human capital.' He calls for regions to not only have a strategy for business, but also a strategy for people. He goes further to suggest, drawing on empirical evidence, that one dimension of this desirable location is predicated on a base of alternative bohemian enjoyment seekers. Florida (2002b, 68) notes that 'places that have a high concentration of bohemians (or alternatively a high concentration of gay people) reflect an underlying set of conditions or milieu which is open and attractive to talented and creative people of all sorts (including those who work in high-technology industries) and thus create a place-based environment that is conducive to the birth, growth and development of new and high technology industries.'

Boland (2007), as well as Storper and Manville (2006), expose the naivety of some politicians and local policy makers for blindly accepting, without fully understanding, these recent discourses as to the best means for achievement of economic development success. Boland (2007, 1023) especially identifies the impact of Michael Porter and Richard Florida as had on economic development as important global voices, particularly in regards to the importance of creativity, the clustering of talent and the competitive advantage that knowledge provides in contemporary economic success. Boland (2007, 1032) argues that these, and other academic expert voices, have played an important role in legitimising and giving weight to a contemporary local economic development 'policy bias towards city-regionalism, competitiveness, the knowledge economy and place marketing' so much so that they have resulted in 'a situation where cities adopt the *same* economic development toolkit'. Rather than local innovation in economic development policy that identifies and optimises local competitive differences so that they may give competitive advantage, the contemporary uniformity of policy often results in the very lack of this competitive innovation and originality.

Compounding this lack of focus on site-specific uniqueness and creativity, local officials and politicians often do not actually understand the implications of their chosen policies, or the links of causality, or lack of them, underlying specific theories. As Storper and Manville (2006, 1252) observe in regards to Florida's strong correlation between talented knowledge workers and economic growth: 'correlation is not causation and, while Florida is doubtless aware of the difference, it seems at least that some of the policy-makers who read his books are not.' Just as Beauregard (1993) observed fifteen years before, economic development is still largely predicated on place marketing for inward investment of capital. However, this is a capital now broadened out to include human as well as financial investment. This inward investment is still largely achieved via stories of success and projecting the right image, or brand, that attempts to differentiate a particular city from the rest, all predicated on the dominant ideas, or orthodoxy, of what makes local economies successful as 'competitive global or world cities'. Yet, this very orthodoxy fails to differentiate. Rather, 'despite the aspirations to create local uniqueness, place marketing frequently results in sameness in both policy and practice', so much so, that these economic development strategies can be argued to be deployable almost inter-changeably between various diverse cities (Boland, 2007, 1028).

A Dash of Lacanian and Zizekian Constructivist Theory

The rest of this chapter draws on a social constructivist derived Zizekian analysis of reality to explain some of these evolving economic development discourses, policies and practices. This theorising will suggest that what underlies the adoption of many of the dominant economic development policy discourses of is a desire for, and seeking of, satisfaction and enjoyment. The constructivist approach is concerned with 'how policies work in practice and the creations of norms, embedded belief systems and knowledge' (Armstrong and Wells, 2006, 266). Much of Zizek's work (1989; 1993; 1997; 1999; 2002a; 2006) draws on the French neo-structuralist psychoanalytical thought of Jacques Lacan (1992; 2007) for its insight. This includes a basic tenet that the symbolic, or language, always fails in attempting complete and comprehensive articulation and this, in turn, frustrates the actor's enjoyment. Not everything can be said, something is always lacking, and there is always an empty remainder, a void not capable of capture by language. Moreover, driven by a desire for the satisfaction of fulfilment and completeness, actors then use fantasy construction, rationalisation and the deployment of empty words – signifiers without explicit meaning – to 'paper over' and obscure, but also to some degree symbolise 'around', this frustrating lack or unsymbolisable remainder. At best, each of these empty words is used to 'palpate what it cannot conceive; it gestures at what it cannot grasp', for each word, at best, can only cover over what is lacking in symbolic representation (May, 2005, 82).

In this light, Zizek and Lacan has been used in the organisational literature by Jones and Spicer (2005), drawing on the concept of the empty signifier, to explain the failure of 'entrepreneurial studies' to come to terms with and succinctly define itself. Here 'the entrepreneur is a marker of this lack; the entrepreneur is indefinable, and necessarily so; the entrepreneur is an "absent centre"' (Jones and Spicer, 2005, 236). The empty and undefinable word 'entrepreneur' covers over this one example of this void in the symbolic. Rather, than discourses on entrepreneurship being stable and coherent narratives focused on a universally agreed core meaning, they are composed of 'paradoxical, incomplete and worm-ridden symbolic' structures that posit 'an impossible and indeed incomprehensible object at its centre' (Jones and Spicer, 2005, 236). This is a void of understanding and meaning – signification – that all with an interest in entrepreneurship strive to search for and comprehensively fill, so that they can understand this valued sublime 'concept' of explicit commercial success. They do so to gain the multiple levels of pleasure and enjoyment that having access to the 'secret' of entrepreneurship would provide. However, they continuously fail to do so, or even comprehensively to identify what is lacking – what remains outside of articulation – about the concept.

Drawing on this understanding of lack, rationalisation and fantasy construction, Zizek argues that the 'more we pride ourselves on being "free thinkers in a free world"', 'the more we blindly submit ourselves to the merciless superegoic command ("Enjoy!") which binds us to the logic of the market' (Vighi and Feldner, 2007, 146). Particularly poignant for economic development, is that this desire for satisfaction and enjoyment resides at multiple levels: firstly, the enjoyment provided by the desired ideal 'guaranteed' to yield economic development success and, secondly, the wider desire to enjoy expressed and materialised in our prevalent consumer habits, themselves. Both conflate with each other under the rubric of economic development to create an environment constituting our materialised social reality, which is largely reflective of our collective desires – a desire for fulfilment that in turn is synonymous with enjoyment.

Enjoyment Provided by the One's that Know

Desire as driven and experienced in the loss or gaining of enjoyment is central to our social reality (Zizek, 1989; 1999; 2002a; 2005; 2006). Just as a seductive (or well advertised) consumer item makes us feel incomplete unless we buy it, this desire for enjoyment also allows an abstract idea, such as the bohemian index, or the search for the secret of entrepreneurship, to catch our interest and fascinate. An idea can 'delude us with its seemingly compelling significance and impose its ideological imperatives upon us' to believe in and identify with that idea (Kay, 2003, p. 54). Such that, if only we do the following – whatever that might be – we can live in a world-class city of talented knowledge workers, or know the 'secret' to be a successful, hence rich, entrepreneur.

Contrary to the classical definition of ideology where illusion is but distorted knowledge, Zizekian ideology is not 'an illusion masking the real state of things but that of an (unconscious) fantasy(s) structuring our social reality itself' so that our ideological beliefs are materialised in all our social actions within society (Zizek, 1989, p. 33). Further, these social fantasies of desire fill out the voids of our deficient social structures by covering over any incompleteness, or dis-ease and dis-satisfaction, through the provision of giving us opportunities to identify with a fulfilling illusion – our local economy will be successful, because our bohemian index is rising, or whatever – hence giving us a sense of security and enjoyment. In Lacan's (2007, 15) and Zizek's (2002a, 2005, 2006) theorising, enjoyment is one of the key elements of the social bond constituting society and the social interactions, links and relationships society constructs where language evokes an effect on all others that in aggregate constitutes society. Indeed, for Zizek (2006, 309) politics and public policy, including economic development, is directly and primarily 'concerned with ways of soliciting, or controlling and regulating' enjoyment.

Something catches the policy-drafters and decision-makers' interest as a significant economic development-related idea, often predicated on ideological belief, when it is sensed and expressed as an object or concept that has the effect of a transcendental illumination or incarnation of impossible potential enjoyment. It is a story of success that can be identified with; hence, it *must* be identified with. It is something that is utterly compelling, say, the desire for a particular solution, or even idyllic ideal, that addresses a known problem, or lack, in the local economic fabric (Zizek, 1989, p.132). It is sublime, it overwhelms, yet often cannot be fully envisaged due to its transcendent intensity, hence Zizek's (1989) title: *The Sublime Object of Ideology*.

For each political decision-maker or policy advisor, in Lacanian thought, 'there is an *ideal economy*, an economy in which needs *would* be met, desires *would* be satisfied, proper human and social development *would be* achieved[:] *If only…*' (Byrne and Healy, 2006, 243). In this regard for this ideology belief to function, there has to be *someone else that knows* and hence 'embody the deeper meaning' to this idea or ideal system (Sharpe, 2006, 111). And for economic development it is the policy gurus, the Porter(s) and Florida(s), the academic *ones that know* the desired answer, that provide what is missing and fills in this lack that in turn will make the ideal of success come true.

Or at least that is the hope, for, at best, the fantasy that the guru has the answer 'protects us from the anxiety of the lack, and it gives a name to—symbolises—the thing that blocks us from getting what we desire' (Byrne and Healy, 2006, 243). In Jones and Spicer's (2005) analysis, the empty thing that we try to grapple with is the essence of entrepreneurialship. In a similar vain, what is crucial for the desiring agent seeking the essence, or secret, of economic development success is that it 'functions through the constitution of this lack (of knowledge, social capital, resources, etc), which as a void gives body to all sorts of fads, theories and rationalisations' (De Vries, 2007, 37). These are provided by the 'ones who must know'. The desire for economic development to be successful thus continues to carry on, even in its continued failure to achieve the desired success.

The Reification of Enjoyment: You Will Enjoy, Not Transgress!

Zupancic (2006, 169) associates Lacan's and consequently Zizek's theorisation of enjoyment with the Marxian theory of commodification and surplus-value via Lacan's concept of surplus-enjoyment (*plus-de-jouir*). Lacan (2007, 177) contends that surplus-value of capital and surplus-enjoyment are historically equivalent, especially in the situation of the traditional authority's, religious or secular, injunction of 'No!', which was particularly prevalent in the emerging early phase of Calvinistic capitalism and a continuing context of traditional state authority into the modern era, perhaps concluding with the fall of the welfare state. This emerged in an historical epoch perhaps best illustrated by Max Weber (2002) who demonstrated how the Protestant work ethic in early Northern European capitalism, not leisure or enjoyment, was the only way to attest the glory of God and demonstrate ones place as predestined for the eternal and everlasting joy of Heavenly life.

Marshall (2007, 110) suggests that, since the 1980s, corresponding to a shift from government to governance and the decline of the welfare state, we have moved from societies of capitalist prohibition to a present-day global society of commanded enjoyment, where literally nearly anything is possible due to technology 'and the prevalence of the market in all facets of social life'. Catlaw (2006, 270) observes that now for public policy administrators the 'challenge, in light of contemporary circumstances, is not to find new ways of inhibiting enjoyment, as neotraditional views would advocate, but of finding ways of making enjoyment possible'.

In contrast to the historical authority and rationality of the state's repressive command to not enjoy as it gets in the way of doing productive work, late capitalism is structured under a rationality of the 'scientific' knowledge deployed by the state and local government, or perhaps the governance of a public-private partnership, through the bureaucratic provision of policy initiatives. Now knowledge and science – or at least the appearance thereof – is necessary to rationalise and legitimise the agency of policy action, not the State or other authority's just arbitrary injunction of negation. This is achieved by expressing a logic of efficiency and expertise (including that of economic development) that does not prohibit enjoyment, but rather channels enjoyment in ways that produces a "bio-politics" (after Foucault) of dissatisfied subjects that have no option, but to seek to gain enjoyment and satisfaction (Marshall, 2007; McGowan, 2004; Zizek, 2004b; Zupancic, 2006).

Individuals 'no longer submit to an exploitative labour market because of some imposed belief – "work harder and your reward will be in heaven" – but because there is no belief, nothing other than the axiom of capital – the desire to buy more, work more, earn more, have more' (Colebrook, 2006, 86). That is the imperative to have more enjoyment, more happiness, for its good for you, your community and the nation! Florida (2002b, 57) argues, drawing on Frank (1997), that the successful clustering of creative economic activity is dependent on a blending of business culture and bohemian culture constituting 'enjoyment and self-actualisation over work' to create a state where 'capitalism has absorbed and integrated what used to be thought of as alternative or cool' into an 'into mainstream economic activity.'

Now 'the power of capitalism does not lie in its repression of our pleasures, but in its coding of all those pleasures into money *and* in producing a surplus value of that code: for we are now enslaved, not by being *denied what we want*, but of being manufactured *to want*' (Colebrook, 2006, 133). In our contemporary global society, the 'moral law' is no longer the imperative that acts as a limitation, stopping us from enjoying too much. Instead, the cultural imperative, the now dominant 'moral law' itself, is the injunction for us to *enjoy*, because 'the ultimate "transgression"' would occur 'should one wish to pursue a life of moderation' (Zizek, 2004b, 174).

Globalised Happiness Whether You Want It or Not

In regards to this transgression, 'a nation *exists* only as long as its specific *enjoyment* continues to be materialised in a set of social practices and submitted through national myths that structure these practices' (Zizek, 1993, 202). This is taken further by the barely challenged international discourse of global capitalisation and the fantasies it now induces in externally structuring each nation state's and their many city-regions' very enjoyment (Stavrakakis, 2003, 63; Zizek, 2004b, 61). Even the ruling British Labour Government, with its 'Third Way' and 'Cool Britannia', in contrast to its tradition of socialism, has placed 'economic globalisation' as 'the most significant factor in shaping Labour Party thinking since the early 1990s' (Allmendinger, 2003, 326). In New Zealand, Australia, Canada, the UK and, no doubt, the USA, key national, as well as local, economic development policy is to ensure that 'our' diverse city-regions are all globally competitive (Gunder, 2006). As McGowan (2004, 193) observes:

> we trust fully in the staying power of global capitalism…The universe of global capitalism is, or so we think, here to stay, and we best not do anything to risk our status within it. Hence, we pledge our allegiance to it, and we put our trust in it. This is the fundamental mode of contemporary obedience to authority…Global capitalism seems an unsurpassable horizon…because we don't want to lose it – and the imaginary satisfaction that it provides.

Illusion resides under this global fantasy of capital where 'the basic feature of' this dominant cultural imperative 'no longer operates on the level of ideals and identifications, but directly on the level of regulating *jouissance*' [the later is the Lacanian term used for 'enjoyment'] (Zizek, 2004b, 113). This is a global capitalism, indeed, where surplus-value is synonymous with surplus-enjoyment supporting the injunction: 'you must enjoy!' In this light, the role of public policy, including that of economic development, is to facilitate enjoyment by providing the correct space – healthy, vibrant, competitive, fit and attractive – where enjoyment, especially for the talented, foot-loose, knowledge workers, can be effectively materialised and maximised under the imperative of global capitalism. The 'need' to attract and retain playful bohemian and talented knowledge workers is central to this imperative of enjoyment, if one wants one's city-region to remain globally competitive!

Consequently, local public governance and the policies of economic development that facilitate this environment of vibrancy and fun are 'nothing more than an ideology that claims to be either "art" or "technology" or "science," depending on the context' (Lefebvre, 2003, 159). This ideology gives the appearance of rational scientific practice in the public interest. It does so by drawing on the academic experts of success – the gurus that know – the Porter(s) and Florida(s) and their related ilk[2]. However, this is an ideology that obscures via selectively deploying only specific facts and also leaving things unsaid. Above all, it gives the appearance of promoting societal efficiency predicated on the concept of satisfaction and enjoyment. However, this is largely a satisfaction of vested interests, the wealthy and the talented – those that can inwardly invest financial or human capital (i.e. themselves) – whose needs must be understandably catered to and accommodated, regardless of cost, to everyone else. This largely excluded the less talented, more knowledge-challenged workers that constitute the majority of any workforce in a city-region. Workers who likely are less mobile than the footloose talented knowledge workers the economic development policies set out to attract in the first place (Gunder, 2006, 216).

For economic development, social reality is indeed divided! Just as Beauregard (1993) suggested fifteen years ago, economic development related policy continues to partition reality. The only interests continuously served by economic development are those capable of the provision of inward capital investment: both financial and now human.

This is exacerbated further in the current milieu of consumerist post-democracy personified by the concept global capitalism. 'Post-democracy is founded on an attempt to exclude the political awareness of lack and negativity from the political domain, leading to a political order which retains the token institutions of liberal democracy but neutralises the centrality of political antagonism' (Stavrakakis, 2003, 59). In response to the dominant 'logic' of global competitiveness, academic technocratic experts and their disciples, including economic development practitioners, perhaps with some public-private governance 'input' or 'leadership', shape, contextualise and implement public policy mainly in the interest of this dominant hegemonic bloc. This is constructed under the logics and knowledges of bureaucratic discourses (see Gunder, 2004), with an objective to remove existing or potential economic blight, 'dis-ease' and disfunction detracting from local enjoyment and global competitiveness (Gunder, 2005; McGuirk, 2004) – for who can argue against this crucial need!

Of course, the hegemonic network, or bloc, initially shapes the debate drawing on appropriate policies of desired success, such as the needs of bohemians, knowledge clusters, or talented knowledge workers, as to what constitutes *their* desired enjoyment and what is therefore lacking in local competitiveness. In turn, this defines what is blighted and dysfunctional and in need of economic, or other, remedy. This is predicated on a logic, or more accurately a rhetoric, that a lack of a particular defined type of enjoyment, or competitiveness (for surely they are one and the same) is inherently unhealthy for the aggregate social body. This lack and its resolution is generally presented as a technical issue, rather than as a political one. Consequently, the technocrats in partnership with their 'dominant stakeholders' can ensure the impression of rationally seeking to produce happiness

2 The cynical reader might observe that this author's 'one that knows' might be Slavoj Zizek.

for the many, while, not to mention, achieving the stakeholders' specific interests (Gunder and Hillier, 2007, 469).

Facilitating this is the avoidance of critical policy debate challenging the favoured orthodox position and policy approach. Consequently, 'the safe names in the field who feed the policy orthodoxy are repeatedly used, or their work drawn upon, by different stakeholders, while more critical voices are silenced by their inability to shape policy debates' (Boland, 2007, 1032). Here the economic development analyst continues to ideologically partition reality by deploying only the orthodox 'successful' economic development response. This also maintains the dominant, or hegemonic, *status quo* while providing 'the lead role as a cover and shield against critical thought by acting in the manner of a "buffer" isolating the political field from any research that is independent and radical in its conception as in its implications for public policy' (Wacquant, 2004, 99). At the same time, this adoption of the hegemonic orthodoxy tends to generate similar policy responses for every competing local area or city-region, largely resulting in a zero sum game (Blair and Kumar, 1997).

The bio-politics of contemporary economic development are predicated on enjoyment – you will enjoy! – not the prior duality of repression/freedom of the Weberian capitalist master's injunction: 'No, you cannot do that!' The achievements of traditional progressive goals were ones of freedom to act against the repression of the negative injunction. Contemporary injunctions are to enjoy – or at least to sustain our happiness – regardless of what we actually desire. Yet, consumer happiness ultimately in Zizekian thought is not a class of truth, but, at best, an ontological class of being where:

> 'happiness' relies on the subject's inability or unreadiness fully to confront the consequences of its desire: the price of happiness is that the subject remains stuck in the inconsistency of its desires. In our daily lives, we (pretend to) desire things which we do not really desire, so that, ultimately, the worst thing that can happen is for us to get what we 'officially' desire. Happiness is thus hypocritical: it is the happiness dreaming about things we do not really want. (Zizek, 2002b, 59–60)

Economic development continues to be desired because it maintains the dominant *status quo*, by appearing to attempt to increase this happiness of material wellbeing for all. This is, firstly, because the state and its local governments and governance structures have to be shown to be doing something to justify their existence. Secondly, and perhaps more importantly, because public sector actions that give the appearance of doing something that seeks to improve the local economy underpins the primal desire of most subjects in society for a safe and assured happy future of security and prosperity. This is even if local economic development agencies and their practitioners can only deliver this as a fantasy-scenario by providing a potential of a limited material increase in happiness for some, even when this may not really be what is actually wanted, rather than as an impossible reality that would actually sate the wants and desires of everyone (Gunder, 2003a; 2003b).

This is a fantasy predicate on an obedience to a shallow, but perhaps sometimes obtainable, consumptive quantitative imperative to be materially happy, which may, when it does occur, be at the expense of actual qualitative psychic desires for self-determination and the more authentic contentment and satisfaction that this may possibly provide!

Conclusion

Beauregard (1993, 280) concluded his chapter on economic development theory with the statement that his work was 'only a beginning' 'to raise consciousness about the constitutive rules of economic development to facilitate a more critical understanding.' Fifteen years on, this chapter has continued Beauregard's beginning by noting the new emergent discourses of success deployed in contemporary economic development. In particular, this chapter has drawn on the Lacanian and Zizekian constructivist literature to illustrate the important role that human enjoyment and desire plays in these economic development discourses.

Enjoyment underlies human behaviours of capitalist consumption, but more fundamentally, it explains at least some of the dimensions as to why our policy decision makers identify with and deploy 'trusted and (perceived) true' dominant discourses of economic development success for their local initiatives. This is done even when the near universal application of the same orthodox discourses may result in a 'zero sum' gain for all concerned, as each local city-region deploys the same or nearly same, economic development policies in an attempt to gain 'unique' competitive advantage over all others local economies under globalisation.

Indeed, fifteen years on from Beauregard's work, economic development practice appears to continue as business as usual, perhaps with some newer stories and strategies of success, provided by the 'academics that know'. As well, the economic development core practice of seeking inward investment has perhaps been expanded to include human capital as well as that of financial capital. Yet, the partitioning of reality continues. Economic development practitioners, policy makers and their political decision makers continue to see and largely have regard to only what they desire: that is successful inward investment. For it is their hegemonic choices, driven by their desires for satisfaction and enjoyment, which indeed materialises our local economic development responses, as well as many other dimensions of our social and spatial realities. In turn, this indeed gives those involved with the creation of local economic development policy and practices a perceived sense of security and enjoyment that they are doing the 'right' thing. For it is what everyone else is doing, so it must be correct thing to do in our globally competitive world!

References

Allmendinger, P. (2003), Rescaling, Integration and Competition: Future Challenges for Development Planning, *International Planning Studies*, 8(4), 323–328.

Amin, A. (1999), An Institutional Perspective on Regional Economic Development, *International Journal of Urban and Regional Research*, 23(2), 365–378.

Amin, A. (2002), Spatialities of Globalisation, *Environment and Planning: A*, 24(3), 385–399.

Amin, A. (2004), Regions Unbounded: Towards a New Politics of Place, *Geografiska Annaler*, Series B, 86(1), 33–44.

Armstrong, H., Wells, P. (2006), Structural Funds and the Evaluation of Community Economic Development Initiatives in the UK: A Critical Perspective, *Regional Studies*, 40(2), 259–272.

Beauregard, R. (1993), Constituting Economic Development: A Theoretical Perspective, in R. Bingham, R. Mier (eds) *Theories of Local Economic Development: Perspectives From Across the Disciplines*, London, Sage, 267–283.

Beaverstock, J., Taylor, P., Smith, R. (1999), A roster of world cities, *Cities*, 16(6), 445–458.

Blair, J., Kumar, R. (1997), Is local economic development a zero-sum game? in R. Bingham and R. Mier (eds) *Dilemmas of Urban Economic Development: Issues in Theory and Practice*, Thousand Oaks, CA: Sage, 1–20.

Boland, P. (1999), Contested Multi-level Governance: Merseyside and the European Structural Funds, *European Planning Studies*, 7(5), 647–664.

Boland, P. (2007), Unpacking the Theory-Policy Interface of Local Economic Development: An Analysis of Cardiff and Liverpool, *Urban Studies* 44(5/6), 1019–1039.

Bracher, M. (1993), *Lacan, Discourse, and Social Change,* Ithaca: Cornell University Press.

Brenner, N, (1999), Globalisation as Reterritorialisation: The Re-Scaling of Urban Governance in the European Union, *Urban Studies*, 36(3), 431–451.

Byrne, K., Healy, S. (2006), Cooperative Subjects: Towards a Post-Fantasmatic Enjoyment of the Economy, *Rethinking Marxism*, 18(2), 241–258.

Catlaw, T. (2006), Authority, Representation, and the Contradictions of Posttraditional Governing, *The American Review of Public Administration*, 36(3), 261–287.

Colebrook, C. (2006), *Deleuze: A Guide for the Perplexed*, London: Continuum.

Cortright, J., Mayer, H. (2004), Increasingly Rank: The use and Misuse of Rankings in Economic Development, *Economic Development Quarterly*, 18(1), 34–39.

De Vries, P. (2007), Don't Compromise Your Desire for Development! A Lacanian/Deleuzian rethinking of the anti-politics machine, *Third World Quarterly*, 28(1), 25–43.

Duffy, H. (1995), *Competitive Cities: Succeeding in the Global Economy*, London: Taylor and Francis.

Florida, R. (2002a), The Economic Geography of Talent, *Annals of the Association of American Geographers*, 92(4), 743–755.

Florida R. (2002b), Bohemia and economic geography, *Journal of Economic Geography*, 2, 55–71.

Florida, R. (2003), *The Rise of the Creative Class: And How It's Transforming Work, Leisure, Community and Everyday Life*, New York: Basic Books.

Florida, R. (2004), *Cities and the Creative Class*, London: Routledge.

Frank, T. (1997), *The Conquest of Cool: Business Culture, Counterculture, and the Rise of Hip Consumerism*, Chicago: University of Chicago Press.

Gunder, M. (2003a), Passionate Planning for the Others' Desire: An Agonistic Response to the Dark Side of Planning, *Progress in Planning*, 60(3), 235–319.

Gunder, M. (2003b), Planning Policy Formulation from a Lacanian Perspective, *International Planning Studies*, 8(4), 279–294.

Gunder, M. (2004), Shaping the Planner's Ego-Ideal: A Lacanian Interpretation of Planning Education, *Journal of Planning Education and Research*, 23(3), 299–311.

Gunder, M. (2005), Obscuring Difference Through Shaping Debate: A Lacanian View of Planning for Diversity, *International Planning Studies* 10(2), 83–103.

Gunder, M. (2006), Sustainability: Planning's Saving Grace or Road to Perdition? *Journal of Planning Education and Research* 26(2), 208–221.

Gunder, M. Hillier, J. (2007), Planning as Urban Therapeutic, *Environment and Planning: A*, 39(2), 467–486.

Huggins, R. (2003), Creating a UK Competitive Index: Regional and Local Benchmarking, *Regional Studies*, 37(1), 89–96.

Jessop, B. (1999), *Reflections on globalisation and its (il)logic(s),* Department of Sociology, Lancaster University, http://www.lancs.ac.uk/fass/sociology/research/resalph.htm#ik, accessed 22 August 2007.

Jessop, B. (2000), The Crisis of the National Spatio-Temporal Fox and the Tendential Ecological Dominance of Globalising Capital, *International Journal of Urban and Regional Research*, 24(2), 323–360.

Jones, C., Spicer, A. (2005), The Sublime Object of Entrepreneurship, *Organization*, 12(2), 223–246.

Kay, S. (2003), *Zizek: A Critical Introduction*, Cambridge: Polity.

Lacan J. (1992), *The Ethics of Psychoanalysis,* London: Routledge.

Lacan, J. (2007), *The Seminar of Jacques Lacan, Book XVII, The Other Side of Psychoanalysis: 1969–1970*, London: Norton.

Landry, C. (2006), *The Art of City Making*, London: Earthscan.

Lefebvre, H. (2003), *The Urban Revolution,* Minneapolis: University of Minnesota Press.

Lever, W., Turok, I. (1999), Competitive Cities: Introduction to the Review, *Urban Studies,* 36(5/6), 791–793.

Marshall, G. (2007), Commanded to Enjoy: The Waning of Traditional Authority and its Implications for Public Administration, *Administrative Theory and Praxis*, 29(1), 102–114.

May, T. (2005), *Gilles Deleuze: An Introduction*, Cambridge: Cambridge University Press.

McCann, E. (2004), 'Best Places': Interurban Competition, Quality of Life and Popular Media Discourse, *Urban Studies,* 41(10), 1909–1929.

McCann, E. (2007), Inequality and Politics in the Creative City-Region: Questions of Liveability and State Strategy, *International Journal of Urban and Regional Research,* 31(1), 188–196.

McGuirk, P. (2004), State, strategy, and scale in the competitive city: a neo-Gramscian analysis of the governance of 'global Sydney' *Environment and Planning A*, 36(6), 1019–1043.

McGowan, T. (2004), *The End of Dissatisfaction?* Albany: SUNY.

Porter, M. (1995), The Competitive Advantage of the Inner City, *Harvard Business Review*, 73(3), 55–71.

Porter, M. (2000), Location, Competition, and Economic Development: Local Clusters in a Global Economy, *Economic Development Quarterly*, 14(1), 15–34.

Porter, M. (2003), The Economic Performance of Regions, *Regional Studies*, 37(6/7), 545–578.

Sandercock, L. (2004), Towards a Planning Imagination for the 21st Century, *Journal of the American Planning Association*, 70(2), 133–141.

Sharpe, M. (2006), The Aesthetics of Ideology, or 'The Critique of Ideological Judgement' in Eagleton and Zizek, *Political Theory*, 34, 95–120.

Storper, M and Manville, M. (2006), Behaviour, Preferences and Cities: Urban Theory and Urban Resurgence, *Urban Studies*, 43(8), 247–1274.

Stavrakakis, Y. (1999), *Lacan and the Political*, London: Routledge.

Stavrakakis, Y. (2003), Re-Activating the Democratic Revolution: The Politics of Transformation Beyond Reoccupation and Conformism, *parallax*, 9(2), 56–71.

Turok, I. (2004), Cities, Regions and Competitiveness, *Regional Studies*, 38(9), 1069–1083.

Vighi, F. and Feldner, H. (2007), Ideology Critique or Discourse Analysis? Zizek against Foucault, *European Journal of Political Theory*, 6(2), 141–159.

Wacquant, L., (2004), Critical Thought as Solvent of *Doxa*, *Constellations,* 11(1), 97–101.

Weber, M. (2002), *The Protestant Ethic and the Spirit of Capitalism*, Los Angeles, Roxbury.

Zizek, S. (1989), *The Sublime Object of Ideology,* London: Verso.

Zizek, S. (1993), *Tarrying with the Negative,* Durham: Duke University Press.

Zizek, S. (1997), *The Plague of Fantasies,* London: Verso.

Zizek, S. (1999), *The Ticklish Subject,* London: Verso.
Zizek, S. (2002a), *For they know not what they do: Enjoyment as a political factor*, London: Verso.
Zizek, S. (2002b), *Welcome to the Desert of the Real,* London: Verso.
Zizek, S. (2004a), *Organs without Bodies,* London: Routledge.
Zizek, S. (2004b), *Iraq: The Borrowed Kettle,* London: Verso.
Zizek, S. (2005), *The Metastases of Enjoyment*, London: Verso.
Zizek, S. (2006), *The Parallax View*, Cambridge: MIT Press.
Zupancic, A. (2006), When Surplus Enjoyment Meets Surplus Value, in J. Clemens, R. Grigg (eds) *Jacques Lacan and The Other Side of Psychoanalysis*, London: Duke University Press, 155–178.

Chapter 15
Moving the Discipline Beyond Metaphors

James E. Rowe

This chapter examines the importance of metaphors and stories in the development of theory for the practice of local economic development. As indicated in the previous chapters, other than Porter's and Florida's contributions, very few new theories have been developed in the fifteen years since the publication of Bingham and Mier's iconic 1993 book. The objective of this chapter is to urge the discipline to move beyond metaphors and to spur scholars on to explore the "potential for thinking differently with respect to the [relationship between] theory and practice" in economic development (Leach and Boler, 1998, p. 150). It will also explain why a poststucturalist or a constructionalist approach is better suited for the development of an explanatory theoretical framework and why a traditionalist or positivistic approach is not.

The Importance of Metaphors and Stories

Mier and Bingham[1] (1993) argued, and this writer agrees, that metaphorical analogies are the best way to engage an economic development practitioner and that metaphors are a solid foundation from which to build new theory. In the intervening time, the significance role of metaphors[2] and stories in economic development strategies, advertising and promotional material has continued.

As a way forward, theorist should consider Flyvbjerg's concept of normative idealism (Flyvbjerg, 1998; Flyvbjerg and Richardson, 2002). This concept was originally presented by Banfield (1971) in 1959 when he suggested that a normative ideal is an inherent part of all planning. He also noted that there are some difficult tensions between this normative ideal and the real world. When looking for the normative aspects of planning "…it is hard to see how references to such a model can be avoided or, indeed, why its lack of realism should be considered a defect" (Banfield, 1971, p. 149). In support, Hillier (2003, p. 41) argues in relationship to collaborative planning that "empirical research from planning practice…is increasingly demonstrating [that] the ideals of communicative rationality and

1 When Bingham and Mier co-edited their iconic book in 1993, they, perhaps, never envisioned the advent of poststructuralism or that it would validate their main premise 24 years later.

2 Metaphors are the main mechanism through which we comprehend abstract concepts (Lakoff, 1992, p. 39).

consensus-formation are rarely achieved". This implies that it is important for the practitioner to manage the expectations of his or her stakeholders because it is essential to "establish reciprocal understanding" of what can realistically be achieved (Flyvbjerg, 2001, p. 90).

Theory has always been about how it should be done and less about what one does (Beauregard, 2005, p. 203); consequently, it is inevitable that the rhetoric of economic development often returns to storytelling, communicative action and facilitation. In this writer's opinion, storytelling and communicative based planning can best be articulated with metaphors. Deleuze argues that the very idea of metaphors or representation has underpinned thinking and philosophy. We act as though there is a literal world that needs to be conveyed by the metaphors or representations generated by minds. Philosophers see themselves as using metaphors to describe an objective world (Colebrook, 2002b, p. 68).

Economic development practitioners often devote their energies to marketing their areas to potential investors. To do so, they tell stories and search for 'generative metaphors'[3] that will capture the imaginations of investors, elected officials and the public (Aay and Van Langevelde, 2005; Buss, 1999; Mier and Fitzgerald, 1991). These metaphors are not necessarily based on empirical analyses but become indispensable rhetorical strategies. The marketing material produced by most economic development agencies describes possibilities, and not necessarily specific trends, based on facts (which are inherently rhetorical). Consequently, the discipline becomes more complex and muddled because of the lack of a theoretical framework to explain the use of metaphors. In a similar vein, in order to overcome the absence of a strong theoretical framework, Amin and others have effectively used metaphors to describe the urban environment in numerous publications (Amin, 2004; Amin and Thrift, 2002).

Generative metaphors are essential to the task of confronting ambiguity and are thus a key to the integration of scholarship and professional practice because they liberate the imagination and engender new understanding of problems and approaches to their solution (Trevor, 1996). Schön and Rein (1994) argues that generative metaphors[4] are both frames of reference and processes for bringing new perspectives into existence. There are ways of seeing one thing as another and, in doing so, enabling the redefinition or resetting of a problem (Schön, 1979). The concept can be further elaborated as follows:

> Generative metaphor – a process by which a familiar constellation of ideas is carried over (*meta-pherein*, in the Greek) to a new situation, with the result that both the familiar and the unfamiliar come to be seen in new ways. One thing is seen as another – A is seen

---

3 A metaphor is an expression which means or describes one thing or idea using words usually used for something else with very similar qualities. Generative refers to the power to produce or generate.

4 Bent Flyvbjerg (2001, p. 80) has even been bold enough to state that metaphors may function as a focal point for the founding of schools of thought.

> as B – just as in the familiar drawings of the Gestalt psychologists a figure may be seen as a vase or the conjunction of two profiles, as a young woman or an old one, as a duck or as a rabbit. When A is seen as B, the existing description of B is taken as a putative redescription of A (Schön and Rein, 1994, pp. 26–7).

Generative metaphors are fluid and open-ended, and their imagery is refined within specific contexts.

This open-ended imagery leads to the conclusion that economic development draws on a complex web of coexisting and conflicting knowledge bases. This can be partially explained by understanding Laclau's concept of an *empty signifier** which was derived from Lacan (Laclau, 2006; Zerilli, 1998). An empty signifier is often a proper name and forms a vacant placeholder for particular contents: "The universal is an empty place, a void which can be filled only by the particular, but which, through its emptiness, produces a series of crucial effects in the structuration/destructuration of social relations" (Laclau, 2000, p. 58). As such, Laclau's idea of an empty signifier is similar to and is based on the Lacanian idea of the symbolic master signifier. The structure of the empty signifier thus functions as the site where the various particulars struggle for hegemony.

This structure of the empty signifier seems a good way to describe the functioning of the signifier *economic development* in the discourse of this book. The name *economic development* is indeed a rubric under which all possible displacements (interpretations) are gathered. As an empty signifier, the term operates as the placeholder to accommodate a variety of heterogeneous demands. These vary from different understandings of the discipline to distinct images such as rhizomes, *nomads** and *plateaus**. One may consider economic development to be an empty signifier because as Laclau (2000c, p. 185) stated, it is a "signifier with no necessary attachment to any precise content". This can be interpreted as meaning that the discipline lacks a theoretical base. Because of this lack, practitioners are placed in the position of always seeking to hegemonically fill this lack.

The lack can be filled by moving the profession beyond stories and metaphorical analogies and begin to develop a theoretical base for the discipline[5]. The pathway toward developing a theory via metaphorical analysis has been clearly delineated (Cresswell, 1997, p. 330; Mier and Bingham, 1993, pp. 301–302; Ortony, 1993). Bingham and Mier (1993, p. xvi) have suggested that:

5 The stories, generative metaphors and untruths used in promotional material could be considered just creative writing by some and images of fantasy by others (for a good explanation of fantasy as it relates to utopian city planning – see Gunder, 2005d). For Deleuze "*Truth* may well seem to be a more modest being from which no disorder and nothing extraordinary is to be feared…for it is, after all, only *pure knowledge*" (Deleuze, 1994, p. 135, my emphasis).

> Alternative visions require a new social construction of reality – new patterns of perception embedded in narrative habits and patterns of seeing. So inspirational story telling, we believe, takes priority in economic development policy and strategy formulation. Metaphors provide the inspirational spine to the stories and thus a framework for incorporating diverse theories of development into practical application.

Metaphors are known as vehicles for the transfer of concepts, ideas and notions from one domain to another (Chettiparamb, 2006, p. 75; Martin, 1999, p. 224). This writer suggests that now is the time for the economic development profession to move the discipline beyond simple rhetoric. Consequently, the next chapter will delineate a poststructuralist theoretical framework based on Deleuzian philosophy that will provide insights into the practice of local economic development. However, before progressing with developing this meta-theory, it is essential to gain an appreciation of stories and metaphors.

The practice of economic development can best be understood in terms of storytelling; of abandoning what Harding calls "the longing for 'one true story' that has been the psychic motor for western science" (Harding, 1986, p. 193).

> Recognising the fundamental limitations of science and scientific methods…[one] suggests that it perhaps makes more sense to treat scientific communication as storytelling. Instead of trying to find objective truth, perhaps it is more meaningful to check the narrative coherence of scientific research by asking two questions: Does the story hang together? Does the story ring true? (Sui, 2000, p. 328).

For Nietzsche (1986, p. 219) objective truth does not exist and has become "a mobile army of metaphors, metonyms and anthropomorphisms – in short, human relations, which have been enhanced transposed and [rhetorically] embellished" because only interpretations exist.

Sandercock (2003, p. 12) stated that "stories can often provide a far richer understanding of the human condition, and thus of [economic development]… than traditional social science and, for that reason alone, deserve more attention". Storytelling and communicative action can best be articulated with metaphors. Metaphors enable people to understand the incomprehensible by substituting a *common-sense* fact for the incomprehensible (Cresswell, 1997, p. 332). They shape the way we perceive an issue and debate the solution. The problem, however, with metaphors is that they lead us to believe that *we* think by likening one thing to another, as though thought were simply a form of recognition and comparison added on to an already objective reality (Colebrook, 2002b, p. 70).

Deleuze contends that there is no difference between images, things, and motion (Deleuze, 1995, p. 42). Therefore, metaphors can take on the heterogeneity of the multiple. Because of one's desire to succeed, especially in the context of daily practice in a globalised economy, an economic development practitioner often creates his or her own reality with metaphors when promoting the virtues of their particular patch. Beauregard (1993, p. 276) stated that these:

> metaphors are not necessarily based on empirical analyses but become essential rhetorical strategies. Hence, knowledge is politically vacuous until it is situated in a framework of meanings that motivate investors to act.

An often used metaphor in economic development describes the process as building a growth machine (Holupka and Shlay, 1993, pp. 179–180). A growth machine is often a coalition of local government, some unions, and place bound business interests like utilities, newspapers, real estate developers, and retail establishments pursuing their agenda of urban renewal or regional development and the creation of safe middle-income enclaves. The growth machine is an interconnected web of interests that is largely taken for granted by practitioners at least partially because they are often a part of it. Deleuze's concept of '*war machines**' and '*body without organs**'[6] fits nicely with this line of reasoning (Deleuze and Guattari, 1987). This implies that the practitioner needs to recognise that rhetorical descriptions written as promotional material are essentially stories that are designed to lure potential investors and are not necessarily based on facts.

One should note that Deleuze and Guattari had strong views on marketing and advertising and how it relates to philosophy as per the following:

> This is our concern, we are the creative ones, we are the idea men! We are the friend of the concept, we put it into our computers. Information and creativity, concept and enterprise; there is already an abundant bibliography. Marketing has preserved the idea of a certain relationship between the concept and the event. But here the concept has become the set of the product displays…and the event has become the exhibition that sets up various displays and the "exchange of ideas" it is supposed to promote. The only concepts are the exhibitions and the only events the products that can be sold (Deleuze and Guattari, 1994, p. 10).

This implies that…Deleuze's (as well as Guattari's) influence reaches across a broad range of disciplines, theories and philosophy. His ideas are easily adapted to a vast range of thoughts. This implies that the Deleuzian mantra of experimenting and creating new and innovative ideas can be applied to advertising, promotion and marketing as well as established academic fields such as planning, geography, architecture, anthropology and economic development.

Metaphors have been creatively deployed to understand everything from urban form to the globalisation process in New Zealand (Amin and Thrift, 2002; Pawson and Le Heron, 2005; Sui, 2000; Tuan, 1978). Metaphors have also been used to influence public debate, policy, and theory. Wyatt argues that metaphors have more than a descriptive function and also carry normative connotations (Wyatt, 2004). The writings of Deleuze and Guattari seem to provide theoretical metaphors

6 A body without organs (BwO) is a term for the changing social body of desire. Desire seeks new channels and different combinations to realise itself, thus forming a *BwO*. Desire is not limited to the affections of a subject.

which describe many things including the non-commercial aspects of the Net. For instance, the *rhizome** metaphor captures how cyberspace is organised as an open-ended, spontaneous and horizontal network. Their Body-without-Organs phrase can even be used to romanticise cyber-sex (Barbrook, 2003).

Deleuze once suggested that we should kill metaphors (Deleuze and Guattari, 1986, p. 70) because the very idea of a metaphor implies that there is a literal objective world that we then think about through an image or figure. When Deleuze denies that any of the terms he uses are metaphors or even so much as figuratively conceived it is because to his mind they are conceptualisations (Buchanan, 2000, p. 60). Deleuze also rejects the idea that 'all we have are metaphors' for this suggests that there is a real world forever lying out of the reach of our mental image of the world. This leads one to conclude that metamorphosis is the contrary of metaphor (Deleuze and Guattari, 1986, p. 22). Consequently, one should consider treating the metaphors of economic development as "metafictions[7] – self-conscious artefacts that invite deconstruction and scepticism" (Gough, 1993, p. 622).

The use of metaphorical concepts as assessment tools for evaluating social phenomena is well established in the literature (Chen, 2005; R. Davies, 2004; Innes and Booher, 1999; Kostianinen, 2002). The metaphor of a network is a good example of this type of research. Horelli (2002, p. 4) elaborated by writing that:

> Presently, the network has become established as a metaphor for the general organisational and technological order which has been created by a variety of interdependent processes characterised by complexity, self-organisation, coevolvement and emergence. Unlike the *machine*, which was the dominant metaphor in the industrial society, the network unfolds in two ways. On the one hand, the network refers to the wholeness of communication, i.e. the system of interdependent nodes and links. On the other hand, it contains dynamic elements and processes that reject any uniformity. Consequently, the network metaphor allows the examination of a variety of different theories, techniques and practice within the same framework.

She went on to analyse her case by initiating a metaphorical assessment of the emerging network of young people in the North-Karelia region of Finland. Her next step was to investigate the spatial and temporal aspects of the emerging network and finally undertaking an analytic assessment of the evaluation process. This type of research demonstrates the effectiveness of metaphorical assessment methodologies and their potential applicability for understanding the practice of local economic development.

The potential of metaphors as a tool to develop new ways of thinking has been delineated in the geography literature (Barnes, 1991, 1996; Buttimer, 1982, 1993; Graham, 1982; Livingstone, 1981; Tuan, 1978). Cresswell stated that:

---

7 A detailed explanation of metafiction can be found in Waugh (Waugh, 1984).

> [Economic development] engagements with metaphor have been restricted to its use in language and text, within the discipline…a more liberal view of metaphor as thought and action will enable [economic development practitioners] to develop a fuller appreciation of human action in space. The significance of metaphor to [economic development] extends, in other words, well beyond the use of metaphors…The [economic development] interpretation of metaphors as they are thought and acted out in the realms of politics and ideology can do much to delineate the praxis of everyday life. Indeed, by critiquing and transforming established metaphors or by suggesting new ones, [economic development practitioners] might provide alternative and more provocative way of thinking and acting (Cresswell, 1997, p. 343).

According to Cresswell (p.332) metaphorical analogies thus generate ideas which provide leaps in understanding that in turn lead to theorising. This book asserts that these stories and metaphorical analogies can lead to a theory that offers a framework for understanding the practice of economic development by viewing them through a Deleuzian lens (Rowe, 2007).

The importance of metaphors and stories in economic development, geography and urban planning has been previously noted in the literature (Bingham and Mier, 1993; Cresswell, 1997; Eckstein and Throgmorton, 2003; Sandercock, 2003; Sui, 2000; Tuan, 1978). The literature also indicates that if economic developers want to be more effective in translating knowledge to action then practitioners should pay more attention to the craft of storytelling and learn to use metaphors more effectively (Sandercock, 2003, p. 20). Metaphors and stories are useful tools for the economic development practitioner; however, theorists within the discipline have failed to expand metaphorical analysis and other tools into theory. Therefore, as the literature indicates, metaphors and stories are a good starting point for developing alternative theory and must be incorporated into any framework or general theory of local economic development because they have become a crucial resource in forging new theory (Chesters and Welsh, 2005, p. 192).

A Poststructural Theoretical Framework

In order to move the discipline beyond metaphors, this writer encourages the economic development fraternity to open their minds to alternative viewpoints and embrace the challenge to develop a theoretical framework for understanding the practice of economic development. This can be accomplished by theorists expanding their bag of tools by thinking outside the square to include poststructuralist methodologies. From a Deleuzian critique this is necessary because in the "discourse of creativity this means thinking, being creative, in new ways and not in ways prescribed and recognised by our current understanding" (Jeanes, 2006, p. 129) of theorising.

I strongly recommend that an economic development professional attain a comprehensive understanding of the traditional theories discussed in Part 3 in order to be an effective practitioner. In addition, this writer argues for an alternative (poststructuralist) approach to understanding the discipline that challenges many commonsense notions, standard codes and orthodox beliefs. From a Deleuzian viewpoint the commonsense, conventional and orthodox world is ultimately illusory. "Genuine [understanding]…occurs through signs which takes us beyond the illusion of habit and common sense to the truths of what Proust calls *essences* and Deleuze labels *differences*" (Bogue, 2004, p. 328). What escapes orthodox thought is difference, or the genuinely *new*, which can only be engaged through an *imageless thought* (Bogue, 2004, p. 333). In order to generate new connections and conceptual transformations that move beyond existing frameworks, one has to "want to do something with respect to new uncommon forces, which we don't quite yet grasp, who have a certain taste for the unknown" (Rajchman, 2000, p. 6). Thus, the orthodox approach can be conceptualised as the negation of *difference*. As a result, one of the key outcomes of this book is to challenge the orthodox understanding (beliefs, opinion or *doxa*) of the practice of economic development and develop a genuinely new framework for understanding and perhaps even theorising the discipline.

According to Gare (1995), a strict poststructuralist approach would involve many separate and unrelated debates responding to specific issues or local experiences. As argumentation and research methodology is advanced, one should develop a more encompassing logic of inquiry (B. Grant and Giddings, 2002; McLennan, 2002, p. 485). Consequently, this writer believes that a meta-theory of local economic development is needed to bridge the gap between the disparate ancillary theories offered by economics, geography, planning for economic development practice. The literature indicates that although there is no clear, hierarchical, tree-like sequence of theories culminating in a meta-theory describing economic development, there is a complex web of interrelationships between and across the diverse facets of economic development that would be described by Deleuze to consitute a *rhizome*, defined as "an acentred, non-hierarchical, non-signifying system without a general and without an organising memory or central autonomon, defined solely by a circulation of states" (Deleuze and Guattari, 1987, p. 21). Such a rhizomatically derived meta-theory[8] would be locally based and bottom-up and will be argued to be able to explain the disconnect between economic development strategies, initiatives and the occurrence of real world economic activities (Alpin, 2000, p. 280).

Increasingly critical social science research investigating problems of economic and regional development has moved from quantitative analysis into the realm of qualitative and case-study mythologies (Johnston and Plummer, 2005). However, the "*qualitative turn* taken by some in critical regional [and economic development] studies may only be just beginning, and there is a great deal of creative methodological work yet to do in deepening its explanatory penetration" (Peck, 2003, p. 736). Hence, in order to develop an explanatory framework for

8 This meta-theory may be applicable to varying aspects of planning practice and other fields of endeavour.

understanding the practice of economic development this writer suggests that one should employ poststructuralist research methods, *actor-network theory** (ANT) and case-study[9] methodologies.

Poststructuralism rests on an assumption that no-one can stand outside the traditions or discourses of their time. As Pratt (2000, p. 626) explains, "a poststructuralist conceptualisation both frames and regulates social reality, it literally brings reality into being", and by doing so, "profoundly disrupts the distinction between representation and pre-discursive reality". From this perspective, a poststructuralist approach offers a valid way forward. The poststructural subject can be described as being a relaxed and flexible person who constitutes his or her own social and spatial reality (Ernste, 2004, p. 441). Poststructuralist thinkers broadly see:

> the world as heterogeneous, composed of a vast plurality of interpretation in which knowledge and truth are contingent and therefore ultimately undecidable. In this world, identity is inherently decentred and fluid because [it is] constituted in unstable relations of difference (Dunn, 1998, p. 175).

For this reason, "the search for grand narratives [such as an explanatory theory for the practice of economic development] will be replaced by more local, small-scale theories fitted to specific problems and specific situations" (Denzin and Lincoln, 1994, p. 11) such as a framework for understanding the practice of local economic development.

The commonsense view of discourse is the spoken language people use to represent reality. In contrast, discourses in poststructuralist theory are interrelated systems of social meanings that "systematically form the objects of which they speak" (Foucault, 1972, p. 49). Language therefore is not a stable, transparent representation of reality. It is rather an historical and unconscious force that structures the realities we experience and the self that does the experiencing. In this sense, discourses offer individuals ways to understand and speak about the world at the same time as actually constituting those individuals, speaking through them as their subjects. This line of reasoning would appear to lead Foucault toward *structuralism*. However, whereas structuralists search for homogeneity in a discursive entity, Foucault (2005, p. 389) focuses on differences. As discussed above, this writer argues for the need for shaping a theory to understand the chaos of markets, global forces and multiple actors as they relate to the practice of local economic development. Consequently, this chapter will establish that the practice of local economic development is a complex transdisciplinary field of endeavour that can best be understood by embracing the Deleuzian concept of difference.

---

9 As per Flyvbjerg (2004, pp. 297–8) case studies are essential in order to demonstrate and test an explanatory framework because practitioners need real world examples to understand the relationship between theory and practice.

The Deleuzian concept of *difference* embraces chaos and complexity because "difference finds its own concept in the posited contradiction: it is here that it becomes pure, intrinsic, essential, qualitative, synthetic and productive; here it no longer allows indifference to subsist" (Deleuze, 1994, p. 45). Consequently, Deleuze approached problems such as 'How to theorise local economic development?' as something that does not have a single simple solution because a problem is something that defines a field of different drives or pressures as problematical because each solution merely transforms the problem and creates new challenges (Williams, 2003, p. 57). For Deleuze, a problem is determined because it cannot be distinguished from a chaotic state. This is important because as Deleuze stated (as quoted by McMahon, 2005, p. 42) "if philosophy is to have a positive and direct relations with things, it is only to the extent that it claims to grasp [an understanding of the practice of local economic development]...in its difference from all that is not it" and that the problem of difference is both "methodological and ontological." Consequently, the challenge for Deleuzian researchers is to develop a new perspective in order to resist *transcendence** (Stagoll, 2005, p. 73). In this writer's opinion, this can only be accomplished by *thinking outside the square* of orthodoxy by striving to develop a new way of thinking that has the potential to gain *immanence* by folding theory into practice.

Addressing the Complexity of the Chaotic Market, Global Forces and Multiple Actors

This writer asserts that a constructionalist/poststructuralist approach addresses the complexity of the chaotic market, global forces and multiple actors because poststructuralist methodologies will always be partial and subjective, even contradictory, because meanings are "multiple, unstable and open to interpretation" (McCouat and Peile, 1995, p. 10). This leads to what Deleuze would describe as a:

> becoming (genesis) but a becoming other (hetro), and it does so in response to an other (chaos). Neither...[economic development] not philosophy are chaotic, but they would be nothing more than mere opinions if they did not allow an element of chaos to enter in and transform and mobilse things (Colebrook, 2002a, p. 70).

From a Deleuzian perspective, this issue can be addressed through the doctrine of *hylomorphism**. Deleuze, through this doctrine, stresses the need to impose order upon chaos. According to Smith (2004) hylomorphism *folds* the chaotic mass of clay into a mold in order to create *immanence**. In this situation, the clay can be conceptualised as the practice of local economic development and the mold as rhizomatic *econphilosophy** (see next chapter). This reinforces the notion that the practice of local economic development is complex and sometimes chaotic and at the best of times is difficult to manoeuvre through the *assemblage* of forces that impact upon the practitioner.

This writer argues that a constructionalist/poststructuralist approach based on difference can and should be developed drawing on Foucault's (2005, p. 377) statement that "all knowledge…proceeded to the ordering of its material by the establishment of differences and defined those differences by the establishment of an order". In other words, Foucault believed that a 'human science' needs to be codified according to its differences. This writer has argued throughout this book that a theory of economic development based on difference can be developed by embracing Deleuzian philosophy because the concept of difference resonates with the complex and chaotic discipline of local economic development.

McMahon (2005, p. 42–43) believes that Deleuze's concept of difference equates with the "true goal of philosophy" and should be tied to the concept of identity. In other words, one should develop theory based on difference and identity. Deleuze (as cited by McMahon, 2005, p. 42) stated that 'If philosophy is to have a positive and direct relation with things, it is only to the extent that it claims to grasp the thing itself in what it is, in its difference from all that is not it". This means that one should address differences outside the concept in question by relating them to the concept of identity because as Deleuze (1994, p. 262) asserted it is "ceasing to be thought [and] difference dissipate into non-being".

This writer will utilise poststructural methodologies to deconstruct/deploy Deleuzian concepts in the next chapter in order to delineate the path toward developing a meta-theory for understanding the practice of local economic development. According to Grant and Perren (2002), a meta-theory can be translated as the philosophical assumptions made by researchers before they construct theories. The meta-theory will be developed in the concluding chapter by presenting and developing a rhizomatic *econphilosophy* of economic development. A number of methodological tools will be presented that will enable one to visualise emerging spatial economic activities as rhizomes which in turn can be visualised as mushrooms (or economic opportunities) popping up on the landscape. The metaphorical tools such as the rhizome, if embraced, will facilitate practitioners to understand the need for constantly reinventing their local communities by developing new and innovative initiatives and approaches to solve their unique local problems. The meta-theory will describe a new way of understanding the complex issues of economic development that finds theory folded into practice. Widder as quoted by Hillier (2007, p. 9) stated that "the *standard of success* for any critical theory is the degree to which it overcomes simplifications of identity and representation". A key aim of this book is to offer a viable framework for understanding the practice of economic development which will be relevant to scholars and practitioners.

Latour and others further refined poststructural methodology with *Actor Network Theory** (ANT) (Latour, 2005; Law and Hassard, 1999). ANT is an interdisciplinary approach to the social sciences and technology studies which is closely related to this research in terms of *complexity* and locality, activity and systems theories. The ANT perspective attempts to explain and interpret social and technological *evolution* by integrating human and non-human actions into the same conceptual framework. As a result, humans and non-humans are sometimes both referred to as *actants*. According to Ernste (2004, p. 448) poststructural insights can be combined with ANT through post-metaphysical and post-dualistic conceptualisations of actors (economic development practitioners) and their actions (economic development strategies and their action plans).

Traditional scientists use deductive reasoning to generate ideas that are tested in the real world. In scientific research, the researcher moves in a systematic fashion from the definition of a problem and the selection of concepts on which to focus (Polit, Beck, and Hungler, 2001, p. 13). Experimental-type research uses primarily deductive forms of human reasoning. Naturalistic inquiry primarily uses inductive and abductive forms of reasoning. Deductive reasoning involves moving from a general principle to understanding a specific case. A deductive reasoning approach is used to describe, test or predict the application of theory and rules to a specific phenomenon. As a result, it is crucial to distinguish social science models from natural science laws because the former yields predictions in an idealised world (classical economists often regarded this as a *natural order*). For example, despite the universal law of gravity, the reasons that objects such as birds or airplanes can fly can be readily understood if the physics are properly explained. Accordingly, "a law applies to all cases, a model to *ideal,* that is, to *particular* cases" (Boudon, 1991, p. 67).

In contrast to nature science, social science cannot produce a predictive theory of the world but, as argued in this book, social science has the potential to develop an explanatory framework (Caterino and Schram, 2006, p. 3). To recap, most traditional transcendental social science research encompasses aspects of the following:

- Positivism which assumes an objective world in which findings can be replicated and be applied generally; this is the dominant approach across science and engineering, but has proven inadequate, to date, in theorising the practice of economic development;
- Interpretive social science which deals with social and individual meaning systems; it has a clear applicability to social and cultural factors, and some institutional factors; and
- Critical social science which is an action research model, often with Marxist influences, aimed at changing the situation which is being studied through the understanding and involvement of the actors.

Since none of the above enjoys convincing empirical support (because of questions of causality), one can argue that in order to develop an explanatory framework as alluded to above, one has to embrace a constructionist approach. Compared to the law-oriented and idealising notions of theory predicated on transcendental ideas, the constructivist approach entails a very different notion of knowledge. The deductive-nomological ideal provides a strict separation between scientific knowledge and everyday knowledge. According to the constructivist position, in contrast, the line of demarcation between science and everyday knowledge is fuzzy (Markusen, 2003). Consequently, social science theory is not in principle different from everyday knowledge which is why Deleuze (2006, p. 2008) stated that "theory does not express, translate, or serve to apply practice: it is practice".

Most poststructuralist approaches imply a constructivist notion of theory in which the basic structure of everyday knowledge is conceptualised as discourses, which are in turn analysed by means of analogies often drawn from linguistics (Cobb, 1999; Kaufman, 2004). Social science theories are embedded in such discourses. As a consequence, the social sciences influence the practices of institutions, media, professions and disciplines of modern society. Constructivists argue that multiple theories will lead to better explanations (Glaser and Strauss, 1967). However, it must be emphasised again, that a constructivist approach does not generate general theories, although by resisting decontextualisation, they often provide strong explanatory frameworks (Dessler, 1999). In contrast, critical theory has focused more on ethical foundations and less on concrete paradigms involved in the explanatory efforts of applied social science.

Theory is a statement that seeks to explain or predict a particular phenomenon. Empiricism refers to observing and/or experimenting, while objectivity assumes that the research can be replicated and the facts are not distorted by personal feelings or bias (Doel, 2001; Gregory, 1991). When researchers critically examine an existing theory to see if observed phenomena are consistent with what the theory predicts, they are using a deductive approach (Ward and Holman, 2001, pp. 48–49). These models are science focused and biology based. It has shaped the way Western science has viewed and conducted research since the Renaissance. The models are based on an assumption of scientific rationality, an emphasis on objective, numerical measurement that highlights physical and chemical data. Researchers employing the scientific method believe that knowledge can be experimentally proven. It is identifiable, measurable and statistically deduced (Senior and Vivesah, 1998).

Engaging the Practitioner

I believe that a constructionalist/poststructuralist approach can engage economic development practitioners and, if applied, provide a better understanding of the discipline. A constructionalist or a poststructalist approach is concerned with factors and outcomes, and these ideas are thoroughly enmeshed in thinking about experimentation and questionnaire design (Crisp et al., 2004). This approach can be defined as the degree to which a given account of the world or self is sustained across time and it is not dependent on the objective validity of the account but on the vicissitudes of social process (Gergen, 1994, p. 51). Deleuze's philosophical method is a kind of constructivism that can be presented as the geography of reason (Semetsky, 2007, p. 198). Constructivism to Deleuze and Guattari (1994, p. 7) "requires every creation to be a construction on a plan that gives it an autonomous existence. To create concepts is, at the very least, to make something" because "philosophy is a constructivism, and constructivism has two qualitative different complementary aspects: the creation of concepts and the laying out of a plane" (Deleuze and Guattari, 1994, pp. 35–6).

It is essential to understand that constructuralism does not prove causality because it does not produce a mechanical template that can be reproduced in different geographic localities. As a result, poststructuralists seek to develop an alternative set of assumptions that recognises the impossibility of determining universal truths. As Denzin (1994, p. 184) maintains:

> it challenges [the] desire to secure a fully centred human subject comfortably situated in a world of roles, statuses, norms, values and structured social systems. It also intends to expose the underlying ideological presuppositions that organize contemporary research and theory…

and thus, a constructionalist/poststructuralist approach has the potential to engage the economic development practitioner by offering a meta-theory that helps to bridge the gap between theory and practice.

Does Economic Development need an Overarching Meta-theory?

This writer argues that local economic development, as an emerging academic discipline, needs an overarching meta-theory in order to be relevant. McLennan (2002, p. 484–6) has indicated that as "inherited academic forms of argumentation and research methodology becomes more fluid and multiple, pressure mounts to constitute a more encompassing logic of enquiry", although most theorists still "tend to favour description and evaluation". Consequently, this writer asserts that an explanatory framework is required to bridge the gap between theory and practice.

A meta-theory is needed because social scientific interpretation is not cumulative and produces no equivalent body of predictive, universalist or totalising theory. Rather, its *raison d'être* is contextual, situational and its methodology is a "concrete practical rationality" (Flyvbjerg, 2001, p. 29). This writer maintains that economic development needs a meta-theory because the borrowed theories of other disciplines fail to adequately address the complexities and chaos of the field. This writer argues that the discipline needs a meta-theory that is pragmatic, understandable, flexible and adaptable in order to respond to ever changing mix of challenges that constitutes the practice of local economic development. According to Easter (2005), the Deleuzoguattarian ontology is grounded in difference, process and immanence and thus, resonates strongly with the practice of local economic development.

The Need for the Development of a Critical Appraisal Framework

This section will make the case for a rhetorical coherent argument for the development of a pragmatic appraisal framework[10] for economic development. It will also explain why traditional evaluation frameworks that employ empirical tests are not appropriate for assessing economic development programmes. It will provide evidence of *reterritorialisation**, *folding** and *assemblages** that can be used as methodological tools for understanding the discipline.

The need to develop an effective assessment framework for economic development has been identified as a key priority since the late 1980s (Bennett, 1988, p. 47) and subsequently, as a result,

> State and local governments have increased their focus on investments in economic development in recent years. With increased effort comes increased desire to determine the quality and results of that effort. Managers need to be able to regularly identify the strengths and weaknesses of individual program[mes]. Yet, effective means for assessment of program[me] quality and outcomes are lacking (Hatey et al. as quoted by Czohara, 2004, p. 3).

It has also been shown that the lack of a robust theoretical understanding of the economic development discipline "leads to a weak intellectual basis for the development of new strategies" (Hillier, 2007, p. 75). Traditional evaluation frameworks have attempted to measure the effectiveness of economic development programmes or strategies by measuring the relative improvements over time in several key economic indicators such as the growth in new jobs (Milkman et al., 1978, pp. 14–15). Subsequently, economic development strategies[11] and initiatives are often considered successful if they appear to have a positive effect on the business climate (Reese and Fasenfest, 1997, p. 197) underpinned by the general belief that more jobs must be good (Fasenfest, 1997, p. 285). However, "simple job counting is hardly an adequate evaluation technique, and will not ensure that these efforts retain support" (Felsenstein and Persky, 2007, p. 25). Some cynics have even argued that many economic development programmes are not rigorously evaluated because they are designed to be visible but not necessarily to enhance the local economy (Dewar, 1998, p. 85).

A key question to be addressed in any evaluation is if the benefits of a programme or initiative outweigh the costs incurred (Bartik and Bingham, 1997, p. 249). Other questions are whether the programme goals were accomplished

---

10 A framework is the conceptual underpinnings of a study. Not every study is a based on a theory or conceptual model, but every study has a framework. In a study based on a theory, the framework is referred to as the theoretical framework (Polit, Beck, and Hungler, 2001, p. 146).

11 Deleuze viewed strategies as "conceived or seen possibilities" (Deleuze, 2003, p. 94).

and what would have happened in the absence of the programme[12] (Bartik, 2002). Such questions are designed to address causality or to measure the effectiveness of a programme, but in this writer's opinion, traditional evaluations have become a "quagmire of good intentions and bad measures" (Clarke and Gaile, 1992). Deleuze would have suggested that without proof of causality, statistics used as measures are just *random influxes of chaotic data* (Colebrook, 2002a, p. 79). In a similar vein, Latour (2003, p. 35) believes that practitioners should be more concerned about "associations which allow connections to be made" then attempting to prove causality. This is important because most measures fail to prove causality and location decisions are based on many factors that are out of the control of the local economic development practitioner. For example, a better and more quantifiable measure may be to evaluate the number of successful grant applications submitted or the number of businesses that graduate from the local incubator (Osama, 2006).

Most assessments employ survey methods to ascertain if the service, tax incentive or initiative was useful to the recipient[13] (Turok, 1989, p. 588). Bartik suggests that more rigorous evaluations are feasible if they are done through random experimentation using statistical analysis with comparison and focus groups that are linked to regional econometric models (Bartik, 2002, p. 33). The assessment of options, both quantitative and qualitative[14], considers the performance of each option against a range of criteria and examines the arguments used to justify the selection of the criterion (Davies, 2006, p. 429). However, most researchers are in agreement that successful performance measures need to be relatively understandable, relevant and measurable (Hatry et al., 1990).

In the philosophy of science, empiricism is dependent upon one's experience. One of the strengths of quantitative research and positivism is that it produces hard numerical data (that's easy to count) which in turn demonstrates an ordered system but a regional market comprising millions of actants in a globalised environment is inherently not an ordered or striated system, however desirous this may be for some. However, positvism requires research to be replicable, provides cause and effect with simple mathematical results. This is fundamental because the scientific method in the natural sciences requires all hypotheses and theories to be able to be tested against real world observations. Within this dualism of positivism versus constructionism the positivist side is easily recognised by their use of "formal propositions, quantifiable measures of variables, hypobook testing, and

12 In poststructuralism, such questions pursue a rhizomatic consequentialist approach to solving problems.

13 In the New Zealand context, since grant opportunities are limited and tax incentives are not available, an evaluation framework needs to consider the quality of service, number of businesses assisted as a percentage of total businesses and if the service actually helped the business grow.

14 Qualculation blurs the distinction between qualitative and quantitative techniques (Callon and Law, 2005).

the drawing of inferences about a phenomenon from a representative sample to a stated population" (Klein and Myers 1999, p. 69). The emergence of a positivist tradition which relies on empirical work and its statistical evaluation can probably be explained by many factors such as the natural science background of many of the researchers.

However, economic development is a social and not a natural science (Flyvbjerg, 2001). Consequently, this writer argues that because of the difficulties of measuring the success of various initiatives, it would be more appropriate to use Deleuzian terms for dealing with dynamic complexity and chaos than traditional methodologies. This book argues that the demands for performity accountability are a meaningless process that negates the intangible benefits of the practice of economic development. As a consequence, this calls for the development of new pragmatic qualitative appraisal theory derived from alternative philosophical viewpoints. This assertion is supported by Flyvbjerg (2001, p. 25) who believes that "it is…not meaningful to speak of *theory* in the study of social phenomena, at least not in the sense that *theory* is used in natural science".

Quantitative research controls extraneous variables and the data can be assessed by standardised testing and is therefore considered more reliable than qualitative studies (Carr, 1994). A weakness is that it does not explain why people act as they do and that often people are treated merely as a source of data (Caterino and Schram, 2006, p. 5). Another weakness in quantitative research is that the more tightly controlled the study, the more difficult it becomes to confirm if the research situation reflects real life. The very components of scientific research that demand control of variables can lower the generalisability of the study. Deleuze traced qualitative difference or difference in kind (or difference in degree) to a fluid continuum of intensity, thereby avoiding Bergson's argument that qualitative difference is itself being differentiated. As Deleuze wrote, it: "show[s] the way in which a thing varies qualitatively in time" (Deleuze, 1988, p. 32).

Traditional quantitative research requires a researcher to propose a theory and then subject it to empirical testing. The conduct of quantitative research is concerned with applying theories and techniques (both descriptive and inferential) to assist in the manipulation of data. The capacity to count and aggregate data with precise methods is the basic principle underlying quantitative research (Saltman and O'Dea, 2002, p. 175). It is essential that the sample is representative to the population as a whole. It is, however, generally recognised that "no quantitative method in isolation can capture the complexity of regional [and local economic] development" (Wetzstein, 2007, p. 41).

For example, in order to measure creativity Richard Florida had to create new indicators using regression analysis and other advanced statistical tools. One such unique indictor considered what people did with their degrees instead of just measuring average education levels (Marlet and van Woerkens, 2004, p. 24). Such qualitative and sophisticated quantitative methods provide useful indicators to a region's economy but often do not address issues of (or prove) causality or if the programme initiatives actually created any jobs or increased wealth in the community. In support of my argument, Storper and Manville (2006, p. 1252) has stated that "correlation is not causation and while Florida is doubtless aware of the difference, it seems" many are not. Consequently, this book argues from a Deleuzian perspective that a pragmatic qualitative appraisal framework should seek to develop an understanding of the processes and underlying concepts of economic development because causality (in most cases) cannot be proven by the empirical measurements used by Florida and others.

This writer also argues that, from a constructionalist viewpoint, traditional assessment methodologies employing quantitative research do not provide an adequate framework from which to theorise the discipline. The fundamental idea of constructionism is that we do not live in a world of objective realities but in a world made meaningful by interaction. Meaning is constructed in communication, stories and discourses (Thorgmorton, 1993). Individual and collective realities correspond because of the shared use of narratives. At its core constructionism is a doctrine which states that social constructions not only describe reality but constitute it (Latour and Woolgar, 1979). Accepting these constructionist premises means that we no longer think in terms of objective reality but in terms of signs that acquire their meaning in communication and discourses which produce the narratives in which we describe ourselves and the world. Castells (2000, p. 403) states that "there is no separation between *reality* and symbolic representation. In all societies humankind has existed in and acted through a symbolic environment". The last section in this chapter discusses the merits and pitfalls of performance-based and performance-measured evaluations.

Performance-becoming Oriented Concepts for Understanding

From a Deleuzian perspective, this leads one to conclude that economic development strategies and initiatives should be based on *performance-becoming* instead of *performance-measured* outcomes because performativity[15] accounts for the "unfolding creation of happenings in everyday life as we encounter, relate to and negotiate [with] other agents in the world" (Rycroft, 2005, p. 252). As a result, Dewsbury (2000, p. 488) argues that performativity comes through convergences and ruptures and "often it is our surroundings that appropriate what we do…such that we are forced into 'never-before-occuring' situations that 'become us'". This means that any action orientated becoming has to be designed to consider the context, constraints and the unique local conditions faced by practitioners. According to Dewsbury (2000, p. 475) "general performance, *practice*…is constituted in the

15 Performativity can be considered part of the spectrum of connecting or associative practices which might affect difference and movement towards alternatives (Le Heron, 2005). For further discussions on performativity see Butler (1997), Casper Brauun (2004), Kraftl (2007), Latham and Conradson (2003), Lyotard (1984), Nash (2000) and Thrift and Dewsbury (2000). For a different application, it is useful to compare performance based planning in the United States, Australia and New Zealand (Baker, Sipe, and Gleeson, 2006).

performance". Carrying this thought further, Crouch (2003, p. 1946) suggested that there should be "a focus on the nuances and facets of performativity, and the uncertainties and possibilities that performativity may produce; using the notion of [performance based criterion]…in a Deleuzian sense of folds, complexity and possibilities". Thus, in a performance[16] becoming concepts for understanding, criterion[17] would be concerned with their transcendence[18], converting constraints into opportunities, and inventing new trajectories, new responses of unheard-of futures (Massumi, 1992, p. 101). A practitioner can begin to convert constraints into opportunities by using the techniques delineated in this book.

This suggests that "attempts to evaluate or measure performance or performativity[19] are fated to be problematic snapshots or precarious stabilisations of inherently unstable and dynamic conditions" (Hillier, 2007, p. 296) because performance evaluations are always open to *de-* and *reterritorialisations* of *lines of flight*. As a result, establishing indicators against which an economic development agency's performance can be measured and evaluated is difficult. The purpose according to Albrechts et al. (2003, p. 293) is to "develop a quality portrait or profile giving a deeper insight into the qualities [of an initiative or an EDA] and to create a language for discussion and negotiation, and finally, to provide a sound…basis for a decision" to continue funding. Nevertheless, governments are still establishing performance standards in an attempt to measure the effectiveness of economic development agencies despite knowing that local practitioners have no control over the macro factors that drive the economy (Czohara and Melkers, 2004, pp. 6–25).

This writer argues that, despite all the sophisticated quantitative and qualitative techniques of forecasting and evaluating programmes, the available tools for the most part fail to prove causality or explain why the desired outcomes are often not achieved. It is also apparent that there is a poor correlation between economic development strategies and real world economic events. Therefore innovative action orientated becoming tools need to be developed that consider the relationship between the drivers of new economic activity with the strategies

16 Others have suggested that performance represents an idea rather than an operational standard (Mastop and Faludi, 1997, p. 817).

17 Tentative criteria may be developed from practical experience and judgement in order to anticipate potential becomings (Deleuze and Guattari, 1987, p. 251). These criteria may be applied as part of one's daily practice and the wisdom garnered from one's professional experience may be able to provide insights into crafting an appropriate appraisal framework. According to Schön (1983, pp. 42–3) this process includes experience, trial and error, intuition, and muddling through.

18 Foucault (1972, p. 203) attempted to break free from traditional Western thought by becoming a "subjection to transcendence" which transcends or lies outside. In this sense, transcendence can be equated with the truth.

19 "Performativity provides a particular focus to the possibility of opening up, in a Deleuzian sense, to the unexpected and the divergent in the 'excess' of multiple possibilities of what people do" (Dewsbury as quoted by Crouch, 2003, p. 1949).

and initiatives implemented by the practitioner. In essence, this writer is arguing that local economic development "needs tools for understanding and practising [a] complex and elusive" (Law and Urry, 2004, p. 404) discipline. Deleuzian philosophy may provide the way forward that will create an "open set of critical tools…evaluations and…creations (Semetsky, 2003, p. 27) in which challenges are "viewed as multiplicities of differential relations which stimulate creative thinking and innovation" (Hillier, 2007, p. 313).

Conclusions

This writer argues that conventional or positivistic social science research approaches cannot develop theory for economic development because positivism attempts to objectively observe phenomena and measure such phenomena using structured techniques. Such a general theory is not possible because, as demonstrated above, positive (or negative) economic growth often occurs regardless of the best efforts of the local practitioners. As a consequence, existing evaluation methodologies that measure statistical growth over time often fail to consider that many factors are almost entirely out of the control of local practitioners and, as a result, do not accurately reflect on or assess the effectiveness of economic development programmes or their strategies.

This chapter has also demonstrated that positivistic social science inquiry requires traditional quantitative research standards of statistical significance and as a result, is of little relevance to the practitioner. This research has also suggested that it has proven difficult to prove causality between economic growth over time and the initiatives available to implement an economic development strategy and the best efforts of the local practitioner. Therefore, in order to develop an alternative theoretical framework for understanding the discipline, one needs to embrace poststructural/constructionalist methodologies. This chapter has also demonstrated that economic development practitioners can be engaged by moving the discipline beyond metaphors.

References

Aay, H. and Van Langevelde, A.B. (2005), "A Dooyeweerd-based approach to regional economic development". *Tijdschrift voor Economische en Sociale Geografie 96*(2), 184–98.

Albrechts, L., Schreurs, J., and van den Broeck, J. (2003), "In search of indicators and processes for strengthening spatial quality: The case of Belgium". *Built Environment 29*(4), 288–95.

Alpin, G. (2000), "Environmental rationalism and beyond: Toward a more just sharing of power and influence". *Australian Geographer 31*(3), 273–87.

Amin, A. (2004), "Regions unbound: Towards a new politics of place". *Geografiska Annaler 86B*(1), 33–44.

Amin, A. and Thrift, N. (2002), *Cities Reimagining the Urban*. Cambridge: Polity Press.

Baker, D., Sipe, N., and Gleeson, B. (2006), "Performance-based planning: Perspectives from the United States, Australia, and New Zealand". *Journal of Planning Education and Research 25*(4), 396–409.

Banfield, E. (1971), "Ends and means in planning". In A. Faludi (ed.), *A Reader in Planning Theory* (pp. 139–50). New York: Pergamon Press.

Barbrook, R. (2003), *Deleuzoguattarians – The Holy Fools*. Retrieved 15 February, 2006, from http://libcom.org/library/deleuzoguattarians-barbrook.

Barnes, T.J. (1991), "Metaphors and conversations in economic geography: Richard Rorty and the gravity model". *Geografiska Annaler 73B*(2), 111–20.

Barnes, T.J. (1996), *Logics of Dislocation: Models, Metaphors, and Meanings of Economic Space*. New York: The Guilford Press.

Bartik, T.J. (2002), *Evaluating the Impacts of Local Economic Development Policies on Local Economic Outcomes: What has been Done and What is Doable?* Kalamazoo: The W.E. Upjohn Institute for Employment Research.

Bartik, T.J. and Bingham, R.D. (1997), "Can economic development programs be evaluated?" In R.D. Bingham and R. Mier (eds), *Dilemmas of Urban Economic Development: Issues in Theory and Practice* (pp. 246–77). Thousand Oaks, CA: Sage.

Beauregard, R.A. (1993), "Constituting economic development: A theoretical perspective". In R.D. Bingham and R. Mier (eds), *Theories of Local Economic Development* (pp. 267–83). Newbury Park, CA: Sage Publications.

Beauregard, R.A. (2005), "Introduction: Institutional transformations". *Planning Theory 4*(3), 203–207.

Bennett, R.J. (ed.) (1988), *Local Economic Development: Identifying the Research Priorities*. Swindon: Economic and Social Research Council.

Bingham, R.D. and Mier, R. (eds) (1993), *Theories of Local Economic Development: Perspectives from Across the Disciplines*. Newbury Park, CA: Sage Publications.

Bogue, R. (2004), "Search, swim and see: Deleuze's apprenticeship in signs and pedagogy of images". *Educational Philosophy and Theory 36*(3), 327–42.

Boudon, R. (1991), *Theories of Social Change*. Cambridge, UK: Cambridge University Press.

Buchanan, I. (2000), *Deleuzism: A Metacommentary*. Durham, NC: Duke University Press.

Buss, T.F. (1999), "The case against targeted industry strategies". *Economic Development Quarterly 13*(4), 339–56.

Butler, J. (1997), *Excitable Speech: A Politics of the Performative*. London: Routledge.

Buttimer, A. (1982), "Musing on Helicon: Root Metaphors and Geography". *Geografiska Annaler 64*(2), 89–96.

Buttimer, A. (1993), *Geography and the Human Spirit*. Baltimore: John Hopkins University Press.

Callon, M. and Law, J. (2005), "On qualculation, agency, and otherness". *Environment and Planning D: Society and Space 23*, 717–33.

Casper Brauun, J. (2004), "A nonhumanist disposition: On performativity, practical ontology, and intervention". *Configurations: A Journal of Literature 12*(2), 229–61.

Castells, M. (2000), *The Information Age: Economy, Society, and Culture* (2nd edn Vol. 1), Oxford, UK: Blackwell.

Caterino, B. and Schram, S. (2006), "Introduction: reframing the debate". In S. Schram and B. Caterino (eds), *Making Political Science Matter: Debating Knowledge, Research and Method* (pp. 1–13), New York: New York University Press.

Chen, H.-T. (2005), *Practical Program Evaluation: Assessing and Improving Planning, Implementation and Effectiveness*. London: Sage.

Chesters, G. and Welsh, I. (2005), "Complexity and social movement(s): Process and emergence in planetary action". *Theory, Culture and Society 22*(5), 187–211.

Chettiparamb, A. (2006), "Metaphors in complexity theory and planning". *Planning Theory 5*(1), 71–91.

Clarke, S.E. and Gaile, G.L. (1992), "The next wave: Postfederal local economic development strategies". *Economic Development Quarterly 6*, 187–98.

Cobb, T. (1999), "Applying constructivism: A test for the learner as scientist". *Educational Technology Research and Development 47*(3), 15–31.

Colebrook, C. (2002a), *Gilles Deleuze*. London: Routledge.

Colebrook, C. (2002b), *Understanding Deleuze*. Crows Nest, NSW: Allen and Unwin.

Cresswell, T. (1997), "Weeds, plagues, and bodily secretions: A geographical interpretation of metaphors of displacement". *Annals of the Association of American Geographers 87*(2), 330–45.

Crisp, B., Anderson, M., Orme, J., and Lister, P. (2004), Learning and teaching assessment: reviewing the evidence. *Social Work Education 23*(2), 199–215.

Crouch, D. (2003), "Spacing, performing, and becoming: Tangles in the mundane". *Environment and Planning A, 35*, 1945–60.

Czohara, L. and Melkers, J. (2004), *Performance Measurement in State Economic Development Agencies: Lessons and Next Steps for GDITT* (No. FRC Report No. 92), Atlanta: Georgia State University.

Davies, G. (2006), "The sacred and the profane: Biotechnology, rationality, and public debate". *Environment and Planning A, 38*, 423–43.

Davies, R. (2004), "Scale, complexity and the representation of theories of change". *Evaluation 10*(1), 101–121.

Deleuze, G. (1988), *Bergsonism* (H. Tomlinson and B. Habberjam, Trans.). New York: Zone Books.

Deleuze, G. (1994), *Difference and Repetition* (P. Patton, Trans.). New York: Columbia University Press.

Deleuze, G. (1995), *Negotiations, 1972–1990* (M. Joughin, Trans.). New York: Columbia University Press.

Deleuze, G. (2003), *Francis Bacon: The Logic of Sensation* (D. W. Smith, Trans.). London: Continuum.

Deleuze, G. (2006), *Foucault* (S. Hand, Trans. 7th edn). Minneapolis: University of Minnesota Press.

Deleuze, G. and Guattari, F. (1986), *Kafka: Toward a Minor Literature* (D. Polan, Trans.). Minneapolis: University of Minnesota Press.

Deleuze, G. and Guattari, F. (1987), *Thousand Plateaus: Capitalism and Schizophrenia* (B. Massumi, Trans.). Minneapolis: University of Minnesota Press.

Deleuze, G. and Guattari, F. (1994), *What is Philosophy?* (H. Tomlinson and G. Burchell, Trans.). New York: Columbia University Press.

Denzin, N.K. (1994), "Postmodernism and deconstructionism". In D. Dickens and A. Fontana (eds), *Postmodernism and Social Inquiry* (pp. 182–202). New York: Guilford Press.

Denzin, N.K. and Lincoln, Y.S. (1994), *Handbook of Qualitative Research.* Thousand Oaks, CA: Sage.

Dessler, D. (1999), "Constructivism within a positivist social science". *Review of International Studies 25*, 123–37.

Dewar, M. (1998), "Why state and local economic development programs cause so little economic development". *Economic Development Quarterl 12*(68–108).

Dewsbury, J.-D. (2000), "Performativity and the event: Enacting a philosophy of difference". *Environment and Planning D: Society and Space 18*, 473–96.

Doel, M.A. (2001), "la. Qualified quantified geography". *Environment and Planning D: Society and Space 19*, 555–72.

Dunn, R.G. (1998), *Identity Crisis: A Social Critique of Post-Modernity.* Minneapolis: University of Minnesota Press.

Easter, D. (2005), *Research literature review: Using sense-making methodology to study the culture wars.* Retrieved 28 December 2006, from http://communication.sbs.ohio-state.edu/sense-making/meet/2005/meet05easter_lit.pdf.

Eckstein, B. and Throgmorton, J. (eds) (2003), *Story and Sustainability: Planning, Practice and Possibility for American Cities.* Cambridge, MA: MIT Press.

Ernste, H. (2004), "The pragmatism of life in poststructuralist times". *Environment and Planning A, 36*, 437–540.

Fasenfest, D. (1997), "Commentary: Evaluations yes, but on whose behalf?" In R. D. Bingham and R. Mier (eds), *Dilemmas of Urban Economic Development: Issues in Theory and Practice* (pp. 284–8). Thousand Oaks, CA: Sage Publications.

Felsenstein, D. and Persky, J. (2007), "Evaluating local job creation: A 'jobs chains' perspective". *Journal of the American Planning Association 73*(1), 23–34.

Flyvbjerg, B. (1998), "Habermas and Foucault: thinkers for civil society?" *Journal of Sociology 49*(2), 210–33.

Flyvbjerg, B. (2001), *Making Social Science Matter* (S. Sampson, Trans.). Cambridge, UK: Cambridge University Press.

Flyvbjerg, B. (2004), "Phronetic planning research: Theoretical and methodological reflections". *Planning Theory and Practice 5*(3), 283–306.

Flyvbjerg, B. and Richardson, T. (2002), "Planning and Foucault: In search of the dark side of planning theory". In P. Allemdinger and M. Tewdwr-Jones (eds), *Planning Futures: New Directions for Planning Theory* (pp. 44–62). London: Routledge.

Foucault, M. (1972), *The Archaeology of Knowledge and the Discourse on Language* (A. Sheridan Smith, Trans.). New York: Pantheon.

Foucault, M. (2005), *The Order of Things: Archaelogy of the Human Sciences*. London: Routledge.

Gare, A.E. (1995), *Postmoderism and the Environmental Crisis*. London: Routledge.

Gergen, K. (1994), "The social constructionist movement in modern psychology". *American Psychologist 40*, 266–75.

Glaser, B.G. and Strauss, A.L. (1967), *The Discovery of Grounded Theory*. New York: Aldine De Gruyter.

Gough, N. (1993), "Environmental education, narrative complexity and postmodern science/fiction". *International Journal of Science Education 15*(5), 607–625.

Graham, E. (1982), "Maps, metaphors and muddles". *The Professional Geographer 34*(3), 251–60.

Grant, B. and Giddings, L. (2002), "Making sense of methodologies: A paradigm framework for the novice researcher". *Contemporary Nurse 13*(1), 10–28.

Grant, P. and Perren, L. (2002), "Small business and entrepreneurial research: Meta-theories, paradigms and prejudices". *International Small Business Journal 20*(2), 185–211.

Gregory, D. (1991), "Interventions in the historical geography of modernity: Social theory, spatiality and the politics of representation". *Geografiska Annaler: Series B, Human Geography 73*(1), 17–44.

Gunder, M. (2005), "The production of desirous space: Mere fantasies of the utopian city?" *Planning Theory 4*(2), 173–99.

Harding, S. (1986), *The Science Question in Feminism*. Ithaca, NY: Cornell University Press.

Hillier, J. (2003), "Agonising over consensus – Why Habermasian ideals cannot be 'real'". *Planning Theory 2*(1), 37–59.

Hillier, J. (2007), *Stretching Beyond the Horizon: A Multiplanar Theory of Spatial Planning and Governance*. Aldershot, UK: Ashgate Publishing Limited.

Holupka, C.S. and Shlay, A. (1993), "Political economy and urban development". In R.D. Bingham and R. Mier (eds), *Theories of Local Economic Development* (pp. 175–90), Newbury Park, CA: Sage Publications.

Horelli, L. (2002, 10–12 October), *Network Evaluation from the Everyday-life Perspective – A Tool for Capacity Building and Voice.* Paper presented at the European Evaluation Society, Seville, Spain.

Innes, J. and Booher, D. (1999), "Consensus building and complex adaptive systems: A framework for evaluating collaborative planning". *Journal of the American Planning Association 65*(4), 412–23.

Jeanes, E.L. (2006), "'Resisting creativity, creating the new'. A Deleuzian perspective on creativity". *Creativity and Innovation Management 15*(2), 127–34.

Johnston, A. and Plummer, P. (2005), "What is policy-oriented research?" *Environment and Planning A, 37*, 1521–6.

Kaufman, D. (2004), "Constructivist issues in language learning and teaching". *Annual Review of Applied Linguistics 24*, 303–319.

Klein, H.K., and Myers, M.D. (1999), "A set of principles for conducting and evaluating interpretive field studies in information systems". *MIS Quarterly, 23*(1), 67–94.

Kostianinen, J. (2002), "Learning and the Ba' in the development network of an urban region". *European Planning Studies 10*(5), 613–31.

Kraftl, P. (2007), "Utopia, performativity, and the unhomely". *Environment and Planning D: Society and Space 25*, 120–43.

Laclau, E. (2000), "Identity and hegemony: The role of universality in the constitution of political logics". In J. Bulter, E. Laclau and S. Zizak (eds), *Contingency, Hegemony, Universality: Contemporary Dialogues on the Left* (pp. 44–89). London: Verso.

Laclau, E. (2006), "Why constructing a people is the main task of radical politics". *Critical Inquiry 32*, 646–80.

Lakoff, G. (1992), *The Contemporary Theory of Metaphor*. Retrieved 5 November 2006, from http://www.cardiff.ac.uk/encap/clcr/gordon/lakoff.pdf.

Latham, A. and Conradson, D. (2003), "The possibilities of performance". *Environment and Planning A, 35*, 1901–1906.

Latour, B. (2003), "Is re-modernization occurring- and if so, how to prove it?" *Theory, Culture and Society 20*(2), 35–48.

Latour, B. (2005), *Reassembling the Social: An Introduction to Actor-Network-Theory*. Oxford, UK: Oxford University Press.

Latour, B. and Woolgar, S. (1979), *Laboratory Life: The Social Construction of Scientific Facts*. London: Sage.

Law, J. and Hassard, J. (eds) (1999), *Actor Network Theory and After*. London: Blackwell Publishing.

Law, J. and Urry, J. (2004), "Enacting the social". *Economy and Society 33*(3), 390–410.

Le Heron, R. (2005), "Academic economic geography and sites of economic geography practice: Examples and reflections from New Zealand". In R. Le Heron and J. Harrington (eds), *New Economic Spaces: New Economic Geographies* (pp. 220–32), Aldershot, UK: Ashgate Publishing Limited.

Leach, M. and Boler, M. (1998), "Gilles Deleuze: Practising education through flight and gossip". In M. Peters (ed.), *Naming the Multiple: Poststructuralism and education* (pp. 149–72). London: Bergin and Carvey.

Livingstone, D.N. (1981), "Meaning through metaphor: Analogy as epistemology". *Annals of the Association of American Geographers 71*(1), 95–107.

Lyotard, J.-F. (1984), *The Postmodern Condition: A report on Knowledge*. Minneapolis: University of Minnesota Press.

Markusen, A. (2003), "Fuzzy concepts, scanty evidence, policy distance: The case for rigour and policy relevance in critical regional studies". *Regional Studies 37*(6/7), 701–717.

Marlet, G. and van Woerkens, C. (2004), *Skills and Creativity in a Cross-section of Dutch Cities*. Discussion paper series no. 04–29. Utrecht: Tjalling C. Koopmans Research Institute.

Martin, J.-C. (1999), "Deleuze's philosophy of the concrete". In I. Buchanan (ed.), *A Deleuzian Century?* (pp. 241–8), Durham, NC: Duke University Press.

Massumi, B. (1992), *A User's Guide to "Capitalism and Schizophrenia": Deviations from Deleuze and Guattari*. Cambridge, MA: MIT Press.

Mastop, H. and Faludi, A. (1997), "Evaluation of strategic plans: The performance process". *Environment and Planning B: Planning and Design 24*, 815–32.

McCouat, M. and Peile, C. (1995), "The micro politics of qualitative research traditions". In M. McCouat and C. Peile (eds), *Qualitative Research: Beyond the Boundaries* (pp. 2–16). Fremantle, WA: Curtin University of Technology.

McLennan, G. (2002), "Quandaries in meta-theory: Against pluralism". *Economy and Society 31*(3), 483–96.

McMahon, M. (2005), "Difference, repetition". In C. Stivale (ed.), *Gilles Deleuze: Key Concepts* (pp. 42–52). Montreal: McGill-Queens University Press.

Mier, R. and Bingham, R.D. (1993), "Metaphors of economic development". In R.D. Bingham and R. Mier (eds), *Theories of Local Economic Development: Perspectives from Across the Disciplines* (pp. 284–304). Newbury Park, CA: Sage Publications.

Mier, R. and Fitzgerald, J. (1991), "Managing economic development". *Economic Development Quarterly 5*, 268–79.

Milkman, R., Toborg, M., Perez, U., and Boyd, B. (1978), *Evaluating Economic Development Programs: A Methodology Handbook*. Washington, D.C.: Lazar Management Group.

Nash, C. (2000), "Performativity in practice: Some recent work in cultural geography". *Progress in Human Geography 24*, 653–64.

Nietzsche, F. (1986), "On truth and lies in an extra moral sense". In M. Taylor (ed.), *Deconstruction in Context*. Chicago: University of Chicago Press.

Ortony, A. (1993), *Metaphor and Thought* (2nd edn). Cambridge, UK: Cambridge University Press.

Osama, A. (2006), "Using a balanced scorecard to measure your economic development strategy". *Economic Development America* Fall, 26–9.

Pawson, E. and Le Heron, R. (2005), "Making contemporary economic landscapes". In J.E. Rowe (ed.), *Economic Development in New Zealand* (pp. 15–29). Aldershot, UK: Ashgate Publishers Limited.

Peck, J. (2003), "Fuzzy old world: A response to Markusen". *Regional Studies 37*(6/7), 729–40.

Polit, D., Beck, C., and Hungler, B. (2001b), *Essential of Nursing Research: Methods, Appraisal, and Utilization* (5th edn). Philadelphia: Lippincott.

Pratt, G. (2000), "Post-structuralism". In R.J. Johnston, D. Gregory, G. Pratt, M. Watts and D.M. Smith (eds), *The Dictionary of Human Geography*. Malden, MA: Blackwell Publishers.

Rajchman, J. (2000), *The Deleuze Connections*. Cambridge, MA: MIT Press.

Reese, L.A. and Fasenfest, D. (1997). "What works best?: Values and the evaluation of local economic development". *Economic Development Quarterly 11*(3), 195–207.

Rowe, J.E. (2007, 12 July), *Towards a Rhizomatic Econphilosophy of Economic Development.* Paper presented at the Association of European Schools of Planning annual conference, Naples.

Rycroft, S. (2005), "The nature of Op Art: Bridget Riley and the art of nonrepresentation". *Environment and Planning D: Society and Space 23*(351–71).

Saltman, D. and O'Dea, N. (2002), "Quality and quantity". In C.A. Berglund (ed.), *Health research* (pp. 174–90). Melbourne: Oxford University Press.

Sandercock, L. (2003), "Out of the closet: The importance of stories and storytelling in planning practice". *Planning Theory and Practice 4*(1), 11–28.

Schön, D. (1979), "Generative metaphor: A perspective on problem-setting in social policy". In A. Ortony (ed.), *Metaphor and Thought* (pp. 254–83). New York: Cambridge University Press.

Schön, D. (1983), *Reflective Practitioner: How Professionals Think in Action.* New York: Basic Books.

Schön, D. and Rein, M. (1994), *Frame Reflection*. New York: Basic Books.

Semetsky, I. (2003), "Deleuze's new image of thought, or Dewey revisited". *Educational Philosophy and Theory 35*(1), 17–29.

Semetsky, I. (2007), "Towards a semiotic theory of learning: Deleuze's philosophy and educational experience". *Semiotica 164*(1/4), 197–214.

Senior, M. and Vivesah, B. (1998), *Health and Illness*. London: Macmillan Press.

Smith, D.W. (2004), "Review of Deleuze and Geophilosophy". *Continental Philosophy Review 37*(3), 375–81.

Stagoll, C. (2005), "Difference". In A. Parr (ed.), *The Deleuze Dictionary* (pp. 72–3). New York: Columbia University Press.

Storper, M. and Manville, M. (2006), "Behaviour, preferences and cities: Urban theory and urban resurgence". *Urban Studies 43*(8), 1247–74.

Sui, D. (2000), "Visuality, aurality, and shifting metaphors of geographical thought in the last twentieth century". *Annals of the Association of American Geographers 90*(2), 322–43.

Thrift, N. and Dewsbury, J.-D. (2000), "Dead geographies – And how to make them live". *Environment and Planning D: Society and Space 18*, 411–32.

Throgmorton, J.A. (1993), "Planning as a rhetorical activity". *Journal of the American Planning Association 53*, 334–47.

Trevor, J.B. (1996), *Logics of Dislocation: Models, Metaphors, and Meanings of Economic Space*. New York: Guilford Press.

Tuan, Y.-F. (1978), "Sign and metaphor". *Annals of the Association of American Geographers 68*, 363–72.

Turok, I. (1989), "Evaluation and understanding in local economic policy". *Urban Studies 26*, 587–606.

Ward, J. and Holman, D.A. (2001), "Who needs to plan?" In C.A. Berglund (ed.), *Health Research* (pp. 47–61). Melbourne: Oxford University Press.

Waugh, P. (1984), *Metafiction: The Theory and Practice of Self-conscious Fiction*. London: Methuen.

Wetzstein, S. (2007), "Managing for a prosperous Auckland? Critical reflections on regional interventions for growing New Zealand's economic centre". *Sustaining Regions 6*(1), 28–49.

Williams, J. (2003), *Gilles Deleuze's "Difference and Repetition": A Critical Introduction and Guide*. Edinburgh: Edinburgh University Press.

Wyatt, S. (2004), "Danger! Metaphors at work in economics, geophysiology, and the internet". *Science, Technology and Human Values 29*(2), 242–61.

Zerilli, L. (1998), "This universalism which is not one". *Diacritics 28*(2), 3–20.

Chapter 16
Towards an Alternative Theoretical Framework for Understanding Local Economic Development

James E. Rowe

> Philosophy "should be in part…a very particular species of detective novel…in that concepts resolves local situations" in the sense of writing "at the frontiers of our knowledge, at the border which separates our knowledge from our ignorance and transforms the one into the other" (Deleuze, 1994, pp. xx–xxi).

The above-referenced quotation was written by Deleuze in his Preface to *Difference and Repetition.* This leads to some of the immanent implications of this work and demonstrates how Deleuzian concepts might generate transformative possibilities for theorising economic development. Laurel Richardson (2001, p. 35) once stated that "I write in order to learn something that I did not know before I wrote it". In a similar vein, this research too can be construed as a kind of detective novel that leads one to discover an alternative theoretical framework for understanding the practice of local economic development that is useful for resolving problems and is applicable in diverse local situations. The key point to note is that the practice of local economic development can be considered a Deleuzian concept that can be understood by exploring the theory of difference.

To commence, one should take Deleuzian concepts and trace *lines of flight* into the turbulence and complexity of economic development, searching for *smooth spaces** in which something new might be discovered (St. Pierre, 2004, p. 287). In this journey of discovery, this writer has gained insights and understanding but recognises that further study is needed to appreciate all the meanings and implications of Deleuze's work. Deleuze emphasised that "there's nothing to explain, nothing to understand, nothing to interpret" (Deleuze, 1995, p. 9) because it carries us "across our thresholds, toward a destination which is unknown, not foreseeable, not pre-existent" (Deleuze and Parnet, 1987, p. 125).

The ideal for this book or any poststructuralist work of theory:

> would be to lay everything out on a plane of exteriority of this kind, on a single page, the same sheet: lived events, historical determinations, concepts, individuals, groups [and] social formations (Deleuze and Guattari, 1987, p. 32).

Deleuze and Guattari, as quoted by Smith (2005, p. 191), advocates for "a process and not a goal" allowing the potential for new discoveries and creations. Deleuze and Guattari went on to say that a book (a book can be considered a rhizome) is an assemblage and as such it is unattributable: "It is a multiplicity – but we don't know yet what the multiple entails when it is no longer attributed, that is, after it has been elevated to the status of the substantive" (Smith, 2005, p. 184). Consequently, any theory of economic development must have a philosophical grounding that connects it to the history of philosophical ideas (Gregoriou, 2004, p. 235).

The literature indicates that one cannot separate valid knowledge and procedures from actors who are deemed legitimate carriers of that knowledge, or conceive of ideas and information as anything but socially embedded (Shdaimah and Stahl, 2006). The concept of function has very different meanings in literature and in philosophy. Aesthetic figures (and the style that creates them) have nothing to do with rhetoric. They are sensations: precepts and affects, landscapes and faces, visions and becomings[1]. One should define a philosophical concept precisely by its becoming, and even in the same terms (Colombat, 1999, p. 211). Deleuze called this kind of philosophy *pragmatics* because its goal is the invention of concepts that do not add up to a system of belief or an architecture of propositions that you either agree with or you don't, but instead leads one to think, experience and experiment (Massumi, 1992, p. 8). Accordingly practice, applied to an economic development practitioner, needs to be innovative and new initiatives need to be constantly developed that may be successful in their unique local context. This is because every region or city is different and "there is no general prescription" (Deleuze and Parnet, 2002, p. 144) as to what strategy or initiative may produce the new jobs and economic prosperity that every community tends to seek.

According to Deleuze, a philosopher's task is "to create concepts that are always new" even if others may not know "the problems to which those concepts are a response [to]" (Deleuze, 1995, p. 136). Deleuze and Guattari are not interested in concepts in order to determine the essence of something – "Rather they are interested in the concept as a vehicle for expressing an event[2], which allows them to introduce novelistic methods into philosophy" (Peters, 2004, p. 224), because a concept always "speaks the event, [and] not the essence" (Deleuze and Guattari, 1994, p. 21). This is important because Deleuze conceptualised events as "floating on the surface of bodies that cannot be said to *ex*-ist, but rather to *sub*-sist or *per*-sist in the relations between bodies" (Poxon and Stivale, 2005, p. 67). Deleuze went on to state that events, including ideas and acts, subsist in both the past and the future

1 The notion of *rhizomic becomings* has also been tied to the study of emergent knowledge dynamics in contexts of innovation to explore new and emergent patterns, channelling interpretation toward the discovery of new combinations and creative assemblages in knowledge (Zhao, 2005).

2 Deleuzian events present new practices and new ways of thinking about problems (Fraser, 2006).

in becoming (Deleuze, 1990). In this sense, an event is the actualistion of the *virtual**. The opening of a new business park, a corporate head office relocation or developing an innovative initiative might be considered such an event.

> Deleuze likes to describe his enterprise as the creation of concepts, as the continual and unending proliferation of ideas, thoughts, reflections [and] positions. Deleuze's thought is kaleidoscopic. 'Twist' it and new positions and possibilities emerge (Tormey, 2005, p. 426).

Concepts are fragmentary wholes comprised of components; they exist in relations to other concepts on the same plane; every concept has a history and a becoming; they are "only created as a function of problems which are thought to be badly understood or badly posed" (Peters, 2004, p. 219).

The problem, as stated in the introductory chapter, is the lack of a theoretical framework for understanding the practice of economic development. Deleuze (1989, p. 280) offers a way forward by stating that "the theory of [economic development]...does not bear on the [discipline]...but on the concepts of the [discipline]...". Economic development in itself is "a practice of images, [metaphors] and signs" (1989, p. 280) that are not limited to a concrete phenomenology of signs and images. Rather, because economic development's "concepts are not given in the [discipline]...philosophy must produce [a] theory [of economic development] as conceptual practice". Every concept has components and is defined by them, therefore it is a combination or a *multiplicity*, but Deleuze (1989) goes on to indicate that every multiplicity is not a concept.

This line of reasoning leads one to conclude that economic development is a Deleuzian *multiplicity.* It is also can be considered an event or a series of events and therefore a potential concept. This writer argues that economic development is a combination of many disciplines; yet to this point, it is unclear if economic development can be considered a Deleuzian concept. Deleuze would have responded to the question by viewing the discipline from a neutral point (or an Archimedean point of reference- see below) and systematically study the factors (symptoms) that influence and impact upon the discipline and develop a framework for understanding by approaching the problem in the same manner that a medical doctor studies symptoms when developing a treatment for a disease. When a doctor examines a patient with a "group of symptoms, his diagnostic task is to discover the corresponding concept" of the disease (Smith, 2005, p. 182). The process of symptomatology in medicine can similarly be applied to economic development. If diagnosing a group of symptoms can be considered concept creation in a Deleuzian sense – than theorising the multiplicity of factors and activities that constitute economic development might also be a Deleuzian concept because the "symptomatological method" promotes "*lines of flight* inherent in every...multiplicity" (Smith, 2005, pp. 190–191).

From a Deleuzian viewpoint, the process and practice of economic development should not be thought of as an economic problem that calls only for more quantification but a philosophical one that demands the creation of new concepts (Buchanan, 1999, p. 115). Every concept has components and is defined by them, therefore it is a combination or a *multiplicity*, but Deleuze and Guattari go on to indicate that each multiplicity is not a concept. Accordingly, as previously stated, a theory cannot dispense with concepts and, for a theory of economic development, the central concept has to be economic development itself (Friedmann, 1987, p. 35). Deleuze argued that concepts are useful for creating *new connections for thinking*, opening up whole new *planes of thought* (Deleuze and Guattari, 1994, p. 139) and that "there is no concept with only one component" (Deleuze and Guattari, 1994, p. 15).

If economic development is viewed as a concept, it must invariably have more than one component – which in turn defines the concept as such. A concept relates back to other concepts in its history and in its present *condition* of becoming. Related to this, a concept has components which can be grasped as concepts themselves. Secondly, "the concept…renders components inseparable within itself. Components, or what defines the consistency of the concept, its endoconsistency, are distinct, heterogeneous, and yet not separable" (Deleuze and Guattari, 1994, pp. 15–20). Deleuze insists:

> for, according to the Nietzschean verdict, you will know nothing through concepts unless you have first created them – that is, constructed them in an intuition specific to them; a field, a plane and a ground that must not be confused with them but that shelters their seeds and the personae who cultivate them (Deleuze and Guattari, 1994, p. 7).

This idea is reiterated when Deleuze and Guattari (p. 21) speak of the concept as "an act of thought…operating at infinite (although greater or lesser) speed". Thirdly, they indicate that a concept will be regarded as the point of coincidence, condensation or accumulation of the components which form part of it. Metaphors [see previous chapter] and metonymies are central to the application of these concepts (Gunder, 2003).

Deleuze proposed that a theoretical framework is just like a bag of tools, filled with so-many prostheses for enhancing, extending and intensifying thought and action (Doel, 1996, p. 429). To continue this line of thought, Deleuze had earlier stated that:

> We have done with all globalising concepts. Even concepts are haecceities, events. What is interesting about concepts like *desire**, or machine, or assemblages is that they only have a value in their variables, and in the maximum of variables which they allow. We are not for concepts as big as hollow teeth, THE law, THE master, THE rebel (Deleuze, 1993, p. 254).

This should be interpreted as:

- *We have done with all globalising concepts* – means that a theoretical framework or meta-theory should produce a tool kit that will enable the practitioner to conceptualise the challenges and opportunities that derive from such forces as globalisation and international monetary policy;
- *Even concepts are haecceities*, events* – this statement means that one needs to understand key concepts such as globalisation and learn how to maximise an area's competitive advantage, etc. *Haecceity** is a term used to denote a *nonpersonal individualisation* of either a body or an environmental assemblage, a block of space-time (see Appendix).
- *What is interesting about concepts like desire, or machine, or assemblages is that they only have a value in their variables, and in the maximum of variables which they allow* – a practitioner can utilise these terms to help visualise a innovative way forward or a new approach to a problem. This helps to explain why performance based becoming tools assist one to a better understanding of the discipline of local economic development; and that,
- *We are not for concepts as big as hollow teeth, THE law, THE master, THE rebel* – Deleuze is saying that the first part (as big as hollow teeth and THE law) means that he believed that there is not and cannot be a universal theory for economic development; the second part (THE master[3] and THE rebel) – means that he is urging practitioners to not blindly follow others (so-called experts with packaged solutions[4]) and to be a rebel by *thinking outside the square* in order to craft innovative solutions for unique local problems because there are no blueprints for success.

Consequently, this writer argues for the development of a new framework that offers an alternative concept of economic development based on context, judgement and practical knowledge (Flyvbjerg, 2001, p. 24). The framework will develop the rhizome concept (and other Deleuzian concepts such as multiplicity, folds, nomads, machines and *bodies without organs**) into tools that can be used to understand and visualise the practice of economic development.

Understanding Key Deleuzian Concepts

This writer commenced the journey toward a practical understanding of the discipline of economic development with the concept of a *rhizome.* As discussed in the introduction, a rhizomatic analysis does not follow traditional scientifically rigorous channels of inquiry. Instead, such an analysis is concerned with mapping

3 The 'master' in this quotation is, perhaps, an example of a Lacanian master signifier.

4 Many communities adopt popular solutions as advocated by leading economic development gurus such as Richard Florida and Michael Porter without a clear understanding of the theory or the odds of success (see Chapter 14).

connections between rhizomes. Mapping rhizomatic connections involves various and often contradictory works, ideas and concepts. Random rhizomatic connections can be drawn together to "connect diverse fragments of data in ways that produced new linkages and revealed discontinuities" (Honan, 2004, p. 270). Patton (2000, p. 37) once quoted Deleuze as asserting that "philosophy is the theory of multiplicities" because of the multiplicity of diverse fragments of information.

Rhizome is a figurative term used by Felix Guattari and Gilles Deleuze in *A Thousand Plateaus: Capitalism and Schizophrenia* (1987) to describe non-hierarchical networks of all kinds. The concept of rhizome (a subterranean network of meandering roots in connection with various hypertextual possibilities) can be developed into a theoretical framework that may be applied to local and regional economic development. Deleuze and Guattari stated that:

> A rhizome as a subterranean stem is absolutely different from roots and radicles. Bulbs and tubers are rhizomes. Plants with roots or radicles may be rhizomorphic in other respects altogether. Burrows are too, in all their functions of shelter, supply, movement, evasion, and breakout. The rhizome itself assumes very diverse forms, from ramified surface extension in all directions to concretion into bulbs and tubers…The rhizome includes the best and the worst: potato and couchgrass, or the weed (Deleuze and Guattari, 1987, pp. 6–7).

The rhizome (see Figure 16.1 opposite) concept is useful for rethinking the notion that knowledge can be traced back to one logical or central source, able to be plotted carefully on the tree structure, or organised within various hierarchies (Deleuze and Guattari, 1981).

> A rhizome does not represent, but only maps our ways, paths and movements. The presentation in the mode of mapping does not assume this map's representing the proverbial territory as given in a strict sense. Deleuze used *tracer* (in French) to indicte the subtlety of what it means to draw a map. The verb *to* draw means – rather than to *copy* – to *create* because what is drawn…does not pre-exist the act of drawing (Semetsky, 2007, p. 200).

The rhizome is also often used as a concept exemplified by metaphors (Gregoriou, 2004, p. 242). Jacobs (2007, p. 268, emphasis in the original) emphasised this point by stating that:

> The multifarious activities that constitute [economic development] can be seen…as links between…ensembles of activity or patchworks are through what Deleuze and Guattari term the *rhizome*, a metaphor that they use to *map* the connections between agents, material objects and the local.

Figure 16.1 A tangle of rhizomes
Source: Copyright owned by and printed by permission of Warren Sellers.

Tree logic[5] operates within a defined space or territory, enclosed by chronological and hierarchical boundaries (Deleuze and Guattari, 1987). Rhizomic thought continually needs more space to spread out. Instead of fixing contributions to knowledge onto appropriate branches (see Figure 16.2) on a tree (where they can be indexed, catalogued and referred to later), rhizomic thought is analogous to the transferral of information via the internet. It is similar to a flow that moves

5 Tree logic is an alternative to the rhizome model. Deleuze and Guattari describe this model in terms of 'root' or 'tree logic'.

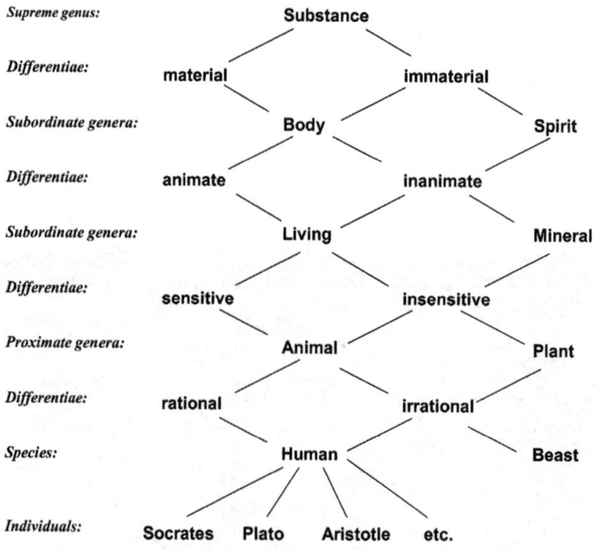

Figure 16.2 Tree structure of knowledge

Source: Tree of Porhyry drawn by Peter of Spain (1329).

haphazardly and usually ephemerally across a network. A rhizomatic tangle is a *system of relays* of potential enquiries. Rhizomatic styles of thinking have no fixed centres or order and can be visualised as a multiplicity of expanding and overlapping connections (Deleuze and Guattari, 1987, pp. 3–26).

Plateaus and Folds

Deleuze and Guattari (1987) referred to plateaus as rhizomes and stated that "We call a plateau any multiplicity connected to other multiplicities by superficial underground stems in such a way as to form or extend a rhizome" (Deleuze and Guattari, 1987, p. 22). They continue to explain this phenomenon by stating that

> a plateau is always in the middle, not at the beginning or the end. A rhizome is made of plateaus. Gregory Bateson uses the word plateau to investigate something very special: a continuous self-vibrating region of intensities whose development avoids any orientation toward a culmination point or external end (Deleuze and Guattari, 1987, pp. 21–2).

The concept of plateaus can also be conceptualised as a level of understanding. For example, the concept of globalisation (see Chapter 5) can be visualised as a plateau that must be scaled in order to gain a solid understanding of the forces that impact the discipline. Similarly, the theories underpinning competitive advantage, locations and clusters (see Chapters 6– 8) are also plateaus that must be climbed in order to be an effective and knowledgeable economic development practitioner.

Deleuze's concepts of the *fold*, or *desire**, for example, "helps us to think about the very difference or power of life; the concept is an event of life and difference that confronts, thinks or gives consistency to difference" (Colebrook, 2002, p. 85). The fold is a metaphor which has been developed and used by Foucault in his various writings. It has been further developed and given its due weight by Deleuze (Deleuze, 2006; Weiskopf, 2002, p. 85). This act of enfolding and unfolding reduces its metaphorical determination (Lopez, 2004, p. 109) which is driven by a desire for anonymity which amounts to a praxis or to an active becoming or to the drawing of a *line of flight** (Düttmann, 2002, p. 174). In this case, *desire* refers to this impersonal and universal synbook which produces organisms, societies, economic and linguistic systems (Colebrook, 2002, p. 121).

The concept of a *fold* has been discussed in detail by Deleuze (1993; 2006, pp. 94–123) and has been tied to economic development by Dovey and Sandercock (2002) and others (Hansen, 2000; Kaup, 2005; Neilson, 2003). The Dovey and Sandercock (2002) paper documented the complex relationship between public and private roles in redevelopment by folding in the perplexing question of the public interest in relation to the Melbourne dockland project. Hansen (2000) tied folding to what the author described as creative *involution**. Neilson (2003) bridged the concept of globalisation to aging by folding both into politics, and Kaup (2005) folded and tied European Baroque inspired architecture to development. Thus,

> to think is to fold, to double the outside with a coextensive inside. The general topology of thought, which had already begun *in the neighbourhood* of the particular features, now ends up in the folding of the outside into the inside" (Deleuze, 2006, p. 118).

Deleuze (2006, p. 116) further elaborated this line of thought by stating that "to think means to experiment and to problematise".

*Nomads, Smooth and Striated Space**

Other Deleuzian metaphors such as *nomads* imply mobile meanings, shifting connections, temporary encounters, and a world of intertextual richness and detail (Doel, 1996). A nomadic thinker opens new connections and experiences new *becomings*, and thus, thinks differently (Jeanes, 2006, p. 129). Deleuze and Guattari also celebrated the nomad culture, a temporary culture that picks up and moves on after a period of time. "Nomadic thought defines itself by the lines of flight, by its boundaries, its edges, through the range of anomalies" (Deleuze and Guattari, 1987, p. 104), and the milieu of a nomadic subject is smooth (Saldanha, 2006, p. 6). The *rhizome* is like this nomadic culture, as it is constantly in flux, movement and change. The rhizome isn't constrained by boundaries or rules and follows its own paths.

Smooth space consists of points as relays between lines; striated space consists of lines between points. Smooth space facilitates immanence and the *new*; while *striated space** channels *immanence** as fixed dimensions in the abstract of transcendental ideals (Hillier, 2005, pp. 285–6). Consequently, government policies are initiatived in the striated space of a structured bureaucracy. As Deleuze and Guattari (1987, p. 474) explains, "smooth space and striated space – nomad space and sedentary space – the space in which the war machne develops and the space instituted by the State apparaturs – are not the same nature". Space is about order, structure, the regular, routine and identity. It is characterised as *logos*. Smooth space "is defined dynamically, in terms of transformation instead of essence" (Deleuze and Guattari, 1987, pp. 361–362). Smooth space is in the realm of *nomos*, and is all about movement across points. This is important because one has to create smooth space between the striations of an economic development strategy in order to respond to the chaotic void of the market.

Duration, Territorialisation and Actuality*

Duration (*durée)* as it relates to time is about the process of becoming because "clock time abstracts from the notion of duration by distorting its continuity" (Stagoll, 2005, p. 79). Clock time can be conceptualised as being linear. This is the opposite of Aion time[6] (non-linear) in which the:

> present is nothing; it is a pure mathematical instant, a being of reason which expresses the past and the future into which it is divided. Briefly, *there are two times, one of which is composed only of interlocking presents; the other is contantly decomposed into elongated pasts and futures* (Deleuze, 1990, p. 62, emphasis in the original).

Deleuze (1988, p. 37) stated that "Duration is not merely lived experience: it is also experience enlarged or even gone beyond; it is already a condition of experience" he went on the state that, "pure duration offers us a succession that is purely internal, without exteriority without succession".

Modes of regional engagement can be understood using Deleuzian concepts of deterritorialisation and reterritorialisation (Patton, 2000). Deleuze uses *territory* in a metaphorical sense to depict sites of political engagement and their lines of power, practices, and institutions. Relatively permanent disruptions to these sites and what is performed in them are *deterritorialisation* processes. Establishing new or replacement engagement relationships involve *re-territorialisation* processes. Clearly, acts of deterritorialisation and re-territorialisation can never be complete. One always incites the other. It has become "less about territorial boundaries…and more about connection and flow" (Law and Urry, 2004, p. 403).

6 Deleuze (1990, p. 63) stated that Aion time "is always and at the same time something which is just happening and something about to happen, never which is happening".

The virtual and actual both constitute reality, while being actualised in the event. Actuality is unfolded from potentiality and the "diverse actualisations of the virtual…[can be] understood as solutions" (Boundas, 2005, p. 297) or events. "From any actual or unfolded term it should be possible (and, for Deleuze, desirable) to intuit the richer potentiality from which it has emerged" (Colebrook, 2005b, p. 10).

Deleuzian Metaphorical Tools for Understanding

This section will delineate the context for the development of a set of criteria that will become useful tools for furthering a practitioner's understanding of economic development. This writer believes that Deleuzian concepts such as rhizomes, folds, plateaus, deterritorialisation and lines of flight refer to spatial relationships between economic forces or physical facilities and can also be seen as ways of visualising them. These and other Deleuzian metaphorical concepts can be considered methodological tools that can be used as key indicators for a performance becoming-understanding of an economic development programme as discussed in the previous chapter.

The meta-theory proposed in this book has the potential to particularly bridge the gap between theory and practice by offering practitioners the methodological tools in which they can approach local problems with innovative solutions on solid theoretical grounds. This writer asserts that there is a need for a critical qualitative appraisal framework. Such a framework is needed because, as discussed in the previous chapter, the causal relationship between growth and economic development strategies (and the best efforts of the local practitioner) is weak or non-existent. The lack of causality results from *folding* the forces of globalisation, international corporate location decisions, central government tax and labour policies, and interest rates into the mix of factors that strongly influence the discipline but are out of the control of the local practitioner. In order to employ the tools developed in this chapter effectively, a practitioner has to begin by embracing rhizomatic thinking and discarding their previous arborescent thinking patterns. This means that they have to *think outside the square* in order to understand that there are no easy answers or packaged solutions to improve their community's economic prosperity.

A set of criteria (metaphorical tools) that can be used for developing a performance based understanding for economic development programmes is delineated in Table 16.1. This writer suggests that these tools can enhance one's understanding by helping the practitioner to visualise novel approaches to local challenges and as a consequence, open new possibilities that lead "to new understandings and the appearance of new meanings" (Semetsky, 2003 as cited by Hillier, 2007, p. 269). The major challenge is to convince practitioners to think rhizomatically and to embrace change and difference.

Table 16.1 Key Deleuzian metaphorical tools for an economic development theory of understanding

Deleuzian Terminology	Concise Definition *	Example of Application
Arborescence	Refers to structured and hierarchical thinking.	This writer uses the term to describe traditional structured patterns of thinking that inhibit innovative thought.
Assemblage	A grouping or collection of anything.	A network of branch manufacturing plants can be considered an assemblage.
Flow	A movement of ideas, concepts or people.	Richard Florida (2006) used the term to describe the movement of knowledge workers to cities that have Bohemian lifestyles.
Line of Flight	Refers to the direction of a movement, marketing programme or one's personal ambitions. The key question is "towards what destination" (Deleuze and Parnet, 1987, p. 120).	For instance, if one wants to become a professional, he or she will have to channel their line of flight (career path) by entering and completing the appropriate university programme.
Multiplicity	Based on Bergsonism, Deleuze defined it as both extensive numerical combinations and continuous intensive changing nature of a subject.	Bogue (2005) described the characteristics of a nomadic multiplicity as an unlimited and undivided space or a metamorphic flux and also as a qualitative multiplicity with an identity that is irreducibly plural and affective.
Nomad	A nomadic thinker wanders about a topic just as a nomadic herdsman moves from one oasis to another.	Jeanes (2006) used the nomadic metaphor to show how such thinking opens new connections, experiences and thus, produces innovative thought processes.
Plateau	It's an elevated natural feature of the landscape and metaphorically it can be a goal, a new level of understanding or an objective that one strives to achieve.	This book used the term to describe a series of concepts such as globalisation that a practitioner has to understand in order to develop an effective strategy.
Reterritorialisation	Amin (2004) uses the term to describe the changes in governance brought about by the reconfiguration regions as a result of devolution.	A good analogy would be the changed boundaries after a local government amalgamation.

Table 16.1 *continued* **Key Deleuzian metaphorical tools for an economic development theory of understanding**

Deleuzian Terminology	Concise Definition *	Example of Application
Deterritorialisation	Deterritorialisation is movement that produces change.	O'Neill and McGuirk (2005) used the analogy of deterritorialisation to describe the changing economy and institutions in the Sydney basin.
Rhizome	A rhizome can be likened to the interconnections of the internet.	Rhizomes are used by this writer to visualise new business parks, warehouses or shopping centres popping up on the landscape like flowers in the spring.
Smooth Space	Refers to an easy flow between ideas or concepts.	A good analogy is to imagine the smooth space of the globalised economy as chaotic or a complex web of divisions and confluences.
Striated Space	Refers to structured or rough space.	Striating space can be visualised as attempts to inscribe some form of fixity into flux, to draw lines and situate the local by delineating aspirations, goals and actions in the form of new initiatives.

* See the appendix for a more comprehensive definition of the various terms.

The criteria are strengthened because practitioners can easily visualise concepts such as flows, plateaus and territorialisation because they are derived from geologic and geographic physical features. Other concepts such nomadic flows of skill workers moving into the smooth space of an entrepreneurial community are also easy to visualise. These visual images resonate with the goals and objectives of most economic development strategies. This requires imagination, new and different thinking (*out of the square*). As stated in the previous paragraph, convincing practitioners and traditional positivitistic academics to embrace alternative philosophical viewpoints is a major challenge and its main weakness. This writer suggests that, if embraced, rhizomatic econphilosophy and the criteria listed has the potential to assist practitioners to be able to appraise local initiatives and as a result, will enable the practitioner to garner new insights into the discipline.

Using metaphorical analogies for understanding the practice of economic development leads to what is known as a *hermeneutic circle*. This refers to the circle of interpretation that result from explaining some philosophical concepts through metaphors. According to this theory, when endeavouring to understand a complex discipline such as local economic development, it isn't possible to really understand any one part of a concept as it relates to the discipline such as globalisation until you understand how it relates to other concepts such as competitive advantage. Consequently, this means that it also isn't possible to understand the whole without also understanding all of the parts. *Hermeneutics** is a way of explaining and expressing how understanding and interpreting philosophical concepts is an ongoing process which takes time to develop (Shklar, 2004). As more information about the concept is acquired, an interpretation gradually changes to incorporate the new found information.

Using the example described in the proceeding paragraph, these tools can be used to help one to understand why some companies are now transferring portions of their production to China and other lower cost centres. For example, the forces of globalisation encouraged Fisher and Paykel (a New Zealand whiteware manufacturer) to move their washer machine production from the Auckland region to Thailand because of lower wages. In white goods manufacturing, labour inputs are a significant portion of the total cost of production. In Deleuzian terms, this means that despite New Zealand's competitive advantage for design and engineering (an *assemblage* of expertise) and its long term commitment to stay in New Zealand, the firm decided that it would be more profitable to move production to a lower cost centre by changing its corporate *line of flight** by developing a *multiplicity* of production centres in other less costly locations. In a sense, this relocation is a good example of a footloose business in a rapidly *reterritorialising* industry.

Why Deleuze is Relevant to Economic Development

The proposed meta-theory will be designed to provide a theoretical perspective on the theory of economic development that enables a better understanding of the practice of local economic development. The meta-theory will be derived from a poststructural theoretical framework that offers an explanation for the poor correlation between strategies, action plans and the seemly random spatial-temporal occurrence of economic development activities. To this writer's knowledge, a Deleuzian framework has never been employed to theorise local economic development; although it has previously been applied to archaeological theory, resource management issues in Canada, architecture, planning theory, Tasmanian governance, global cities and Sydney's political economy (Doel and Hubbard, 2002, pp. 357–9; Frichot, 2006; Hillier, 2007; Hipwell, 2004, pp. 359–62; Jacobs, 2007; O'Neill and McGuirk, 2005; Shanks and Hodder, 1995, pp. 35–6; R. G. Smith and Doel, 2007; Tilley, 1993, pp. 18–20). Jean Hillier's (2007) *Stretching Beyond the Horizon* is especially important because it presents the first theory of spatial planning and governance based almost entirely on the works of Gilles Deleuze.

This chapter argues that economic development when viewed through a Deleuzian lens becomes clearer because "Deleuze and Guattari did not use philosophy to interpret [economic development]…or [economic development]… to explain philosophy" (Colebrook, 2002, pp. xxvii–xxviii). This is noteworthy because the Deleuzian philosophy of difference offers new ways of thinking about economic development by providing insights into the complexity and chaos of capitalism while affording alternative ways of thinking about economic development policies or strategies. It has the potential to become a theoretical foundation underpinning a new paradigm[7] (Shaffer et al., p. 70) because it develops a set of methodological tools that enables academics and practitioners to bridge the gap between theory and practice and to explain the disconnect between strategies, action plans and the occurrence of real world economic activities. It has also been shown that Deleuzian philosophy encourages the creation of innovative initiatives to address unique local situations. Therefore, this chapter posits that economic development as viewed though a Deleuzian lens offers a conceptual framework that merits critical debate and further research.

Archimedean Point of Reference

This writer has concluded that the discipline of economic development lacks an Archimedean point of reference from which to view the field as a whole. In my search for an Archimedean point of reference, the Deleuzian concept of *geophilosophy** was explored. Deleuze and Guattari explicitly referred to their own philosophical method as *geophilosophy*, privileging geography over history and stressing the value of the *present-becoming* (Semetsky, 2004, p. 230). Therefore:

> Philosophy is a geophilosophy in precisely the same way that history is a geohistory from Braudel's view…Geography wrests history from the cult of necessity in order to stress the irreducibility of contingency (Deleuze and Guattari, 1994, pp. 95–96).

Deleuze, as quoted by Badiou (2000, p. 90), stated that the idea is to make "the past active and present to the outside so that something new will finally come about". Therefore, seeking to create something new, this author has coined the term *econphilosophy* to describe the connection between economic development and philosophy, spurred on by Deleuze's penchant for inventing new terms for his neologisms (Gough, 2004, p. 253).

In developing the argument for a meta-theory for local economic development, this writer borrowed metaphorical terms and several common clichés from many different sources to describe the relationship between economic development theory and practice. Econphilosophy endeavours to tie philosophy to the spatial and practical activities that encompass the practice of economic development. In a similar vein, Jessop (2000, pp. 328–9) employed the concept of ecological

7 A new paradigm can be developed in the "form of an innovative experiment or analytical treatment that, by its very success, implied a particular way to understand and study the subject in question" (Schram, 2006, p. 29).

dominance in his explanation of globalisation. Others such as Wilson (2006) tied ecological and urban systems research to complexity theory[8] just as Deleuze and Guattari borrowed the notion of the *rhizome* from biology (Schuh and Cunningham, 2004).

Deleuzian econphilosophy offers a viable ontological and epistemological framework for the economic development discipline and as such provides a new way of perceiving and understanding its practice. It gives us the tools to analyse and intervene in the mixture of smoothing and striating forces at work in the complex space of economic development (Bonta and Protevi, 2004, p. 39). Econphilosophy describes a theory folded[9] into practice and that, more importantly, provides a framework, tools and the methodology to analyse and understand the practice of economic development. It also portrays a new way of understanding complex issues that provides ontologically similar accounts for human and non-human endeavours. Econphilosophy concerns itself with systems that are sometimes simultaneously human and nonhuman, organic and inorganic, composed of part-objects from a variety of systems that are subject to change at various time-scales. Econphilosophy develops a platform for understanding the disconnect between theory and practice and offers an explanation for the occurrence of random and unpredictable economic activities. It also provides a logical framework for understanding the psychological drivers that motivate the economic development practitioner.

The argumentation for this chapter continues with two seemingly competing tendencies (the globalisation of economic activity and the localisation of industries), which have captured the interest of scholars, economic development professionals, and policymakers in recent years (Peck and Tickell, 2002). While trends towards globalisation of industries and companies appear to reduce the importance and distinctiveness of (subnational) regions, a tendency towards localisation of certain industries and economic activities appears to do exactly the opposite (Porter, 1990). The simultaneous globalisation and localisation tendencies have created policy challenges for national and local governments (Raco et al., 2006, p. 478). One response to these challenges has been a dramatic proliferation of regional development policies based on regional clusters of firms [see Chapters 6–8] and industries (Porter, 2000), despite the fact that local boosterism and the promotion of local clusters and knowledge industries have not reduced regional disparities in many areas[10] (Amin, 2005, p. 624).

This research promotes a variant of Deleuzian geophilosophy (coined econphilosophy) as a viable ontological and epistemological framework for

8 Complexity science provides "a source of insight into the nature of virtual multiplicities" (Mackenzie, 2005, p. 52).

9 In this sense, folding creates a new awareness of both theory and practice (Anderson, 2006, p. 739).

10 This book argues that packaged solutions such as Porter's concept of clusters do not necessarily produce the desired results in all localities (see Chapter 8).

understanding economic development (Deleuze and Guattari, 1994, pp. 85–116). One has to think differently in order to act differently[11] (Foucault, 1990, p. 9). Deleuzian econphilosophy allows one to consider a complex systems approach "to break free of conceptual deadlocks, circumvent crises of representation and the textualist trap, overcome imposed dichotomies and challenge subdisciplinary boundary-drawing" (Bonta and Protevi, 2004, p. 38). By 'becoming-deleuzian' the sociocultural strata open up through various activities that might be designated as *rhizomatic* (Massumi, 1996). Massumi (p. 401) argues that Deleuzian philosophy "challenges the reader to do something with it" and that, through this pragmatic rather than dogmatic insistence, "readers are invited to fuse with the work in order to carry one or several concepts across their zone of indiscernibility with it, into new and discernibly different circumstances".

This author suggests that Deleuze married poststructuralism to complexity theory in *A Thousand Plateaus*[12]. The union has produced an econphilosophy of immanence, through careful observation and attunement to what is going on mixed with cautious experimentation. Deleuzian econphilosophy provides the tools to analyse and intervene in the mixture of smoothing and striating forces at work in the complex spaces we inhabit (Bonta and Protevi, 2004, pp. 38–43). This philosophy can offer a framework for understanding economic development by employing the Deleuzian concepts of rhizomes, desire machines, multiplicity and *bodies without organs* that will lead to the development of an alternative theoretical framework of economic development.

The driving force behind econphilosophy is the endeavour to provide a steady bridge between human and physical divisions that often surface in the contemporary real world of economic activity. Because economic development is so complex, "There can be – there *must* be – a Deleuzian cultural ecology, a post-poststructuralist biogeography, a Deleuzian geomorphology..." (Bonta and Protevi, 2004, p. 39) and, by extension, a Deleuzian meta-theory of economic development. This writer suggests that a Deleuzian theoretical framework incorporating econphilosophy can provide an important new contribution to the understanding of economic development. Such a new framework would best be established by sharing concepts[13] between disciplines in an attempt to discover new ways of interpreting the changing economic landscape and the role of the economic development practitioner in influencing it.

---

11 Thinking and acting differently means that the practitioner has to develop or craft an economic development strategy and implement an action plan designed to address local problems by thinking rhizomatically.

12 It should be noted that neither complexity theory nor poststructuralism were conceived when *A Thousand Plateaus* was originally published in 1980.

13 "Concepts are relative with respect to their nature, and absolute with respect to their location, i.e., the space occupied by the concept on its immanent conceptual plane" (Penner, 2003, p. 50).

Econphilosophy proposes a new way of understanding the complex issues of economic development that finds theory folded into practice and that, more importantly, provides ontologically similar accounts for human and non-human endeavours[14]. Econphilosophy concerns itself with systems that are sometimes simultaneously human and nonhuman, organic and inorganic, composed of part-objects from a variety of systems that are subject to change at various time-scales.

Econphilosophy has to be read through the lens of complexity theory[15]. Mark Bonta and John Protevi in *Deleuze and Geophilosophy*[16], explored the connections between Deleuze and Guattari's thought and complexity theory. They explained that:

> Researchers in complexity theory[17] investigate the way certain material systems in the inorganic, organic, and social registers attain both higher levels of internal complexity and a 'focus' of systematic behaviour without having to rely on external organizing agents (Bonta and Protevi, 2004, p. 3).

Econphilosophy demystifies the creativity of open systems by extending these capacities to organic and non-organic domains, and by contending that humans will always be subject to systemic structural stratification at the same time that they might be engaged in moments of creative openness.

Deleuze and Guattari (1994) described philosophy as the *creation* of concepts[18] through which knowledge can be generated. As Peters (2004) points out, this differs from the approaches taken by many traditional philosophers who are more concerned with the clarification of concepts:

14 This is important because it provides a theoretical explanation for both the occurrence of random economic activities and for the actions of the practitioner.

15 Complexity theory involves notions, problems and results about complexity (of predicates, functions, proofs) and is deep-rooted in mathematical logic and (good) theorems. Bounded arithmetic and propositional logic are closely interrelated and have several explicit and implicit connections to computational complexity theory. Central computational notions (Turing machine, Boolean circuit) are crucial in metamathematics of the logical systems and models of these systems are natural structures for concepts of computational complexity (Krajicek, 1995).

16 Bonta and Protevi connect geography and philosophy through complexity theory while Byrne ties complexity and planning theory together (Byrne, 2003).

17 "Complexity theory refers to a body of knowledge which assimilates contributions from many disciplines, including the natural…and social sciences" (Chettiparamb, 2006, p. 73).

18 "If one concept is 'better' than an earlier one, it is because it makes us aware of new variations and unknown resonances, it carries out unforeseen cuttings-out, it brings forth an Event that surveys us" (Deleuze and Guattari, 1994, p. 28).

> Against the conservatism, apoliticism and ahistoricism of analytic philosophy that has denied its own history until very recently, Deleuze and Guattari attempt [a] geography of philosophy, a history of geophilosophy, beginning with the Greeks. Rather than providing a history, they conceptualise philosophy in spatial terms as *geophilosophy*. Such a conception immediately complicates the question of philosophy: by tying it to geography and a history, a kind of historical and spatial specificity, philosophy cannot escape its relationship to the City and the State. In its modern and postmodern forms it cannot escape its form under industrial and knowledge capitalism (Peters, 2004, p. 218).

Deleuze and Guattari created unique methodological tools for analysing flows or movements across space. For Deleuze "concepts such as *assemblage, deterritorialisation, [folds], lines of flight, nomadology, [plateaus],* [*reterritorialisation*] and *rhizomes* clearly refer to spatial relationships" (Gough, 2005, p. 2) between real world economic activities and can be seen as ways of visualising them. This researcher interprets these concepts as tools for *thinking outside the square* in order to understand the practice of economic development. As a consequence, in order to apply these tools one must distinguish *rhizomatic* thinking from *arborescent* conceptions of knowledge as hierarchically articulated branches of a central stem or trunk rooted in firm foundations. Rhizomatic thought, on the other hand, can be presented as a more appropriate way forward across a diversity of knowledge and methods of inquiry. Traditional thought and writing has a centre or subject from which it then expresses ideas. Rhizomatics, by contrast, makes random, proliferating and decentred connections (Gough, 2005).

It is important to note that many Deleuzian concepts such as rhizomes, plateaus, striations, lines of flight and folds have inherently *spatial* connotations because they are metaphors derived from geologic and geographic physical features. This inherently spatial imaginary emerges "from both the movements of bodies and the images those bodies produce of each other" (Colebrook as quoted by Thrift, 2007, p. 55). Economic development's contextual particularity is also intrinsically *spatial* because the discipline is fundamentally concerned with the creation and location of economic activity at a particular geographical location and the resulting flow-on effects for society. Therefore, this writer chose geophilosophy (which was subsequently refined into econphilosophy) to assist the reader to visualise relationships between spatial economic activity and the strategies, initiatives and activities of the practitioner. It should be noted that Foucault also embraced spatiality and deployed a multiplicity of spatial metaphors in his writings (Harvey, 2007, p. 45).

For example, metaphorically when referring to geologic formations, rhizomes can grow on plateaus that have been developed over centuries from a multiplicity of deposits that have been layered into striations that have subsequently been folded into mountains. In a similar vein, metaphors can be used to describe a common economic development scenario. The decision to locate and build a new economic activity such as a branch manufacturing plant can be made by corporate headquarters located in another country because the corporation wants to channel its *lines of flight* by opening new markets. The said corporation makes the decision to expand in a foreign market because its own domestic market has *plateaued* and the firm has grown to the stage that it wants to compete with a *multiplicity* of international firms and markets. The corporation and its branch plants have become an *assemblage* of interconnecting parts that have become *folded* into the globalised economy. Real world examples of this story are exemplified by the recent closing of the Ion wheel manufacturing facility in Manukau, New Zealand (despite its profitability) because of its parent company's bankruptcy in Australia; and Fisher and Paykel's decision to relocate its washer machine production from Auckland to Thailand for both distribution and labour cost efficiencies. These two cases are examples of corporate folding and changing lines of flight.

This makes sense if one understands that arborescent thought stifles and constrains the development of a discipline such as economic development (Drummond, 2005). Therefore, this researcher suggests that we engage in a metamorphosis from an arborescent way of thinking to a rhizomatic one because by thinking rhizomatically, one is open to "new connections, creative and novel becomings that will give…[a practitioner] new patterns and triggers of behaviour" (Bonta and Protevi, 2004, pp. 62–63). As Umberto Eco explains, "the rhizome is so constructed that every path can be connected with every other one. It has no centre, no periphery, no exit, because it is potentially infinite. The space of conjecture is a rhizome space" (Eco, 1984, p. 57). The space of economic development can also be understood as a *rhizome space*.

Conclusions

This is important because "we inhabit a world where the actual is always haunted by possibility, by the virtualities folded within its emergence" (Massumi as quoted by Latham and Conradson, 2003, p. 1902) and economic development, as an emerging academic discipline needs to differentiate itself from planning, economics and geography and develop its own core theory. Practitioners and academics need to "convince…[these] disciplines that our sub-field is important and vigorous" (Markusen, 2000, p. 288). The literature clearly confirms that economic development as a transdisciplinary field of study lacks a unifying theoretical framework. This writer, in an attempt to fill the gap, has formulated a platform from which to theorise the discipline.

In the preface, I lamented the lack of an explanatory framework for understanding the practice of local economic development. Early in my career I managed to successfully function as an economic development practitioner without considering the theoretical implications of my daily practice or for the initiatives and strategies that I was charged with implementing. Being young and naïve, I did not understand why theory is important or how theory could improve my performance as a practitioner. Despite this lack, I was successful in securing government grants and I was involved in a number of high profile industrial relocations and expansions. As a result, I was able to advance my career because I was a good salesman with a flair for developing successful grant applications (Blakely and Bradshaw, 2002, p. 375). Essentially, my performance indicators were based on my ability to influence new job creation by attracting footloose businesses and garnering grants[19]. Many of my former colleagues were not as lucky and, as a result, have drifted into other fields of endeavour.

This research demonstrates that local economic development practitioners, especially in a small country like New Zealand, operate in a different context, scale and political environment compared to those in the USA or European Union and consequently should not be judged by traditional measures. However, in order to be successful regardless of geographic location, practitioners need to be proactive and not be reactive by trying to *make things happen* (Deleuze, 2005, pp. 71–2). As explained in the introduction and illustrated throughout the book, *muddling through,* uncritically adopting *best practice* initiatives and *being seen to be doing something* is a recipe for failure. This means that local economic development practitioners should strive to create a culture where *becoming-proactive* is the norm because "being innovates; being is differentiated, [and] because being differentiates" (Hallward, 2006, p. 13).

As a result of this research, I have concluded that an economic development agency or the actions of a practitioner should be judged on its or their ability to deal with chaos. Stakeholders should ask if the organisation or individual is *stirring things up* by taking risks and creating possibilities for success because an economic development practitioner should be "someone who creates their own impossibilities and thereby creates possibilities" (Deleuze, 1995, p. 133). This means that a practitioner should be a mediator[20] who addresses the challenges of achieving the impossible "because without a set of impossibilities, you won't have the *line of flight*, the exit that is creation, the power of falsity that is the truth" (Deleuze, 1995, p. 133, my emphasis).

The discipline has changed significantly since I began my career as an economic development practitioner in the 1970s. Being a good salesman is no longer enough to be successful in today's competitive globalised world. Today an economic development practitioner needs higher skill levels and a greater understanding of the multiple disciplines that interact in the coalface of daily practice than I needed at the beginning of my career. Consequently, practitioners can no longer afford to work in a theoretical vacuum. Hopefully, this book will provide some insights into the theory underpinning the discipline and generate critical debate and further theoretical research.

---

19 Securing grants has been just as important for advancing my career in Australia and New Zealand as it was in the United States.

20 A mediator is an enabler, fixer, catalyst or one who stirs things up (Osborne, 2004, p. 440). In a Deleuzian context, a mediator is one who deals with chaos well and endeavours to accomplish the impossible (which defines the average job description of an economic development practitioner).

References

Amin, A. (2004), "Regions unbound: Towards a new politics of place". *Geografiska Annaler 86B*(1), 33–44.

Amin, A. (2005), "Local community on trial". *Economy and Society 34*(4), 612–633.

Anderson, B. (2006), "Becoming and being hopeful: Towards a theory of affect". *Environment and Planning D: Society and Space 24*, 733–52.

Badiou, A. (2000), *Deleuze: The Clamor of Being* (L. Burchell, Trans.). Minneapolis: University of Minnesota Press.

Blakely, E. and Bradshaw, T. (2002), *Planning Local Economic Development, Theory and Practice* (3rd edn). Thousand Oaks, CA: Sage.

Bogue, R. (2005), "Nomadic flows: Globalism and the local absolute". *Concentric: Literary and Cultural Studies 31*(1), 7–25.

Bonta, M. and Protevi, J. (2004), *Deleuze and Geophilosophy: A Guide and Glossary*. Edinburgh: Edinburgh University Press.

Buchanan, I. (1999), "Deleuze and cultural studies". In I. Buchanan (ed.), *A Deleuzian Century?* (pp. 103–117), Durham, NC: Duke University Press.

Byrne, D. (2003), "Complexity theory and planning theory: A necessary encounter". *Planning Theory 2*(3), 171–8.

Chettiparamb, A. (2006), "Metaphors in complexity theory and planning". *Planning Theory 5*(1), 71–91.

Colebrook, C. (2002), *Understanding Deleuze*. Crows Nest, NSW: Allen and Unwin.

Colebrook, C. (2005), "Actuality". In A. Parr (ed.), *The Deleuze Dictionary* (pp. 9–11), New York: Columbia University Press.

Colombat, A.P. (1999), "Deleuze and the three powers of literature and philosophy: To demystify, to experiment, to create". In I. Buchanan (ed.), *A Deleuzian Century?* (pp. 199–217). Durham, NC: Duke University Press.

Deleuze, G. (1988), *Bergsonism* (H. Tomlinson and B. Habberjam, Trans.). New York: Zone Books.

Deleuze, G. (1990), *The Logic of Sense* (M. Lester, Trans.). New York: Columbia University Press.

Deleuze, G. (1993), *The Fold: Leibniz and the Baroque* (T. Conley, Trans.). Minneapolis: University of Minnesota Press.

Deleuze, G. (1995), *Negotiations, 1972–1990* (M. Joughin, Trans.). New York: Columbia University Press.

Deleuze, G. (2005), *Pure Immanence* (A. Boyman, Trans.). New York: Zone Books.

Deleuze, G. (2006), *Foucault* (S. Hand, Trans. 7th edn). Minneapolis: University of Minnesota Press.

Deleuze, G., and Guattari, F. (1981), "Rhizome". *Ideology and Consciousness 6*, 49–71.

Deleuze, G. and Guattari, F. (1987), *Thousand Plateaus: Capitalism and Schizophrenia* (B. Massumi, Trans.), Minneapolis: University of Minnesota Press.

Deleuze, G. and Guattari, F. (1994), *What is Philosophy?* (H. Tomlinson and G. Burchell, Trans.). New York: Columbia University Press.

Deleuze, G. and Parnet, C. (1987), *Dialogues* (H. Tomlinson and B. Habberjam, Trans.). New York: Columbia University Press.

Deleuze, G. and Parnet, C. (2002), *Dialogues II*. London: Continuum.

Doel, M.A. (1996), "A hundred thousand lines of flight: A machinic introduction to the nomad thought and scrumpled geography of Gilles Deleuze and Felix Guattari". *Environment and Planning D: Society and Space 14*, 421–39.

Doel, M.A. and Hubbard, P. (2002), "Taking world cities literally: Marketing the city in a global space of flows". *City 6*(3), 351–68.

Dovey, K. and Sandercock, L. (2002), "Hype and hope". *City 6*(1), 83–101.

Drummond, J. (2005), "The rhizome and the tree: A response to Holmes and Gastaldo". *Nursing Philosophy 6*(4), 255–66.

Düttmann, A.G. (2002), "…and…and…Deleuze politics". *Angelaki: Journal of Theoretical Humanities 7*(3), 171–6.

Eco, U. (1984), *Postscript to the Name of the Rose* (W. Weaver, Trans.). New York: Harcourt, Brace and Jovanovich.

Florida, R. (2006), *What really drives economic development?* Retrieved 28 February, 2007, from http://creativeclass.typepad.com/thecreativityexchange/2006/11/what_really_dri.html.

Flyvbjerg, B. (2001), *Making Social Science Matter* (S. Sampson, Trans.). Cambridge, UK: Cambridge University Press.

Foucault, M. (1990), *History of Sexuality: Use of Pleasure* (Vol. II). New York: Vantage Books.

Fraser, M. (2006), "Event". *Theory, Culture and Society 23*(2–3), 129–32.

Frichot, H. (2006), "Showing vital signs: The work of Gilles Deleuze and Felix Guattari's creative philosophy in architecture". *Angelaki: Journal of Theoretical Humanities 11*(6), 109–116.

Friedmann, J. (1987), *Planning in the Public Domain: From Knowledge to Action*. Princeton, NJ: Princeton University Press.

Gough, N. (2004), "RhizomANTically becoming-cyborg: Performing posthuman pedagogies". *Educational Philosophy and Theory 36*(3), 253–65.

Gough, N. (2005), *Geophilosophy and methodology: Science education research in a rhizomatic space*. Retrieved 17 July, 2006, from http://www.bath.ac.uk/cree/resources/noelg_SAARMSTE_ch.pdf.

Gregoriou, Z. (2004), "Commencing the Rhizome: Towards a minor philosophy of education". *Educational Philosophy and Theory 36*(3), 233–51.

Gunder, M. (2003), "Planning policy formulation from a Lacanian perspective". *International Planning Studies 8*(4), 279–94.

Hallward, P. (2006), *Out of this World: Deleuze and the Philosophy of Creation*. London: Verso.

Hansen, M. (2000), "Becoming as creative involution?: Contextualizing Deleuze and Guattari's biophilosophy". *Postmodern Culture 11*(1).

Harvey, D. (2007), "The Kantian roots of Foucault's dilemmas". In J. Crampton and S. Elden (eds), *Space, Knowledge and Power: Foucault and Geography* (pp. 41–7). Aldershot, UK: Ashgate Publishing Limited.

Hillier, J. (2005), "Straddling the post-structuralist abyss: Between transcendence and immanence?" *Planning Theory 4*(3), 271–99.

Hillier, J. (2007), *Stretching Beyond the Horizon:A Multiplanar Theory of Spatial Planning and Governance*. Aldershot, UK: Ashgate Publishing Limited.

Hipwell, W.T. (2004), "A Deleuzian critique of resource-use management politics in Industria". *The Canadian Geographer 48*(3), 356–77.

Honan, E. (2004), "(Im)plausibilities: A rhizo-textual analysis of policy texts and teachers' work". *Educational Philosophy and Theory 36*(3), 267–81.

Jacobs, K. (2007), "Territorial modes of governance and the discourses of community reaction in the State of Tasmania". *Space and Polity 11*(3), 263–77.

Jeanes, E.L. (2006), "'Resisting creativity, creating the new'. A Deleuzian perspective on creativity". *Creativity and Innovation Management 15*(2), 127–34.

Jessop, B. (2000), "The crisis of the national spatio-temporal fix and the tendential ecological dominance of globalizing capitalism". *International Journal of Urban and Regional Research 24*(2), 323–60.

Kaup, M. (2005), "Becoming-Baroque: Folding European forms into the new world Baroque with Alego Carpentier". *CR: The New Centennial Review 5*(2), 107–149.

Krajicek, J. (1995), *Bounded Arithmetic, Propositional Logic, and Complexity Theory*. Cambridge, UK: Cambridge University Press.

Latham, A. and Conradson, D. (2003), "The possibilities of performance". *Environment and Planning A 35*, 1901–1906.

Law, J. and Urry, J. (2004), "Enacting the social". *Economy and Society 33*(3), 390–410.

Lopez, A. (2004), "Deleuze with Carroll: Schizophrenia and simulacrum and the philosophy of Lewis Carroll's nonsense". *Angelaki: Journal of Theoretical Humanities 9*(3), 101–120.

Mackenzie, A. (2005), "The problem of the attractor". *Theory, Culture and Society 22*(5), 45–65.

Markusen, A. (2000), "Two frontiers for regional science: Regional policy and interdisciplinary reach". *Papers in Regional Science 81*, 279–90.

Massumi, B. (1992), *A User's Guide to "Capitalism and Schizophrenia": Deviations from Deleuze and Guattari*. Cambridge, MA: MIT Press.

Massumi, B. (1996), "Becoming-deleuzian". *Environment and Planning D: Society and Space 14*, 395–406.

Neilson, B. (2003), "Globalization and the biopolitics of aging". *CR: The New Centennial Review 3*(2), 161–86.

O'Neill, P. and McGuirk, P.M. (2005), "Reterritorialisation of economies and institutions: The rise of the Sydney basin economy". *Space and Polity 9*(3), 283–305.

Osborne, T. (2004), "On mediators: Intellectuals and the ideas trade in the knowledge society". *Economy and Society 33*(4), 430–47.

Patton, P. (2000), *Deleuze and the Political*. London: Routledge.

Peck, J. and Tickell, A. (2002), "Neoliberalizing space". *Antipode 34*, 380–404.

Penner, M. (2003), "Normativity in Deleuze and Guattari's concept of philosophy". *Continental Philosophy Review 36*, 45–59.

Peters, M. (2004), "Geophilosophy, education and the pedagogy of the concept". *Educational Philosophy and Theory 36*(3), 217–26.

Porter, M. (1990), *Competitive Advantage of Nations*. London: Macmillan.

Porter, M. (2000), "Location, competition, and economic development: Local clusters in a global economy". *Economic Development Quarterly 14*(1), 15–34.

Poxon, J. and Stivale, C. (2005), "Sense, Series". In C. Stivale (ed.), *Gilles Deleuze: Key Concepts* (pp. 65–76). Montreal: McGill-Queens University Press.

Raco, M., Parker, G., and Doak, J. (2006), "Reshaping spaces of local governance? Community strategies and the modernisation of local government in England". *Environment and Planning C, Government and Policy 24*, 475–96.

Richardson, L. (2001), "Getting personal: Writing-stories". *International Journal of Qualitative Studies 14*(1), 33–8.

Saldanha, A. (2006), "A geophilosophy to come". *Theory and Event 9*(4), 1–8.

Schram, S. (2006), "Return to politics: perestroika, phronesis, and post-paradigmatic political science". In S. Schram and B. Caterino (eds), *Making Political Science Matter: Debating Knowledge, Research, and Method*. New York: New York University Press.

Schuh, K. and Cunningham, D. (2004), "Rhizome and the mind: Describing the metaphor". *Semiotica 149*(1/4), 325–42.

Semetsky, I. (2004), "Experiencing Deleuze". *Educational Philosophy and Theory 36*(3), 227–31.

Semetsky, I. (2007), "Towards a semiotic theory of learning: Deleuze's philosophy and educational experience". *Semiotica 164*(1/4), 197–214.

Shaffer, R., Deller, S., and Marcouiller, D. (2006), "Rethinking community economic development". *Economic Development Quarterly 20*(1), 59–74.

Shanks, M. and Hodder, I. (1995), "Processual, postprocessual and interpretive archaeologies". In I. Hodder, M. Shanks, A. Alexandri, V. Buchli, J. Carman, J. Last and G. Lucus (eds), *Interpreting Archaeology, Finding Meaning in the Past* (pp. 3–29), London: Routledge.

Shdaimah, C. and Stahl, R. (2006), "Reflections on doing phronetic social science". In S. Schram and B. Caterino (eds), *Making Political Science Matter: Debating Knowledge, Research and Method* (pp. 98–113), New York: New York University Press.

Smith, D.W. (2005), "Critical, clinical". In C. Stivale (ed.), *Gilles Deleuze: Key Concepts* (pp. 182–93), Montreal: McGill-Queens Press.

Smith, R.G. and Doel, M.A. (2007), *A New Theoretical Basis for Global-city Research: From Structures and Networks to Multiplicities and Events*. Retrieved 8 June, 2007, from http://www.lboro.ac.uk/gawc/rb/rb221.html.

St. Pierre, E. (2004), "Deleuzian concepts for education: The subject undone". *Educational Philosophy and Theory 36*(3), 283–96.

Stagoll, C. (2005), "Difference". In A. Parr (ed.), *The Deleuze Dictionary* (pp. 72–3), New York: Columbia University Press.

Thrift, N. (2007), "Overcome by space: Reworking Foucault". In J. Crampton and S. Elden (eds), *Space, Knowledge and Power: Foucault and Geography* (pp. 53–8), Aldershot, UK: Ashgate Publishing Limited.

Tilley, C. (1993), "Introduction: Interpretation and a poetics of the past". In C. Tilley (ed.), *Interpretative Archaeology* (pp. 1–27), Oxford, UK: Berg.

Tormey, S. (2005), "A 'critical power'?: The uses of Deleuze". A review essay. *Contemporary Political Theory 4*(4), 414–30.

Weiskopf, R. (2002), "Deconstructing 'the iron cage' – Towards an aesthetic of folding". *Consumption, Markets and Culture 5*(1), 79–97.

Wilson, A.G. (2006), "Ecological and urban systems models: Some explorations of similarities in the context of complexity theory". *Environment and Planning A 38*(4), 633–46.

Zhao, F. (2005), "Entrepreneurship and innovation in e-business: An integrative perspective". *The International Journal of Entrepreneurship and Innovation 6*(1), 53–60.

Appendix I

Arborescence/arborescent – The virtual model of the tree used directly or indirectly to trace a hierarchy. The term also can be related to traditional ways of thinking and researching a problem and has a centre or subject from which it then expresses ideas. For Deleuze, this type of striated or structural thinking stifles creativity (Stagoll, 2005a).

Actants – the term was coined by Bruno Latour. "Actants have a kind of phomenic rather thatn a phonetic role: they operate on the level of function, rather than content. That is, an actant may embody itself in a particular character (termed an *acteur*) or it may reside in the function of more than one character in respect of their common role in the story's underlying 'oppositional' structure. In short, the deep structure of the narrative genertes and defines its actnats at a level beyond that of the story's surface content" (Hawkes, 1977, p. 89).

Actor Network Theory (ANT) – ANT's rich methodology embraces scientific realism, social constructivism, and discourse analysis in its central concept of hybrids, or 'quasi-objects', that are simultaneously real, social, and discursive. Developed as an analysis of scientific and technological artefacts, ANT's theoretical reichness derives from its refusal to reduce explanations to either natural, social, or discursive categories while recognising the significance of each (see, e.g. Latour, 1993, p. 91). Following the work of Hughes, ANT insists that "the stability and form of artefacts should be seen as a function of the interaction of heterogeneours elements as these are shaped and assimilated into a network" (Law, 1990, p. 113).

Assemblage – An assemblage is a multiplicity; a network of meshed lines and is a form of functional connections and flows of force and power relations which construct the social. Machinic assemblages are 'not fixed structures, but sites of continuous organisation and disorganisation (Bogard, 2000, p. 273). It can also be described as an intensive network or rhizome displaying 'consistency' or emergent effects by tapping into the ability of the self-ordering forces of heterogeneous material to fold together.

Becoming – "The Deleuzoguattarian concept of becoming implies the pathways along which an entity or concept may be transformed whilst retaining some resemblance to its former self. Becoming is linked rather to the unpredictable, indeterminate, never accomplished actualisation of virtualities" (Hillier, 2005, pp. 280–281).

Body without Organs – "The Body without Organs is a limit. In particular, it is the limit at which all the flows which constitute the world flow completely freely, each into the others, so that no distinctions exist among them any longer. Deleuze and Guattari described a world in which everything flows and everything is made of flows: not only water, air, magma, blood, paint, electricity, not only grass, earth, sun, but ideas, people, culture, books, conversations flow. What allows us to distinguish these flows from each other, to single out one or another is a threshold or a point which separates each of them. Every flow is made by cutting off another flow, by restricting or drawing off a flow" (Evans, 1996).

Desire – "is the material process of connection, registration and enjoyment of flows of matter and energy coursing through bodies in networks of production in all registers, be they geologic, organic or social" (Bonta and Protevi, 2004, p. 76).

Deterritorialisation (along with territorialisation and reterritorialisation are the three moments of Nomadology) –

> territoriali[s]ation has to happen within a capitalist economy, which produces anti-production, or excess that must be reterritoriali[s]ed back into the economy. The economy is a territoriali[s]ing machine, so deterritoriali[s]ation is absolutely necessary and also has to happen, however everything under capitalism can not be territoriali[s]ed. (Parr, 2005).

It can be described as a move away from a rigidly imposed hierarchical, arborescent context, which seeks to package things (concepts, objects, etc.) into discrete categorised units with singular coded meanings or identities, towards a rhizomatic zone of multiplicity and fluctuant identity.

Difference – According to Stagoll (2005b, p. 73, my emphasis) "Deleuze's difference-in-itself releases difference from domination by identity and sameness". In this situation, "…identity must always be referred to the difference inherent in the particulars being *swept up* in the process of constructing a relationship between them. To realise this is [it is necessary] to meet the challenge of developing a new perspective in order to resist *transcendence.*

Duration – Duration (*durée*) was adopted by Deleuze from Bergson in order to develop his philosophy of difference. According to Stagoll (2005, p. 80) "Duration is always presenting the givenness of one'e experience. It does not transcend experience, and neither must it be derived philosophically…because duration as lived experience, brings together both unity and difference in a flow of connections".

Econphilosophy – Econphilosophy is a term coined by this writer which endeavours to tie philosophy to economic development that includes spatial and other connotations. While geophilosophy refers to Deleuze and Guattari's attempt to reorient philosophy from a concentration on temporality and historicity to spatiality and geography, this book employs the concept of rhizomatic econphilosophy to view the practice of economic development through a Deleuzian lens (see geophilosophy).

Empty Signifier – "The empty signifier is the discursive centre, what Laclau and Mouffe (1985) calls a nodal point, i.e. a privileged element that gathers up a range of differential elements, and binds them together into a discursive formation. But it is only by emptying a certain signifier of its content that this process can be achieved. Its emptiness makes it possible for it to signify the discourse as a whole. The power of a certain signifier is therefore coterminous with its emptiness. It is only through this emptiness that it can articulate different elements around it, and thus produce a discursive formation" (Wrangle, 2007).

Event – For Deleuze, an event "carries no determinate outcome, but only new possibilities, representing a moment at which new forces might be brought to bear…thinking and creating are constituted simultaneously." (Stagoll, 2005, p. 88). Deleuze (1990, p. 65) also stated that an event is "always in disequilibrium, presents one of its sides as the sense of propositions and the other as the attribute of states of affairs."

Folding – "The French noun for fold '*le phi*' has a philosophical lineage in a family of words such as com*pli*cation, im*pli*cation, multi*pli*cation, re*pli*cation, suggesting that multiples are folded in complex ways rather than simply added on. Similarly, to explicate is to unfold or explain, while something pliant is foldable. Folding brings new connections as once-distant entities are now juxtaposed. It generates new energies as folds are never pre-formed or given. They have no transcendent rules or final solutions. Folds literally com*pli*cate. They express a multi*pli*city" (Hillier, 2007, p. 60).

Geophilosophy – Deleuze and Guattari "seek to reorient philosophy from a concentration on temporality and historicity to spatiality and geography (Bonta and Protevi, 2004, p. 92), because "thinking takes place in the relationship of territory and the earth" (Deleuze and Guattari, 1994, p. 85). As a result, "universality pertains to the capitalist world market as a multiple network of simultaneous (although uneven) relations rather than to capitalist history as a single line of temporal development" (Holland, 2005, p. 60).

Haecceity – "Deleuze and Guattari use the term…where the universe pours in, flow out- an unlimited One-All, universal-singular" (Seigworth, 2005, p. 160). Deleuze and Guattari (1987, pp. 260–261) defined the term in its cartography by its longitude (the 'speeds and slowness' of its material flows) and by its latitude (its set of affects).

Hermeneutics – Originally hermeneutics referred to the process of interpreting religious writings. Notable exceptions include most structuralist and poststructuralist criticism. These non-hermeneutic approaches focus not on discovering what a text means but rather on how meaning is deployed or subverted.

Hylomorphism – Hylomorphism is the doctrine that the process of production is the result of an imposition of a transcendent form (morphe) upon an immanent matter (hyle), an order imposed upon chaos, like a mold imposed on a mass of clay (Smith, 2004, p. 377).

Immanence – In philosophical terminology, immanence is an act of being within a conceptual space. Immanence is a concept in the Deleuzian sense which is a way of connecting new ideas and possibilities for thinking. Immanence is also necessarily connected with other Deleuzian concepts, concepts that open up the new style of thought.

Involution – Deleuze borrowed the term from mathematics. As opposed to evolution, "involution describes a creative process whose field of production does not depend on differentiation, but rather involves a dissolution of form that…makes possible the 'dance of disparate things' through transversal modes of becoming" (Hansen, 2000, pp. 15–16).

Line of Flight – A line of flight is "the threshold between assemblages, the path of deterritorialisation, the experiment; in complexity theory terms, a move that triggers a bifurcation…or a vector of escape…between milieus" (Bonta and Protevi, 2004, p. 106).

Master Signifiers – Master signifiers are "any signifier that a subject has invested his or her identity in – any signifier that the subject has identified with (or against) and that thus constitutes a powerful positive or negative value" (Bracher, 1993, p. 111). They are often empty signifiers open to contested meaning (see empty signifier).

Multiplicity – "On the plane of consistency, multiplicities are the virtual patterns and thresholds of systems, defined by singularities and laid out in diagrams by an abstract system that cannot change past thresholds of intensity of flows…without a qualitative change in systems behaviour that is a becoming" (Bonta and Protevi, 2004, p. 117).

Nomadlogoy/Nomads – Bonta and Protevi (2004, p.119) define nomads as "the geography, geohistory, or logos of the rhizome and war machine, as opposed to history, the logos of the State: 'nomads have no history; they only have a geography'".

Plateaus – Lorraine (2005b, p. 206) describes plateaus as a "continuous, self-vibrating region of intensities that does not develop in terms of a point of culmination or an external goal. Plateaus are constituted when the elements of a region are not subjected to an external plan of organisation. An external plan imposes the selection of some connections rather than others from the virtual relations among the elements that could be actualised, actualising varying capacities to affect and be affected in the process".

Rhizome – Rhizome is a figurative term used by Felix Guattari and Gilles Deleuze in *A Thousand Plateaus: Capitalism and Schizophrenia (1987)* to describe non-hierarchical networks of all kinds. To paraphase Deleuze (1987, p. 6–7), a rhizome is similar to the root system of certain types of grasses or tubers that are essentially a mass of interconnected radicals which can be illustrated by and compared to the internet.

Smooth Space – "Smooth space is the space of intensive process and assemblages, as opposed to the striated space of stratified or stable systems" (Bonta and Proveti, 2004, p. 143–144). Deleuze and Guattari (1987, p. 494 as quote by Lorraine, 2005, p.253–254) stated that "smooth space haunts and can disrupt the striations of convential space, and it unfolds through an infinite succession of linkages and changes in direction that creates shifting mosaics of space-times out of the hetergeneous block of differenct milieus."

Striated Space – Striated space is "space marked by striae (striations); metric or measured space…[and] is the product of stratifications, especially as effectuated by the State apparatus…Striation results from stratification, the overcoding, centralisation, heirarchisation, binarisation, and segmentation of the free movements of signs, particles, bodies, territories, spaces an so on" (Bonta and Protevi, 2004, p. 151).

Transcendence – In philosophical usage, the act of being above or beyond something else either empirically, that is, in space or power, or ontologically, in mode of being (Bonta and Protevi, 2004, p. 162). In Kant's theory of knowledge, being is beyond the limits of experience and hence unknowable.

Virtual – "In Deleuze's ontology, the virtual and the actual are two mutually exclusive, yet jointly sufficient, characterisations of the real. The actual/real are states of affairs, bodies, bodily mixtures and individuals. The virtual/real are incorporeal events and singularities on a plane of consistency, belonging to the past – the past that can never be fully present" (Boundas, 2005, pp. 296–297).

War Machine – A war machine "is the counterforce to the State's stratification machine, which forms hierarchical, centralised, and overcoded social formations" (Bonta and Protevi, 2004, p. 165). Deleuze stated that "the war machine's form of exteriority is such that it exists only in its own metamorphoses; it exists in an industrial innovation as well as in a technological innovation, in a commercial circuit as well as in a religious creation, in all flows and currents that only secondarily allow themselves to be appropriated by the state" (Deleuze and Guattari, 1987, p. 360).

References

Bogard, W. (2000), "Smoothing machines and the constitution of society". *Cultural Studies 14*(2), 269–94.

Bonta, M. and Protevi, J. (2004), *Deleuze and Geophilosophy: A Guide and Glossary*. Edinburgh: Edinburgh University Press.

Boundas, C.V. (2005), "Virtual/virtuality". In A. Parr (ed.), *The Deleuze Dictionary* (pp. 296–8). New York: Columbia University Press.

Bracher, M. (1993), *Lacan, Discourse, and Social Change*. Ithaca, NY: Cornell University Press.

Colebrook, C. (2005a), "Actuality". In A. Parr (ed.), *The Deleuze Dictionary* (pp. 9–11). New York: Columbia University Press.

Deleuze, G. (1990), *The Logic of Sense* (M. Lester, Trans.). New York: Columbia University Press.

Deleuze, G. and Guattari, F. (1987), *Thousand Plateaus: Capitalism and Schizophrenia* (B. Massumi, Trans.). Minneapolis: University of Minnesota Press.

Deleuze, G. and Guattari, F. (1994), *What is Philosophy?* (H. Tomlinson and G. Burchell, Trans.). New York: Columbia University Press.

Evans, A. (1996), *Body without Organs Definition*. Retrieved 16 April, 2006, from http://webpages.ursinus.edu/rrichter/bwodefinition.html.

Hansen, M. (2000), "Becoming as creative involution?: Contextualizing Deleuze and Guattari's biophilosophy". *Postmodern Culture 11*(1).

Hawkes, T. (1977), *Structuralism and Semiotics*. Berkeley: University of California Press.

Hillier, J. (2005), "Straddling the post-structuralist abyss: Between transcendence and immanence?" *Planning Theory 4*(3), 271–99.

Hillier, J. (2007), *Stretching Beyond the Horizon: A Multiplanar Theory of Spatial Planning and Governance*. Aldershot, UK: Ashgate Publishing Limited.

Holland, E. (2005), "Desire". In C. Stivale (ed.), *Gilles Deleuze: Key Concepts* (pp. 53–64). Montreal: McGill-Queens University Press.

Latour, B. (1993), *We Have Never Been Modern*. Brighton, UK: Harvester Wheatsheaf.

Law, J. (1990), "Technology and heterogeneous engineering: The case of Portuguese expansion". In T.J. Pinch (ed.), *The Social Construction of Technology Systems: New Directions in Sociology and History* (pp. 111–34). Cambridge, MA: MIT University Press.

Lorraine, T. (2005a), "Plateau". In A. Parr (ed.), *The Deleuze Dictionary* (pp. 206–207). New York: Columbia University Press.

Lorraine, T. (2005b), "Smooth space". In A. Parr (ed.), *The Deleuze Dictionary* (pp. 253–4). New York: Columbia University Press.

Parr, A. (2005), "Deterritorialisation/reterritorialisation". In A. Parr (ed.), *The Deleuze Dictionary* (pp. 66–9). New York: Columbia University Press.

Seigworth, G. (2005), "From affection to soul". In C. Stivale (ed.), *Gilles Deleuze: Key Concepts* (pp. 159–69). Montreal: McGill-Queens University Press.

Smith, D.W. (2004), "Review of Deleuze and Geophilosophy". *Continental Philosophy Review 37*(3), 375–81.

Stagoll, C. (2005a), "Arborescent schema". In A. Parr (ed.), *The Deleuze Dictionary* (pp. 13–14). New York: Columbia University Press.

Stagoll, C. (2005b), "Becoming". In A. Parr (ed.), *The Deleuze Dictionary* (pp. 21–2). New York: Columbia University Press.

Stagoll, C. (2005c), "Difference". In A. Parr (ed.), *The Deleuze Dictionary* (pp. 72–3). New York: Columbia University Press.

Stagoll, C. (2005d), "Duration (Duree)". In A. Parr (ed.), *The Deleuze Dictionary* (pp. 78–80). New York: Columbia University Press.

Stagoll, C. (2005e), "Event". In A. Parr (ed.), *The Deleuze Dictionary* (pp. 87–8). New York: Columbia University Press.

Wrangel, C. (2007), *Towards a Modified Discourse Theory Pt. 1: Laclau's 'Empty Signifier'*. Retrieved 15 September 2007, from http://thatsnotit.wordpress.com/2007/05/03/towards-a-modified-discourse-theory-pt-1-laclaus-empty-signifier/.

Appendix II

A Summary of the Criteria used to Analyse BM's Subjective – Objective Dichotomy

	SUBJECTIVISM			OBJECTIVISM		
Ontological Assumptions	Reality as a projection of human imagination	Reality as a social construction	Reality as the realm of symbolic discourse	Reality as contextual fields of information	Reality as a concrete process	Reality as a concrete structure
Epistemological Assumptions	To obtain phenomenological insight, revelation	To understand how social reality is constructed	To understand patterns of symbolic discourse	To map contexts	To study systems, processes and change	To construct a positivist science
Assumptions about Human Nature	Man as pure spirit, consciousness, being	Man as the social constructor; the symbol creator	Man as an actor; the symbol user	Man as an information processor	Man as an adapter	Man as a responder
Favoured Metaphors	Transcendental	Language game	Theatre, Culture	Cybernetic	Organism	Machine
Examples	Exploration of pure subjectivity	Hermeneutics	Symbolic analysis	Contextual analysis	Historical analysis	Surveys

Adapted from Morgan and Smircich (1980)

Appendix III

A Summary of the Criteria used to Analyse BM's Radical Change – Regulation Dichotomy

	RADICAL CHANGE			REGULATION		
Assumptions about change to society	Every society is at every point subject to forces of radical change	Every society experiences periods of revolution and periods of stability	Every element in society is subject to incremental but continuous change	Every element in society has facilitates change to the existing social order	Every element in society responds to change imposed upon it	Every element in society is relatively stable and change occurs infrequently
Assumptions about the structure of society	Every element in society renders a contribution to internal disintegration	Every element in society displays contradiction and paradox	Every element in society is in a constant state of structural flux	Every element in society displays surface flux which obscures general structural principles	Every element in society is part of an organic system	Every society is a well integrated structure of elements and each element has a function
Assumptions about the degree of conflict in society	Every society at every point displays dissensus and conflict	Every society is based on the coercion of some of its members by others	Every group in society protect their own interests and are in open conflict with other groups	Every element of society is determined by power relationships between individuals and groups	Every functioning social structure is based on negotiation between the demands of its stakeholders	Every functioning social structure is based on a consensus of values among its members
Favoured Metaphors	Anarchy and chaos	Transformation revolution	Tribal factions	Morphogenic	Organic	Mechanistic
Examples	Analysis of anarchy and chaos including action	Critical analysis of the status quo including action to transform	Critical analysis of the status quo	Analysis of functional autonomy	Analysis of the latent functions of society	Analysis of laws governing society

Index